Sport and Body Politics

There is more to Japanese sport than sumo, karate and baseball. This study of social sport in Japan pursues a comprehensive approach towards sport as a distinctive cultural sphere at the intersection of body culture, political economy, and cultural globalization. Bridging the gap between Bourdieu and Foucault, it explains the significance of the body as a field of action and a topic of discourse in molding subject and society in modern Japan. More specifically, it provides answers to questions such as how and to what purposes are politics of the body articulated in Japan, particularly in the realm of sport? What is the agenda of state actors that develop politics aiming at the body, and to what degree are political and societal objectives impacted by commercial and non-political actors? How are political decisions on the allocation of resources made, and what are their consequences for sporting opportunities and practices of the body in general? Without neglecting the significance of sport spectatorship, this study takes a particular angle by looking at sport as a field of practice, pain and pleasure.

Wolfram Manzenreiter is Professor in the Department of East Asian Studies at the University of Vienna.

Routledge Research in Sport, Culture and Society

1 **Sport, Masculinities and the Body**
Ian Wellard

2 **India and the Olympics**
Boria Majumdar and Nalin Mehta

3 **Social Capital and Sport Governance in Europe**
Edited by Margaret Groeneveld, Barrie Houlihan and Fabien Ohl

4 **Theology, Ethics and Transcendence in Sports**
Edited by Jim Parry, Mark Nesti and Nick Watson

5 **Women and Exercise**
The Body, Health and Consumerism
Edited by Eileen Kennedy and Pirkko Markula

6 **Race, Ethnicity and Football**
Persisting Debates and Emergent Issues
Edited by Daniel Burdsey

7 **The Organisation and Governance of Top Football Across Europe**
An Institutional Perspective
Edited by Hallgeir Gammelsæter and Benoît Senaux

8 **Sport and Social Mobility**
Crossing Boundaries
Ramón Spaaij

9 **Critical Readings in Bodybuilding**
Edited by Adam Locks and Niall Richardson

10 **The Cultural Politics of Post-9/11 American Sport**
Power, Pedagogy and the Popular
Michael Silk

11 **Ultimate Fighting and Embodiment**
Violence, Gender and Mixed Martial Arts
Dale C. Spencer

12 **The Olympic Games and Cultural Policy**
Beatriz Garcia

13 **The Urban Geography of Boxing**
Race, Class, and Gender in the Ring
Benita Heiskanen

14 **The Social Organization of Sports Medicine**
Critical Socio-Cultural Perspectives
Edited by Dominic Malcolm and Parissa Safai

15 **Host Cities and the Olympics**
An Interactionist Approach
Harry Hiller

16 **Sports Governance, Development and Corporate Responsibility**
Edited by Barbara Segaert, Marc Theeboom, Christiane Timmerman and Bart Vanreusel

17 Sport and Its Female Fans
Edited by Kim Toffoletti and Peter Mewett

18 Sport Policy in Britain
Barrie Houlihan and Iain Lindsey

19 Sports and Christianity
Historical and Contemporary Perspectives
Edited by Nick J. Watson and Andrew Parker

20 Sports Coaching Research
Context, Consequences, and Consciousness
Anthony Bush, Michael Silk, David Andrews and Hugh Lauder

21 Sport Across Asia
Politics, Cultures, and Identities
Edited by Katrin Bromber, Birgit Krawietz, and Joseph Maguire

22 Athletes, Sexual Assault, and "Trials by Media"
Narrative Immunity
Deb Waterhouse-Watson

23 Youth Sport, Physical Activity and Play
Policy, Interventions and Participation
Andrew Parker and Don Vinson

24 The Global Horseracing Industry
Social, Economic, Environmental and Ethical Perspectives
Phil McManus, Glenn Albrecht, and Raewyn Graham

25 Sport, Public Broadcasting, and Cultural Citizenship
Signal Lost?
Edited by Jay Scherer and David Rowe

26 Sport and Body Politics in Japan
Wolfram Manzenreiter

Sport and Body Politics in Japan

Wolfram Manzenreiter

LONDON AND NEW YORK

First published 2014
by Routledge
711 Third Avenue, New York, NY 10017

Simultaneously published in the UK
by Routledge
2 Park Square, Milton Park, Abingdon, Oxfordshire OX14 4RN

Routledge is an imprint of the Taylor and Francis Group, an informa business

First issued in paperback 2015

Library of Congress Cataloging-in-Publication Data
Manzenreiter, Wolfram.
Sport and body politics in Japan / by Wolfram Manzenreiter.
pages cm. — (Routledge research in sport, culture and society)
Includes bibliographical references and index.
1. Sports—Japan—History. 2. Sports and society—Japan—History. 3. Human body—Social aspects—Japan. 4. Human body—Political aspects—Japan. 5. Culture and globalization—Japan. I. Title.
GV655.M36 2013
796.0952—dc23
2013006696

ISBN 978-0-415-84040-8 (hbk)
ISBN 978-1-138-95289-8 (pbk)
ISBN 978-0-203-76735-1 (ebk)

Typeset in Sabon
by IBT Global.

Contents

Figures

Tables

Acknowledgments

Ever since I started doing research on sport in Japan, I knew that there would be a monograph of some kind at the end of the engagement. With the years passing, I could visualize the book, but I had no idea what its precise focus was going to be. In the end, writing this book has lasted quite a while. Its content is based on more than a decade of researching sports in Japan and East Asia. Its earliest chapters were drafted at a time when the study of sport as a social institution and a cultural expression was primarily taken up by scholars from the narrow fields of Sport History or Sport Sociology only. Back in the late 1990s, when the study of sport barely raised interest among Area Studies specialists, a small group of Japanese sport researchers and Japanese Studies scholars with a genuine interest in sport phenomena gathered at the National Museum of Ethnology in Senri to start a dialogue that has continued until today. The first chapter is a direct outcome of that kick-start meeting. All the others are indirectly linked to this historical event from which a truly transnational and transdisciplinary network has emerged, bridging the gaps between the study of sport, Japanese Studies and social theory. The network has gradually expanded, throughout Japan and beyond, as well as within Sport Studies and Japanese Studies.

While working on sport I have been lucky enough to meet a great many kind and intelligent people whose curiosity, enthusiasm and know-how have helped me to realize this book. Such encounters, detours and explorations into very different intellectual camps made me realize that the study of sport actually is a study of global modernity. What is probably neither a very surprising nor challenging insight, particularly when seen from today, was very comforting to me along the way. I felt encouraged to reread my earlier writings that touched upon political and historical issues as well as questions of geographical or anthropological interest, and combined my discussion of the body and modernity within the framework of globalization. Taking up the threads and weaving them together has been the objective of this book, which I would like to dedicate to our common cause: making sense of sport.

You meet a lot of people when working on a research topic for fifteen years in and out of the various circles and societies of sport researchers. Not all of the encounters have been as memorable and stimulating as others; but most of them have involved meeting very nice people—and the very rare exceptions won't find their names listed below! If you feel your name deserves mentioning here, and it isn't, it is quite likely that you are right. Blame it on me, but don't be cross with me for what is merely a memory lapse.

I want to express my gratitude and appreciation to Susan Brownell (University of Missouri), Florian Coulmas (German Institute of Japanese Studies), Claudia Derichs (Marburg University), Julian Dierkes (British Columbia University), Harald Dolles (University of Gothenburg), Dong Jinxia (Beijing University), Jerry Eades (Asia Pacific University), Karin Fischer (Johannes Kepler University Linz), Carolin Funck (Hiroshima University), Kostas Georgiadis (International Olympic Academy), Allen Guttmann (Amherst College), Hirose Ichirō (RIETI), Barbara Holthus (German Institute of Japanese Studies), John Horne (University of Central Lancashire), Steven Jackson (University of Otago), William W. Kelly (Yale University), Kiku Kōichi (Tsukuba University), Koh Eunha (Korea Sport Science Institute), Lola Martinez (SOAS, University of London), Matsuda Keiji (Tokyo University of Arts), Andreas Niehaus (Ghent University), Nogawa Haruo (Juntendo University); Gertrud Pfister (Copenhagen University), Anette Schad-Seifert (University of Düsseldorf), Kim Schimmel (Ohio State University), Sugimoto Atsuo (Kansai Gakuin University), Christian Tagsold (University of Düsseldorf), Takahashi Yoshio (Tsukuba University), Takeda Hiroko (Tokyo University), Lee Thompson (Waseda University), Xin Xu (Cornell University), Yamashita Takayuki (Ritsumeikan University) and all those others that have been joining forces in various collaborative projects throughout the years. I also want to thank the three anonymous reviewers; Max Novick and Jennifer Morrow from Routledge and Eleanor Chan from IBT/Hamilton for their professionalism; and my colleagues and students from the Department of East Asian Studies at University of Vienna for their support over the years. The biggest thank you of all, as always, goes to my family. I promise; the next book will be out much faster!

Introduction

Researching Sport and the Political Economy of the Body in Japan

INTRODUCTION

As in every other advanced modern society, sport has come to occupy a prominent position in the everyday life of the Japanese. Actively participating in sport (*suru supōtsu*), as well as watching others excelling in sport (*miru supōtsu*), consumes substantial proportions of free time and consumption spending of many contemporary Japanese. For others, doing precisely the same act of performing and observing others' sport performance is a major source of their income, that is a profession or a business. Sport is a major generator of communication among many Japanese, as it provides an endless stream of news and numbers, of stories and gossip that account for a remarkable share of media content delivered by Japan's daily newspapers, sport journals, television and radio broadcasters, and other media such as the internet. Sport is also a central topic of unmediated communication, as it composes rich content for face-to-face interactions all over the country. Anyone observing informal conversations between inhabitants of a farmer village on Hokkaidō in Japan's upper north, town and city dwellers of the metropolitan areas in Kantō or Kansai in the centre of mainland Japan or the members of a fishing community in Japan's subtropical south of Okinawa, is very likely to listen to similar conversations about baseball teams, soccer players and sumo bouts, which are the most popular professional sports attracting nationwide attention. Apart from differences resulting from regional and seasonal climate change and from functional as well as social demands, many Japanese regularly dress in sport clothes or casual wear fashioned as sport clothes. A sportive outfit, including domestically produced apparel and internationally well-known brand names, is widely accepted nowadays in many social situations beyond the realms of physical exercise and leisure. Health, fitness and body consciousness are not only highly fashionable; they signify an active lifestyle. To be interested in sport, and much more to be active in sport, has almost become a normative marker of cultural citizenship in contemporary Japan. As this study shows, this has not always been the case, but rather is related to more general trends of society in a globalized world.

Sport indeed can be viewed as one of the most successful export products of the Old World. Over the past 500 years, Western civilization has exported numerous social, cultural, political and economic institutions to the rest of the world, often assisted by military force or enforced by economic supremacy. The hegemonic power of the Western bloc framed the processes by which its own cultural institutions turned into apparently universal principles. Worldwide, states, nations and people have largely consented to the regulatory framework of the nation-state and its associated principles of parliamentarianism, democracy, egalitarianism, market capitalism and the like. Yet in terms of spread, compliance and acceptance, hardly any institution has proved to be more successful, pervasive and persistent than sport. While representative political participation, free entrepreneurship, equal employment opportunities and even basic human rights are often highly contested and the subject of severe dispute, there seems to be almost unanimous consent to the veneration of physical prowess on the playing fields and the excitement generated by sportive games and contests. No matter what cultural belief and value systems give order and meaning to a particular society, people everywhere are highly likely to approve of the aesthetics of the sporting body, the narratives of symbolic competition, the moral economy of fair play and the symbolic and often also material value of victory and sporting records.

OUTLINE OF A RESEARCH PROGRAMME ON SPORT AND THE POLITICAL ECONOMY OF THE BODY IN JAPAN

Hence this study on sport in Japan is equally a study of cultural globalization—which is one of the three key terms framing my analysis on sport and body politics in Japan (the others are body culture and political economy). By doing this, I don't aspire to deliver a comprehensive account of the history of sport in Japan. Cornerstones of such a task have been accomplished by physical educators (Takenoshita and Kishino 1959; Kishino et al. 1973) and historians (Kimura 1975; Kimura Ki 1978; Kōzu 1995); more recently, Guttmann and Thompson (2001) spawned the first monograph on Japanese sport history in a foreign language, analysing Japan's modern sport experience in terms of two intersecting processes of indigenization and sportification. These historical studies without doubt have their merits and deserve acclamation for their extensive archival work and attention to detail. Yet dealing with a field as broad as sport, the narratives are often fragmentary and anecdotal, while many of them are largely descriptive and in the positivist tradition. Taking a historical anthropological approach to sport as a cultural expression rooted in social relations, Kelly (1998a, 1998b, 2000, 2004, 2009, 2011) has extensively written on Japanese baseball, particularly the Hanshin Tigers. Resonating with my own understanding of researching sport and body culture in Japan are also the ethnographic study of body culture and femininity within Tokyo fitness clubs by Spielvogel (2003), the cultural-historical exploration of celebrities in Japanese sports by Frost (2010) and Guthrie-Shimizu's (2012) work on transpacific relations in baseball. A comparative reading of their findings and the historical accounts mentioned before would suggest that sport, whether taken as a cultural expression or a social field, a market or a symbolic arena of political struggles within and between societies, is always a historical construct and a figuration subjugated to manifold transformative forces emerging from within and without Japanese society. My own study, trying to surmount the shortcomings of undertheorized histories and compartmentalized approaches, pursues a comprehensive approach towards sport as a distinctive cultural sphere at the intersection of body culture, political economy and cultural globalization.

A social scientific study of sport in a particular locality—such as Japan—faces two basic and apparently contradictory challenges. First, how can it get hold of a phenomenon that pretends to be universal but is actually highly specific in origin and in the way it is practised and understood at a given time and place? Most Japanese dictionaries feature a highly generalized definition of sport as 'body movements conducted for the pursuits of pleasure, competition or physical fitness'. If this abstract expression, which is a quote from the widespread *Daijirin* dictionary, can be taken as a proxy for the common conception of sport in Japan and by the Japanese, there is no reason to assume that there is anything specific about sport in this place. However, each of the concrete activities subsumed under the cover term of *sport* can be dismantled as a system consisting of particular forms of body practices, body control, training routines, rules of game and conduct and the ritualized handling of equipment and localities. Consequentially, the great variety of physical games and sport practices—ranging from the popular contest of *nawabiki* (tug-of-war) and martial arts like kendo or karate to lifestyle sports of surfing and spectator sports such as professional baseball and long-distance relay races (*ekiden*), as well as the huge diversity of ways of performing one of these sports according to situational definitions like the level of the game, the formality of its rules and the purpose of its participants—defies a premature definition. If the variability of sport in time and place were ignored, the definition would be either very diffuse or highly reductionist. As Dyck (2000:19) has noted, 'to insist upon reducing all of the fascinating variation [. . .] to shore up a general analytic definition of sport would be to risk losing the object in the art of trying to be "sociological" about it'. Keen to avoid the pitfall of sociology marred by Eurocentric bias, Giulianotti asked for a critical analysis of sport in society as a comprehensive survey of the 'categorical range of sporting practices, and the interconnections between these practices and power relations, community identity codes of social conduct, and metaphysical belief systems' (Giulianotti 2005:xiii). When looking at sport within the particular framework of Japanese society, it therefore is mandatory to identify the processes and agents involved in the social construction process that give meaning to certain activities and phenomena as sport. As we will see, forces from within sport and beyond, from inside of Japan and from abroad, are equal participants in the process of boundary-making.

Second, how can it come to terms with an intrinsically fuzzy field that is loosely demarcated by the label of 'Japan' or 'Japanese', while dealing with a phenomenon that is arguably the prime example of globalization? Speaking of sport in Japan or Japanese sport, the geographic and cultural allocation of 'Japan' is, contrary to first thought, far from being unproblematic. The label 'Japan' may refer to the state as the institution which claims to monopolize the legitimate use of power within a given territory, a claim which is often changing and disputed and hardly ever encoded. Or it may refer to the nation, as a populace held together by a particular kind of lasting identity that encompasses common myths of origin, historical memories, a common culture, conceptions of common rights, duties and economic opportunities and, above all, attachment to a given territory (Hargreaves 2000). Both notions are neither stable nor distinct. In the course of the 'short twentieth century' (Hobsbawm 1994), during which Japan turned into a colonial power, the territory of Imperial Japan and the conception of being Japanese changed a number of times. Even after the geographic boundaries of Japan were reduced once more to the archipelago it had spawned prior to the imperialist period, nationality remained contested territory. Japan, as any other multiethnic society, commands over a hegemonic national identity that is not fully inclusive. The concept of nation may be of global applicability, but because of the vast cultural variability in the construction of nations, nationality and nationalism, a full account of the peculiarities of the situation in which specific nationalities are operating is demanded (Bairner 2001).

Moreover, what makes the debate even more complicated is the fact that the history of and present-day sport in Japan cannot be adequately grasped without considering the manifold relations with the world of sport beyond Japan. Colonial empires, missionary regimes and international trade provided the premises for the early stage of the global spread of sport. Modern sport thus entered the non-Western world as a disciplinary regime, colonizing mind and bodies, consciously as well as subconsciously (Bale and Cronin 2003). In postcolonial times, the 'global media sport complex' (Maguire 1999)—consisting of international sport organizations, multinational media and communication networks and the global consumer industry—succeeded the early prompters as a powerful alliance of principal agents seeking to spread sport all over the world. Pursuing their own interests, these institutional actors accomplished the task of globalizing sport, thereby constructing the sanitized cosmopolitan air of universal sport and disguising its vernacular roots and local shoots.

As an anthropological project, a social scientific study of sport in Japan would locate the inquiry in particular times and places to find out the commonalities of body practices, games and contests that this society subsumes under the notion of sport and/or alternative concepts—and by the same token, identify the categorical differences and boundaries that are giving shape to a field of common interest. As a sociological project concerned with the particular social phenomenon of sport, the study would have to demonstrate how the production and consumption of sport is reflecting the social structure of society in time *and* in transition. The macro-sociological analysis of the political economy of sport and the body is loosely based on the assumption that society is segmented according to relations of ownership (Marx 2003 [1872]); social facts (Durkheim 1971 [1915]); or the interplay of wealth, prestige and power (Weber 2010 [1921–1922]), separating the various groups of society from each other and integrating them at a more distant level of aggregation, such as class, the local community or national society. Following the tradition of these giants of sociological theorizing, researchers have argued that sport is functionally equivalent to religious belief and ceremonies in producing organic solidarity across group boundaries in post-traditional society (Bromberger 1995), or that sport contributes to the alienation of the working class (Vinnai 1972) and the disguise of the oppressive forces of class relations in capitalism (Brohm 1978), or that sport is nothing but a microcosm of society, shaped and characterized by the same premises (Guttmann 1979).

A critical investigation into sport can, and in my eyes should, attempt to bridge the gap between local memories, archives and national knowledge systems, on the one hand, and transnational discourses and universal theories that consciously transcend the particularistic boundaries of Western epistemology on the other. Rather than strictly separating the structural from the actors-based approach as well as the symbolic from the material analysis, I argue for an integrated research programme that combines questions and insights of both fields of inquiry and theoretical claims. Figure I.1 shows the basic components and dynamics of interrelatedness mapping out the cornerstones of a praxeologist theory of body culture. In order to understand sport and body culture, we have to understand how within a certain field consciously and routinely performed practices of the body are legitimized by meanings and how these 'normalized' practices are giving shape to those structures and institutions in which they are taking place. Equally, we have to analyse how practices present and re-present meanings that are embodied in structures which in the first place have a major effect on the way in which practices can occur. The circular dynamic of this comprehensive understanding of body culture is frequently challenged by impacts coming from outside the field. These can turn into ruptures that enforce adaptation of practices, meanings and institutions, ultimately leading to transformation of the entire field of body culture.

A multidisciplinary research programme on sport and body culture that is focusing on the dynamic interrelationship of practices, meanings and structures would strive to find answers for questions on the roles of sport and

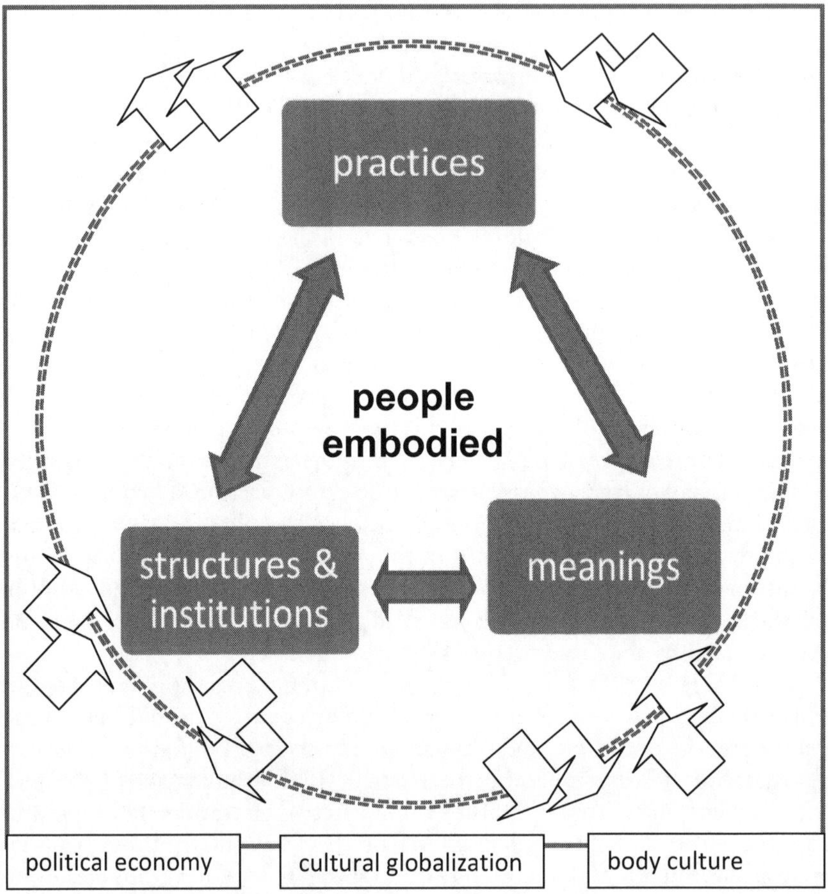

Figure I.1 A model of body culture.
Source: own creation, modeled after Liepins 2000.

body practices in regulating the social fabric of subject and society. More specifically, how and to what purposes are politics of the body articulated in Japan, particularly, but not exclusively, in the realm of sport? What is the agenda of state actors that develop politics aiming at the body? How are political decisions on the allocation of resources made, and what are their consequences for sporting opportunities and practices of the body in general? To what degrees are political and societal objectives impacted by the 'sport industrial complex', consisting of sport organizations, the sport industry and sport media, and other non-state actors? Such an approach would be concerned with the investigation of sport and the body in Japan as a distinctive place in contrast to other localities *and* the analysis of structural relations that shape the practice of sport in various social groups, all the while paying attention to Japan's relative positioning within the global political economy.

CULTURAL GLOBALIZATION

Cultural globalization, *body culture* and *political economy* are the three key terms framing this analysis of sport in Japan. The preceding section already indicated that a study on sport in a given locality is by necessity also a study on international relations and cross-cultural exchange. To be more precise, by studying sport in Japan, I wish to demonstrate that dynamics of globalization are influencing body cultures in Japan as elsewhere around the world, and the driving force behind this transformation is rooted in political economy. These key concepts and their particular value for analysing sport in modern and late modern societies will be addressed in the following sections. Here I will start with a short explanation of cultural globalization and its twofold nature: One dimension refers to the worldwide spread of culture, the second to the way in which culture is impacted by globalization.

Globalization became the dominant concept within the social sciences to frame the social, political and economic processes of the post–Cold War world system. Since the mid-1980s and the early 1990s at the latest, an increasing number of mindful observers noticed the rise of a new world economy that came to be characterized by the growing influence of global capital, the increased importance of transnational markets for financial services and specialized services for international investments and the new international division of labour based on low-paid and flexible labour relations. These changes of the economy were accompanied by the decreasing influence of national governments in the regulation of economic processes. Technological innovations such as world-encompassing computer and telecommunication networks facilitated the creation of transnational markets and their never-ceasing operations (Sassen 1998:xxvi). Within this scenario, sport has become inextricably linked to agents, structures and processes of global capitalism (Wright 1999).

In line with the economy, culture emerged as the second most important field of analysis for globalization theory. Notwithstanding the conceptual discord with historical traits—capitalism has always been global—and the nature of the effects of globalization (cf. Robertson 1990 vs. Giddens 1990), most commentators concur on the common notion 'of one single world or human society, in which all regional, national, and local elements are tied together in one interdependent whole' (Holton 1998:2). Accordingly, globalization is conceived as 'a process or a set of processes which embodies a transformation in the spatial organization of social relations and transaction—assessed in terms of their extensity, intensity, velocity and impact—generating transcontinental or interregional flows and networks of activity, interaction and the exercise of power' (Held et al. 1999:16). If culture is understood in its broadest sense as 'that complex whole which includes knowledge, belief, art, morals, law, custom, and any other capabilities and habits acquired by man as a member of society' (Edward B. Tylor [1871], quoted in Brumann 1999:3), then an understanding of cultural globalization would conform with globalization in its general usage. What else are economy, politics and social institutions if not parts of the inventory of the humanly created world? Hence to obtain a heuristic surplus from the conceptualization of cultural globalization, I suggest using a 'cognitive' definition of culture that emphasizes the mental orientations and predispositions that enable men to relate to each other in a meaningful way. A vintage example has been provided by symbolic anthropology that defines culture as the 'historically transmitted pattern of meanings embodied in symbols, a system of inherited conceptions expressed in symbolic forms by means of which men communicate, perpetuate, and develop their knowledge about and attitudes toward life' (Geertz 1973:89). According to Tomlinson (1999:105), the complex and multiform interrelations, penetrations and cultural mutations that characterize globalization are leaving their imprints on styles of cultural experience and identification everywhere. Cultural globalization hence impacts habits and attitudes of people around the world, yet without necessarily leading to uniform standards of behaviour and belief.

The impact of global economic flows on the culture of sport has been assessed in contrasting ways. Key notions of the debate, such as cultural imperialism (Tomlinson 1991) and cultural diffusion (Guttmann 1994), hybridization (Houlihan 1994) and homogenization (Harvey, Rail and Thibault 1996), glocalization (Robertson 1994) or grobalization (Andrews and Ritzer 2007), vary widely on directivity, processuality and agency. Considering the leading role of US business, Donnelly (1996) conceived of sport as another cultural form by which the world's nations are subjugated to American cultural hegemony. Refuting the 'Americanization' claim, Bairner (2001:14) doubted that 'the Americans have gone anywhere near to achieving the success of the British in terms of the actual export of games'. He even claimed that sport sociologists have been prominent in the struggle to ensure that the globalization process should not become identified with a relentless and irresistible surge toward total homogenization (Bairner 2001:11). Similarly, Maguire (1999:93) challenged the top-down unilateral power structure of homogenization. Instead of looking for one-directional flows, he insisted on multidirectional flows of cultural exchange and suggested that we should understand globalization 'in terms of attempts by more established groups to control and regulate access to global flows and also in terms of how indigenous peoples both resist these processes and recycle their own cultural products'. The key dichotomy emerging from his argument, 'diminishing contrasts, increasing varieties', echoes Appadurai's earlier observation 'that both sides of the coin of global cultural process today are products of the infinitely varied mutual contests of sameness and difference' (1990:308).

SPORT, PLAY AND CULTURE

As we know from the rich programme of sport media, sport nowadays consist of an ever-increasing pool of different sport forms. At the same time, however, regional differences and local particularities of sport practices diminish, as both local traditions (of folk games) and local versions (of world games) adjust to the dominant model of Western sport, outlined in Allen Guttmann's (1979) well-known explanation of the nature of modern sport. A closer look at the phenomenon of modern sport in any particular locality soon reveals the dialectics of universalism and particularism at work. While the global political economy under Western hegemony has played a crucial role in the dissemination of sport without doubt, a number of universal conditions have also facilitated the adoption and adaptation of sport all over the globe. I see these universalities rooted in the corporeality of sport, which I will address in the next section, and sport's intrinsic characteristics of the two interrelated binary pairs of certainty and uncertainty and the juxtaposition of sameness and difference.

Most, if not all, modern sports are based on the certainty of the claim that starting conditions are the same for all contestants. Once the race or the game is under way, certainty changes into uncertainty, as the goal of the game is to extract difference out of sameness: difference measured in seconds, centimetres, goals or points that draw the line between victory and defeat. The open nature of sport as a 'real-life event' that can change direction anytime creates thrill and suspense, giving birth to what Bette and Schimank (2000) identified as the particular aesthetic dimensions of sport. With rituals or ritual-like behaviour marking start and finish of the competition, or ceremonies heralding the temporary discontinuity of the rules of everyday life, sport is placed within a clearly demarcated spatial-time-frame constituting what could be called 'secondary life' in Bakhtin's (1987) terms. Yet as any ritual does, sport symbolically refers to the social order of the 'primary life', both in form and content (Alkemeyer 1997; Gebauer and Alkemeyer 2001). The symbolic message of the sport contest may conflict with the official ideology or the folklore theory of a community about its 'natural order' and underlying rationalities of hierarchy and power inequalities. Tensions and contradictions are formally mitigated because the performance of sport itself is ritually and symbolically separated from everyday life. Ever since anthropologists started to pay attention to the symbolism involved in the production of meaning, they have argued that any society has developed its own set of rituals and cultural media that function to maintain structure—or to subvert it (van Gennep 1960 [1909]; Geertz 1987; Turner 1982). Like initiation rites, spiritual ceremonies, carnivalesque spectacles and dramatic performances, the cultural form of sport constitutes such a powerful cultural device that can serve to instil certain orientations to the world in individuals, in the first instance through the symbolic manipulation of the body, in the second through the bodily manipulation of symbols.

Despite a long tradition of anthropological interest in ritual, it was the cultural historian Johan Huizinga who rated the inventive power of play and its impact on cultural change as the central and distinguishing feature of man. His seminal study on the culture of play (Huizinga 1955 [1938]) clearly demonstrated that all societies have known how to transform the basic play drive into a cultural expression by giving order to the movement of the body. Shared experience of the practising and trading of the knowledge how to play the game from one group to another subdued the chaos of natural play to the rules of social play. But in contrast to the folk games of premodern times, the sport of the 20th century was for Huizinga merely a corrupted aberration of cultural creativity, having lost most, if not all of its original play-like qualities to the allures of profit-making. Writers in the tradition of Critical Theory echoed his negative assessment. 'Sport is not play but ritual in which the subjected celebrate their subjectedness', wrote Theodor Adorno (1991:77) for whom sport represented the prime example of everything he despised in mass culture.

The universalism in play was also acknowledged by the French anthropologist Roger Caillois. His study *Les jeux et les hommes* (1958) expanded Huizinga's original observations in order to categorize societies according to the games their people prefer. He developed a matrix of types of game, based on whether the element of competition (*agon*), chance (*alea*), simulation (*mimicry*) or vertigo (*ilynx*, or inebriation) is dominating the stock of games held by society. At a second level of analysis, he differentiated between spontaneous, creative play (*paidia*) and rule-bound games (*ludus*). Even though most games tend to belong to more than one category, the typology enabled him to classify social entities by marking the structural analogies between a society's stock of games and its value system and normative orientation. As most sports are characterized by a competitive moment (*agon*) and rules (*ludus*) that help to determine the outcome of a contest, they fit well into the value system of liberal societies (as well as into capitalist economies, which is why Adorno disdained the passion for sport as the real mass basis of the dictatorial power of the masters of mass culture). Examples for Japan's traditional games with fundamental rules and a strong competitive stance include horse riding, archery, fencing with sword sticks, sumo wrestling, boat racing and *gichō*, a team game roughly comparable to field hockey; all of these activities flourished from the later Heian period (794–1185) well into the Edo period (1600–1867).

It must be noted that access to most of these pre-sport activities was restricted to specific segments of premodern Japanese society. In addition, the games and contests were usually part of a larger form of ceremony or ritual that directed their particular meaning away from the apparent triviality and make-believe of the world of play. The seriousness of non-play was even more pronounced in martial arts (*bugei*), which is the element of traditional body culture that Japan probably has become most famous for. Yet the way martial arts have turned into combat sports, and judo even into an Olympic sport, illustrates the way body cultures change and travel. The increasing mobility of people, texts and images of the 19th century did not only induce the reform of many Japanese martial arts in line with major didactic and ideological principles that were inherited from the competitive body cultures of the dominant West, but it also triggered their international diffusion. Highly personalized networks of knowledge that still mirrored the traditional dyadic master–disciple relationships within the world of martial arts characterized the early stage of the dissemination process. But in order to achieve worldwide recognition as modern sports, traditional reign later had to be replaced by bureaucratic rule, to borrow Max Weber's phrase. The Japanese martial arts received a huge promotional thrust once the established organizations in charge of education and preservation formally renounced their control rights in favour of centralized national and international sport federations. The deterritorialization of culture, stripping off the colour of local or parochial traditions and systems of thought, is an important prerequisite for a cultural forms' successful global diffusion, no matter whether it travels east or west (cf. Frühstück and Manzenreiter 2001). Yet deterritorialization does not imply the end of locality, rather it signifies its transformation into a more complex cultural space (Tomlinson 1999:149).

THE BODY IN CULTURE

Within this scenario of cultural transfer, bodies—as the corporeal interface between self and society—are of crucial importance for the performative acts of presentation and representation. As Susan Brownell (1995:11–13) argued in her ethnographically and historically grounded exploration of modern Chinese body culture, the structured body movements of sport will generate a moral orientation toward the world, if they are assigned symbolic and moral significance and if they are repeated frequently enough. The universe of sport, ranging from physical education at schools and workouts in fitness gyms to conspicuous styles of sport-related consumption and the highly mediatized spectacles of professional sport, provides a variety of widely accepted and commonly accessible venues for shaping, consuming and negotiating bodies and is therefore highly significant for a political economy centring on the body. Reading sport as cultural practice or performance thus requires understanding the fundamental relationship between subjective acting and objective conditions and the impact of the individual's action on the construction of these conditions.

The body has been noted and described as a signifier of cultural difference by travellers and ethnographers of all times. Yet it was Marcel Mauss (1989) who first elaborated on the socially mediated nature of any consciously or unconsciously initiated movement of the body. His ground-breaking essay 'The Techniques of the Body', originally published in 1934, turned the attention of the social sciences towards the constructed nature and cultural rooting of even the most profane everyday practices, such as walking or hand movements. The disciplining of physical and emotional drives into appropriate categories of behaviour and the ability to perform the bodily tasks as expected by one's society are all predicated on the deliberate separating of the body from its 'natural', undisciplined state. The French sociologist argued that the entire inventory of body movements is formed by 'education' and 'contact' (with the social environment), and he called the ways in which people in their respective society know how to use their bodies according to situational requirements, the 'techniques of the body'.

The notion of 'habitus', that helped Mauss to understand the human being as a totality in which the tangible aspects of human life are related with the body and its material experience, the techniques of work, control of emotion and the enactment of ritual and ceremonial performances, has been used by authors as different as Hegel, Weber, Durkheim, Polyani, Elias and Levi-Strauss. It was Pierre Bourdieu (1987), however, who sharpened the concept of habitus as an explanatory concept as well as an analytical tool. For his sociology of social practice, habitus became the central pillar, referring to a complex set of dispositions, a habitual way of being, that rests upon the objective conditions everyday life is subjugated to, such as race, class, wealth, etc., as well as the cultural expressions, media, rituals, games, etc., that represent society's stratification. The habitus is constructed through and manifested in the shapes of bodies, gestures and everyday usages of the body ranging from sitting and eating to ways of walking, running and using the body in sport. Moving beyond the subject–object dichotomy of sociological theory, Bourdieu (1990:53) grasped habitus as 'a system of structured (and) structuring dispositions, which is constituted in practice and is always oriented towards practical functions'.

The conception that the body and its movements are shapeable and in fact have to be shaped rigorously in order to achieve progress and mastery has been central to most traditional Japanese crafts, including the martial arts. As O'Neill (1984) summarized, the precise imitation and repetition of set models of action, as demonstrated by teachers, is the method of learning in all the traditional performing arts of Japan, and by way of extension, a preferred model of appropriation in Japanese culture. Instructors usually rely on non-verbal and kinetic modes of training. Beginners, but also advanced students, are expected to learn a craft, a movement or other body techniques by carefully observing and imitating the performance of their superiors. *Kata*, patterns of movements which in the case of martial arts contains a series of logical and practical attacking and blocking techniques, were developed as mnemonic vehicles through which the skill, or technique, could be passed down from one generation to the next. In the peaceful Edo period, the ultimate purpose of lethal effectiveness waned in significance, and the Confucian ethic of self-cultivation became a more appropriate frame of meaning. *Kata* in early modern martial arts thus came to emphasize exact form, not immediate effectiveness. Even in modern Japan, when the martial arts of feudal times were reinvented as physical education of the modern subject, the learning style of imitation and frequent repetition remained among the dominant patterns of practice. *Kata* served the body to memorize the techniques properly, *randori* and *kumite*, the free sparring practice, served to revise the practical knowledge and to confirm that the disciplined body was ever able to act instinctively.

If the body moves in unison with the demands of the moment, a perfect balance between skills and challenge is achieved. In the words of martial arts, the practising subject enters a state of no-mind (*mushin*). The sensual experience of *mushin* somehow corresponds with the state of flow, an intrinsically motivating and optimally rewarding condition into which an individual enters when he or she is fully immersed in an activity that is testing the limits of his or her skills, yet without putting it under stress (Csikszentmihalyi 1975). Linking Japanese martial arts techniques of the body with the phenomenological view of the body as it is experienced, Cohen (2006:77–78) argues that the practice of progress achieved by the endless repetition of movements does not simply lead to perfection, but to profound changes in the 'body-self'. Standing in the tradition of Zen, the ultimate goal of martial arts is supposed to achieve non-dualism through practice. Among Japanese martial art practitioners, the transcendence of consciousness is explained as a result of the individual's efforts to develop a sense of inner self. This requires the accomplishment of an outer self which is in harmony with the social order and the environment (Cox 1990:68–70); without subjugating the self to the primacy of the collective over the individual, such a balance cannot be achieved.

Similar observations on routine training methods, pedagogical philosophy and collective orientations have been made for a great number of sports in Japan, particularly within institutions of formal education. Herrigel (1953:44) noted that practice, repetition and repetition of the repeated are distinctive features for long stretches of the way to mastery in archery. Kelly (1998b) carefully plotted the way Japan's 'king of homeruns', Oh Sadaharu, learnt to swing the bat in endless sessions of repetitive drills and supervised practice. Field notes from sport lessons and training hours with school sport clubs in Japan reveal that also today a great proportion of time is consumed by repetitious training exercises performed over long periods of time with little or no variation. Writing on school football, Dalla Chiesa (2002) concluded that football is more about work than play. The way it is practised in training as well as in competitions actually serves to shape the players' moral (*seishin*) and social skills, utilizing the body as a somatic or corporeal tool. The social frame of the school sport club (*bu*) conveys a sense of stability and certainty to them which might be a surrogate for the absent pure pleasure of play. When coaching a Japanese university rugby club, Light (1999) noted that his students often referred to concepts that are subjectively understood and learnt through the body such as the notion of *seishin* (which Light translates as human spirit), *seishin ryoku* (spiritual power) and *gaman* (restraint). The regimes of training adopted by team players typically require commitment of the individual, group ethos and neglect of the self, perseverance and endurance of hardship, and reflect a general belief in the need to learn specific patterns. These are all characteristics highly valued by Japanese society and are also values that underpin education in contemporary Japan.

To summarize the debate on sport and body culture, sports are like any kind of cultural performance media of the 'somatisation of the social' (Bourdieu 1992) in a double sense. On the one hand, they are embodiments of objective conditions such as material, social and symbolic structures. On the other hand, they are performing media of embodied attitudes, worldviews or what Bourdieu called 'cultural dispositions'. The corporeal experience of sport practice mediates between the private world of everyday body techniques and the public world of shared performances. Sport engagement thus must be read as strongly related to an individual's habituation. Analysing the type of relation to the body a particular sport favours or demands, whether it is endurance, aesthetics, power, speed or skilfulness, reveals a lot about the way certain sport resonate with the tastes of particular social aggregates (Bourdieu 1986). But it would be premature to conclude that the place and meaning of sport in society are simply imposed from above by forces like the educational system, mass media or popular culture industries, as their appropriation and realization ultimately are open to debate, resistance and renegotiation. As cultural manifestations, the appearance of sport and the meanings associated with the rule-conducted and playful, yet in many cases also competitive and achievement-oriented practices of the body, have been changing with time and space, as well as the societies that created them. This is all the more the case under the condition of globalization.

POLITICAL ECONOMY OF THE BODY

Globalization, as we have seen, is more than just a commercially driven process aiming at the creation of a global market for products whose popular consumption leads to the standardization of cultures that were once distinctive. As argued elsewhere, globalization should also be understood as a 'practical logic', or a logic in practice that has come to be diffused on a planetary scale (see Manzenreiter and Horne 2004). In the sense of the taken-for-granted assumption, or orthodoxy, of the contemporary time, it corresponds to the notion of *doxa*, which Bourdieu (1977:168) explained in his *Outline of a Theory of Practice* as the unquestioned consensus based on 'theses tacitly posited on the hither side of all inquiry'. Acknowledging globalization as a 'pseudo-natural objective' accepted by people worldwide as 'the way things are' does not imply placing it merely in the sphere of consciousness or ideas, as this would fail to take its real-life dimensions as well as its historicity into account. Yet by emphasizing the relative importance of economic capital and the capitalist modes of production, distribution and exchange within the nodes and hubs of a globalized world, globalization must be acknowledged as an outcome of social and economic struggles, not from a moralizing point of view, but from a theorizing angle.

In as far as downplaying the struggles between social actors or systematically neglecting the social conditions of cultural products and production are concerned, Bourdieu has been most critical of the work by Michel Foucault. Bourdieu's radical repudiation of discourse analysis and structuralist semiology explicitly addresses Foucault's formulations on the intertwining of knowledge and power which, 'for want of taking into account agents and their interests, and especially violence in its symbolic dimensions', remain abstract and idealist (from *The Rules of Art*, quoted in Callewaert 2006:78). Despite Bourdieu's fundamental discomfort with Foucault's methodology, his theoretical contributions to the history of ideas, the micro-physics of power and the political economy of the body in particular deserve recognition as helpful tools for making sense out of how practices of the body and social structures are interconnected by way of 'discourses', ideas and meanings. These are genuine elements of the realm of culture, but Foucault's analysis clearly shows that they are political, too, since knowledge and power are inseparably interlinked.

Foucault's analysis is based on historical shifts of 'epistemes', or systems of knowledge that characterize a specific historic epoch: 'In any given culture and at any given moment there is only one episteme (system of knowledge) that defines the conditions of the possibility of all knowledge' (Foucault 1970:168). The tectonic shift towards the episteme of modernity, following upon the Renaissance episteme of resemblance and the Baroque episteme of representation, became evident in new ways of thinking about man as natural being and his body and human life in terms of biology. In the Classical Age of resemblance, knowledge of the body consisted of knowing it in relation to the divine order of the world through a seemingly endless chain of analogies, emulations, sympathies and congruencies. Knowledge in the age of representation, by contrast, became systematically ordered in networks of identity and differences. The knowledge facilitating the taxonomical and utilitarian perception of the body took shape in the foundations of the human sciences, including modern medicine, psychology, criminology, population studies and political economy (Amariglio 1988).

Political economy in its broadest sense should be foremost understood as a reference to its classical understanding as theoretical framework for varying approaches seeking to explain the relations between economic processes and social or political conditions. More of importance to this study is its conception in a more practical sense that conceives of political economy as a method to safeguard the accumulation of wealth of a nation and as such a particular form of governmental intervention which emerged in the transition 'from a regime dominated by structures of sovereignty to a regime dominated by techniques of government' in the 18th century (Foucault 2007:142). The emerging techniques of power were essentially centred on the individual body, to take control over it and increase its productive force through exercise and drill. The body of the modern subject was principally regarded as useful and docile; still each and every body had to be disciplined and subjected to the greater utilities it served.

Linking new forms of scientific knowledge with the new regime of the civic state, Foucault grasped political economy as the governing principle of bureaucratic rationality that restlessly pursues increases in efficiency: Its techniques of power 'were also techniques for rationalizing and strictly economizing on a power that had to be used in the least costly way possible, thanks to a whole system of surveillance, hierarchies, inspections, bookkeeping, and reports—all the technology that can be described as the disciplinary technology of labor' (Foucault 2003:240). Political economy is not simply knowledge aiming at the enrichment of the state, but the 'knowledge of processes that link together variations of wealth and variation of population on three axes: production, circulation, consumption' (Foucault 2007:450). The body of the populace not only provided labouring bodies to production, but also desiring bodies to the market. As power in Foucauldian terms is the cumulative effect of all social positions, rather than the privilege or possession by a single class of social actors, it achieves its goals without force, brutal oppression or open ideology. The corresponding strategies consist of diffuse, invisible technologies of power, embedded in the pores of everyday life, stretching into the most intimate zones of the body. Under the ubiquitous impact of the 'micro-power', the body is constantly placed in the political: 'Power relations have an immediate hold upon it, they invest it, mark it, train it, torture it, force it to carry out tasks, to perform ceremonies and to emit signs' (Foucault 1977:25). Because the political allocation of the body is tied to its economic utility, Foucault explicitly introduced the term of the political economy of the body.

A Foucauldian archaeology of knowledge spanning the past five or more centuries would reveal that in Japan the body has been similarly placed in varying epistemes shifting with the ages. To my knowledge, such a project is still wanting, and even a very first draft sketching its contours is certainly beyond the capabilities of this introduction. Such a task would have to carve out the analogies and networks between the living body and the metaphysics of the dominating Buddhist worldview of medieval times and how the emphasis on unreality of things has been systematically interlinked with the lack of sovereign state power, the major landholding structure of *shōen* (autonomous estates or manors) with its complex hierarchies of rights to income from the land, the omnipresence of warfare and death, the manifold uncertainties Japanese of all social origins experienced in this world and the historically unique prevalence of naturalist depictions of the human body in works of art, such as the oversized but hyperrealist wooden body sculptures of the *niō* (guarding figure) placed at many temple gates, the graphic depictions of corpses in the process of decay and decomposition (*kusō-zu*), or Ikkyū's poems on dying and burial rites (Yōrō 1996:203–204).

A history of thought for the following period would certainly take for its starting point the many tractates of Neo-Confucianism, which provided a heavenly sanction for the highly formalized social order of the Edo period (1600–1868). A system of thought explaining reality as well as issues of social responsibilities strongly harmonized with the needs of the centralized Tokugawa bureaucracy (*bakufu*) and its total authority over social mobility, economic activities, religious affairs, education and everyday life. This social philosophy, strongly shaped by the school of Zhu Xi (in Japanese *shūshigaku*) and Taoist traditions, was rooted in the idea that reality is shaped by the dynamic between the principle (*ri*) giving the universe its structure and its manifestations through energy or vital force (*ki*). Hence Neo-Confucianism equated the rigid corporate order of the four classes and the reciprocity of social relations with the cosmic harmony of the universe; similarly, health and well-being were also considered as an ephemeral state taking place only when the delicate balance between body and its environment had been achieved (Ohnuki-Tierney 1989:62). Kaibara Ekiken's famous tract *Yōjōkun* (Lessons on leading a healthy life, 1713; Kaibara 2010) described the appropriate techniques of the body and its underlying principles in great detail. With the help of dieting, exercises, mental control, sexual restraint and art of breathing, man was capable of achieving the balance and circulation of the vital power so that he or she could live for the entire predetermined span of life. As the body was regarded as a gift from heaven and earth, forwarded by father and mother, taking care of one's health was intimately related to filial piety and the maintenance of the cosmic order.

The Edo period concept of health did not separate body from mind and spiritual well-being. Health and longevity were maintained by an integrated body 'as a small universe in relationship with nature as a larger universe' (Takizawa 2011:5). Accordingly, traditional medicine of Chinese origin (*kanpō*) was concerned with making use of the five phases in nature (*gogyō*: wood, fire, earth, metal and water), which were equally constitutive factors in creating the universe. The cultivation of the self, based on a regular lifestyle in accordance with moral and ritual rules, linked personal health with social health, and human development with cultural refinement and society at large: Body care was clearly understood by Kaibara and his contemporaries as contribution to society at large. This was even more pronounced in the early 19th century, when the publication of self-cultivation texts (*yōjōron*) proliferated more than ever. At a time when the social reality of power and wealth was hardly in line with the ideals of Neo-Confucian doctrine, these manuals revealed a shift from a focus on disciplinary body techniques, such as self-restraint, body exercise and mental control, to a focus on coordination and quality of life by emphasizing the needs and tasks of morality, domestic economy and education (Takizawa 2011:7–8).

Japanese-style physiocratism during the Edo period did not recognize the value of the individual: While land and agriculture provided the economic base of the state and income for the nobility, the smallest unit of any economic planning was the family whose labour in the fields yielded the rents that contributed to the collective tax load of the village. Only the 'great transformations' of the 19th century separating the age of Japan's modernity from its antecedent period made it possible to speak of a political economy centring on the body. Western state theory radically changed the relationship between the individual and the social order. The strategies utilized by the Meiji government complied with the previously outlined technologies of bureaucratic rule by and large. The modern institutions of compulsory education and conscription army served as powerful tools to transform the peasant body and conduct according to the needs of modern 'statefare' (governance). Cultivation of one's self continued to be seen as standing in the service of the larger collective. But under the impact of Western sciences and medical knowledge in particular, the comprehensive view on health and illness in relation to the cosmic order was replaced by a compartmentalizing perception of the body divided in its parts.

It must be noted that the body politics of the modern or premodern epistemes never exerted the same effect, nor were they equally endorsed by all segments of society. For example, the confinement of body movements, postures and attitudes was most prominent among the samurai and urban upper classes but hardly filtered down to the lower levels of society, which also rebelled against the later ban of nudity in public by the Meiji government (Nomura 1990:262). Public health measures against cholera, such as isolation hospital, conflicted with the more familiar diagnosis of causes and cures of similar symptoms by *kanpō* physicians, who practised Chinese herbal medicine, and often provoked open protest and even popular riots (Suzuki and Suzuki 2009:189). Despite of the suppression of *kanpō* medicine and the enforced normalization of public health according to Western scientific knowledge on health and the body, Taoist belief and Shintoist symbolic notions of purity and impurity continued to inform folklore understandings of illness and health care among the Japanese deep into the 20th century (Ohnuki Tierney 1984).

ABOUT THIS STUDY

All of the following chapters contribute to the programme I have briefly outlined here. Each chapter was originally drafted to address a particular theoretical problem or to answer a specific research question. But they all resonate with the common programmatic of coming to terms with the interaction of universal, global and local forces that shaped the way sport in Japan has been understood ever since the country opened for cultural exchanges with the Western world. Dealing with the numerous cultural, social, political and economic relationships and processes—including transcultural iconographies, global labour migration, new technologies of governance and border-crossing capital flows—that affect cultural globalization demands a variety of approaches and multidisciplinary analysis. Hence this study consists of methodologies from the fields of sociology, anthropology, management studies, political science, cultural studies and history. Sociology, as John Horne (2006:15) aptly reminded the readership of his study on sport in consumer culture, is better qualified than most other disciplines for making sense out of sport: The discipline of sociology is inherently theoretical and comparative, interested in social and historical contexts and encourages empirical research that employs a variety of perspectives and models to gain new insights into the fabrics of social life.

The first part on 'Configurations of Modernity: Sport, the Body and the Nation' contains three chapters that deal with the early stages of the history of modern sport in Japan. This period was of crucial significance for providing fertile ground for the cultural import and the direction of its further development. The first chapter, using the method of historical comparison, delineates the process of institutionalization in Japan and Austria, which were both latecomers in the modernization process. Looking at actors, organizations and institutions, from fields as dispersed as politics, economics and science, that were involved in opening new spaces for the practice of sport, this chapter identifies the transfer routes, networks of actors and their interests that finally led to the establishment of sport in these places. The comparison of two case studies that started from very different cultural outsets yet had a number of structural similarities provides empirical evidence for the interlude of universal forces and particular factors behind the dynamics of cultural change. Regional asymmetries that emerged during the institutionalization process are also addressed by Chapter 2 on the spatial provision and arrangement of sport spaces in early 20th-century Japan. This chapter transcends developments in sociology, anthropology, social history, social geography and political economy to reconstruct the emergence of a public–private sport infrastructure. Historical accounts and early data collected by the public bodies in charge of sport and physical exercise suggest the weight of the Japanese government as the principal agent behind the designation of space for the Japanese sport landscape, particularly because space is a limited and highly contested resource in modern societies. Chapter 3 then takes a closer look at the role sport played in supporting the totalitarian regime of the imperialist state. The Japanese government initiated various techniques to discipline and mould the population into a servile and compliant mass. Sport played a crucial role for physical disciplinization, as well as moral guidance, but less for nationalist indoctrination. In further contrast to the fascist states in Europe, which this analysis only implicitly refers to, the totalitarian state tolerated new ideas and usages of sport for commercial interest that had been brought forward by the new mass entertainment industries of the interwar period.

Inquiry into the ways the state has been using the politics of the body to steer its people continues throughout the following five chapters in the second part on 'New Roles, New Faces: Sport in the Service of Various Masters'. While this part is the most sociological, insofar as the questions addressed and theories employed are concerned, each of the studies acknowledges that historical background provides significant information to contextualize the main argument. Chapter 4 takes a closer look at the contribution of school sport to the production and reproduction of a hegemonic gender order. The analysis of curricula of physical education and statistical data on school sport clubs enrolment shows that both national education politics and the 'hidden curriculum', which is deeply tainted by the gendered worldview of Japanese society, have had a lasting impact on the gendering of sport involvement. The next three chapters also take issue with state politics centring on the body and the implementation of sport and health politics. Chapter 5 is concerned with the funding of the Japanese sport infrastructure today under the framework of Japan's sport for all policy; Chapter 6 demonstrates how Japanese state authorities have been employing sport to address the challenges of aging and old age in contemporary Japan; and Chapter 7 places the government's concern with fighting obesity in the context of sociological debates about risk, reflexivity and governance in late modernity. The final chapter of this part examines Japan's experience in hosting the 2002 FIFA World Cup and what kind of benefits were anticipated and actualized by the hosting authorities. Drawing on macroeconomic data and an ex post survey among bureaucrats from the host cities, this case study provides evidence about the failure of the commonly purported yet hardly ever realized economic benefits of hosting a sport mega-event. All the chapters in this part clearly show that state interest in sport is no longer restricted to the moulding of a national body and that sport is confronted with a great variety of new expectations. Sport today is increasingly seen as potentially providing a 'feel-good' factor that central and local governments are eager to capitalize on. Furthermore, the political class has also come to value and employ sport as a tool to fix some of the most urgent problems of contemporary society, such as unemployment, regional economic disparities, underfunded public budgets and the future of a fragile public health system. In its attempt to respond to such crises, the state also uses the core strategies of neoliberal rule: privatization, deregulation and liberalization, albeit in a particular way that fits with Japanese institutions.

The third and final part of the book on 'Global Dimensions: Sport and Geo-Politics of the Body' does not necessarily focus on Japan and Japanese actors alone. Instead of looking at the Japanese sport system from the inside, these studies locate Japan and the usage of sport in the East Asian region into the contexts of international relations and global power asymmetries. Drawing on assumptions derived from world systems theory, Chapter 9 argues that debates on the symbolic meaning and the political usage of sport in East Asian diplomacy have oscillated between postcolonial nation-building and the politics of regional integration. Historical accounts and recent events clearly show that Japan as well as other nation-state actors in the region and elsewhere have utilized the global game of football as a vehicle for the acquisition of power and the expression of status in the international community of states. Adding postcolonial discourse to the world systems approach, Chapter 10 critically explores the difficulties of articulating national identity and equal representation at spectacular sport mega-events such as the FIFA Football World Cup and the Summer Olympic Games. The under- and oftentimes misrepresentation of East Asia and its traditional notions of body culture within the world sport system is largely caused by the institutional design and parochial ideology of the powerful international non-governmental organizations in charge of world sport and its major events and competitions. The difficulties of coming to terms with representing the nation vis-à-vis the dominant West are amplified by the sport NGOs' reliance on financial, technical and moral assistance from corporate sponsors, transnational media industries and humanitarian actors seeking to employ the sport spectacle for their particular needs. The power of transnational capital and corporations that bypass national state regulations and capitalize on uneven development and other asymmetries is addressed in Chapter 11 on the position of East Asia within the border-crossing production networks of global sport apparel and equipment makers. Searching for commonalities and congruencies among the various approaches and findings of the individual chapters, the epilogue will turn once more to the implications of bringing together the fields of body culture, political economy and cultural globalization. That the notion of the 'global' is most pronounced throughout the chapters in this final part of the book reaffirms my argument that the sociological study of sport in Japan is a study of and in globalization. Hence while this book deals empirically with the manifold facets of a phenomenon in a particular place, its theoretical framework never loses sight of the wider global cultural and political economy within which people live and nation-states operate.

Part I

Configurations of Modernity

Sport, the Body and the Nation

1 Modern Bodies, Capital Cities
The Institutionalization of Sport in Late Nation-States[1]

INTRODUCTION

Empirical studies of the meaning of sports in contemporary Japan point out the multilayered complexity of attitudes and expectations with which sport is confronted (Asada and Kataoka 1975; Ehashi 1979; Niwa and Kaneko 1983; Niwa 1985; Kusaka and Maruyama 1988; Sanbonmatsu 1979, 1994). Depending on the kind of sport involvement, the particular kind of sport, the social framework of sport participation or the distribution of standard social variables, sport participants tend to put more emphasis on either one or more of the following features with which sport is commonly associated: social integration, health care, enhancement of physical attractiveness, testing one's physical limits or obtaining a sense of relaxation, entertainment or excitement. The quantitative research methods employed for the majority of these surveys are extremely helpful for understanding the comparatively high significance of the social group by which individuals are socialized into sports. Although there is a considerable lack of comparable empirical data sets on sport consciousness for any period prior to the 1980s, I think that the relative importance of the social environment of sport practice justifies the argument that the diversification and pluralization of attitudes towards sport is a rather recent phenomenon of consumer society. Since the 1970s, when private enterprises in Japan awoke to the promising prospects of the sport market, they successfully managed to establish their sport-related products as lifestyle markers and to fragment the sport market into smaller sub-units according to the diverging lifestyle designs of their customers (cf. Tokunaga and Ōhashi 1982; Sugimoto 1995).

This development, which might be characterized as typical for any late modern society, does not necessarily require us to reject the notion of a specific Japanese understanding of sport as outlined by critical sport sociologists and education specialists such as Nakamura Toshio (1981, 1995), Kawaguchi Tomohisa (1962, 1966) or Seki Harunami (1997). In fact, the aggregation of the survey results mentioned above supports the assertion that the traditionally dominant sport ideology (Uesugi 1982) emphasizing competitiveness, self-abnegation, group dependency, spirituality, will for power and lack of rationality has been at work in many social contexts of sport throughout the 20th century. In order to obtain insight into the origin of the Japanese notion of sport and to understand why this particular sense of sport achieved and maintained predominance against competing sport ideas, I suggest taking a closer look at the very early years of modern sports in Japan. Specifically, such an analysis should centre on the parameters of social agency, social distribution and social legitimization within the institutionalization process of sport.

This chapter is going to explore the way in which sport that once had been a preserved leisure activity of a small elite in Victorian England became part of the commonly shared culture of Japan and Austria. In methodological terms, this study of the early years of modern sport in Japan will develop its arguments on the basis of a historical comparison that puts these remote places into the context of the political economy of the 19th century. In terms of political and economic development, both imperial Austria and Japan justifiably are said to be late-developing nations. Notwithstanding the delay of the industrial revolution and the transformation of the political system, the Austrian as well as the Japanese people experienced severe changes in the second half of the 19th century. Both the March Revolution (1848) in Austria and the Meiji Restoration (1868) in Japan were crucial for the emergence of modern nation-states in the long run. Short-term effects, however, proved to be adversary as the power hegemony of aristocracy managed to ride out the turmoil in a refreshed way. Thus the most important 'revolutions' in the modern history of the two nations contributed to delaying the development of equality, civil rights and opportunities of political participation.

However, it goes without saying that the everyday life of the people was deeply affected by the continuous progress from feudal society to the pre-stages of modern society. As a consequence of the dynamics of political and social change, the relationships between the individual and the collective were to be redefined. Within the newly shaped state–subject relationship, the body was assigned a crucial role: The 'modern body' in the context of this chapter is not only a metaphor for the individual's capacity to reflect upon his or her body, particular the body in motion. At the same time, 'modern body' signifies the increasing interest of the state in the physical bodies of its subjects. The close relationship between the emergence of modern sports and the nation-state has been observed by sport sociologist Inagaki Masahiro. He stated that the import of the foreign cultural device had to traverse three stages until the practice finally became part of the indigenous cultural inventory. Firstly, rules have to be standardized and accepted throughout the country. Secondly, organizations that are in charge of affairs related to a particular kind of sport on a national scale must be established. And, finally, national competitions and tournaments have to be conducted (Inagaki 1987). The model of cultural accommodation, of which the framing dates are outlined in Figure 1.1, will be tested further in the discussion that follows.

Imperial Japan Constitution of 1889	Late developing nations	**Imperial Austria** Constitution of 1867
martial arts + folkloristic games / popular entertainment	vernacular body practices	body practices of the nobility + folk games
since 1850s	first exposure to sport	since 1840s
since 1860s sports and gymnastics	initiation	since 1840s Turnen (PE) since 1860 sports
?	adaptation ▼ appropriation	?
1911: Dainippon Taiiku Kai (~ NOC; 1912 Stockholm)	institutionalization	1908: Joint Sport Committee (~ NOC)

Figure 1.1 'Black box' cultural accommodation: Historical timeline of the institutionalization of sport in Japan and Austria.

Impact and timing of such transformations differed considerably within Japan and Austria, and it is justified to state that domestic discrepancies were by far larger than differences between these nations. The farming population in the remote areas in Japan's northeast or the Austrian Alps were comparatively weakly exposed to technological progress, the development of traffic routes and communication infrastructures or the emergence of national media. Yet the inhabitants of the capitals of Vienna, of which the population doubled in the second half of the 19th century, and Tokyo, already then counting more than one million inhabitants, were placed at the forefront of the modernization of everyday life. Capital cities as a hotbed of international encounters, new fashions and lifestyles play in general a seminal role in processes of cultural diffusion. Both Vienna, capital of the Habsburg Empire, and the new metropolis of Meiji Japan, Tokyo, spearheaded the nationwide development transforming vernacular traditions of body culture under the influence of modern sports.

The spread of modern sports started in England and reached via neighbouring countries even the most distant places in the world. The new cultural practice disseminated from the centres of political and economic power to the peripheries, from the capitals to the smaller cities and rural areas (cf. Figure 1.2a, 1.2b). The aspiration of imitating the lifestyle of the 'leisure class' as well as the worldview based on rationalism and accountability were characteristic traits of the new English middle class, whose members reinvented folk games and transformed rural traditions according to their own class logic. Thus sports turned into a powerful cultural device for the new elites of the countries that spearheaded the path to modernity. This is no less true for the latecomers.

Cultural flows have been discussed in terms of cultural imperialism (whereby the colonizer forces the colonized party to subjugate to its practices, norms and values, e.g. Tomlinson 1991; Galtung 1991), cultural diffusion (formerly parochial practices spill over to neighbouring regions and countries in concentric waves, e.g. Guttmann 1994; Norden 1998), or cultural hegemony (dominance is achieved and maintained by negotiating power relations between all parties involved, e.g. Hargreaves 1986; Yamashita 1997). Similar to the worldwide spread of American popular

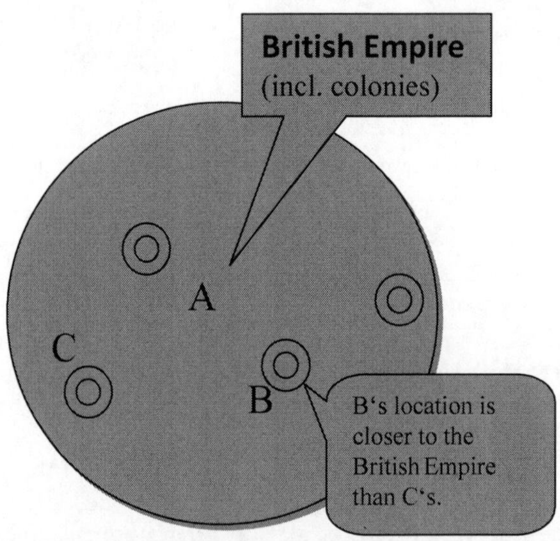

Figure 1.2a A-B-C dissemination model: The geography of distance.

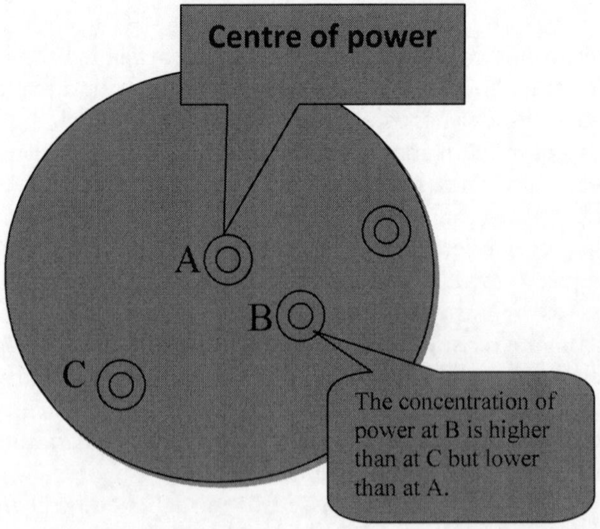

Figure 1.2b A-B-C dissemination model: The geography of power.

culture, the global expansion of modern sports has repeatedly been criticized as cultural imperialism. However, as I am going to discuss, this approach has its own shortcomings. First, it assumes a one-sided power relationship with an almighty state on top and marionette-like subjects at the bottom. Second, it fails to take into account the particular interests of the subjects that are less submissive and disempowered than the one-sided approach assumes. In consequence, a more benevolent concept such as cultural diffusion is better placed to take the power structure of the modern nation-state, where the nation is the sovereign, into consideration without neglecting the role of agency. Therefore I attempt to analyse which actors, organizations and institutions from fields as dispersed as politics, economics and science were involved in opening places for enacting the cultural practice of sport. The comparison of two case studies on the institutionalization process that start from very different cultural outsets yet have a number of similarities, is a promising endeavour in order to get hints at the interlude of general forces and particular factors behind the dynamics of cultural change. By looking at the specific traits of modern sports in these two 19th century capitals, I will discuss channels of import, agents of change, political interests and social organizations related to the early period of institutionalization of sport in the modern nation-state. Contrary to the notions of path-directed modernization and the levelling power of globalization, the comparative analysis of national sportscapes clearly argues in favour of a balanced approach paying attention to the impact of vernacular traditions and local culture.

MAKING SENSE OF 'SPORT'

The term 'sport' was hardly known in either Japan or Austria during the first half of the 19th century, and neither was the idea of sport. Even in England, throughout the 18th century the word 'sport' signified almost exclusively gaming or hunting. The meaning of play-like activity, pleasure and competition started to spread abroad in the first half of the 19th century. But it took more than 50 years for Austria, and in the case of Japan almost a century, until the concept of sport was fully understood by people in Japan and Austria. On July 1, 1880, the first number of Vienna's earliest sport newspapers was published by the Austrian pioneer of sport writing and sport enthusiast Victor Silberer (1846–1924). The name of the weekly, *Allgemeine Sport-Zeitung*, indicated that by this time the modern meaning of sport was commonly known, at least known enough for sales promotion, even if actual sport participation was low (Maruna 1998:188). In Japanese, quite different words were used to equalize English sport: The earliest English-Japanese dictionary from 1814, the *Angeria gorin taisei* by Motoki Shōzaemon, translated sport as *shōka*, *nagusami*, meaning amusement. References to amusement (*tawamure*), play (*yūgi*), hunting (*kari*) or fishing (*gyo*) predominated in the 19th century. According to Abe Ikuo's seminal study of the etymology of the term of 'sport' in Japan (Abe 1988), it was only in the Taishō period (1912–1926) that references to the contemporary usage of the word started to appear in Japanese-English dictionaries. Athletic sports were mentioned first in Ernest Satow's *An English-Japanese Dictionary of the Spoken Language* (1904). While Satow's translation, undō, corresponded with the usage at higher institutions, Inouye's *English-Japanese dictionary* (1915) listed a new word, *kyōgi*, that emphasized the competitive aspect. Japanese monolingual encyclopedias included the loanword of sport only from the 1930s. The *Daigenkai* (1932) explained *supōtsu* as *kōgai yūgi* (outdoor games) or *yagai undō kyōgi* (outdoor athletics). The *Great Heibonsha Encyclopedia* from 1934–1935 already hinted at the conceptual problems of explaining a term used and instrumentalized for so many different purposes as physical education, mass training and hedonistic pleasure (Abe 1988:16–19).

The fact that sport derived from the English language does not mean that play and physical exercise prior to the global spread of sport had been limited to the Anglo-Saxon cultural sphere. When Francis Ottiwell Adams joined the first American Legation at Edo as secretary, he observed that only the higher levels of the domain school system educated their pupils in physical education: The three-year middle school course included daily lessons in either fencing, wrestling or spear exercise, and a monthly practice on horseback under the guidance of expert instructors. At the high school level, 'the students spent more time in the gymnasium and on the riding-course, becoming proficient in riding, wrestling, archery, fencing, long and short spear exercise, and the various arts by which an unarmed man may defend his life and injure his enemy, were parts of the curriculum' (Adams 1914:445). In Imperial Austria, skills- or strength-contesting games such as horse riding and fencing, but also swimming and *Jeu de Paume*, a precursor of modern tennis, were also widely popular particularly because they served to educate the nobility and to teach their sons in martial arts and war strategy well.

Yet we have good reasons to believe that only present-day observers regard these activities as sports. At the time when the term of 'sport' was imported into the vocabularies of Japanese and German, both languages did not have an equivalent cover term matching the connotation of modern sport. The vacancy is not restricted to the linguistic inventory. On the conscious level, the capacity (and the need) to assign all these activities to a single, higher-ranking category did not exist. Defining sports on a synchronic level is difficult enough because of the continuous transformation process. Complications grow once the historical perspective is added: British sport sociologists advise wisely against all attempts to fixate form and content of sports, as they develop in line with the changes of time and societies (Horne, Tomlinson and Whannel 1999).

CENTRAL SPORTS AND MARGINAL SPORTS

Separate from conceptualization problems on a cognitive level, differences between modern sport and its precursors from ancient times to the early modern period clearly occurred in functional terms. Allen Guttmann's (1979) comparison of historical sports phenomena has led to the well-known insight that modern sports were clearly marked by seven factors: secularization, equality, specialization, rationalization, bureaucratization, quantification and a quest for records. Whereas premodern sport games were primarily related to external purposes such as religious rites or communal affairs, modern sports emerged in the modernization process as self-centred institutions. The aristocratic idea of 'sport for the purpose of sport' was symbolized by the highly contested amateur status that excluded the early professionals in sport from participating at the Olympic Games. As the regulation restricted the right to participate only to the noble and the wealthy (Fetscher 1996:132), it factually expelled the working class, who possessed neither the material nor immaterial resources required for sincere involvement, from participation at official contests. In Japan, where the first body in charge of the national sport regulation was remodelled according to European sport organizations and the International Olympic Committee in particular, effects were basically the same. The Greater Japan Amateur Sports Association (Dainippon Taiiku Kyōkai) neatly differentiated professional competitors (*shokugyō kyōgisha*) from semi-professionals (*jun shokugyō kyōgisha*), instructors (*kyōgi shidōsha*) and regular competitors (*futsū kyōgisha*): Workers were defined as quasi-professionals and thereby generally excluded from any event organized by the association; the association entitled itself the right to concede exceptions on a case-to-case basis (Kaga 1978:148–149).

Martial arts serve as a good example to illustrate the differences between the universal principles of modern sport and the locally rooted sport cultures of premodern times. While martial arts originally had to fulfil the purpose of warfare (fighting and killing), the practical value of fighting skills dwindled under the lasting hegemonic rule of the Tokugawa. Control over basic or better skills of martial arts remained closely connected to the class of the *bushi* (samurai) because these capabilities were the solemn basis of their superior positioning within the Confucian class system of the Edo period. Consequently, accessibility to the *dōjō*, the training ground of a school, was exclusively limited to members of the warrior class. At least this was the principle. In reality the separation between classes became less strict once the economic base of society started to shift. In the long course of the peaceful Edo period, expertise in warfare and real-life fighting were devalued. Thus some impoverished masters of martial arts were forced to regard their skills as a craft for earning a livelihood and opened their dōjō for wealthier merchants (Manzenreiter 2005). Given the rich political and social context represented by the functional transformation of sword fencing, Norbert Elias (1982, 1989), who interpreted the emergence of modern sport as a response to the state's monopolization of physical violence, certainly would have taken the appeasement of the warrior class and the 'sportification' of their skills as indicative of the civilizing process in a non-European context.

The samurais of the warring centuries were generalists rather than specialists as they were expected to excel in any of the martial arts. However, the trend towards specialization increased over time when mastery in martial arts was no longer the basic prerequisite of the warrior class's craft but a tool for self-development and self-completion. During the relatively peaceful Edo period, schools (*ryūha*) that specialized in a single craft emerged and competed with rival schools for adherents. Intra-school contests provided the opportunity to exhibit proof of individual skills and the superiority of style-specific techniques—as such, their promotional value was priceless—but they were often forbidden by local sovereigns (Hurst 1998:179). The typical instruction method relied on the close relationship between master and pupil, oral tradition and close imitation. Licenses (*menkyō*) were granted to the successful apprentice at various stages of the education permitting them to perform certain techniques and finally teach the art in the name of the school. The licensing system was also a vague scale of expressing skills and strength, but the awarding system was far from being standardized. The final license permitted the establishment of one's own training centre (*dōjō*). Due to fragmentation and separation, new schools emerged, amounting to many hundreds in the late Edo period (Hurst 1998:177–189).

The trends towards specialization and functional re-orientation helped to secure the survival of the otherwise useless art. But many of Japan's autochthonous martial arts were threatened to fall into oblivion after the country set out for its modernization programme in the Meiji period (1868–1912). When the country was opened for cultural imports from the West, preserving its own heritage was not in vogue. It is the merit of a single man that Japan's indigenous contribution to the world of sports remained. During his student years at Tokyo University, Kanō Jigorō (1860–1938) met the German medic Erwin von Baelz, who was in service of the Japanese government to contribute to the establishment of modern medical sciences in Japan. Like many other foreigners, Baelz unconsciously reflected upon his own humanist educational ideals and thus was prompted to lament the one-sided emphasis on intellectual education among students and blunt disregard of the necessity of physical exercise. Kanō, who was studying various techniques and styles from the many schools of *jūjutsu*, was encouraged by the German medic to preserve the traditional heritage of martial arts. Assembling techniques from the styles he had studied, Kanō refashioned traditional martial arts in line with the internal structural principles of Western sports. Thus he constructed a new kind of martial art that he deemed suitable for modern society. The introduction of a neatly differentiated ranking system, the internal reward structure of *kyū* and *dan* grades, clear-cut competition rules, a rational training system and modern instruction techniques linked the tradition of jūjutsu with modern sport and contributed to the attractiveness of his *kōdōkan jūdō*. But judo was designed to be more than just a sport. Kanō developed an extensive theory underlying the practice of judo and emphasized its social and ethical merits. Sport practice thus was closely related to the educational process of character building and the individual's contribution to the good of the nation (Niehaus 2003; Inoue 1992, 1998). In the long run, Kanō's concept was successful enough to influence many of the reinvented martial arts such as *kendō*, *karate-dō* or *aikidō* that were adapted to the basic scheme outlined by Kanō. The sportification of martial arts thus began in Japan, albeit inspired by direct exchanges with Western educationalists, and reached its climax when far away from the Japanese soil, the decision fell to make Judo an Olympic sport. Having spread to the West since the turn of the century, Japanese martial arts became the first internationally acknowledged contribution from non-Western origin to global body culture. Yet in direct comparison to the Western-style central sports, such as football, basketball, volleyball or track and field, Japan's own judo, karate and kendo are just marginal sports, even on a domestic level.

TURNEN AND GYMNASTICS

In Habsburg Austria, the right to sports was primarily a prerogative of the ruling class. Their offspring was instructed at military academies, which were opened only to the youth of the nobility, in the art of riding, fencing and swimming. In the middle of the 19th century, these educational institutions played a crucial role in the transformation of body culture. First, schools such as the military academy at Vienna were opened to wealthy commoners in the aftermath of the March Revolution of 1848, and thus contributed to the levelling of class differences. Second, they provided the space for testing and spreading newly introduced sports activities. Two different currents acted contemporaneously upon the young bodies. English sports reached this part of central Europe only in the second half of the century, while German-style gymnastics were already practised in 1838. Albert von Stephani (1810–1844), who had studied in Berlin with Ernst Eiselen (1792–1846), started to teach gymnastics to the students of the Theresianum academy in Vienna in 1838. The multi-ethnic empire of Austria struggled hard to maintain a balanced treatment of its people. Officials eyed the new practice suspiciously, particularly because the German Turner movement had been started by Ludwig Jahn (1778–1852) as a nationalist reaction against the Napoleon occupation. Twenty years earlier, the Austrian chancellor Metternich had even recommended to the Prussian king the abolition of the Turner movement for political reasons.

Therefore the practice of turnen was introduced under the less ominous name of gymnastics. In 1861, gymnastics became part of public schooling through an edict of the municipal government of Vienna. In 1868 the Ministry of Education declared gymnastics as a compulsory subject in all elementary schools, and the education of sport instructors began in 1871 (Strohmeyer 1998b:45–47). School gymnastics were based on strictly regulated and standardized movements, suppressed individuality and promoted group consciousness. Therefore, the subject lacked any incentives to develop more than basic skills. Yet these principles corresponded strongly with the educational ideas of the dominant Herbart philosophy, and gymnastics based on emulation soon became the international standard (Größing 1998:202).

The foundation of private unions or societies was detained by the lack of civil rights. Hardly any were established prior to the liberalization of the 1860s. However, when the Austrian constitution of 1867 granted the right of assembly, citizens as well as proletarian workers started to establish their own gymnastic unions and sport clubs in rapid succession. Austrian unions were chiefly involved in the inauguration of the German federation of gymnastic societies in 1868 (Deutscher Turnerbund). Although a similar association for Austria was formed in 1872 under the name of 'Turnkreis 15', Austria remained part of the all-German federation until 1904. According to Inagaki Masahiro (1995), gymnastics flourished especially in the Northern part of Europe because the late developers, Germany, Sweden and others regarded gymnastics as useful and effective tools to catch up to the leading nations. Meiji Japan also adopted gymnastics for precisely the same purpose of nation-building. Bureaucrats as well as educators soon realized the potential of educating the nation through physical training. While the 'pugnacious body' of the elitist samurai had been the ideal of the body culture in feudal Japan, modernizing Japan preferred the 'docile body' of the masses, trained in calisthenics.

Gymnastic training that already had been taught at various fief schools (hankō) during the 1860s was actively promoted by the modernist and intellectual Fukuzawa Yukichi (1835–1901) at his private institution of higher education, Keiō Gijuku (today better known as Keiō University; Shirahata 1994, 1999). Fukuzawa's writings of the 1860s used either the Japanese words undō and yūgi or the loan word of *jimunasuchikku* (Shirahata 1999:61–62). A first Japanese translation of *taisōjutsu* was available since 1868. This term, consisting of the characters for body (*tai*, *karada*), handle (*sō*, *ayatsuru*) and technique (*jutsu*), is probably rooted in a direct translation from the French *art d'exercer le corps*, which became *karada o ayatsuru jutsu*, or *taisōjutsu* in Sino-Japanese reading. It is speculated that the word *taisōjutsu* was created by Nishi Amane, the founder of modern philosophy in Japan who became later head of the teacher training institute in Tokyo and as such chiefly involved in drafting the Imperial Rescript to Soldiers (*gunjin chokuyu*) (Shimizu 2001:81–82).

At public schools, the compulsory subject of gymnastics was implemented at elementary school level as early as 1872. The Education System Order of 1872 (*gakusei*) that laid the foundation for the establishment of Japan's first modern education system listed the subject of gymnastics (*taijutsu*, since 1873 *taisō*). A first instruction manual of six volumes was translated from French in 1873. In order to define content, purpose and methods of teaching for courses in physical education, George Adams Leland, an authority on physical education from Amherst College, Massachusetts, was invited to Japan in 1876 by the vice minister of education, Tanaka Fujimaro (1845–1909), who was in charge of conducting the establishment of the national school system. Starting in 1878, Leland suggested a lighter version of gymnastics (*kei taisō*, also normal gymnastics, *futsū taisō*) which aimed at promoting health and was deemed to be more suitable to the average Japanese physique. This approach paralleled Tanaka's new education policy aiming at a less centralized system of higher flexibility and more awareness of Japanese traditional values. Leland also supervised the foundation of a special research and education college for sport teachers, the Physical Education Training College (Taisō Denshūsho), the education of the first instructors specialized on physical education and the compilation of a standardized syllabus (Takenoshita and Kishino 1959:9–11).

Basically two currents of interest determined the physical education policy in early Meiji Japan. Liberal-minded educationalists such as Izawa Shūji (1851–1917), who served as the first director of the Physical Education Training College in Tōkyō, and Tsuboi Gendō (1852–1922), the former interpreter of American Marion Scott, who had been recruited to innovate teaching methods and administration in the early 1870s, sympathized with the humanist thought and pedagogic philosophy of Herbert Spencer and Johann Heinrich Pestalozzi. They advocated a holistic approach to education that acknowledged the unity of mind, body and soul. Physical education thus was an indispensable part of educating the individual character (Irie 1988:37–40).

However, a second string of military gymnastics was introduced by Mori Arinori (1847–1889), one of the leading intellectuals of his time who served as minister of education from 1885 until to his assassination in 1889. Mori was also influenced by the writings of Spencer, but he emphasized the merits of physical education for the nation as a whole. His firsthand experiences from visits to America and England made him believe that the prosperity of a nation relied on the education of the masses rather than on the promotion of the individual. Inspired by the school education he had observed abroad, he attempted to foster national pride and collective identification among the masses. He rejected Leland's concept of light exercises (*kei taisō*) and promoted the spread of military gymnastics (*heishiki taisō*), including marching, the use of school uniforms, military lifestyle and organization of dormitories and sport days. Mori, though a patriot, was nonetheless no militarist in the strict sense of the term. Along with many of his contemporaries, Mori considered patriotic feelings to be of utmost importance for educating the modern subjects of the state. Military exercises, as well as employing members of the military for educational purposes, were effective tools for achieving this aim (Kimura 1975).

In his Report to the Throne on Military Style Physical Education (*Heishiki taisō ni kansuru jōsōbun*, probably 1887), Mori placed the objectives of his ministry within the general policy of development based on economic wealth and military strength (*fukoku kyōhei*), and he wanted military instructors to teach the arts of marching and physical drill to the young students. The military itself was gladdened by this policy shift. In pursuit of a much more straightforward policy that demanded physical strength as well as subordinated minds, the army pressured hard to extend its influence on the educational system. Army officers were accepted at the Physical Education Training College as early as 1881 and soon started to teach gymnastics at public schools, which suffered from the scarcity of sport instructors. In 1886, Mori's recommendations were put into practice and the number of hours dedicated to physical education at the compulsory school level was raised to five or six hours a week. The proportion of military gymnastics increased substantially, but only within certain limits determined by educators and medical scientists serving in advisory boards of the Ministry of Education. Some deemed the comparatively hard exercises to be inappropriate and even dangerous for the children's physical state. With similar arguments referring to physiology rather than to education sciences, the advisory boards rejected all proposals of adding martial arts to the curricula of public schools (Takenoshita and Kishino 1959:78–79). Although a strong lobby advocated the recognition of the Japanese traditional sports, particularly in the wake of nationalist sentiments spurred by Japan's victorious military acts abroad, it was only in 1911 that the modernized, reinvented martial arts of judo and kendo were officially admitted as an optional part of physical education at middle and higher schools (Hayashi 1982, 1984).

About the same time, Nagai Michiakira composed the first curriculum for physical education in 1913. During his own school years at Kōbe Elementary School, Ibaraki Normal School and the Tokyo Teacher Training College Nagai experienced the various styles of normal and military gymnastics and playful sports. His biography reveals that his initial doubt about the applicability of military education was mitigated by his short military service in 1893, which convinced him of the necessity to revise school education as a kind of pre-military education (Shimizu 2001:83–84). Thus military gymnastics, together with active games and Swedish gymnastics, a new style from Scandinavia that was popularized in Japan since the 1890s by Kawase Motokurō and Inokuchi Aguri, among others, formed the basic content of the first syllabus of physical education. A latent collectivist orientation and nationalist purposes were at the roots of his strictly functionalist approach towards physical education and in marked contrast to the more playful conceptions of *yūgi* and *undō*, as they were propagated by Kanō in his later years as principal at the Tokyo Higher Normal School. In Nagai's widely read *Manual of Physical Education at School* (*Gakkō Taisō Yōgi*) which was also published in 1913, the well-balanced development of each part of the body, the completion of each of its functions, the capacities of fast action and endurance and disciplined and cooperative behaviour were outlined as the basic principles of school sport (Shimizu 2001:89–90).

Hence since the late 1880s, physical education was clearly seen as standing in the interest of the collective, the nation or the state. The emphasis on repetitive drill exercises, in line with military-style elements such as marching or armed exercises, the compulsory military service which was introduced in 1873 and tightened once more in 1887 and the nationalist *kokutai*-ideology indicated that the ultimate purpose of physical education was seen in the formation of 'diligent workers and strong soldiers'. Sport sociologist Inagaki (1995) argued that because of the repetitive practising of collective movements, gymnastics were a powerful device to instil group orientation and consciousness of hierarchy. Already at the turn of the 20th century, Austrian poet Peter Rosegger (1843–1918) commented on the social function of gymnastics:

> On the level of the individual, 'turnen' is nothing else than a device of education and health promotion. As a methodical mean to instruct companionship, national virtues by commonly shared achievements, it gains political significance. As such, it cannot be over-esteemed. (Rosegger 1894, quoted in Strohmeyer 1998a:216)

SCHOOL SPORT AND CLUB SPORT

For the majority of the people of Austria and Japan, the experience of active sport participation remained limited to physical education lessons in compulsory education. English sport games, in contrast, were restricted to British residents and, in the case of Vienna, to the upper class. Outdoor games and ball sports were added to the physical education programme of public schools only in 1890. At that time, Tsuboi Gendō's textbook called *Rules of Outdoor Games* (*Kogai yūgi hō*, 1885) was widely circulated among Japanese teachers. But it is not known to what extent football, baseball or less sophisticated games that were described in this book were actually taught. Schools in general still lacked specialized educators, appropriate equipment and the necessary open space. Austria's education law from 1869 prescribed every school to have an exercise ground, whereas Japan's law was revised accordingly only by the Elementary School Ordinance in 1890 (Kamiwada 2001:171). Compulsory schools were abundant in late 19th-century Tokyo, but the majority of the school facilities did not even possess a schoolyard (Masai 1997). In such cases, physical education was either taught in open public spaces, such as nearby shrine grounds, public parks and the riverside, or simply inside the school building or the classroom (Yoshimi 2001:52). Schools in the periphery had no shortage of space but few funds. For many schools in rural Japan, it was impossible to get hold of the basic equipment. Rural schools that suffered from the Great Depression in the impoverished peripheries even failed to buy balls and bats for a decent game of baseball (Kōzu 1980). For these reasons, until the 1920s, for most of those living in Imperial Japan the meaning of sport, in terms of sport practice, was practically close to synonymous with calisthenics.

Exceptions took place at the cultural interfaces between Japanese society and the outside world. Non-Japanese in the service of the young Meiji state did not only import urgently needed technological knowledge; they also brought everyday lifestyles, leisure activities and cultural practices into the newly opening country. At the 'treaty port' of Yokohama, sport clubs such as the Amateur Athletic Association, the Race Club, the Rifle Association, the Rowing Club or the Cricket Club were functioning as early as 1866 (Fält 1997). The social organization form of the 'club' accompanied the global spread of sports. Kōbe, which was opened to foreigners in 1867, saw the founding of particular clubs for riding, track and field, cricket and sailing within the first two years, and golf clubs, tennis clubs, football and mountaineering clubs followed en suite (Tanada 1988). Despite the proliferation of sport clubs, however, the impact on the host country in the Far East remained limited. In most cases, membership was restricted to foreign residents (cf. Fält 1997:6–7), and the rare Japanese visitors usually belonged to the upper stratum of society. This minority had more opportunities for exposure to Western culture and lifestyles than the overwhelming majority of the Japanese (Hashizume 1987), and it was tempted into emulating the social frame of the *kurabu* as the preferred organizational mode for modern leisure activities (Shirahata 1985).

In Austria, too, English residents living in the capital of Vienna were the primary cultural brokers that imported English sports. Members of the diplomatic corps and employees of British companies contributed to the establishment of sport clubs from the 1860s onwards. They were core members of the early sport clubs such as the boat club 'Bahn frei' (1862), the Skating Club (1867), the First Wiener Athletic Club of weightlifters (1st WAC, 1880), Vienna Cricket Club (1882), Wiener Lawn Tennis Club (1885), Vienna Football Club (1894) or the track and field Wiener Athletik Club (WAC, 1896). In contrast to the German-style gymnastic societies that covered a much larger selection of sports, the English-style sport clubs focused on a single sport. Until the late 19th century, sport clubs were chiefly maintained by the middle classes. The working classes tended to form unions of more general character, and sport clubs or circles emerged as branches of the gymnastic unions; later they also developed circles and clubs of their own (Norden 1998:56).

Premodern Japan knew a number of social associations similar to English clubs or German unions, especially in the world of arts and religion. However, social groups in the realm of body culture, such as the schools of martial arts (*ryūha*) and the sumo ringer stalls (*sumōbeya*), fulfilled social functions exceeding by far the usual range of sport clubs. Social relationships in *ryūha* were based upon the principle of fictive kinship rules; thus they shared with households and other social organizations a number of organizational and ritual aspects designed to foster community feelings and continuity, philosophical concepts, teaching methods and means of transmitting the basic assets from one generation to the next (Hurst 1998:177). Similarly to the *sumōbeya*, strict hierarchical principles structured interpersonal relations and interactions. An organizational form better suited to mitigate the tensions arising from the gap between status achievements in competitions and the usual position was offered by the Western model of the club.

Except for the foreign enclaves and the school sport clubs, the Shinbashi Athletic Club of 1878 was the first 'real' sport club to be founded in Japan. The founder of this baseball club, Hiraoka Hiroshi, was attracted by baseball while studying in America. He returned home with a rulebook and the equipment sponsored by A. Spalding, the American entrepreneur and promoter of the game. Hiraoka and other members of the Shinbashi Athletic Club, who trained every Saturday in Shinagawa, were employees of the national railway company at the Shinbashi Station. At the same time of the establishment of the private Shinbashi Athletic Club, students at the Tōkyō Kaisei Gakkō founded a rowing club, which became later known as the Tokyo University Boat Club (established in 1877). Baseball clubs were founded in 1884 at Keiō University and Meiji Gakuin University. When Kōdōkan founder Kanō Jigorō served as director of the Tokyo Teacher Training College in the 1890s, he introduced a general sport club (*undōkai*) with eight branches. Judo, of course, was included, but so were lawn tennis, bicycle riding and baseball. Membership to at least one club was required from all trainee teachers. Modern companies, together with educational institutions, public administration offices and the army, became chief promoters of sport club activities in the later Meiji period and in successive years. While in Europe sport clubs were established as self-administered and autonomous interest groups, their Japanese counterparts were usually developed within the social framework of a larger organizational unit. This tendency soon developed into a characteristic trait of the social landscape of sport in Japan.

In a certain sense, access to sport was thus far more restrictive and regulated than in the West. Except for rare exceptions since the early years of the 20th century—the Japan branches of the YMCA or YWCA opened facilities for basketball, volleyball or swimming in Tokyo and Kyoto on a membership system—the secondary and tertiary institutions of the educational system remained the most important supplier of sport opportunities. The institutions of higher education were the only locations where direct interactions between Westerners and Japanese had significant consequences on the promotion of sport. Most universities and high schools had a large staff of academics from abroad who had been invited to build up the modern education and science systems. They played a crucial role in the introduction of sports because of the direct and frequent interaction with their Japanese students.

Foreign teachers such as the English Frederick W. Strange at the Daigaku Yobimon (later First High School in Tokyo) in 1875 (Abe and Mangan 2003:100), and the Americans Horace Wilson at the Kaisei Gakkō (later Imperial University of Tokyo) in 1872 and Albert Bates at the Kaitaku Shika Gakkō (later Agricultural University of Sapporo) in 1873 introduced their national pastimes and other sports to their pupils (Whiting 1989:27). With the successive introduction of track and field sports (1873), football (1874), skating (1876), rowing (1877), tennis (1878), rugby (1896), hockey (1906), volleyball (1908) and basketball (1908), most modern sport games were quite well known among the educational elite at the end of the Meiji period (cf. Kishino et al. 1973). However, these sports were not part of the regular syllabus. The actual menu of sport activities depended on initiatives from the teaching staff in charge of nominally supervising the extracurricular activities (*bukatsudō*) of the semi-autonomous student clubs (*undōbu* or *kōyūkai*). Due to structural impediments regulating the accessibility to upper schools, only a tiny fraction of the population could actively participate in sport: The total number of students enrolled at the eight high schools and four universities in 1918 was a mere 15,520, while a further 200,000 were enrolled at secondary schools (Takemura 1998).

The resulting numerical discrepancies between the universal elementary school and the intensely limited institutions of higher education created elitist perceptions, hierarchical structures, severe competition, inter-school rivalry and a new self-image of a privileged youth standing at the top of the social order. In particular, the school sport clubs of the national high schools that were introduced by Mori Arinori in the 1880s were extremely elitist and self-centred. The meaning of sport created and reproduced within this social framework was strictly instrumental; participation at sport activities and competitions was devoted to the honour of the home institution, which was the primary focus of identification. The tradition of autonomous self-administration and physical self-discipline, which was borrowed from the English public boarding school system, and the Neo-Confucianist, samurai class background of the teaching staff merged into the ethos of 'muscular spirituality' (Kiku 1984:10–11; Shimizu 2002:130–134). Stoic endurance, strict obedience and self-sacrificing rigour were core qualities of the elite ethos furnished within the sport clubs. While the 'budofication' of Western sport (Kiku 2007) certainly helped to facilitate the adoption of sport, it also fatally shaped the way sport in Japan has been assessed thereafter.

THE EMERGENCE OF A NATIONAL SPORT

A number of factors deserve attention in order to explain adequately why baseball emerged as the new national sport in Japan. At the beginning of the 20th century, baseball started to spread through the entire nation, as it turned into an official subject of mass education, an appealing option of mass entertainment and a favourite advertisement tool of the mass media. Baseball first evolved as elite club sport at the institutions of higher education. In particular the baseball club of the First Higher School at Tokyo (Ichikō), established under the supervision of F. W. Strange in 1886, gained wide attraction after a series of victories over rival school teams and even American teams in the early 1890s. Beating the foreigners at their own game comprised a surprising experience that matched the rising patriotic sentiments of nationalist currents within the population and the ever-ambitious military. Popular folklore attributed the success to the demonstrative fighting spirit (*konjō*) of the Ichikō players (Whiting 1989:28–34). Throwing several hundred curveballs in a row or firing series of fastballs at the catcher from a mere five- or six-metre distance belonged to the standard repertoire of training sessions at Ichikō. The inner model of the Ichikō sport club, including the social organziation, the spiritual connotation and the moralizing attitude, happened to become mandatory for all kind of sports inside and outside of the school system (Taniguchi 2003:81). The overemphasis on winning, dedication and identification with the team, the school and the nation was not restricted to the so-called 'Pride Baseball', but became a characteristic feature of all school sports. Kimura Ki (1978), Kusaka Yūko (1985), Kiku Kōichi (1989) and other writers on the history of Japanese baseball have demonstrated that the Confucian background of the early generation of schoolteachers and their educational ideals contributed to the emergence of a particular sport ethic among their students.

Inter-school competitions started in 1887 with a boat race on Tokyo's Sumidagawa. Baseball tournaments were dominated by the Ichikō team until the turn of the century when it was overpowered by both Keiō and Waseda university teams. In 1903, these clubs inaugurated their own semi-annual tournament that drew thousands of spectators to the ball parks. In 1905 the special series came to a sudden standstill that lasted for 20 years after supporters of the clubs went on the rampage through the capital. However, inter-school games continued when in 1914 a three-university league was formed with the addition of Meiji University. This league was finally extended to the Big Six College Baseball League in 1925, including Hōsei, Rikkyō and Tōkyō University (Kelly 2000:106). Every leg of the league games attracted huge audiences in the capital of Tokyo. The pioneering researcher on urban life in prewar Japan, Gonda Yasunosuke, observed that sport had come to play a considerably important role in popular amusement. Massive demand for popular entertainment was fuelled by the socioeconomic results of mass production, capital centralization and urbanization, which were all more or less immediately affected by the wars of the first two decades (Gonda 1921, 1931, quoted in Shimizu 2001:94–95).

The development towards the commodification of sport finally led to the establishment of Japan's first professional baseball league in 1935. Private railway companies and national newspapers were mainly involved in this process, although the relationship between the mass media and sports dates back to the early years of the century. Newspaper publishers were soon aware that sports news could help to enlarge circulation and readership, so they began to promote all kinds of sports events and tournaments from relay races and marathons to ski races and swimming contests. In 1915, for example, the Ōsaka Asahi Shinbun publishing house inaugurated a new national middle school baseball championship tournament, which soon became Japan's most central sport event (Kelly 1998a).

In contrast, football (soccer) is the Austrian counterpart of baseball in the national sport culture. The first football club was the First Vienna Football Club ('Vienna'), founded in 1894 by English football enthusiasts and a small number of Austrian members. Soon, however, Austrians from the middle and upper classes that venerated anything of English origin took the lead in setting up new football clubs: More than 40 clubs were founded in the three years from 1898 to 1900. Tournaments attracted a regular spectatorship of several thousand people who were willing to spend money on an entrance ticket, a programme bulletin and some snacks. The club management, eager to capitalize on the mass attraction of football, was therefore rather more interested in selling football matches against attractive teams, preferably from abroad, than in organizing a national league. In order to prevent good players from leaving, they were offered the chance to earn cash options. The Austrian Football Federation tried in vain from 1904 to maintain the English gentleman-amateur status ideal. At this time most of the Viennese clubs were busily constructing new stadiums and less inclined to abstain from the expected profits from some tens of thousands of spectators. It took seven years until the first tournament league was finally established in 1911–1912. However, both the First and the Second Division consisted only of teams from the Austrian capital, Vienna.

Initial attempts to keep the sport restricted to the middle and upper class were doomed to fail. The club statutes of the Vienna Football Club still excluded workers and day labourers explicitly from membership. Ticket prices and prescribed areas in the stadiums were meant to keep the proletarians at a distance. However, even before the formation of Vienna's classic workers' football clubs (such as Rapid in 1898) began, a distinctive kind of football culture emerged. When the working-class youth adopted the sport, an undomesticated version of football, which was neither officially acknowledged nor administered and often even prohibited, it was played on the grass of the public parks, at the outer fringes and the open spaces outside of downtown Vienna, in backyards and the narrow alleys of suburban

Vienna. For these players, the adored star athletes of the big city clubs were god-like, and they trained hard to imitate their styles and techniques. Their own 'clubs', martially named as Hispaniola, Herkules, Einheit (unity) or Gewalt (power), were hotbeds of resistance against the dominant culture of the adult world and the football establishment. For these young players, football had no relationship with England but definitely was local property (Marschik 1998:170–174).

In Germany, where football was introduced approximately at the same time, the dominant Turner movement tried hard to avert the spread of the 'savage game'. In Austria, however, no autochthonous body culture had to defend its territories against the cultural import. Precisely for that reason, Vienna was able to turn into a Central European football capital comparatively early. By the time of World War I, the development towards a national sport was finished by the military that adopted football, firstly for recruitment, then for training purposes and later for diversion purposes at the front. After the war, hundreds of thousands were familiar with the game and its rules (Marschik 1998:182).

SPORT ASSOCIATIONS

The close integration into the education system and the particular social organization of extracurricular club activities had a lasting effect on the development of sport in Japan. The elementary stage of becoming a social institution was completed in both countries at approximately the same time as the inauguration of administrative bodies in charge of supervising the activities of athletes, sport clubs and regional associations. In Austria, a Joint Commission for Sport Interests was formed in 1908 in the wake of preparing a celebration of the emperor's long-term rule; this commission also represented Austria at the IOC. In Japan, Kanō Jigorō was approached by a Belgian diplomat in the name of the IOC. Because of his prominent public position—until the end of the Meiji period, he served as teacher and principal at various higher schools, including the prestigious First Higher School and the leading teacher training college in Tokyo, and he regularly attended advisory boards of the Ministry of Education—he was the natural choice when the International Olympic Committee searched for a suitable candidate to establish a national branch in Japan in 1909.

As the Ministry of Education and the private sport association Nihon Taiiku Kai (founded in 1891) refused to support Kanō's task of selecting athletes for the Olympic Games, he had to rely on resources provided by the main institutions of sport activities—the higher schools and universities. When the Dainippon Taiiku Kyōkai (Great Japan Amateur Sports Association) was founded with Kanō as its first president in 1911, the majority of positions on the board of the association were occupied by school educators. During the early years, two major problems had to be faced: First, the lack of a solid base of membership, and, second, the lack of funds and the high dependency of financial contributions by public and private organizations. The initial funds of 15,000 yen were granted by the *zaibatsu* companies Mitsui and Iwasaki, under the condition of returning parts of the fund if the association was capable of obtaining an income of its own (Kōzu 1978:51–52). The problem of membership was gradually solved during the formation process of nationwide single sport associations that started during the early 1920s. The second problem, however, remained a burden throughout the history of the association. Several amendments of the statutes during the first period following the inauguration were primarily designed to explore new resources of funding. As a consequence, the proportion of board members representing the interests of government and capital increased considerably. Especially during the late 1930s and early 1940s, when sport was instrumentalized for nationalistic purposes, the former gained in relative significance: More than 90 per cent of the operational budget was received from the government (Fujita 1988).

CULTURE AND THE SOCIAL ORDER: SOME FINAL OBSERVATIONS

In this chapter, I have demonstrated how the perception and the disposition of the individual and the collective body were transformed in line with the cultural import of Western sport. As the discussion of the case studies of Japan and Austria has shown, the capitals spearheaded the introduction of sport. Although places such as Yokohama or Kōbe had a much larger foreign population, they played a very minor role in the process of appropriation. Both countries were in a similar fashion exposed to the two main currents of English sport and German turnen that finally would merge within the new national body cultures of Japan and Austria. The comparison of these two case studies asserts that geographical proximity is less important than a simplified dissemination model implies. Political conditions, such as the right of assembly, local strategies of absorbing cultural imports, the climate of innovation and overall changes of lifestyle and attitudes, as well as the power of the innovators to reach the various layers of society, are of far greater importance than the position on a geographic map. Thus we have a strong argument in favour of a model based on the relevance of developments within the wider environment.

The historical analysis stresses three aspects of seemingly universal quality. It stresses the particular role of national systems, such as the education system and mass media, to contribute to rapid diffusion, although its abilities to reduce time lags between centre and peripheries have been rather restricted. The comparative analysis underlines the particular influence of the local environment in which cultural practices are integrated. Despite nationally or internationally acknowledged rules, the practice of a sport may bear very different meanings, depending on who is participating when and under what conditions. The way in which sport is open to such differing interpretations is very likely a major reason for its capacity to reach global audiences. Finally, the fragmentation of modern society along the lines of economic and social power is mirrored in the modern sport landscape. The way sport-related spaces are allocated, managed, opened and closed for particular sections of society tells a lot about the way power and submission are distributed within a society. In both case studies, class-specific differences in sport participation have been widely discussed, while the heaviest burden of discrimination certainly was loaded against women. With the exception of gymnastics, they were systematically excluded from most sports during the period of investigation.

Although it is far from being complete, this short history has attempted to outline the major agents, acts and processes that were crucial for the institutionalization of modern sports in Japan up to the early 1930s. Even if many Japanese at that time had little or no opportunity to participate actively, sports were no longer unknown or unintelligible to them. Sports had become part of their culture. One significant fact should be clear from my analysis: In contrast to most European countries, where the state guaranteed far-reaching autonomy to the organizations concerned in regard to the supervision of sport rules, competitions and club regulations (Bourdieu 1986), the Japanese state itself entered the stage as an exceptionally strong player. Probably this active role was necessary because the Japanese tradition lacked a cultural equivalent which could have easily been substituted by the new set of practices. Furthermore, the Meiji leaders' vision of a modern Japan included a Western-style education system plus physical education. Although direct interactions with sporting Westerners hardly had any major impact on the introduction and diffusion of sports, the West as 'self-referential Other' was of utmost importance. Because sport was introduced to Japan as a foreign, unknown concept, practices as well as ideas were naturally adjusted to more familiar values, standards of behaviour and organizational patterns. The close interconnection with the national education system as the foremost channel of sport diffusion did not only promote the perception of sport as an educational tool, but it also increased the susceptibility of sport to be used instrumentally for external purposes. I argue that these general conditions—culture and education—that were evident throughout the early institutionalization process of sport, can be seen as the clue for the persistent endurance of the dominant sport ideology until recent times.

As my overview has shown, the process of institutionalization was never under entire control of one particular agent. Sport historians such as Takenoshita Kyūzō and Kishino Yūzō (1959), Kimura Kichiji (1975) and Irie Katsumi (1986) have described the changing power relations overshadowing the Monbushō's physical education policy as a permanent tug-of-war between the military and its ultranationalist allies on one side and medical professionals and liberal-minded educationalists on the other. Although no final decision was achieved until the early 1930s, the outcome of the power struggle was predetermined. Only the most radical critics dared to challenge the authority of the tennō state, while most educationalists were confined within the ideological framework prescribed by the Imperial Constitution in 1889 and enforced by the Imperial Rescript on Education. Proclaimed on October 30, 1890, the *kyōiku chokugo* glorified the values of loyalty and filial piety and established them as absolute principles of formal education. The Monbushō distributed certified copies to all schools of the country where it was publicly displayed next to the portrait of the emperors (*goshinei*) at special occasions. School principals were instructed to read the Rescript to students on such occasions as national holidays and graduation ceremonies. As such, it served as a powerful instrument of political indoctrination for over half a century until the end of World War II.

Even the values of self-improvement and individualism that flourished in the discourse on free education during the Taishō years, shaping the practice of physical education of teachers such as Iwamoto Genjirō, Tachibana Susumu and Kawaguchi Hideaki, were easily converted into the oppressive norms of subjugating the self to the good of the nation. The double structure of sport as an exclusive preserve of the educational elite, on the one hand, and compulsory military calisthenics for the masses, on the other hand, converged into a nationalist concept of sport. As a later chapter will show, Japan's prewar version of Sports for All encouraged mass participation in a similar way and for similar purposes as mass recreation programmes did in the European fascist states of Italy and Germany.

Finally, as stated earlier, the story told here is far from being complete. An alternative way of looking at the history of sport would rather emphasize the productivity and creativity of the practitioners—which I actually suggested in my previous research on the social construction of Japanese mountaineering (Manzenreiter 2000). Contributions by Yoshimi Shunya (1993, 1999), Jin Fumio and Kurosu Mitsuru (1986) on the history of sport diffusion also underline the existence of creativity at work: These authors have argued that sport became an item of Japanese culture once it had successfully found a place within the cultural field of spectacles and popular festivals (*matsuri bunka*). In particular Yoshimi convincingly demonstrated that urban residents in Japan did not subjugate themselves to the national ideology embodied within the local or regional sport festivals (*undōkai*) but, rather, adopted the sports day as just another new holiday in a regular cycle of annual events. The material basis provided by this kind of historical analysis remains weak, but the growing body of academic knowledge will lead to a deeper understanding of conditions and relations of power and resistance during the institutionalization process of sport in modernizing Japan.

2 Creating Space
Urbanity and Modernity in the Japanese Sport Landscape[1]

INTRODUCTION

The sociological study of the institutionalization process of modern sport has been largely concerned with questions of agency, authority and control: Who has been involved in importing and disseminating the new body culture, and how has it been interpreted and repackaged to make it compatible with the social fibres of modern Japanese society? What has not been considered so far are material and spatial aspects of this body culture going global. Most, if not all, sports require more than just knowledge of rules, consent with the basic ethics and belonging to a social group or organization that provides sport opportunities. Highly specialized practices as they are need special equipment and particular spaces that have to be established. Yet space is a limited resource in modern society, particularly in its urban conglomerates, and the rationalization of space is a characteristic trait of modernity and capitalism alike (Bale 1993a:121).

My spatial interest in the Japanese sport landscape has been triggered by the renowned historian of sport Allen Guttmann challenging the critical perspective of most participants at the international conference on 'Sports and Body Culture in Modern Japan' in spring 2000 (Kelly with Sugimoto 2007). Guttmann questioned the prevalent mode in which sport was assessed as a tool in the service of an oppressive state system rather than as a joyful, enriching and positive contribution to human life. There is little doubt that both interpretations are justified in their own terms, even if we assume in the tradition of the Frankfurt School and its elitist polemic against sport and popular culture that joy and pleasure are mediated products of cultural industries that skillfully manipulate consumers' taste, interests and expenditures (Kausch 1988:24). Guttmann's critical intervention has been, however, a full about-turn from an older observation made by John Hargreaves in the mid-1980s. The English sociologist noted that the majority of sport sociologists neglected the important part sport plays, even if unintended, in reproducing power relations in society (1986:2) because they regarded sport primarily in positive terms, as it fulfils various positive functions. Yet since Hargreaves published his own influential book on sport, culture and power, Antonio Gramsci's notion of hegemony, which delivers the theoretical foundation of the cultural studies approach, emerged as one of two major influential currents in late 20th-century sport sociology (cf. Gruneau 1983; Takahashi 1995; Yamashita 1995, 1997; the second one is figurational sociology; e.g. Elias and Dunning 1989; Kiku 1997; Maguire 1999). The Cultural Studies approach suggests researching sport as 'a site of ideological struggle where individual lives and experiences are involved in a process of interpretive negotiation with the surrounding social structures' (Andrews and Loy 1993:269).

The paradigmatic shift might provide one explanation for Guttmann's uneasiness; a second one might have been the inherent difficulties of some papers to address individual experience and subjective meaning when looking at the larger structural patterns of society. Particularly in the case of historical studies, sources produced by key players such as government agencies, sport associations or the media industries are much easier to access and to assess than the comparatively rare testimonies of contemporary affections and emotions. With other words, there is ample material to reconstruct the amount of school hours and the content of sport curricula for students at public or private schools for any given period of time. But we hardly know how and what students felt during the repetitious routines of physical exercise lessons as it is much more difficult to get access to testimonials that have not been mitigated for commercial or propagandistic purposes. While I don't want to question the value of firsthand accounts from the popular press, school journals, the membership magazines of public youth associations or pedagogic literature, I want to explore a different approach that traces back the formation of the Japanese sport landscape. In order to enrich the evidence provided by standard historical sources, and in order to overcome the biased proportion of such resources, I will have a look at the spatial provision and arrangement of sport in early 20th-century Japan.

In my reading, the Japanese sport landscape is understood as the totality of space devoted to the experience of sport within a given social entity, such as a community, a municipality, a prefecture or a nation. We can expect the relations and structures of the inhabitants and usages of these social spaces to be of crucial importance for the construction of the sport landscape, precisely because space is limited and therefore a contested resource. Space in general is an essential part of sport. Generations of scholars have been struggling with the inherent difficulties of defining the notion of sport. But at least one basic condition is beyond all doubt: Sport always requires physical energy input, i.e. a certain effort by sporting individuals that put their bodies into motion. No matter whether a certain kind of sport requires speed, strength, skills or aesthetics, in all cases excellence is contested by the body of the individual athlete or the collective body of the team in relation to space. Sport activities such as running or rowing are not just about bridging a certain distance, but also about traversing a limited space as fast as possible. Shot-putting or jumping require getting as far or high as possible in unlimited space. Football team players or tennis players have to defend their home space against any hostile intrusion while trying to break into the opponents' territory as often and decisively as possible. One key factor of the emergence of modern sport as a social institution has been the rigid definition of the spatial boundaries in which sport is performed. The development of modern sport has been characterized by the separation of specific space earmarked for sportive purpose (Bale 1993b:135), as the modern quest for rationalization and standardization required the normative definition of proper space usage (Nakamura 1991:8–9). At the same time, the spatial segregation of 'inside the field', where the action is, and 'outside' propelled the process of role differentiation among athletes and between main actors (i.e. athletes, referees) and side actors (i.e. spectators and others) (Nakamura 1994b:113–118).

Ever since modern sport was introduced to Japan, sport participants, including athletes, educators and spectators, had to explore new spaces for the sake of the new cultural practice. While some outdoor activities only required the reformulation of the legitimate use of open space, such as mountains, rivers, the seaside or municipal parks, most modern sports are in need of more elaborated facilities that require the temporary or permanent designation of space. This is particularly the case if the practice of sport is considered primarily in terms of achievement orientation—which is not necessarily the case. Bale and Sang clearly stated with reference to track and field sports that 'physical education and leisure may embrace running, throwing and jumping but neither the bodies nor the landscapes of physical education or leisure are configured in the same ways as Olympic bodies and landscapes' (1996:20). But in the context of modernity's general dislike of ambiguous use of space, modern sport requested its own exclusive territory, indicative of order, standardization and control.

I comply with the basic idea that the same activity might either be part of a symbolic universe based on the central ideology of modernity or belong to the completely different realm of play and leisure. Yet in modern society, elite sport and mass sport are linked to each other by numerous threads, including the discursive employment of sport for non-sportive usages by politicians, the media and consumer industries. There is no doubt that the rise and fall or popularity of a given spectator sport inevitably leads to increase or respectively decrease in amateur sport participation or sport mimicry outside of the formalized field of sport participation. For this reason, my interest in the sport landscape will have to transcend the narrow focus on sport facilities, even if only the former can be quantified on the basis of data at hands. Thinking about sport and space, about the way the Japanese sport landscape emerged, should lead to fresh insights into the role of sport in modernizing Japan, in everyday life as well as within the relationship between the state and the individual in interwar Japan. Based on historical accounts and early data collected from the public bodies in charge of sport and physical exercise during the first decades of the 20th century, on textual and visual sources, I will reconstruct the emergence of a public–private sport infrastructure in Japan.

A SHORT HISTORY OF SPORT FACILITIES IN EARLY MODERN JAPAN

The prehistory of sport facilities in Japan dates back to ancient times and the Middle Ages, given that archery, fencing or horse riding within the particular context of their time can be read as sport activities. In fact, before Japan encountered Western-style modern sport, the semantic label of sport space was only temporarily assigned to most of the spaces that were used at that time for military training or for entertainment of the nobility. Horse races, for example, did not necessarily require designated sites; the highly popular displays of mounted archery, such as *yabusame* or *kasagake*, also often took place in the open expanse of grassland or at sandy beaches. According to records dating back to the mid-Heian period (794–1192), archery contests were held in courtyards, temple or shrine yards, at military training ranges or even indoors. The martial arts probably have the longest history of specialized space usage. Yet prior to the Edo period, training took place largely outdoors, particularly because only this environment resembled battle conditions. Only in later years did practising inside of the *dōjō*, the roofed training hall, become standard routine of the Tokugawa warriors (Hurst 1998:225). Sumo was practised on the spot. The *dohyō*, the upraised earthened sumo ring, was only invented in the Edo period (1600–1868), probably as a response to the governmental attempt to ban the spectacle from the city streets. According to woodblock prints and other depictions of sumo sceneries from the 17th century, until the 1660s the place to fight was demarcated only by the surrounding wrestlers and spectators. The introduction of ropes or straw barrels, that separated the action from the side action, might have contributed to preventing the audience from getting too closely involved with the action (Ikeda 1977:94–97).

The history of modern sport facilities in Japan is first of all a history of school sport facilities. The first sport facility without affiliation to school education was the cycling track in Ueno, which was reconstructed as an athletic field in 1911, about a quarter of a century after the history had begun with the construction of the Godensan athletic ground of Tokyo University in 1887 (Yokomatsu 1996:276). Already in 1875, the necessity of having a sport ground attached to each elementary school was noted in various reports by the Ministry of Education (Monbushō) and regional government regulations. The Second Revised Elementary School Ordinance of 1990 echoed Mori Arinori's earlier promotion of gymnastics, making it a compulsory subject (1885) as it required from every school an athletic ground abutting immediately against the school building. The up-to-now universally applied outline of Japanese school sport grounds was finally standardized with the Ministry's *Pictorial Explanation of the School Architecture and Planning Outline* from 1895 (*Gakkō kenchikuzu setsumei oyobi sekkei taiyō*), which recommended southern or eastern alignment for hygienic reasons (Kamiwada 2001:169–171).

However, even though the general outlay of school facilities became increasingly determined and standardized by ministerial ordinances and other official documents, not every school necessarily came to possess the required amenities. Spatial obstructions due to the lack of city planning turned out to be a major obstacle that was fuelled by the increasing number of pupils attending regular classes. Because of the increasing numbers of students the space available for physical education became increasingly short: The 1899 amendments to the Regulations on School Provisions (Shōgakkō Setsubi Junsoku Kaisei) prescribed the size of a school ground for up to 100 students as 100 *tsubo*, or 330 square metres, at least. Larger schools should calculate a minimum of one *tsubo* per student. Yet due to the reasons outlined in the preceding, the absolute minimum was exceeded in hardly any case but rather regarded as the standard norm for school sport facilities (Kamiwada 2001:172).

Earlier documents of the late Meiji period named the athletic ground gymnastic ground (*taisōjō*), and only in the later Taishō years did the official name of sport ground (*undōjō*) become commonly used. In the meantime, the image of school sport had gradually shifted away from gymnastics to a much broader and inclusive understanding. The growing popularity of baseball and Japan's first attendances at Olympic Games might have been causes underlying the growth in size of sport grounds. According to Kamiwada (2001:174), the dusty, rectangular sport grounds were primarily used for the gymnastic apparatus of Sweden gymnastics, which was the dominant style of physical education at schools in the Taishō and early Shōwa years (i.e. 1912–1940), but also for baseball and track and field athletics. Gymnasiums, by the way, were first introduced as a bad weather alternative to the open sport grounds. In most cases, spatial restrictions and financial burdens caused the double usage of large-scale halls for two different purposes: On the one hand, the building served as an assembly hall for cultural presentations as well as for official school ceremonies that took place at particular school and national holidays. Throughout the year, these halls were used for physical education classes. Depending on the situation, the room was either a gym or a symbolic sanctuary where the Imperial Rescript on Education was read out by school principals at national holidays or during official school meetings. Due to the multiple uses and the hierarchical order of physical and national education, these facilities hardly offered optimal conditions for the purpose of teaching physical education. But the spatial juncture of sport and national ceremony also helped to symbolically reproduce the power structure of the nation-state.

ATHLETES AND SPECTATORS IN THE JAPANESE SPORT LANDSCAPE

Until the Taishō period, modern sport games were basically confined to the institutions of higher education. The general public began to be attracted towards sport when inter-school rivalries started to spread in the early 20th century. Matches between high school sport clubs or university teams drew mass audiences of tens of thousands of spectators gladly embracing the new spectacle. At these rare occasions, people got acquainted with the appeal of sport, but also with the characteristic sport ideology of the clubs centring on strong will, self-abnegation, collective orientation and elitism and the way sport was performed in archetypical fashion.

One related factor that had prepared the ground for the new urban amusement of spectator sport was the modern institution of the local or regional school sport festival (*undōkai*). The history of school sport days in Japan began with the (probably) first *undōkai* ever staged by the Kaigun Heigakuryō in Tsukiji, Tokyo in March 1873. The Naval College, established in 1869 prior to the School System Order of 1872, was one of Japan's earliest institutions of modern higher education and deeply dedicated to the nationalist programme to catch up with the Western nations. As the navy was to be remodelled after the British navy, the influence of English culture and traditions was particularly strong at this college. Archibald Douglas, the naval officer who also introduced football to Japan in 1873, initiated a comprehensive sport festival at the college in 1874; teachers from England were in charge of coaching the students for participation at flat races, long jumps, high jumps, steeple chase or walking matches. The programme also included a number of funny yet competitive games such as blindfold races, races for athletes over 15 carrying a younger student on their back, three-legged races and races with a bucket of water in the hand. What fascinated the spectators most, however, was the turmoil created by the final item, catching a pig by the tail (Hirata 1999:86–98). Over the following years, similar school sport events were occasionally staged throughout the country, e.g. in 1876 again at the Naval Academy, in 1878 (and 1880) at the Sapporo Agricultural College (Sapporo Nōgakkō) or in 1883, jointly organized by Tokyo University and the Yobimon Gakkō (Kimura 1999:131–132).

However, only after Minister of Education Mori introduced the field day as a 'disciplinary tool' for elementary and junior high schools in 1885, did these sport spectacles begin to spread all over Japan. In the first stage of the development, approximately until 1888, the authoritative journal on education, *Dainippon Kyōikukai Zasshi*, regularly featured promotional articles on sport days. Because of the lack of space, and probably also because of the scarcity of instructors and pupils as well, the *undōkai* of the early years were usually co-organized by a number of schools in a region. The students left the school premises in marching order and marched in lock-step, following the national flag, until they reached the field, riverbed and shrine premise where the local *undōkai* was staged. Thus the sport festival constituted a blending of excursion and sport competition. In this instance, teachers or students and their wider social environment could regard the *undōkai* as a contemporary extension of older traditions, such as the cherry blossom viewing or other traditional excursions of *terakoya* schools, private academies or other institutions of learning in early modern Japan (Yoshimi 2001:44). The programme usually consisted of the inevitable ceremonial elements, normal gymnastics, military gymnastics and competitive games. While the students generally competed against each other and were rewarded for individual achievements, they also learnt to represent their age group or the entire school. In the context of sport, inter-school rivalries started to enfold. Even though they were not intentionally sought after, the rivalries between the institutions of higher education, which even led to instances of hooligan-style social disorder in late Meiji Japan, were accepted for their inward-bounded merits of school solidarity and group identification (Hirata 1999:99–100).

Yoshimi Shunya's historiography of the *undōkai* is critically aware of the role of sport as an 'ideology device' (Yoshimi 1999:9) and the way it was instrumentalized for nationalist purposes in Meiji Japan. Depending on the mood of the time, the content of the sport day could vary greatly: from gymnastics to ball games, from athletics to military games, such as flag-taking. The marching formation of the athletes entering the sport field, as well as mass calisthenics, clearly demonstrated the result of a disciplinary education that put the body into the service of the collective. Linking the collective to the nation was simply achieved by the open display of national symbols, including the Imperial Rescript on Education or a photograph of the emperor, which were usually kept in a sealed place, and the *hinomaru* flag. The hierarchical order between winner, runners-up and losers, as well as the highly formalized award ceremony, made the participating children, as well as the spectators, familiar with the modern logic of achievement orientation and its basic ethic of diligence and endeavour (Yoshimi 1993:55–59). However, Yoshimi (1999:41) also provides ample evidence for the people's creativity in interpreting the annual event as a new contribution to the regular calendar of local festivities. The popular adaptation became the more obvious the closer the event was related to the local population. Residents became chiefly involved in preparation tasks of 'their' annual *undōkai*; ambulant merchants opened their shops near the sport grounds, while the local retailers closed business for the day (Yoshimi 1993:62–66). As both levels—compulsory education and popular imagination, or school and amusement—were intertwined by conjunctional relations, the power relations between state and subject and the official family state ideology were reproduced among athletes and spectators.

As various studies have shown (Yoshimi 1999; Kelly 2000; Kiku 1993; Shimizu 1999, 2002), the media industries as well as the modern transport industries played a leading role in promoting sport as a new kind of entertainment in urbanizing Japan. Sport columns appeared in the Japanese newspapers during the late Meiji period; at the same time, a new type of newspaper writer specialized in sport reporting was born. The sportive rivalries between school baseball teams, for example, the semi-annual *sōkeisen* between the new baseball powerhouses Waseda and Keiō, were extensively covered by the newspapers (Kiku 1984; Ikei 1991; Kelly 1998a). The intense identification with the school and the school team were probably responsible for severe social disorder erupting from time to time after the games. When the fan clubs of the two universities went on a rampage through the Ginza in August 1905, the presidents of the universities interrupted the special series; the suspension lasted for two decades. But already in 1914, a new college baseball league consisting of Keiō, Meiji and Waseda University was established. By 1925, Hōsei, Rikkyō and Tōkyō University had joined this league, which expanded to what became known as the Tokyo Big Six College Baseball League.

Such occurrences occasionally caused heated debates and sharp criticism in the press. In August and September 1911, the *Asahi Shinbun* in Tōkyō featured a colourful debate on its pages about the moral hazards of baseball. The so-called 'harms of baseball' controversy (*yakkyū to sono gaidoku*) opened with an essay by Nitobe Inazō, the author (and inventor) of *Bushido—The Soul of Japan* (in 1899–1900; see Nitobe 2001), who dismissed the game as unworthy of truly civilized gentlemen. Only Americans, but no Englishmen or Germans, would engage in that 'pickpocket's sport' where athletes are supposed to steal bases. Another commentator during the 22 days of the controversy lamented the unparalleled waste of valuable space for such a small number of players, and some school teachers criticized the athletes' lack of interest in classroom routines (Nakamura 1995:126–127). The attack was countered by a two-week series in the *Tōkyō Nichinichi Shinbun* in defense of the sport, and also the *Yomirui Shinbun* published a discussion series on the merits and demerits of baseball (Kelly 1998a:107).

THE COMMERCIALIZATION OF SPORT

The number of possible encounters between the people and elite sport and the sport elite increased when the newspaper publishing companies started to exploit the rising popularity of sport for their own profits. Competing for subscriptions, the national newspapers employed sport coverage as a vehicle to redefine themselves as mass media, rather than as merely political newspapers (Kelly 1998a:108; Kelly 2000). Sponsoring sport contests or individual athletes and promoting sport participation among the broader public were meant to spark the interest in sport generally and to capitalize on the increased demand for sport coverage. One of the most outstanding sponsors was the *Ōsaka Mainichi Shinbun* that organized boat races, long-distance running events and track and field meetings from 1905 onwards. In 1908, the newspaper sponsored the National Middle School Tennis Tournament for the first time at Hamadera beach. The seaside resort had been developed by the Nankai Railway Company in 1905. At this location, the *Ōsaka Mainichi Shinbun* also sponsored sailing regattas and student sumo tournaments (from 1909), the National Middle School Swimming Contest (1915) and baseball (1916). In 1913, it sponsored the First Japan Olympic Festival at the newly erected Toyonaka Sport Ground. The facilities thereafter were used regularly for track and field meetings and baseball games (Yoshimi 1999). The *Yomiuri Shinbun*, which established its own professional baseball team in December 1934 and prepared the ground for the inauguration of the Japanese professional baseball league in 1936, began sponsoring sport events at this early time: In commemoration of the 50th anniversary of the capital of Tokyo in 1917, the *Yomiuri Shinbun* sponsored a relay race of two teams from Eastern and Western Japan along the old highway between Kyōto and Tōkyō. The victorious team finished the 516 kilometres in less than 42 hours in what was the first occasion that the term *ekiden* was used in relation to a sport event (Okao 1987:109–110).

The Ōsaka branch of the *Asahi Shinbun*, which only four years earlier had published the debate on the evils of baseball, sponsored the first annual National Middle School Baseball Tournament at Toyonaka Sport Ground in 1915. In the first year, about a quarter of all national middle schools participated in the event which soon became the most celebrated amateur sporting event in Japan; the participation rate doubled in the second year. As the Toyonaka ground soon reached its capacity limit, the *Ōsaka Asahi Shinbun* commissioned the planning of a new stadium in Nishinomiya to be erected on an area of 12,000 *tsubo* (approximately 37,000 sqm) with concrete walls, an iron roof and up to 50 rows at the terraces of the legendary Alp Stand towering above the playing field. As long as construction of the Kōshien, the later Mecca of Japanese high school baseball, was under way, the national baseball meets moved into another sport complex built by the Hanshin Railways Company. Next to the baseball field, the Naruo Sport Grounds offered also facilities for horse racing and track and field athletics, among others. For the 1923 semi-finals, demand was much higher than supply as the number of fans exceeded by far the capacity of the ball park; in order to prevent the masses from social disorder, a second ground was opened for the day and both semi-finals were staged at the same time (Sakaue 1998:21–22). A year later, in August 1924, the new Kōshien opened its gates; it accommodated up to 60,000 visitors. Yet popular demand was so high that the side stands had to be expanded twice (in 1929 and 1936) to accommodate even more spectators. Construction costs of the Kōshien were defrayed between the *Mainichi Shinbun*, which had sponsored its own annual spring baseball tournament (Zenkoku Kōtō Gakkō Yakyū Senbatsu Taikai) in the stadium since 1924, and the Hanshin Railways Company, which controlled public transport to the stadium.

CENTRAL STATE INTERESTS

The growing activism of the media and the new popularity of sport events attracted the attention of local and national authorities. A first nationwide survey on the state of sport facilities was commissioned by the Home Ministry in 1919 under the leadership of Nagai Michiakira. Comparing the state of art in the developed countries of the West with Japan, the committee clearly recommended increasing all efforts to improve physical strength, sanitation and health of the nation. In particular women were considered as suffering from bad health and lack of physical well-being. In more concrete terms, the report, called *Undō, kyōgi, bujutsu, sono ta sekkyokuteki tairyoku zōshin shisetsu shōrei ni kansuru kengi*, published in 1920, recommended: (1) education of the people; (2) construction of sport facilities by regional authorities, with financial support from central government funds; (3) promotion of sport programmes and facilities for public employees and company workers; (4) education of sport instructors and their employment by regional authorities; (5) agitation of sport spirit (*undō seishin*) by public award ceremonies for victorious athletes; and (6) organization of sport events for youth associations, women's associations and military reserve organizations (Kōzu 1978:71–72; see also Sakaue 1998:66–68). As some of these suggestions were realized only a few years later, it is safe to state that this report marked the beginning of a national sport policy reaching beyond the realm of school education.

Already in 1898, Parliament approved to support the work of the Nihon Taiiku Kai, which was founded in 1891 as a private club for sport and gymnastics with 50,000 yen over five years under the condition that the predecessor of the current Japan University of Sports Sciences established sport facilities at 12 location for the education of sport instructors throughout the country. The general scarcity of sport grounds and gyms caused the Monbushō in 1905 to demand the opening of school facilities to the public (Kōzu 1978:88); this is probably the earliest incident of the same request that continued to echo throughout a hundred years of history of sport in Japan.

TRAINING THE BODY

Opening private pools, ski slopes and hiking trails, publishing companies and private railway companies pioneered Japan's leisure industries during the Taishō years (Takemura 1998). Yet ordinary workers hardly had time or money to participate in most of the commercial sport events. Whereas representatives of capital and labour were both well aware of the importance of the workers' physical strength and health, the former were reluctant to take initiatives for the improvement of their workers' living conditions. Only after the workers started to unionize were they provided with opportunities for active sport participation. In 1913, the year after the inception of the Yūaikai by Suzuki Bunji and other labour activists, club branches for physical exercises and recreational activities were established within this first union-like organization. During the reoccurring labour disputes of the early 1920s, the unionists at large companies such as Yawata Steel, Kawasaki Shipbuilding and Mitsubishi Shipbuilding organized regular sport events for the striking workers. The companies soon realized that the extension of social welfare measures, including the provision of sport facilities, was an effective counter-weapon against the spread of unionism and socialism among their workforces. Thus, the company management actively encouraged the establishment of company sport teams and the construction of sport fields immediately after the labour disputes were settled. Since the early 1920s, sports such as baseball, track and field, volleyball and others have flourished on the company level in the modern sector of Japan's economy (Kōzu 1978:58–61).

In 1921, baseball, tennis, swimming, athletics, field trips, strolls and mountaineering were sport activities offered to young male company workers in Ōsaka. Female workers could participate in swimming, strolls and occasional field trips (Ōsaka-shi Shakai-bu Chōsa-ka 1923, quoted in Kaga 1978:152). National intercity tournaments in various sport disciplines, usually sponsored by the national newspapers, started in 1927. Sporting activities and facilities became part of a range of services provided by companies, through which they were able to exercise control over their workers' lives outside the workplace. Corporate sport turned into a characteristic element of paternalist relations between employers and employees. Prominent forerunners included Yawata Steel Industries, Mitsubishi Shipbuilding, the National Railways and the Municipal Administration of Tokyo. They successfully reconstructed their employees' free-time practices and the institutions that supervised their conduct even during time off. The development of corporate sport perfectly matched the new social policy of the government. As we have seen, the government had realized the importance of public health for national wealth as early as the 1890s, but its basic policy line remained unchanged up to the social turmoil of the early Taishō years (Irie 1988). The establishment of a section for social education within the Ministry of Education in May 1919, which later became the Department of Social Education, indicated a new willingness to expand the supply of physical and health education beyond the borders of school institutions.

THE SPORT LANDSCAPE IN NUMBERS

Data on the distribution of sport facilities were first compiled in early Shōwa Japan by the Bureau of Physical Education (Monbu Daijin Taiiku Ka) in 1933–1934 and its later successor in charge of social education, the Bureau of Physical Strength at the Ministry of Health and Social Welfare in

1938 (and 1940) (Kōseishō Tairyoku Kyoku). The very first survey referring to *taiiku shisetsu* (sport facilities) in the title had already been commissioned two decades earlier by the Bureau of School Hygiene at the Ministry of Education (Monbu Daijin Kanbō Eisei Ka 1922). The report was published in 1922 under the Japanese title of 'Summer Sport Facilities in All Japan during 1918, 1919 and 1920'. The term *taiikuteki shisetsu*, however, is misleading as the report does not address permanent facilities, such as sport fields and other open-air facilities to be used primarily in the warm season. The survey rather examined what kind of physical education and health programmes were available to schoolchildren in Japan's prefectures over summer (cf. Figure 2.1). In the first year of the survey, about 770 programmes were registered all over Japan. Yet in some prefectures, including the Northeast and parts of the Southwest, also Kōchi and Yamanashi, no or hardly any courses were available. Over the following two years, the total amount of summer sport programmes almost tripled to 2,132. While this indicates a heightened awareness of the importance of physical activities, we do not know whether the increase in sport programmes also meant increase in reach. For example, course duration on average was much shorter than in 1918, and more than 50 per cent of the total supply was composed of swimming and early morning meetings (*hayaoki-kai*).

These data do not explain why Okinawa, despite its favourable climate and coastlines, was a late-developer, or why the supply in Tokyo actually shrank over the observation period. Without reference to a quantified target

Figure 2.1 Regional spread of public summer sport programmes, 1918–1920.
Source: Data according to Monbu Daijin Kanbō Eisei Ka (1922).

group, the plain enumeration of courses fails to produce new insight into the construction of sport landscapes. We can guess from external knowledge about the economic imbalance in Japan that poverty and scarcity of resources were very likely impediments to the spread of sport programmes. The relationship is unclear, however, as swimming or plain gymnastics do not require mountains of wealth.

Data from the later survey on 'Facilities in All Japan for the Improvement of Physical Strength' are better suited to illuminate the Japanese sport landscape. Published in 1938 and in 1940, the report not only covers core facilities, such as ball parks, stadiums or martial arts *dōjō*; it also pays attention to the usefulness of recreational parks, playgrounds, nature parks and temple sites that can easily be employed as locations suitable for certain sport. Data can also be asked for the accumulation of special sport facilities, kind of ownership and operation and the year of opening. Hence these data provide a fascinating insight into the concept and management of public space in modern Japan (cf. Figure 2.2). While the construction of sport and other recreational parks began as early as in the 1880s, the development gained momentum only in the middle of the Taishō period, which is precisely the same time when the previously mentioned survey on summer sport programmes was launched. Comparatively little attention (and funding) was devoted to the erection of playgrounds and sport parks. Emphasis was put on the opening of recreational parks, nature parks and similar multifunctional rest areas in urbanizing Japan. A substantial mass of sport and recreational parks was only attained in the 1930s.

The distribution of sport facilities was highest in the central area of Chūbu, flanked by neighbouring Kantō and Kinki (Eastern and Western Japan). Yet this subdivision is too generous to answer questions on local availability, which is better addressed by looking at the density of sport facilities in the 46 prefectures of Japan (cf. Figure 2.3). Chūbu's prefectures lost in comparison to the regions of Kantō and Kinki, where Osaka and Tokyo are leading the ranking list. Tochigi and Okinawa did not have any public sport sites at all. Precisely the same prefectures that were late in employing summer sport programmes were also lagging behind with sport facilities: The Northeast, the very Southwest and Shikoku were particularly underequipped with less than five facilities.

Although the public transport system of the 1930s was quite well developed, a ball park in Shinjuku was perhaps out of reach for people living in the slightly distanced cities of Koganei or Hachiōji, which are also part of the prefecture Tokyo. Thus a more precise picture emerges once the focus gets closer to the municipal level. In addition, it arguably makes more sense to consider the area of the sport sites instead of their sheer numbers. According to the results of the Kōseishō survey, there was a high degree of concentration in Shinjuku, Minato-ku and also in Kōtō, while most other parts of the city lacked any sport site. Yet many areas already featured recreational parks and other public open sites that were easily adopted for sport purposes. Central

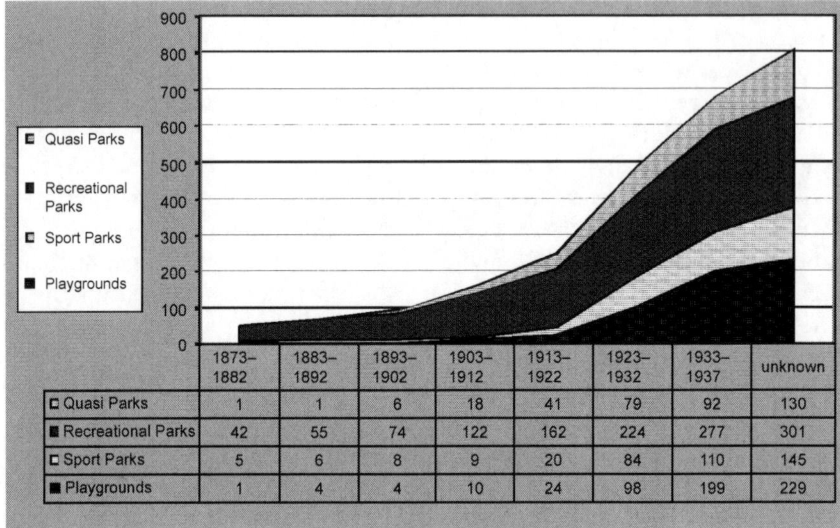

	1873–1882	1883–1892	1893–1902	1903–1912	1913–1922	1923–1932	1933–1937	unknown
Quasi Parks	1	1	6	18	41	79	92	130
Recreational Parks	42	55	74	122	162	224	277	301
Sport Parks	5	6	8	9	20	84	110	145
Playgrounds	1	4	4	10	24	98	199	229

Figure 2.2 Development of sport facilities, 1873–1937.
Source: Data according to Kōseishō Tairyoku Kyoku (1940).

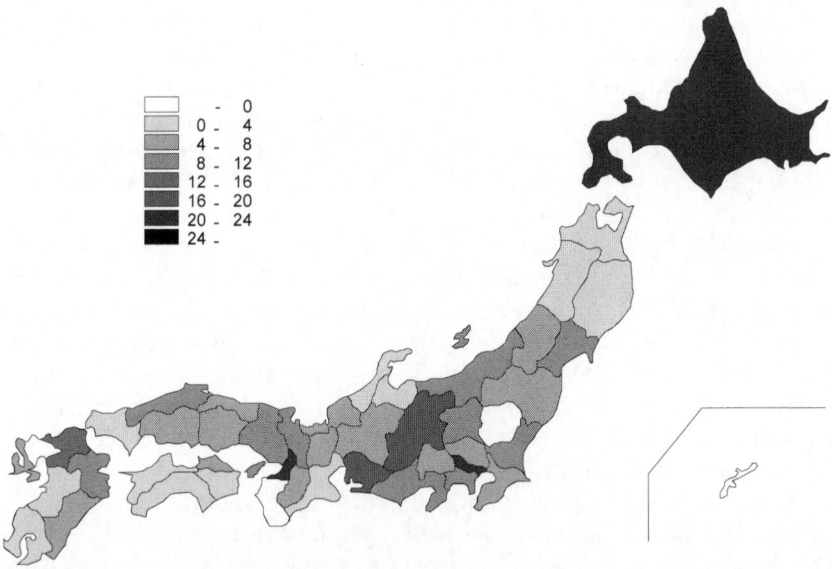

Figure 2.3 Regional spread of ball parks and sport facilities in Japan, 1940.
Source: Data according to Kōseishō Tairyoku Kyoku (1940).

Tokyo featured the highest concentration, particularly in Taitō, Chiyoda and Minato, thanks to large municipal parks such as Ueno Park, Asakusa Park and Hibiya Park. Outside at the fringe of Tokyo City, the amount of public owned and managed space was also considerably larger (cf. Figure 2.4).

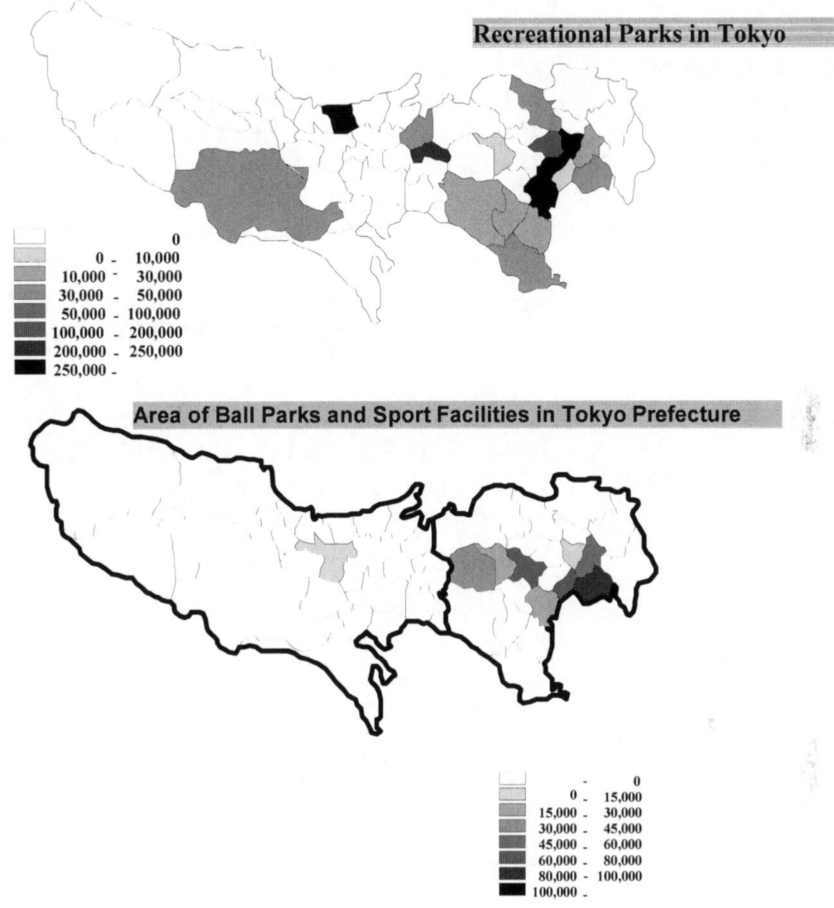

Figure 2.4 Spread and area size of recreational and sport parks in greater Tokyo, 1940 (sqm).
Source: Data according to Kōseishō Tairyoku Kyoku (1940).

Due to its nature and objectives, the ministry's survey has some weak points. The naming of the survey of facilities for the strengthening of the national body clearly states the particular interest of the Bureau of Physical Strength, which opened only in 1938, together with its umbrella organization of the new Ministry of Health. The importance of training the individual body in order to enhance the strength of the collective body was far from being new to Japan. Dating back to Mori Arinori's term in office during the 1880s, this approach had shaped the basic policy of physical education within public schools ever since gymnastics had become a compulsory subject of all primary educational institutions. Mori, Japan's first and probably most influential minister of education, did not have to invent this strategy by himself as it was regular practice of most modern nations in the late 19th century. In the early 20th century, the need to reach out for individual bodies intensified. First of all, Japan's army and Japan's new industries were in need of manpower. Secondly, since the end of World War I demographics in Japan had considerably changed. Rapid urbanization was one of the most eye-catching phenomena in 1938: Between 1920 and the mid-1930s, the number of cities with more than 100,000 inhabitants doubled from 16 to 34, and the urban population tripled from 6.75 million to 17.52 million (Sakaue 1998:44). An additional seven million lived in smaller cities of more than 25,000 inhabitants. In most instances, the growth of cities was far too rapid for planning and control departments. In consequence, housing conditions were often even worse than in the most impoverished rural village. The fight against lack of hygiene, tuberculosis and other unwanted accompaniments of modernization was counted among the most eminent tasks of social policy.

The extensive preface to the study report indicates that officials were fully aware of the dark side of modernization and urbanization. The comments also gave weight to the claim that national sport and body politics in prewar Japan served nationalist interests while aiming at strengthening military power and advancing industrial productivity. The policy approach that shaped the design of the survey is most interestingly expressed by the formula employed by town planners in order to calculate the minimum size of the local sport landscape. In the case of a city of 100,000 inhabitants, the minimum of 210,000 sqm was determined on the basis of a multivariate model which took the availability of alternative sport sites, such as open areas, riversides, streets and parks, into consideration as well as local demographics and sport habits of age groups. Children older than ten were supposed to practise four hours a week, but only 60 per cent were expected to engage actively in sport; at the opposite of the social stratum were adults in their 30s. Participation rate was expected to be as low as 10 per cent, and average length of sport practice was limited to one hour a week.

As the policy approach of the study closed up on urban Japan, villages, towns and cities with a population of less than 25,000 inhabitants were excluded in principle. Living conditions in the countryside were far from being superior to city life. Because the countryside was located in close vicinity to grand nature, however, the need of recreational parks or playgrounds certainly was less severe. Furthermore, investments into local projects relied on local funds. Shortness of public funding, which was a handicap to all local governments, paralysed the local administration and social work in great parts of the low-income countryside, particularly after the economic crises of the 1920s and the Great Depression.

Data do not justify assuming a linear relationship between population size and amount of sport facilities (cf. Table 2.1). While large cities tended to have more facilities than smaller towns, the ratio of citizens and area of sport facilities generally was lower in these conglomerates. In March 1938, 69 small towns with a total population of 2.5 million commanded over 27 sport-specific sites (and 127 non-sport-specific recreational parks), while 30 specialized sites (plus 316 general parks) were to be found in the six big cities with 13.5 million inhabitants. Set against the minimum demand of 2.1 sqm per head as outlined by the Ministry, no city category managed to get close to the bottom line. Particularly bad was the ratio in large cities with 0.13 sqm/head, followed by 0.29 sqm/head in the smallest. Comparatively good conditions of 0.67 sqm/head, though far below the desired minimum, were provided by larger towns of 50,000 to 100,000 inhabitants. On the second rank followed smaller cities with a ratio of 0.48 sqm/head (total average: 0.392 sqm). Apparently both the smallest and the largest urban conglomerates struggled in a similar way, probably because of the delay of infrastructure development in smaller cities and the massive intricacies of coping with rapid population growth in the big cities.

The proportional distribution of different kind of operators tells a lot about the way ownership was immediately related to the targeted user group (cf. Table 2.2). National stadiums or national nature parks were constructed and maintained by the central government; prefectural facilities were primarily opened to the regional population and thus financed by regional government, and the local infrastructure was mainly used by local inhabitants. Central government spending on the expansion of the sport infrastructure only began in the time this survey was published. In fact, the report stated that all the prefectures without a single public ball park or sport ground were just in the process of building large-size multifunctional sport sites, subsidized by funds of the Ministry of Health. In postwar Japan, prefectures were consecutively re-equipped with modern sport sites suitable for international tournaments when they hosted the national sport festival (*kokutai*).

Table 2.1 Cities, Sport Infrastructure and Sport Space per Head in Variously Sized Cities, 1940

	Small Towns	*Towns*	*Cities*	*Big Cities*
Size	*25,000–50,000*	*50,000–100,000*	*100,000–500,000*	*500,000 or more*
Total	69	60	31	6
Inhabitants	2.45m	41.85m	5.55m	13.54m
Recreational parks	127	188	174	316
Area size	13.2m	17.0m	10.0m	14.2m
sqm/head	5.40	4.06	1.81	1.05
Sport parks	27	48	40	30
Area size	0.72m	2.8m	2.7m	1.8m
sqm/head	0.29	0.67	0.48	0.13

Source: Data according to Kōseishō Tairyoku Kyoku (1940), own calculations.

Table 2.2 Ownership of Sport Facilities, 1939

Sport Facilities/ Ownership	*Playgrounds*	*Sport Parks*	*Recreational Parks*	*Quasi Parks*	*Other*	*Total*
State	0	1	0	1	1	3
Prefectures	0	11	32	2	7	52
Municipalities	215	82	255	30	17	599
Private clubs	6	14	0	17	48	85
Corporations	2	37	2	54	24	119
Unknown	6	0	12	26	14	58

Source: Data according to Kōseishō Tairyoku Kyoku (1940).

Privately managed facilities started to emerge during the early Showa years; some of them were commercial enterprises, but the majority was composed of facilities for the exclusive use of members of owner companies or corporations. Public clubs or associations which were at the core of the European institutionalization process of sport, however, were far from being part of the architects' master plan devising modern Japanese society.

The survey also neglected some sport facilities which were not accessible to the wider public. While the National Sports Field at the Meiji Shrine as well as some of the new and privately owned baseball parks that were established in line with the new professional league were featured, all facilities with restrictive terms of accessibility, such as schoolyards, training grounds and buildings managed by schools and other educational institutions, were systematically excluded from the survey.

As I have argued in the first chapter, for most living in prewar Japan actual sport experience was limited to physical education and the framework of the educational system. Sport games were a prerogative of the upper stratum of Japanese society and particularly for those who attended higher education. In mid-Taishō, only a mere 15,500 was enrolled at the eight high schools and four public universities, while 200,000 went to secondary schools. Compulsory education, by contrast, already covered 98 per cent of the population at school age. General emphasis was laid on calisthenics, as all curricula of physical education revealed. Teacher Training Institutes played a pivotal role for the one-sided spread as they were the central place from where physical education instructors spread out to all parts of Japan. Sport games were only partially thought to fit the physical condition of the young students. For example, a widely read textbook on outdoor sport games of the 1930s explicitly described soccer as non-suitable for children and young adolescents.

Local and grassroots sport initiatives were an unofficial but indispensable component of the early institutionalization process of sport in Europe. In Japan, however, the state suppressed any kind of grassroots movement until the years after the Pacific war.

CONCLUSION

As we know from the previous chapter, sport in Japan developed as part of the modernization project. As we have seen from the data, the capital of Tokyo and other large cities spearheaded the introduction of sport sites while the countryside was lagging far behind. The urban environment, however, provided particular difficulties, primarily in relation to the limit of space. The inherent difficulties of the project to assess sport landscapes in quantitative terms became evident rather soon. Doubt on the accuracy of numbers is always justified. Yet my own failure of taking the variability of time into consideration of the conceptualization of sport landscapes is much more severe. It is crucial to differentiate between three different types of sport sites that contribute to the construction of the sport landscape. There are (1) primary sport sites which are especially designed for the purpose of sport and which are of permanent duration; (2) secondary sport sites which primarily have to serve different interests but are temporarily and consciously devoted to sport events; (3) tertiary sport sites which primarily have to serve different interests but are spontaneously and unpredictably opened for sport purposes.

The data I have discussed here stress the overwhelming importance of secondary sport sites for the emergence of the Japanese sport landscape. Now the crucial point seems to be that secondary sport sites such as schoolyards or the Meiji Shrine precincts are designed for clear-cut primary objectives which are embodied by their spatial outline, cultural icons and highly suggestive symbols. Thus these sites enforce the ideological subjugation and adaption of non-primary practices when they are to be staged within their precincts. Read in this way, the prewar Japanese sport landscape was dominated and heavily shaped by national interests of the emperor state ideology. Given that the period under observation lasted for nearly three generations, we can expect that the symbiotic outcome continued to influence even the sport landscape in postwar Japan. As the next chapter is going to show, this definitely was the case when Japan increasingly turned into an authoritarian and militarist state in the 1930s and 1940s.

3 Sport, Body Control and National Discipline in Prewar and Wartime Japan[1]

INTRODUCTION

Sport and body culture as fields of political and nationalist ambitions are characteristic features of totalitarian systems in modern societies. No other political movement knew better how to capitalize on the symbolic values and very practical implications of strong, healthy and superior bodies than the fascist ones that emerged as an essentially new force and a major factor within and outside of Europe during the 1930s. In response to the experiences of World War I, economic crises, political instability and social unrest that continued throughout the postwar decade, fascist ideologies worldwide were regarded as a promising alternative and practical solution across national and social constituencies. Practical, immediate action and the corporeality of direct participation provided a main attraction to anti-intellectual fascism that gained currency, particularly but not exclusively, at bottom level of the fascist organizations. Notwithstanding the many faces fascism had throughout the world, as well as to its followers, the concurrent emphasis on the superior *and* the collective body was a common feature contributing to its success since they resonated with the widespread longing for strong leadership and a secure sense of belonging. The symbolic expression of physical strength, which separated the strong from the weak, and the uniform body, which offered the feeling of home and community to the chosen members, converged into the imagery, rituals and rhetoric of fascist aesthetics. Or, in the words of Juan Linz, fascism satisfied both the romantic desire for the heroic deeds of the individual and the desire for submergence in a glorious collectivity. Its political leaders knew how to employ these needs to subordinate the individuals to the goals of the state and those holding power in it (Linz 1976:23).

The history of Japan and Japanese body politics throughout the first half of the 20th century provide an interesting case study for the analysis of the relations between sport and totalitarianism. In 1931, the year of the invasion of Manchukuo in Northeastern China by the Japanese Imperial Army, marked the end of Japan's short interlude with liberalism and democracy. In addition, the military occupation signified Japan's outset towards the establishment of a seemingly fascist totalitarian regime, which was completed a decade later.

According to Willensky, Imperial Japan's evolution into a fascist state started with Japan's withdrawal from the League of Nations in 1933 and continued with the controversy over the Emperor Organ Theory (*Tennō kikan setsu*) in 1935; the signing of the Anti-Comintern Pact with Nazi Germany in 1936; the promulgation of the National General Mobilization Law (*Kokka sōdōin hō*) in 1938; the New Structure Movement (Shin Taisei Undō) and the dissolution of the political parties in May 1940; the signing of the Tripartite Pact with Nazi Germany and fascist Italy in September of the same year; and then the inauguration of the Imperial Rule Assistance Association (Taisei Yokusan Kai) in October (Willensky 2005:77). During this entire period the Imperial Japanese government used ubiquitous calls for service to the state and allegiance to the ideal of *kōdō*, the way of the emperor, which was outlined already in Kita Ikki's *Nippon kaizō hōan taikō* (Plan for the Reconstruction of Japan) from 1919, to shape and mould the population into a motivated yet servile populace.

Even though Japan in the 1930s and early 1940s was clearly exhibiting all signs of radicalism, militarism, imperialism, ultra-nationalism and racialism, historians, with the noteworthy exception of Marxist researchers, have been largely reluctant to describe prewar and wartime Japan as a fascist state for a variety of reasons. Next to the circumstance that the emphasis on praxis and the anti-intellectual stance of fascism itself inhibited the development of a reasonable political theory, classification attempts have been hampered by the open and explicit refusal of political leaders of the 1930s as well as thinkers from the right to be labelled as fascists. Because of historical preconditions Japan's governing forces lacked the total power of fascist governments elsewhere. Even wartime cabinets were shaken by intra-ministry rivalries; elections were continued until 1942, offering alternative choices for independent candidates or refusing the right to vote; the mass organization failed to control the military and did not entirely permeate civil society (Manzenreiter 2007a). In addition, and this is of importance for the comparative historical research on fascism, the lack of a mass movement thrusting a political party into power and the non-existence of a radical disjuncture between early Shōwa Japan (1926–1945) and its precedent eras have been identified as main arguments to defy the applicability of the term. However, as Alfredo Rocco, the later Italian minister of justice, explained in *The Political Doctrine of Fascism* from 1925, fascism is indifferent to methods but not to ends (Willensky 2005:62). As Maruyama Masao (1963:88) noted already in the early postwar years, in contrast to Germany and Italy, fascism in Japan did not come by force; it succeeded by permeating the existing power structure from inside. On cultural terrain, in contrast to political institutions, Japan's emperor-centred ideology and its obsession with racial superiority was much closer to the main fascist ideologies of Europe. In fact, as Willensky (2005:64) recently argued, the institutional preconditions and intellectual foundations for the fascist transformation of the political system had been laid much earlier (and more thoroughly) than the attempts of the Italian right-wingers to found a doctrinaire base underlying their will to power.

Notwithstanding the conceptual problems that cannot be solved within the limited space of this chapter, it is evident that the Japanese state faced similar challenges in forming a totalitarian aggregate like its European counterparts. It is the task of this chapter to identify the role sport played in this authoritarian enterprise. In the following sections I will delineate various ways in which sport and body politics were employed by the Japanese government to discipline and mould the population into a servile and compliant mass. I will show that the increasingly intense grip on the individual bodies was far from being new in this period but a continuation of a sometimes contradictory and ambiguous policy line initiated already in the mid-Meiji period (ca. 1885–1900). The picture would be incomplete without referring to important counter-currents. The increasing commodification of sport since the early 1920s gave birth to new ideas and usages of sport without provoking explicit actions by state authorities. The resulting question concerning the reason for the Japanese state's relative indifference towards sport during this period will be answered in the final discussion.

THEORIZING THE NATIONAL BODY

The dominant conception of the relation between state, nation and subject at the time was summarized by the powerful notion of *kokutai* (national or state body) that based the Japanese system on the supreme authority of the emperor. One of the most debated challenges to the conventional view of the *kokutai*, Minobe Tatsukichi's theory of the emperor as organ of the state (*Tennō kikan setsu*), also applied the image of the body by designating the emperor as a constitutionally defined organ within the body of the state. Of course, the somatization of the nation or the state has not been a Japanese invention since the image of the body has been used in political theory since Thomas Hobbes, John Locke and other thinkers of the 17th century debated about the nature of the 'body politic'.

In marked contrast to Renaissance thought, the somatization of the national socialist society in 20th century was triggered by a strong anti-intellectualism, which in contrast effected the valorization of the body. According to Hitler's *Mein Kampf*, the entire education system of the national socialist state was to be geared on rearing healthy bodies; mental and intellectual capabilities followed second. Academic schooling was ranked the last position, well behind character development, promotion of willpower, decisive power and responsibility. In some fascist movements, the fetishist concern with the physical was publicly put on display by the very bodies of their leaders, such as Benito Mussolini or Oswald Mosley from the British Union of Fascists (Collins 2000). But with the exception of the leader cult, fascist body politics usually focused on the collective, not on the individual. Reflecting upon the role of physical training within national socialist ideology, the former fast track runner and sport officer of the paramilitary Sturmabteilung (SA), Bruno Malitz, compared sport with conscription and defined sport as a further 'service to the nation' (*Volk*):

> We national socialists want to educate the people through sport. The goal of national socialist sport is the thorough formation of the individual for the purpose of strengthening the national body. (Quoted in Leitgeb 2000:28)

In ideological terms, the somatization of the national socialist society derived from the hyper-inflated ideal of an imagined healthy and vital, in other words sportive national body (*Volkskörper*). Its vitality and energetic power were seen as the root of the expansionary drive into new territories and habitat (*Lebensraum*), hence the special role that the German fascist movement assigned to the body, its education and presentation. Rightist intellectuals in Imperial Japan similarly paid high attention to the question of living space. On the one hand—in political scientist terms of realism—Imperial Japan sought the expansion of Japan's sphere of influence within the Greater East Asia Co-Prosperity Sphere (*Dai Tōa Kyōeiken*), a layered zone of empowered and autonomous states placed like a buffer area around the core of the Japanese islands (Martin 1999). On the other hand, Katō Kanji and other proponents of the Japanese version of physiocratism (*nōhonshugi*) placed their hopes for a new Japan into the Manchurian annexation by the Kwangtung Army. In the vast open spaces of the Manchurian puppet-state they saw a new fertile soil for the surplus energies of those parts of Japan's young rural population that was exceeding demand in their impoverished home regions (Mori 2004).

The conception of the collective body as an agent of political power also tainted some theories of physical education in Japan. The palingenetic myth, a core element of all fascist ideologies heralding the advent of a new man out of the ruins of the old, rotten society, was adopted in the writings of Ueda Seiichi and Sasaki Hitoshi. Like other, not necessarily nationalist-minded intellectuals, they believed that educating the body provided the ultimate precondition for creating 'new man'. According to the social Darwinist law of the strongest, the physically trained new mankind was to be empowered to destroy the social world suffering from the constraints of capitalist society and mechanization, to renew it and find new ways of social living in imperialist expansion (Irie 1986:76). The fascination of reaching the masses by addressing their bodies impacted upon the writings of sympathizers of leftist and socialist ideas as well. Maekawa Mineo, Nakaya Jūji and Yamada Yoshimasa were outspoken critics of the social conditions resulting from modernization and urbanization. While they were in favour of the idea of proletarian sport, which by definition should transgress national borders, they also perceived radical physiocratism as an escape route from the inherent contradictions of modern society.

MOULDING THE MASSES INTO A NATIONAL BODY

For all Japanese governments after the Meiji Restoration in 1868, the modern institutions of compulsory schooling and the conscription army provided the most effective tool for integrating the majority of the Japanese population into the construction of the national body. Particularly the modern mass education system, allowing the authoritarian state encompassing access to the entire young generation, diffused the intense nationalism of the upper classes downwards to all the Japanese. Ever since physical education became a compulsory subject in the early Meiji period, the body and its formation were central policy objects for the development of national identity, loyalty and submission as core values of the authoritarian family state ideology (Manzenreiter 2001). Physical education at elementary school level basically consisted of calisthenics and active games. Particularly the techniques of the former, which were conducted according to military-style orders and afforded the conscious adjustment of individual moves with the bodies of the instructor and fellow students, were well suited to install collective attitudes and deliberate subordination. Body techniques acquired in physical education could be used for public demonstrations of social cohesion as well as for more practical military purposes. Since the 1880s, *heishiki taisō* (military gymnastics using military equipment, mock rifles, marching exercises and combat simulations) was introduced to the school curriculum for higher grades. With the years, pressure to extend the reach of pre-military education increased: In 1917, the Special Council on Education recommended to the Parliament that students above middle school should be trained to be soldiers with patriotic conformity, martial spirit, obedience and toughness of mind and body (Abe, Kiyohara and Nakajima 1992:12). During the Taishō years (1912–1926), liberal educationalists in the councils of the Ministry of Education safeguarded the younger age groups as well as female students against these objectives of the Ministry of Army.

A similar tug-of-war between opposing camps of educationalists and bureaucrats delayed the introduction of martial arts to the national curriculum for about three decades. Physiological concerns with the effects of martial arts on the young bodies accompanied the discussion of the suitability of martial arts for children and youth. Classical *bujutsu* as well as *budō*, the modernized versions of Japan's autochthonous physical culture, were regarded as equally useful for the purpose of indoctrination because of their common emphasis on obedience, endurance and self-discipline. Furthermore, the practice of *budō* allowed the immediate establishment of links with a glorious tradition and the historical continuity of the warrior ethics from feudal Japan. As Reischauer (1970:185) had observed, both primary school and conscription convinced the peasant population, 'who for almost three centuries had been denied swords and other arms, that they too were members of a warrior race' and 'inculcated in them the glory of Japan's great military traditions and the ideal of death on the battlefield in the service of the emperor'.

But only in the 1930s, when the military's influence outweighed liberal reasoning within the cabinet government, were martial arts finally adopted by the official school curricula. In the year of the Manchurian invasion, *kendō* and *jūdō* became compulsory for secondary schooling, and in 1936 for the higher grades of elementary schools, too; since then, girls were also obliged to take courses in *naginata-dō* and *kyūdō*. A year prior to the reform, the Educational Reform Council suggested to the Ministry of Education to abolish the harmful element of competition and championships from all sports; instead it encouraged to stress piety, fortitude, and fairness in accordance with the traditional ideal of *bushidō*.

Members of the National Reserve Army always had been valuable resources to teach the military style of gymnastics, and in 1925 the Ministry of Army finally conceded the right to send serving army officers in to supervise military training (*gunji kyōren*) in middle schools and above. Over the course of the 1930s, the instrumentalist objectives became increasingly clear when sport games mutated into military exercises. At the National Youth Defense Games (*Seinen gakkō kokubō taiiku taikai*), students in uniforms marched into sport grounds that partially resembled battlefields. Held for the first time in 1939 and since then annually, the programme contained competitions in throwing grenades and running with gas masks, stretchers or water buckets, thereby simulating activities of high demand in combat abroad or at the home front. In 1939, the new sport of national defense (*kokubō undō*) was added to the sport curriculum. Within the public education sport system, Western sports were increasingly marginalized and oppressed. Starting from 1940, the Ministry of Education officially allowed students to participate in competitive sport merely for one or two hours a week, and this just on Sundays or holidays; instead the youth was encouraged to study martial arts. The nationalist appropriation of Western sport acquired a rather absurd, yet highly symbolical, dimension when English expressions were replaced by newly coined sport terms in Japanese. This development started in 1936 and was reinforced by the beginning of war against England in the Pacific (Abe, Kiyohara and Nakajima 1992:15).

The administrative organs in charge of school and social education used rational scientific methods in an attempt to prove the effectiveness of their politics. Panel data on the physical fitness of the youth were available since public schools had been obliged to conduct regular examinations in the early 20th century. The results showed an alarming decrease in physical abilities of military conscripts and the general deterioration of health conditions among the young urban generation (see Table 3.1). In the 1930s, the newspapers echoed the army's concern about the loss of military manpower and transferred the issue of public health into the public domain. According to a newspaper report from 1932, 200,000 children in rural areas were chronically undernourished, which seems fairly underrated; nonetheless, it caused the Ministry of Education to nationalize the operation of school nutrition few weeks later (Kishino et al. 1973:156). Shortsightedness (myopia) and chronic diseases of the respiratory organs were labelled as typical school diseases because their occurrence tended to increase with the length of school visit (Yamamoto 1999:39). In order to cope with the ailing national body, the Army Ministry urged for the instalment of a new ministry in charge of health and social welfare and made its establishment one of the conditions for supporting the new cabinet under Konoe Fumimaro.

In 1938, the newly founded Ministry of Health and Welfare took over all competencies related to public health and national fitness, including the provision of sport facilities and the control of sport organizations; only school sport remained under the jurisdiction of the Ministry of Education. The new ministry's Board of Physical Fitness (Tairyoku Ka) enacted the Physical Strength Badge Test (*tairyoku shō kentei*) in August 1939 and promulgated the National Physical Strength Law (Kokumin tairyoku hō) in April 1940. The fitness test aimed at the entire male population between 15 and 25 years; those who had participated in a speed running competition (100 metre), a mid-distance run (2,000 metre), broad jump, throwing a hand grenade, a 50-metre run carrying a sandbag and pull-ups received a badge, indicating the level of their performance. In 1943, the test also was adapted to females from 15 to 21 years of age (Abe, Kiyohara and Nakajima 1992:18).

The National Physical Strength Law regulated that all males under 26 years of age and females under 20 years of age were measured (height, weight, volume of respiratory organs, strength of grip) and inspected for diseases in a way as a ministerial ordinance from 1900 had already requested from all attending public schooling. Whereas in former times data were primarily collected and transferred to the Ministry of Education, they were now interpreted on a case-by-case scale, since the latest law reform from 1938 obliged schools to share the responsibility for improved health conditions with their students. Examination data were forwarded to the students together with concrete recommendations of therapies and general improvement. The score cards listed the individual results together with national and prefectural averages, which invited the individual to perceive his or her ranking in comparison with the collective nation. At the same time, as material objects the sheets symbolized the grip of the state on the individual body and extended state control function into the private sphere of the households and neighborhoods into which students and their family members carried the score cards (Yamamoto 1999:38).

CONTROL STRUCTURES BEYOND THE SCHOOL APPARATUS

With the years, the state authorities' interest in the bodies of the subjects surpassed the limited realm of compulsory and secondary schooling. Particularly useful was the new national mass medium of radio broadcasting and the spread of early morning radio gymnastics (*rajio taisō*), beginning in 1930. Modelled after a scheme devised by life insurance companies abroad, the Japanese broadcast did not simply aim at strengthening the bodies of children and adults alike, but also their minds and sentiments. Through the medium of the radio, the state was practically empowered to reach the entire populace, practising in identical fashion, listening to the same tunes and following the same orders.

The structures of mass organizations facilitated the state authorities' outreach for the bodies of its subjects. Founded in 1930, the All Japan Gymnastics Association (Zenkokumin Taisō Kyōkai) soon matured into a mass organization with some million participants throughout the nation. In 1932, there were 2,950 organizations in 23 prefectures with a total of 1,952,417 participants; in 1934, the association counted 3,218,158 members of 7,052 organizations in 35 prefectures (Sakaue 1998:121). The annual highlight was the *taisō matsuri*, a spectacle of mass calisthenics, which was held at Meiji Jingu Gaienmae Undō Kyōgijo, the national sport ground next to the spiritually symbolic centre of the state, the Meiji Shrine. The national juncture was even more pronounced by holding the festival on November 3, the national holiday commemorating the birthday of Meiji Tennō, the founding figure of the modern Japanese nation-state. The symbolic significance of time and space for the experience of national identity must not be underestimated. Ever since the National Sports Games were held at the National Stadium at the Meiji Shrine for the first time in 1924, their final day concurred with the Memorial Day for the Meiji emperor, which was declared All Japan Sports Day (*Zenkoku taiiku dē*). A visit to the national monument was obligatory for the athletes from out of town when they represented their home region at the national sport festivals in the capital. At the occasion of the national sports day, schools and youth organizations nationwide held sport events. The peripheries were united with the centre from 1932 onwards, when live broadcast from the *taisō matsuri* and the National Sports Games integrated them into the imagined community of sporting Japan.

Many sources from the 1920s and 1930s indicate that the concern with leftist ideas and socialist movements was a major cause for the government to tighten measures of social control over the young generation out of schooling. In the previous chapter, I explained how the corporate sector of Japanese business adopted sports for their paternalist employment policy and that this initiative was in full accordance with the social policy line of the government. Therefore, state control also reached into the sport programmes of private enterprises. The establishment of a section for social education within the Ministry of Education in May 1919, which later became the Department of Social Education, marked for the first time the national determination to extend physical and health education beyond the borders of school institutions. Corporate sports, however, were under the supervision of the Ministry of Home Affairs and its special police department on corporate affairs (Keisatsuchō Kōjō Ka) which also organized sport fests and tournaments. According to a survey of the department from 1934, 11,251 companies with 212,070 workers participated in the official industrial sports day (Sakaue 1998:155). A survey on the state of corporate sports in 1937 gives a somehow opaque picture of the companies' sponsored activities (Kōseishō Tairyoku Kyoku 1940)—methodological shortcomings of the data presentation make it impossible to advance a precise interpretation of the general state of company sports. Yet at least the figures indicate the interest of capital in the physical well-being of their labour resource. The report on the survey also featured a number of research studies from the Research Institute of Labour Sciences in Kurashiki, Okayama, which demonstrated the negative impact of industrial labour on physical development and the consequential need for regular, even obligatory, sport programmes: Comparing female workers and students, the researchers found that 'the rapidity of mental mobility' (*seishin undō sokudo*), i.e. the coordination of hand and eye movements, was slower among industrial workers than among students of the same age group. Another research project suggested that industrial labour inflicts harm upon the balanced growth of the body; particularly the lower limbs reportedly remained underdeveloped. A ministerial ordinance from October 1938 made gymnastics compulsory for company workers (Kishino et al. 1973:168)—which may explain why gymnastics was the most often practised sport activity within corporate sport. Only large companies actually could afford providing their own social welfare programmes. The majority of workers at small and medium-sized industries needed different supply sides.

Together with corporate sports, national youth associations helped establish a framework for moderate mass participation in sport. During the years of World War I, Tanaka Giichi, a high-ranking officer of the Imperial Army and a later prime minister, studied patriotic youth organizations abroad, and upon his return in 1915 he initiated a nationwide network of voluntary youth groups (*seinendan*). Under the directive of the Home Ministry, the Japanese youth organizations consolidated in a centralized organizational structure in 1925. Membership of the local branches of the Greater Japan Federation of Youth Groups (Dai Nippon Rengō Seinendan) was compulsory for every male inhabitant of a respective administrative district if he had completed elementary school and still was under conscription age (Kōzu 1078:45–48). The Federation counted a membership of more than a million in the early 1930s. School directors and members of the reserve army usually served as group leaders and instructors. The basic concern was the moral education of the working youth and their surveillance. Next to military drill exercises, sport comprised a major component at the weekly meetings. By means of physical education, including athletics, gymnastics and *budō*, youths were expected to contribute to the national aims of producing strong soldiers and diligent workers. The actual practice of sport, however, differed considerably depending on the location of the branches. According to surveys from the late 1920s, baseball matches already attracted audiences of some tens of thousands, but active participation was very limited, particularly in rural regions which simply lacked facilities and equipment. *Budō* and gymnastics, which are sports with a low demand of technological thus financial input, therefore were among the most common sport activities in the countryside; mountain climbing, swimming, table tennis and baseball were much more popular among urban *seinendan* branches (cf. Table 3.1).

Similar organizations for the social education of late-teen girls came into existence in 1927 (Dai Nippon Rengō Joshi Seinendan). By the early 1930s, membership exceeded four million for both sexes. By 1928 there were 15,295 youth groups for boys with a membership of 2,534,326 and 13,043 girls' groups with a membership of 1,514,459. The total number of groups amounted to 28,338 with 4,048,785 members (Monbushō 1972). A new organizational structure for youth schools (*seinen gakkō)* was established in 1935 integrating the former youth training centres (*seinen kunrenjo*) and vocational supplementary schools under the supervision of the Social Education Bureau of the Ministry of Education, which received some support from the Ministry of the Army. According to the first article of the 1935 Youth School Ordinance, youth school education aimed at the provision of instruction in discipline and virtue of the mind and body and, at the same

Table 3.1 Sport Activities of Urban and Rural *seinendan* Branch Groups

	Urban (%)	*Rural (%)*
Track and field	25.7	66.2
Mountaineering	23.9	12.6
Swimming	16.2	4.4
Baseball	21.7	3.0
Tennis	6.6	4.2
Table tennis	9.8	2.6
Ski	1.9	1.6
Basketball	1.4	0.0
Camping	3.7	0.3
Budō	22.1	37.4
Sumo	9.1	13.6
Gymnastics	2.4	1.2

Source: Sakaue (1998:44).

time, intended to instruct the working youth in the knowledge and skills necessary for their vocation and everyday life, so as to assist them in the development of the requirements for the members of the Japanese nation. Courses lasted for four to five years and included physical education and military drills for boys.

During the latter half of the 1930s, pressure increased on these and all other youth major organizations, such as the Japan Boy Scout Association (Shōnendan Nippon Renmei, 1922) and the Imperial Association of Boy Groups (Teikoku Shōnendan Kyōkai, 1934), to standardize content, objectives and form of social education along the lines of the state. Ultimately they were forced to merge into one single organization at the end of the decade. In January 1941, the foundation of the Greater Japan Youth and Child Organisation (Dai Nippon Seishōnendan) was celebrated at the Nippon Seinenkan in Tokyo (Sakashita 2003:11). The structure of the organization copied the straightforward control configuration of the national administration system, linking the local level via prefectural sections with the centre of state power. Prefectural sections were headed by governors, and directors of youth schools supervised the activities at local level.

The same design characterized the structure of the Great Japan Amateur Sports Association (Dainippon Taiiku Kyōkai), founded in 1911 and reorganized into a federation of autonomous sports associations and regional branches in 1925. Under its auspices, championships were held and athletes selected for participation at international tournaments. Since the heads of the regional branches were public employees and the association heavily depended on funding from the Ministry of Education, it transformed gradually into an arm of central government (Sakaue 1998:156). When the governmental concentration of body and sport politics culminated at the beginning of the 1940s, the amateur sports federation and its associated member organizations were resolved. All university sport organizations were pooled in one singular sport club (Dai Nippon Gakutō Taiiku Shinkō Kai) at the end of 1941, and all civic sport organizations turned into members of the newly founded Greater Japan Sports Association (Dai Nippon Taiiku Kai, 1942) under the presidency of prime minister Tōjō Hideki, who also headed the Imperial Rule Assistance Association (Taisei Yokusan Kai), the only equivalent of an overarching and all-embracing mass organization during Japan's fascist regime.

CLEAVAGES: MASS SPORT, ENTERTAINMENT AND INTRA-MINISTERIAL COMPETITION

If the discussion were to stop here, the picture of an ever totalitarian and suppressive state would largely confirm with the general idea of fascist body politics. However, sport also came to fulfil leading roles for commercial interests, new lifestyle patterns of the urban middle class and

Japan's public diplomacy. Since the beginning of the century, profit-seeking strategies of modern mass transportation and mass media companies provided the ground for a fairly important supplement to the disciplinary tool of sport in the 1930s. As already mentioned in the previous chapter, the huge interest in inter-school competitions and the rising demand for entertainment for its urban audiences sparked the interest of newspaper publishers in exploiting the rising popularity of sport for their own profits. By hosting sport events, sponsoring tournaments and opening private pools, ski slopes and hiking trails, publishing companies and private railway companies also pioneered the exploration of Japan's leisure industries since the Taishō years (Takemura 1988). In Ōsaka, the Municipal Survey Bureau of Social Affairs (Ōsaka-shi Shakai-bu Chōsa-ka) recorded 48 sport events in 1921 that were sponsored or hosted by local newspapers. Over a period of 185 days, 12,124 athletes and 1,618,818 spectators participated at the media-sponsored events, which totalled an average of 33,978 participants per event (Kaga 1978:151). National intercity tournaments in various sport disciplines, usually sponsored by the national newspapers, started in 1927. Thus Gonda Yasunosuke, the Japanese pioneer of social science research on leisure, noted as early as 1923 that baseball certainly no longer belonged to the elites exclusively since now it fascinated all social classes and mobilized mass spectatorship. Seven years later, Gonda reported in his field research notes the 'unbelievable incident' of empty cinemas throughout the entertainment quarter Asakusa. This extraordinary state was caused by the start of the traditional inter-university baseball match between Waseda and Keiō university teams (*sōkeisen*). Radio broadcasts of the game also interrupted the usual bustling street life. The street corner radio immobilized passersby until the final siren allowed life in Asakusa to return to its normal routine (Kōzu 1995:253).

Given that sport clearly helped to reach a mass audience, particularly the wealthier new middle class, it is difficult to imagine why the media, transport companies and other modern commodity producers, as well as their audiences and customers, should have changed their conceptualization of sport as a commodity for mass entertainment without external pressure. The National Baseball Order from 1932 was an attempt to control the burgeoning popularity of baseball and discipline their fans: The Order on Control and Management of Baseball from 1932 required all organizations to apply for permission for baseball games from the Ministry, and it also prescribed the rules of amateurism and requested the organizing bodies to guarantee disciplined behaviour of the cheering groups. Yet it did not prevent the newspaper publisher Yomiuri Shinbun from setting up its own professional team. With other corporations following the example, eight professional teams began competing for the annual league title in 1937. The highly popular baseball league continued to play their legs until air raids on Tokyo interrupted the league in 1944 (Kiku 1993).

The mass interest in spectator sport gave birth to new special-interest media. Long before the Japanese state's war economy started to control the allocation of resources—which ultimately had a much stronger impact on the suppression of Western sports and the sport entertainment business than the state's ideological reservation—in 1938, the Japanese sport media market was inflated with uncountable new journals, magazines and other print formats catering to the needs of the modern urbanites. In 1936, the *Ōsaka Asahi Shinbun* enlarged its daily sport pages to a total of nine pages that certainly covered more baseball games than military gymnastics. The immense increase of publishing activities during the 1930s was a response to new technologies and new consumption styles as well.

A final factor contributing to the popularity of sport was the increasing visibility of Japan on the international stage when her athletes participated at international tournaments. Particularly successful were Japanese representatives at the Far Eastern Games, which were staged ten times between 1915 and 1934 (Date 2000:206). On an intercontinental level, activities were first more of symbolic value only. After unspectacular results at the Olympic Games of Stockholm in 1912, where just a small delegation of three athletes participated for the first time, and mediocre results in the 1920s, Japan's representatives became increasingly successful in the 1930s. Funds from the imperial family, which started in the mid-Taishō years to remodel itself as a modern ruler by establishing explicit links with the world of modern sport (Sakaue 1998:186), supported the travel abroad of the athlete delegations to the Los Angeles Olympics in 1932 and the following Berlin Olympics. According to the report to the emperor by the president of the amateur sport association, Kishi Seiichi, the success of the Japanese delegation at the 1932 Olympic Games in Los Angeles positively changed the attitude towards Japan in the American press, which had turned increasingly hostile towards Japan after the Manchurian crisis (Sakaue 1998:188). In 1936, the first live coverage ever linked the Japanese audience immediately to the excitement of the tournament. Interest in the Games had been intensified since the announcement that Japan was going to host the 1940 Olympics. Social critic Yamakawa Hitoshi noted a patriotic wave and common understanding of national victory sweeping through the newspapers and the mind of their readers (Ishizaka 2004:112). In official statements, representatives from the Tokyo City Council and the Dainippon Taiiku Kyōkai commented the decision as a public acknowledgment of Japan's national power (*kokuryoku*) and an honourable accolade (Sakaue 1998:224). However, the joint alliance of sport and politics did not last long, and after the war with China broke out, political support started to wane. Particularly the Ministry of the Army interpreted the huge allocation of funds for the Olympics as a waste of resources. Already in 1938, the Games were cancelled, together with the Sapporo Winter Olympics and the World Exhibition, which all had been meant to be part of the official programme to commemorate the 2,600 years anniversary of the Japanese Empire (Collins 2007). The Oriental Games, hosted by Japan at this occurrence, were not much of a substitute since next to Japan only those countries that belonged to the sphere of influence of Japanese colonialism were represented.

CONCLUSION

I have shown in the previous discussion how sport and body politics have been utilized by the Japanese state to mould its citizens into a disciplined and submissive mass. But the sport system was far from being consistent and pervasive, as the final section tried to argue. At no time during the period examined did the state act as a homogeneous and unified body. Quarrels of competency constantly accompanied administrative issues, and body politics resulted from ongoing negotiations between the Ministries of Education, the army and social welfare, including their respective advising committees, lobbyists and pressure groups. The cancellation of the Tokyo Olympics occurred at a time when the expansion of the war into the Pacific was yet to be seen. But the military dominated cabinet politics, and it certainly disagreed with the representational merits of hosting an international sport event. This is a remarkable contrast to the fascist government's symbolic appropriation of the Olympic Games (cf. Alkemeyer 1996).

Capitalist interests differed in some respects from political objectives, and these cleavages were tolerated to a far greater extent than in Western fascist societies. Professionalization of sport was shunned by the German national socialists, but it found acceptance by the Japanese state, who embraced sport spectacles as a kind of high-pressure release valve (*anzenben*) to let off social unrest, economic uncertainty and political frustration. It seems that the state accepted the commercial initiatives since they provided leisure services to the masses which the state could not accomplish. But the national newspapers also served governmental interests, for example, by organizing and staging National Defense Sport Games (*kokubō undō taikai*) or collecting suggestions from their readership on how to raise national strength and fitness in 1937 (Kishino et al. 1973:166).

Generally speaking, sport played a crucial role for disciplinization, as well as moral guidance (*zenshin shidō*), but less for nationalist indoctrination. In this regard I cannot follow Mangan and Komagome (2000), who argued that sports in Japan were at the centre of the induction of the male body (and mind) into martial self-sacrifice. This goal was far more effectively realized within different social contexts, first of all at the school level, and followed by the routines of everyday life in communal self-organization. Within the state ideology, sport fulfilled a complimentary function, and since it was not central, it could be read, practised and used for different, alternating purposes. In sociological terms, this is not a very satisfying explanation, but it neatly describes the core essence of the Japanese sport system as well as my reservations to the unchallenged usage of 'fascism' as a suitable term to categorize the political system of Japan in this period.

The development of Japanese sport, which may be rendered as propelled by the dynamics within the social field of powers, is a result of the competition between all the actors and agents that have to make a certain claim in relation to sport. These actors included athletes, educators, the media, administrative bodies and state authorities in charge of body politics, among many others. Empirical evidence shows that the state had only limited interest, or success, in the total regulation of the field since its ideas of the sportive body were countered by several alternative and opposing practices and interpretations. The state provided the hegemonic ideology of the body. But dominance never occurs without opposition, even in totalitarian systems. It even might be argued that unmediated state oppression naturally provokes resistance and rejection by groups of the people, whereas participatory political systems command over a wider range of 'technologies of governance' that attenuate discrepancies of interest and power in society. The following chapters can be read as a challenge to this simple equation as they are primarily concerned with the new meanings and functions of sport in postwar democratic Japan.

Part II

New Roles, New Faces

Sport in the Service of Various Masters

4 Sport and Gender in the Japanese Classroom[1]

INTRODUCTION

Critical inquiries into the world of sport have disclosed that sport has always been a 'sexual battlefield' in which familiar stereotypes of men and women are communicated and reinforced (Boyle and Haynes 2000:127). Male domination in sport was established as early as the 19th century, when sport emerged as a social institution created by and for men. Biological scientism and the social organization of modernity, in particular the spatial and functional segregation of gender roles, provided the ideological nutrient for the legitimization of gender discrimination in sport. Female subordination was based on a taken-for-granted view of sport as 'natural domain' of men because of the innately different biological and psychological natures of men and women. In contrast to and as complement of the adventurous and competitive-victorious ideal of masculinity, the modern idea of femininity was conceptualized around domestic services provided by women as wives and mothers.

In Japan, as elsewhere, compulsory schooling effectively contributes to the production and reproduction of gender roles. For a number of reasons, physical education classes have been and continue to be at the core of an ideological programme reinforcing the hegemonic gender order. First of all, the subject of physical education is located at the intersection of the two social institutions of school and sport. Second, the wide uniformity of school education, including instructor manuals and teaching styles, guarantees that generational cohorts throughout the country become familiar with similar ideas and messages about being a girl or a boy. Third, the long duration of twelve years, in which more than ninety per cent of Japan's children attend school, coincides with periods of maturation and human development which are crucial for the development of attitudes, values, norms and ideas of selfhood. Fourth, Japan's education industry is fuelled by a societal want of hierarchy, and despite the myth of the classless society, it has always created and continues to produce hierarchical differences between educational institutions with far-reaching consequences (Saitō 2000). Within this institutionalized system of ranking and differentiation based on educational credits, sport arguably serves as a trademark or marketing tool of schools of secondary education which are vying for the same customer base. Sport practice is also related to the reproduction of social stratification insofar as membership in school sport clubs has often been used either as a criterion for the assessment of teamwork capabilities of job applicants or, more bluntly, as a pipeline for personal recruitment through alumni networks. However, for the overwhelming majority of Japanese students enrolled in compulsory education, sports are first of all part of a regular school subject, and as such a basic component of classroom routine. Seen from the perspective of the education system, physical education (PE) is a standard element of the curriculum for a sound and healthy upbringing of pupils. Yet it also reproduces social inequality based on gender differences.

In this chapter I am going to deconstruct physical education as a practice field in which four or five rather independent currents converge and contribute to the production and reproduction of what I call 'body regimes'. Body regimes are here defined as mind-sets of orientation which are incorporated into the (physical) body, consciously as well as unconsciously, by the members of a social community. As they speak through the body to the individual and to the collective, body regimes provide standards of bodily appearance and behaviour and categories of distinction and difference but also of sameness and similarity. Constituting an embodied knowledge about society and one's place within society, body regimes bear structural analogies to the idea of 'habitus' (Bourdieu 1987). This central notion of Pierre Bourdieu's sociology denotes 'a system of structured (and) structuring dispositions, which is constituted in practice and is always oriented towards practical functions' (Bourdieu 1990:53). As part of humans' habitus, body regimes are constructed through and manifested in the shapes of bodies, gestures and everyday usages of the body ranging from sitting and eating to ways of walking, running and using the body in sport. They are normative but not necessarily mandatory. To a certain degree, they are experienced as coercive though no regime rules absolutely unconfined.

In order to comprehend the impact of physical education on the construction of femininities and masculinities in contemporary Japan, we have to give equal consideration to five different contexts which have always been closely interconnected throughout the modern history of school sport and cannot be dealt with separately. Body regimes are contextualized by institutional, organizational, ideological, transcultural and corporeal currents. We first have to look at the education system as a social institution, at its historical formation and the way in which the official ideas of what constitutes a 'grown-up' in Japan are translated into educational curricula and spread by the schools' teaching staff. Second, we have to look at how sportive experience is organized in classroom formations and extracurricular club activities. Third, we will be concerned with the ideological and terminological packaging of sportive experience: What are the dominant ideas of the merits of sport education, and what ideas of gender relations and the relationship between individual and society work behind the practice of school sport? Fourth, we have to be aware of the transcultural context of sport. In Part I, I already referred to the inherent gender logic of sport. In the age of globalization, the local sport experience can hardly be disconnected from the rules monitored by governing transnational organizations and the images transmitted and sold by multinational media corporations. Fifth, and finally, the body, which is the primary target of physical education, is a powerful mnemonic device, as Marcel Mauss (1989 [1934]) demonstrated in his essay on the techniques of the body. The sociologist argued that 'education' and 'contact' with the social environment are giving shape to the inventory of body movements of an individual. The 'techniques of the body' enable the individual to unconsciously employ the body in response to situational requirements in its respective society. Observers of Japanese pre-school institutions have shown how the teaching staff is consciously making use of this corporeal capability in daily life and work routines (e.g. Ben-Ari 1997).

My argument is based on two general assumptions; first, the principal observation of the structured arrangement of economic and cultural capital, which can be gained or lost on the sport ground as well as in any other socially embedded situations, and, second, the reading of sport as a projection screen for the symbolic display of gender order, which itself is a function of power relations in the social fabric of public and private life. What makes sport so peculiar in this regard are its physical appeal and the role of the body that constitutes 'the fundamental principle of division of the social and symbolic world' (Bourdieu 1995:93). A modern subject's notion of self is composed of multiple components, but the body is probably the component most intimate to the self and immediate to the other. Phenomenology teaches us that we *have* a body and at the same time *are* bodies. We can reflect upon our own corporeality, we can dress up, trim our bodies or slim them down; at the same time, we are bodies, for they are the interface to the world we are living in. Without consciously or unconsciously acting upon our bodies and its externalities, there are no meaningful encounters with others (Kameyama 1991). Sport, which can be understood as a particular kind of body performance, is affected by the same antagonistic principle: Athletes train and shape their bodies in training sessions in order to be superior to contenders in competitive encounters.

For analytical purposes, my discussion centres on three different features of sport at school: regular PE classes as required by the curriculum, extracurricular club activities as suggested by the curriculum and the impact of the so-called 'hidden curriculum of physical education'. As I will show, choice and practice are deeply tainted by the impact of the gendered worldview of Japanese society.

PHYSICAL EDUCATION IN THE PREWAR SCHOOL SYSTEM

Sport emerged as a conservative domain for the representation of gender since it became adapted to the needs of compulsory education. At Japanese public schools, the Education System Ordinance of 1872 (*gakusei*) introduced the subject of gymnastics at the elementary school level as early as 1872. Two adversary currents of interest determined the physical education policy in Imperial Japan. Liberal-minded educationalists (Izawa Shūji, 1851–1917, and Tsuboi Gendō, 1852–1922, among others) sympathized with humanist philosophy and advocated a holistic approach that acknowledged the unity of mind, body and soul. Physical education thus was seen as an indispensable part of educating the individual character (Irie 1988:37–40). In contrast to the individual-centred pedagogy, a second school focused on the individual body as an ingredient of the national body. Invented and promoted by the influential thought of social evolutionism, its proponents emphasized the merits of physical education for the nation as a whole. The basic ideas of this school of thought were summarized in the Report to the Throne on Military Style Physical Education (*Heishiki taisō ni kansuru jōsōbun*), written by Minister of Education Mori Arinori (1847–1889) around 1887:

> The wealth and strength of the country will rise to the same extent as the spirit of loyalty to the Emperor and love of our nation prospers. Therefore it is the task of the Minister of Education to nurture this spirit. Physical education has been recognised as being of utmost importance for this purpose and has been added to the curriculum. However, as yet there is no result to be seen because only a few military men have been summoned as instructors and the great majority of school teachers have only had one or two occasions to learn exercises from military men. Generally speaking, the will of school teachers cannot even be spoken of in the same way as that of the military men. The ordinary school teachers do not know how to cultivate an attitude of obedience to a superior authority, to develop an attitude of courage like that of the samurai, nor do they understand how to teach young people to strictly observe rules and regulations . . . The subject of physical education should be separated from the [jurisdiction of the] Ministry of Education and placed under the management of the Ministry of the Army, and pure military style physical education should be carried out by military officers. (. . .) If this was done and the regulations strictly enforced, we will see the development of physical education. Students will take on the superior character of military men. A spirit of loyalty to the Emperor and love of the country will be encouraged. The vital energy for persevering under hard labour will be born. And some day in future when these students are selected for conscription, the results of the military style physical education will be most conspicuous. (Monbushō 1972:chap. 3.1 [1] c)

Hence since the late 1880s, physical education was clearly seen as being in the interest of the collective, the nation or the state. The emphasis on military-style exercises, including marching, armed exercises and repetitive drills, prepared the male students for compulsory military service (introduced in 1873). The communion with the nationalist emperor state ideology indicated that the ultimate purpose of physical education was seen in the formation of 'diligent workers and strong soldiers' as the male supplement to the 'good wife and wise mother'. Their future superiors were trained and shaped within the framework of elite schools at the secondary level. Donald Roden (1980) described in his historical account of *School Days in Imperial Japan* how team games in particular and sport in general were regarded as essential training fields for physical power, controlled aggressiveness, leadership capabilities and moral standards: all of them qualities that differentiated the boys from the men.

According to data compiled by the regional committees in charge of supervising school education, it was only at the beginning of the 20th century that attendance rates at ordinary elementary schools reached saturation level (cf. Table 4.1). The 1872 Education System Ordinance stipulated compulsory school education age as the eight years of school age from 6 until to 14 years (Komatsu 1976:227). Yet the minimum of school attendance varied according to the legal framework, which became stricter and more concise over the years. Only three years after the inauguration of the modern compulsory school education system in 1875, every second boy but only every fifth girl attended school in the scope of the specified minimum. In 1885, two out of three boys, but only every third girl, attended classes regularly.

The 1880 Elementary School Ordinance defined the minimum term of attendance at elementary schools as 16 weeks per year over a period of no less than three years. But in 1886 the School Order declared that parents had the obligation to send their children to school. The 1900 Elementary School Order was even more precise in defining the school-age realm and the persons looking after school-age children (as those who exercise the rights of the parents with respect to those children) in juridical terms. Provisions for excusing or postponing compulsory attendance due to disability, sickness or retardation were elaborated, and for the first time the government took a firm attitude in stating that child labour was not an acceptable excuse for skipping compulsory education. These promulgations were declared before the background of an increasingly positive attitude towards education. In consequence of the Elementary School Order, that also waived school fees, the attendance rates at elementary school improved considerably. In 1900, when the order was released, attendance rates were 90.6 per cent for boys and 71.7 per cent for girls, and ten years later almost every boy (98.8 per cent) and girl (97.4 per cent) received compulsory education (Komatsu 1976; Horimatsu 1975).

Table 4.1 Attendance Rate at Ordinary Elementary Schools, 1875–1915

	Total (%)	*Boys (%)*	*Girls (%)*
1875	35.4	50.8	18.7
1880	41.1	58.7	21.9
1885	49.6	65.8	32.1
1890	48.9	56.1	31.1
1895	61.2	76.7	43.9
1900	81.5	90.6	71.7
1905	95.6	97.7	93.3
1910	98.1	98.8	97.4

Source: Monbushō (1972).

Girls were largely excluded from the nation-centred perceptions within school education. Mass enrolment of female students started only at the end of the 19th century (cf. Table 4.1). At the turn of the century, Inokuchi Aguri and others introduced 'Sweden gymnastics' to Japan as a new variant thought of as more suitable to the Japanese physique in general and to girls in particular. For the following decades, both military and Sweden gymnastics co-existed side by side with games. The first Syllabus of School Gymnastics, proclaimed by the Ministry of Education in 1913, was composed of these core elements. However, the male body continued to be of primary concern. The Diet passed a bylaw in 1917 on the promotion of military gymnastics, following recommendations by the Council for Education: Male 'students above middle school should be trained to be a soldier with patriotic conformity, martial spirit, obedience, and toughness of mind and body' (Abe, Kiyohara and Nakajima 1992). The female body was excluded from the field of martial arts, which were added to the school curriculum in 1931, ending a decade-long debate between militarists, *budō* teachers and pedagogues on the suitability of martial arts for the juvenile body.[2] The liberal climate of the Taishō years (1912–1925) allowed substantial improvements for girls' participation in sport. A survey of the Prime Minister's Office among 2,153 schools (594 boys' schools, 949 girls' schools, 610 vocational schools) showed that in the late 1920s, athletics, tennis, table tennis and volleyball were quite common at the majority of girls' elite institutions of advanced education (cf. Table 4.2).

During the increasingly chauvinist interwar years, girls' participation in physical education classes was redirected towards gymnastics, outdoor games and other activities guiding them towards their future roles as mothers. In the course of general mobilization after 1937, some of the differences in the treatment of the sexes disappeared. The 1942 Syllabus of Physical Discipline (*tairen*) emphasized physical activities dedicated to national defence, such as throwing hand grenades instead of rounders, running with gas masks or with the freight of sandbags or stretchers. With less and less male students available, girls were also prepared for semi-militarist deployment.

Table 4.2 Middle School Sport Clubs in Early Shōwa Japan

	Boys Middle Schools	*Girls Middle Schools*	*Vocational Schools*	*Totals*
Kendo	569	1	508	1,078
Judo	476	0	311	787
Kyudo	119	132	98	349
Sumo	155	0	166	321
Track and field	550	517	453	1,520
Swimming	377	199	197	773
Tennis	546	600	481	1,627
Volleyball	175	563	81	819
Basketball	213	451	127	791
Baseball	450	2	260	712
Table tennis	47	424	114	585
Football	210	0	52	262
Rugby	24	0	5	29
Rowing	73	3	25	101
Ski	72	56	48	176
Skate	10	8	8	26
Others	210	403	220	833
Total	4,276	3,359	3,154	10,789

Note: Survey among 2,153 schools, 594 boys' schools, 949 girls' schools, 610 vocational schools.
Source: Monbu Daijin Kanbō Taiiku-ka 1932, quoted in Sakaue (1998:32).

Postwar reforms immediately prohibited all militaristic physical exercises. *Budō* sport followed suit on November 6, 1945, because of its martial quality and feudalist character in the eyes of the Occupation Forces. Instead, a new understanding of sport was emphasized, stressing its educative qualities for the promotion of democratic attitudes. For the first time, women were given the right to enjoy equal opportunities in education with men, following Article 26 of the Constitution:

> All people shall have the right to receive an equal education correspondent to their ability, as provided by law. All people shall be obligated to have all boys and girls under their protection receive ordinary education as provided for by law. Such compulsory education shall be free.

SPORT IN CONTEMPORARY CURRICULA

When the new school curricula were promulgated in 1947, the physical education subject was expanded to denominate a broader health programme (*hoken taiiku*). Since then, course programmes have been revised about every ten years. Ministry guidelines specify the same amount of time for boys and girls in calisthenics, gymnastics, track and field, swimming and health education. In principle, PE subjects at school are roughly the same for both sexes, regarding the number of hours but with slight differences in the kind of subjects. PE curricula generally state that the subject is meant to raise interest in sport among the students. To accomplish this goal, all curricula neatly register an overall aim and content of classes, according to phase and year of school. A sketchy guideline for the achievement of the goal is also included.

Physical Education and the Life Course at School

As with other school subjects, sport curricula reflect a developmental and hierarchical structure: Basic knowledge and techniques are provided first, followed by more detailed instructions or more specialized exercises in later years. For example, during the first two years in elementary school, pupils are expected to become familiar with rudimentary exercises and simple team games, in order to build up physical strength and to be good friends with others. As in all later stages, a fifth of the entire five hours of physical education per week is dedicated to health education and theoretical knowledge (including sport theory in much later phases). Over the next stages, more skills, exercises and games are added to the catalogue as well as more elaborated ethical and moral standards. During the third and fourth grade, boys and girls are freshly introduced to swimming, apparatus gymnastics and expressive movements. Teachers are expected to pay attention to the awakening awareness of sexual differences, and students shall adapt to the imperatives of rules, develop respectfulness, spirit of cooperation, fairness and the ability of 'giving it all' (*saigo made ni doryoku suru taido*). This list is further extended during the final two years at elementary school, when pupils get acquainted with track and field athletics, new exercises in gymnastics, fitness training, ball sport and creative expressivity.

In order to maintain the effectiveness of classroom teaching and orderliness, teachers instruct their pupils how to follow commands, to keep still, to line up according to height and similar routines. While curricula explicitly recommend teachers pay full attention to local traditions and environmental conditions, the ultimate decision on the extent to which folk games or outdoor activities such as skating, skiing or playing in snow should be included in the course programme is left to the school and the teacher.

PE Curricula in Secondary Education

Until children leave elementary school, boys and girls have been practising sport together. At the secondary level, there is no general guideline recommending either co-educative or separated sport education. However, until very recently physical education classes were usually divided into courses for male and female students, based on the general notion that students should be educated according to their physical abilities and interests. Physical education was thus an outstanding field in the education system where students were confronted with the issue of gender identity. As we will see later, this policy is currently undergoing changes (Itani 2003).

Since national guidelines were revised in 1999, junior high school students of the second and third year have been granted some freedom of choice, and the array of elective subjects has been widely enlarged for high school students (cf. Kreitz-Sandberg 2000).[3] In the lower secondary phase, the subject of physical education (*taiiku*) is renamed health and physical education (*hoken taiiku*). The course outline features eight subgroups, i.e. fitness training, apparatus gymnastics, track and field, swimming, ball games, martial arts, dance and health education (cf. Table 4.3), which are all compulsory during the first year. Fitness training, which is basically geared towards acquiring strength and stamina, and basic sport theory are mandatory in the following years, while students can choose one or two disciplines of apparatus gymnastics, track and field and swimming, and two more out of ball games, martial arts and dance. Health education, which is most clearly pronounced during the final stage of compulsory education, prepares students to take responsibility for their own health and well-being. During the first year, students acquire knowledge about the physical and chemical processes within the maturing body, basic sex education and ways to mental and spiritual well-being. The larger

Table 4.3 Health and Physical Education at Junior High School

A Fitness training	E Ball games
(1) stretching and release	(1) basketball, handball
(2) increase in physical strength	(2) football
B Apparatus gymnastics	(3) volleyball
(1) mat exercises	(4) tennis, table tennis, badminton
(2) horizontal bar exercises	(5) softball
(3) balance beam exercises	F Martial arts
(4) vaulting horse exercises	(1) judo
C Track and field	(2) kendo
(1) running (short, long distance, hurdles, relay)	(3) sumo
(2) wide jump, high jump	G Dance
D Swimming	(1) creative dance
(1) crawl	(2) folk dance
(2) breast stroke	(3) contemporary rhythmic dance
(3) backstroke	H Health education

Source: Monbushō (1999a).

relationship between health and the living environment is addressed in the second year, with an emphasis on healthy nutrition, hygiene instructions, appropriate and reasonable handling of resources, waste reduction and sound lifestyles. Students also receive guidance in first-aid practices. The final year offers tutorials on managing a healthy lifestyle, which includes explanations about the dangers of consuming tobacco, alcohol and drugs, as well as basic information on AIDS and sexually transmitted diseases (Monbushō 1999b).

EXTRACURRICULAR SPORT ACTIVITIES

The sporting experience is not limited to the classroom. A far larger proportion of time, interest and enthusiasm is spent on extracurricular club activities (*bukatsudō*), which constitute an essential part of school life at the secondary level.

Junior Sports Club Network

Elementary school students who want to deepen their sport involvement can join the nationwide network of kids' sport clubs (Monbushō 1999c). The respective organization Supōtsu Shōnendan was established in 1962, just prior to the Tokyo Olympics, for the purpose of sparking interest in sport among the younger Japanese. The name is misleading, as Supōtsu Shōnendan does not exclusively target young boys. Membership is not restricted to elementary school grades, though the majority is likely to stem from this age group. Clubs are open to everyone up to the age of 25, regardless of sex and educational status. Kids' sport clubs focus on sport activities, but they also engage in outdoor activities like camping and hiking; cultural activities such as painting, singing and crafts; and social activities, including volunteering and participation in community projects. The local communities provide basic resources such as training space and voluntary instructors. A statement published on the homepage of the governing body, Japan Amateur Sport Association (Nihon Taiiku Kyōkai), in 2004 revealed the perception of sport enrolment as a useful tool for socialization into community affairs: 'There is considerable interest in clubs as institutions providing important experiences to boys and girls in becoming commendable members of society'.

Kids' sport clubs usually feature a single sport; only a minority of about 5,000 covers more than one kind of sport. Most members are enrolled in sport activities that also rank highest among junior and senior high school students: football, followed by *nanshiki yakyū*, a modified version of baseball, basketball and kendo. While the choice at hands depends largely on the goodwill of people from the local community, the overall concern with male-dominated sport may be one explanation for the low participation rate of girls who comprised only 20 per cent of club members in 2003 (NTK 2003).

Roots and Traditions of School Sport Clubs

When students enter junior high school, they are likely to join one of the self-administered school clubs, which are usually divided into sport clubs and culture clubs. Membership at the *undōbu* or *bunkabu* is voluntary, but the social pressure to join a club and maintain membership status throughout the three years of junior high or senior high school years is immense. Club membership demands a huge amount of time from participants. Sport clubs in particular meet on a daily basis for training sessions, sometimes twice a day before and after classroom hours. Training periods cover the whole week, often Saturdays and Sundays, too, and usually stretch well into school vacation. Physical education curricula also advise teachers to adjust their teaching programme to the local array of extracurricular club activities. The spectrum of clubs depends on school traditions as well as on the availability of supervisors from the teaching staff (*komon*) and a minimum of student members. In recent years, both the fading popularity of school sport clubs as well as the increase of alternative sport organizations beyond school have caused a decrease in numbers of clubs and of students enrolled in these clubs at some schools. Demographic trends will accelerate this process in the near future.

The origin of *bukatsudō* goes back to the early days of the establishment of the modern education system in Meiji Japan and the boarding school system at the national high schools. As Donald Roden (1980) has pointed out, the backbone of the educational system at the higher schools was a social Darwinist ethic that was most obvious in the daily routines of dormitory life and club life. Due to the mostly obligatory boarding school system, students had ample time on their hands, and one of the major ways to fill the free time was offered by club life, particularly in the form of school sport clubs. The quantitative discrepancies between the universal elementary school and the intensely limited institutions of higher education created elitist perceptions, hierarchical structures, severe competition, inter-school rivalry and a new self-image of a privileged youth standing at the top of the social order. The consequences of the fusion of elitist conceit, physical education and Confucian ethics for the shaping of the Japanese understanding of sport as 'muscular spirituality' has been discussed in Chapter 1. The male-only environment added a distinctive flavour to the cocktail. Rituals of masculinity and exercises of asceticism forged the collective solidarity of the student community. In every respect, club life maximized the individual's feelings of dependence on first the team, then the school and, ultimately, the nation.

Women, by contrast, were hardly considered to be serious contenders in sport, althoughat some of the secondary educational institutions for women, clubs had been opened as well since the Taishō years. The progress of women's sport, albeit very slow, was propelled by three different dynamics: State concerns with national health first encountered the pedagogical orientation of liberal-minded educators and their experiences from abroad, and in a later stage these currents met the rise of an urban middle class with new lifestyle interests. However, club activities were limited to those sports deemed to be suitable to the female body, such as tennis, hiking, bicycling or skating. If free time practice only allowed women to 'adopt good manners and get a cheerful spirit' (*yōgi ni totonae, seishin o kaikatsu ni;* Kōtō jogakkō-rei shikō kisoku [implementation statutes for the Law on Girls High Schools] 1901), educators did not see any reason to speak out against women's participation in sport.

From the early 20th century, a rising number of articles in journals devoted to physical education, such as *Undōkai* (The World of Sport) or *Taiiku to Kyōgi* (Physical Education and Competition), echoed a new understanding of sport that was no longer exclusively male-oriented. But these professional discourses reflected a deep-rooted belief in the innate difference between men and women, and these differences were now employed to explain male superiority in sport. Physical educationalist Ōtani Takeichi stated in 1922 that women were lacking the fighting spirit of men. As they did not possess the natural desire for throwing things or wrestling, they should not engage in such activities. In another article, the same authority related the spirit of sportsmanship to the Japanese tradition of *bushidō*. This analogy to the male-centred cultural ideal was also used to explain women's inferiority in sport (Taniguchi 2003:82).

The tradition of the *bukatsudō* survived the postwar reforms of the education system. As my research on mountaineering has shown, school and university sport clubs remained deeply tainted by their prewar legacy until the late 1960s (Manzenreiter 2000). The continuation of clubs relied on the reactivation of former members and instructors as well as on Old Boys' networks that helped to maintain the character of a 'ritual community, set apart from the mundane world around it by its own internal rules and values' (Cave 2004:390). Fierce competition among schools and intense training demand continued to emphasize the values of hierarchy, strict subordination and moral improvement. The downside of a practice which blurs the line between hierarchically ordered discipline and bullying has been documented most drastically in a number of tragic incidences that culminated in the deaths of junior members by the hands of their seniors. Furthermore, when form prevails over substance, practice for the sake of practice may dominate or suppress the joyful experience, as Dalla Chiesa (2002) observed in his years with several football teams at Japanese schools. 'When the goal is not the goal', participation in a football sport club does not impact positively on the youngsters' body and health. The particular lesson students learn from being inside the Japanese institution of *bu* is that total dedication to the team will earn them a safe place on the rooster (or on the social ladder) in the future, no matter how far their physical capabilities are developed (Dalla Chiesa 2002:196–197). School activities thus help schools to attain the goals of adjusting students to a social environment structured by vertical relationships, increasing control over their students, consuming their physical energy and controlling the value orientation of the peer group (Dalla Chiesa 2002:195–196).

However, as Cave has argued, there is also a brighter side to club activities because of their flexible nature and their multifaceted appeal. 'They are a means of school management and control in the widest sense, supplementing the classroom as an arena that allows both discipline and relaxation, and which lets students develop enthusiasms and abilities neglected by the formal curriculum' (Cave 2004:414). Because of the pervasiveness of a club system that managed to cope with decades of immense social change, clubs form the cornerstone in Japan of the widespread acceptance of *seishin kyōiku* (character education), achieved by perseverance (*gaman*), endurance against hardship, self-perfection through emulation and repetition and mutual dependence.

Making Sense of Gendered Club Membership

For reasons waiting to be explained, boys are much more susceptible to the pleasures and hardship of sport club membership than girls, as membership data to the nationwide federations of school sport clubs exhibit. In 2004, 1.87 boys and 1.79 million girls were enrolled at Japan's junior high schools. From the 3.67 million students, 2.39 million or two out of three students joined a school sport club (Chūtairen 2004). As the remaining 35 per cent very likely entered some culture club, this distribution shows the relatively larger appeal of sport to the students and to their social environment. In terms of sex differences, boys outnumber girls not only in total numbers, but also in share of enrolment: Only every second girl, but three out of four boys, are members in a sport club. Sex differences prevail also in terms of sport activities pursed by the students. The National Junior School Sports Association (*Nihon Chūgakkō Taiiku Renmei*) features 18 sport-specific sections, ranging from gymnastics, martial arts and team sport to track and field. Until 2001, football and *nanshiki yakyū* were not allowed for girls; since then, however, girls' participation in these sport activities has met with approval. At the same time, rhythmic gymnastics (*shin taisō*, which is best characterized as variant of gymnastics that places aestheticism over athleticism) has been opened for boys for the first time. Comparing the kind of sport activities boys and girls are attracted by (cf. Table 4.4), girls favour soft tennis, which is practised by 22.4 per cent of all girls enrolled in school sport club activities, followed by volleyball (19.9 per cent), basketball (16.3 per cent), table tennis (9.9 per cent) and badminton (8.5 per cent): Each of these sport activities was found acceptable for female students many decades ago. By contrast, *nanshiki yakyū* attracts a fifth of the entire male sport population (21.2 per cent) and is thus most popular with boys, followed by football (15.0 per cent), soft tennis (14.0 per cent), basketball (12.1 per cent) and table tennis (12.0 per cent). Among the top five sport activities, three are shared by boys and girls. Yet the overwhelming concern of boys with baseball and football causes imbalances in the respective sex ratios.

Table 4.4 Top Ten Club Sport Activities at Junior High School Level

Rank	*Boys*	*Girls*
1	*nanshiki* baseball (21.2%)	soft tennis (22.4%)
2	football (15.0%)	volleyball (19.9%)
3	soft tennis (14.0%)	basketball (16.3%)
4	basketball (12.2%)	table tennis (9.9%)
5	table tennis (12.0%)	badminton (8.5%)
6	track & field (7.2%)	track & field (8.2%)
7	kendo (5.1%)	softball (5.9%)
8	volleyball (4.1%)	kendo (4.2%)
9	judo (2.8%)	swimming (1.8%)
10	badminton (2.5%)	judo (1.2%)

Source: Chūtairen (2004).

Table 4.5 Sex Differences in Sport Enrolment at Junior High School Level

Sport Activity	*Membership Ratio (m/f)*	*Appeal Ratio (m%/f%)*
Track and field	1.3	0.9
Gymnastics	0.5	0.4
Rhythmic gymnastics	0.1	0.01
Swimming	1.3	0.9
Basketball	1.1	0.7
Volleyball	0.3	0.2
Table tennis	1.9	1.3
Soft baseball	480.8	334.9
Handball	1.5	1.0
Football	109.5	76.3
Softball	0.01	0.01
Badminton	0.4	0.3
Soft tennis	0.9	0.6
Sumo	37.0	25.8
Judo	3.4	2.3
Ski	1.5	1.0
Skating	4.6	3.2
Kendo	1.8	1.2
Total	1.4	1.0

Source: Chūtairen (2004); own calculations.

The sex ratio is most clearly unbalanced in the previously exclusively male domains of baseball and football, where boys will continue to outnumber girls for the foreseeable future. Table 4.5 shows two different methods of comparing sport involvement of the sexes. The first column depicts the membership ratio, which simply compares numbers of students of a given sport activity. A value of 1 would indicate perfect balance, a value higher than 1 specifies male prevalence and a lower value specifies female prevalence. The same principle is applied to the appeal ratio, which takes into account the aforementioned difference in population size of male and female club members. Since this value pays attention to the generally lower appeal of sport for girls, the appeal ratio thus is better suited to compare the relative attractiveness of a sport activity for the respective sex. The left column indicates that the number of boys in track and field is 1.3 times higher than the number of girls. But given that boys generally outnumber girls in school sport clubs, this activity seems to be more attractive to girls. Similarly, we can see from the comparison that the conspicuously low participation rate of male students in rhythmic gymnastics is actually an expression of a very low appeal.

Gendered differences in sport participation become more pronounced with rising age. At the senior high school level, the variety of sport activities offered increases considerably, though in terms of popularity, there is hardly any noticeable shift (cf. Table 4.6). According to membership data provided by the All Japan Senior High School Sport Federation (*Zenkoku Kōtō Gakkō Taiiku Renmei*), eight of the ten most popular junior high school sport activities remained among the top ten of both sexes. Boys sympathize most strongly with baseball and football (both slightly less than 16 per cent), followed by basketball (9.9 per cent), tennis (8.3 per cent) and track and field (6.0 per cent). Women's sport is largely made up of the team sports volleyball (14.9 per cent) and basketball (13.4 per cent), followed by badminton (11.6 per cent), tennis and soft tennis (about 9.4 per cent each).

Most eye-catching is the change at the top position of male sport. The junior high school boys' favourite sport vanished entirely from the list and has been replaced by baseball, which is the 'real thing' in comparison to

Table 4.6 Top Ten Club Sport Activities at Senior High School Level

Rank	*Boys*	*Girls*
1	baseball (15.8%)	volleyball (14.9%)
2	football (15.4%)	basketball (13.4%)
3	basketball (9.9%)	badminton (11.6%)
4	tennis (8.3%)	tennis (9.4%)
5	track & field (6.0%)	soft tennis (9.4%)
6	table tennis (5.4%)	kyudo (7.4%)
7	soft tennis (5.2%)	track & field (6.7%)
8	volleyball (5.1%)	softball (5.1%)
9	badminton (4.4%)	kendo (4.4%)
10	kendo (3.8%)	table tennis (3.9%)

Source: Zen-Kōtairen (2004); Kōyaren (2004).

nanshiki yakyū, the variant played at the middle school level. High school baseball has been the most popular spectator sport at the amateur level for the last century, particularly since the national newspaper *Asahi Shinbun* initiated the well-known national baseball tournament in 1916. For largely historical reasons—baseball was the first sport to be organized nationwide and the first professionally managed sport as well—high school baseball is supervised by a distinct federation. Unfortunately, data of the Japan High School Baseball Federation do not differentiate between male and female students, and thus my calculations concerning gender differences in high school sport are not as reliable as I would wish them to be. I adjusted official numbers by taking into account average membership size (2004: 38 per club) and Tom Blackwood's information that since 1997, the year of the first all-female national championship, there have been around 20 female teams throughout the country (2003: 23). I also tried to figure in female managers and supporters of the male teams, estimating conservatively slightly less than two female students per team (total of 8,000).

Sport participation rates considerably decline when students enter high school. A total of 1.45 million students (approximately 50 per cent) continue doing sport. Compared to a participation rate of 65 per cent at the junior high school level, the drop-out rate is quite large and particularly high among girls, as the membership sex ratio of 2.0 indicates. The number of sport activities on offer is twice the number of junior high, but out of 40 sport and games, at least eight are formally secluded for women. Male-only sport activities are water ball, football, rugby, cycling, boxing, weight lifting, sumo and wrestling, while *naginata*, a martial art traditionally associated with female members of the warrior aristocracy, is exclusively open to females (cf. Table 4.7). In both cases, discrimination is not necessarily based on formal criteria of exclusion. The baseball federation rejects female players because the sport is too dangerous and the federation cannot bear the risk of injury (Blackwood 2003:22). In the case of other sports, it is more likely that the lack of same-sex qualified teaching staff reduces the opportunity for girls to maintain a club of their own. Lastly, the exclusiveness may be due to a lack of interest on the part of the students who have similar or more attractive sports to choose from (like kendo instead of *naginata*, for example). For a more detailed depiction of the gendered structure of sport participation at the senior high school level, see Table 4.7.

Rohlen (1983:188) observed in the 1970s that girls belonged to many high school sport clubs but they generally practised and competed separately. This is still the case in most disciplines, although borderlines have become less strict. Blackwood found out that at least five female players had joined baseball teams in 2002, even though they knew that they could not play at tournaments. But in the shadow of the male performers on the ground, there are in fact quite a substantial number of female members of baseball and other team sport clubs. Instead of acting centre stage, they are usually involved in support roles for the male players, washing their

Table 4.7 Sex Differences in Sport Enrolment at Senior High School Level

Sport Activity	*Membership Ratio*	*Appeal Ratio*	*Sport Activity*	*Membership Ratio*	*Appeal Ratio*
Baseball	17.4	8.8	Sumo	M	M
Nanshiki baseball	M	M	Judo	4.2	2.5
Track and field	1.8	1.1	Ski	2.4	1.5
Gymnastics	1.0	0.6	Skating	4.2	2.5
Rhythmic gymnastics	0.2	0.1	Rowing	1.8	1.1
Swimming	1.3	1.3	Kendo	1.8	1.1
Dive jump	1.2	0.7	Wrestling	M	M
Waterball	M	M	Cycling	M	M
Basketball	1.5	0.9	Boxing	M	M
Volleyball	0.7	0.4	Hockey	1.2	0.7
Table tennis	2.7	1.6	Weightlifting	M	M
Soft tennis	1.1	0.7	Sailing	2.1	1.3
Handball	1.6	1.0	Fencing	1.1	0.7
Football	M	M	Karate	1.9	1.1
Rugby	M	M	Archery	1.6	0.9
Badminton	0.7	0.4	Naginata	F	F
Softball	0.2	0.2	Paddling	2.7	1.6
			Total	2.0	xx

Note: M signifies male sport only, F = female sport only; own calculations.
Source: Zen-Kōtairen (2004); Kōyaren (2004).

uniforms, preparing snacks and meals, putting away equipment (Kameda 1995:115). According to a survey by the Japan High School Baseball Federation, 71 per cent of all high school baseball clubs had female 'managers' in charge of all the tedious but badly needed work. Baseball is not unique in this regard. The supportive role of females seems to be a rather common feature of team sport clubs (Itō 2001; Blackwood 2003). When girls are not available for the manager's duties, the behind-the-scenes work is usually executed by someone of lower rank within the club hierarchy, a junior member or someone with little chance to ever play in games.

SOCIETY AND THE HIDDEN CURRICULUM

The discussion so far has shown that patterns of sport participation of Japanese students are significantly gendered. These patterns impact the decision whether to get involved in sport and, if yes, in what kind of sport. The outcome of this process of decision making in turn impacts the way sport and gender are interrelated. Parental adults as role models and peer groups as pressure groups have always been important factors influencing the individual's decision; nowadays the media have come to join them, as Sugimoto (1995:161–163) correctly observed on the impact of the media on the latent curriculum (*senzai karikyuramu*) of physical education. I also argue that the media's impact is particularly strong because in the age of media sport the media appeal of a discipline is decisive for its financial support (e.g. in form of sponsorship), on the one hand, and its capability to draw media audiences and foster fan loyalties, on the other hand. The question of who is represented in the media is no less important than the question of how an athlete is represented.

While cultural industries have been comparatively open to the employment of women, the sport writers' world seems rather closed. Virtually everywhere, argues Jennifer Hargreaves (1994:151), men figure much more than women as media-sport professionals, sport writers and academics in all sport-related fields. The Japanese case is no exception. Among the 46 Japanese newspaper journalists that covered the Sydney Olympics in 2000, Iida (2002:81–83) identified only three women, who contributed a mere 4.1 per cent of 635 articles and not a single photo to the Japanese print media display of the Olympics. While the coverage of women's and men's sports in three national dailies was quite evenly balanced in quantitative terms, it differed considerably in qualitative terms, i.e. the kind of sport featured and its contextualization. Women got frequent press coverage in disciplines that had gained social acceptance long ago, such as track and field or swimming, or in 'typically' feminine sport, such as synchronized swimming and beach volleyball (Iida 2002:79). The women's beach ball team did not advance very far in 2000, yet its photo shots were, together with the synchro swimmer teams, most often displayed on the sport pages. Hence the observable gains women made in the media representation did not always work to their advantage, if the increase were primarily based on the permissive (or compelled) disclosure of the female body to the male gaze. As Alina Bernstein (2002) has commented, the sexualization of female athletes trivializes their achievements and in fact robs them of athletic legitimacy, thus preserving hegemonic masculinity.

Research on the role of sport media in the reproduction of gender stereotypes has found that the coverage is often framed within stereotypes which emphasize social expectations toward the athlete as women rather than as athletic achievers (cf. Iida 2003). According to Hirakawa's (2002) analysis of sport-related TV commercials, women were clearly underrepresented (comprising 14.4 per cent of images) in the spots and staged in comparatively passive or overdetermined roles that can easily be associated with the dominant normative destination of female existence: as wife and mother. While male athletes were typically shown in action, in actual competition or surrounded by fans and admirers, women rarely appeared as active performers, and if they did, then in fairly domestic contexts, running the dog or playing with children. Masculinity was valorized by the celebration of the sport hero in very condensed heroic situations, whereas the sport heroines were deprived of all their heroic features. Again, this narrative technique is far from being exclusively Japanese as Whannel has observed in comparative work on sport heroes and heroines. He also noted that 'sport characteristically provides a space for the eradication, marginalisation and symbolic annihilation of the feminine' (2002:45). It seems that the success of the female athlete causes alert or a sense of crisis in the world of masculine domination. Iida also found that female athletes were often called by pet names and endearing terms stressing their cuteness and 'lovely' dependence on men. As male athletes are referred to in a much more detached and honourable way, the verbal annexation of the female athlete is a linguistic practice that reinforces gender-based status differences.

The prominence of a sport in the media guarantees its retention, as we can see in the correlation of media visibility and appeal of a sport to the young Japanese. If a mass sport is also played on a professional level, it usually should command over a substantial amount of capable and certified instructors. This observation is closely connected with one of the basic problems frequently associated with gender inequality in Japanese sport. In August 2001, the Council of Education explained the low participation rate of girls in kids' sport clubs with the lack of qualified female sport instructors. Girls were said not to shun sport in general but to be disgusted and repelled by the unattractive supply of male-dominated sport games.[4] Looking at the broader picture, Kawaguchi, Ikeda and Miki (1999) stated that more and more female athletes are performing on the world stage, yet 90 per cent of their coaches are male. More and more women take active part in sport classes of social education, yet only 3.5 per cent of their instructors are female. Furthermore, while the number of female teachers is increasing, they are overrepresented in certain subjects and underrepresented in senior positions. Many women teach home economics and Japanese, but few teach science and physical education. Sixty per cent of teachers at primary schools are female, but the number of women promoted to senior positions is very low, given the share of 1 per cent female principals out of the total. In short, concludes the Japan NGO Alternative Report on Women 2000, girls simply lack positive role models among the teachers close to them. There are still many obstacles to overcome in the education system until gender equity is achieved (Japan NGO Report Preparatory Committee 1999).

If we looked more into the actual practice of PE classes, more concrete examples would emerge showing how the actual experience of sport engraves gender differences into the body. An often heard criticism is the name call issue. Teachers have alphabetically ordered name lists (*meibō*) for boys and girls (Itō 2001:128); traditionally, girls had to stand still and wait until the teacher had checked the attendance of their male classmates. This routine seems to be still widely in practice, as well as the habit of having students line up according to body height. This does not necessarily give advantage to the boys as some girls are bigger and taller than boys, but in general this ritualized form of behaviour tends to emphasize the physical superiority of boys. Another point of complaint is the overall concern with the quantitative measurement of individual development (Iida 2000). The basic model is the Ministry's physical strength test (*tairyoku chōsa*), which has been conducted annually since 1964 to ascertain the present conditions of the nation's physical fitness and abilities.[5] Originally this test covered only students at the levels of primary and secondary education, but the coverage has been extended to include the adult population, and many institutions mirror the national survey at the pre-school level. PE curricula advise teachers to adjust the PE programme to the schedule of the test, which is likely to heat up training activities before the day of the survey. Again, the design of the survey, the measurement standards of performance and the way results are computed for public display seem to prove the superiority of the male body.

CONCLUSION

The discussion has shown that physical education is an important site for the construction and consolidation of gender identities within schools. It goes without saying that the Japanese body regime rather complies with collective norms than with the totality of individual choices. Classroom lessons and self-administered club activities function as sites for the gendered display of hegemonic forms of both femininities and masculinities. Differences in sport club enrolment clearly show the tension between dominant and subordinate masculinities and femininities and that these are played out through the acceptance and refusal of different forms of sport activities. Comparing the gendered sport supply at school institutions of early Shōwa Japan and the present, the consolidation of a gendered worldview in sport is remarkably perennial. Sport remained to be primarily a 'homosocial institution enforcing and reproducing the ideals of masculinity' (Okada 2004:42). As Jennifer Hargreaves (1994:279) observed, 'the longer men practically and ideologically have appropriated an activity, the more difficult it is for women to get inside'.

This result contrasts with the general observation of social change. The spread of liberal democratic ideology in the latter half of the 20th century triggered tremendous changes in patterns of leisure and consumption and in the relation between the sexes. It is equally true that the advance of consumer society opened new opportunities for women's participation in sport. Globalization impacts have put masculine hegemony under scrutiny again: The East Asian economic crises, the loss of job security, men's dissatisfaction with corporate employment and the modest increase in career opportunities for women have challenged the gendered division of labour. But the willingness to take sides with neoliberalism has weakened familial patriarchy while social patriarchy gained ground. Looking at women's participation in football in China, Japan and Korea (Manzenreiter 2004a), I argued that capitalism and democracy, on the one hand, and the commercialization and spectacularization of football, on the other hand, have brought about contradictory effects of 'civilizing' and 'suppressive' power. While the globalization of sport has given some impetus to changing gender relations in several nation-states, male sport continues to flourish as the unquestioned standard of sport. In consequence of economic market principles overgrowing traditional culture-based principles of gender discrimination in sport, power relations between the sexes were disguised and the male prerogative was preserved.

Spielvogel (2003) argues that social inequalities between the sexes contribute to the ubiquitous dieting in high schools, on campuses and in fitness clubs where most aerobics instructors and members reflect the national preoccupation with weight and being slim. Given the Japanese ideological emphasis on the fluid boundaries between self and the other, dieting and food refusal serve women as powerful means to resist and comply with gender inequality and age-appropriate gender roles. Her study reconfigures the Japanese fitness club as a confluence of historical transformations, in which constructions of sport shifted from expressions of patriotism and national solidarity to those of individuality and lifestyle directed particularly at the female body (Spielvogel 2003:60). The emphasis on youth, associated with sexiness and vulnerability, good proportions and shapely legs, is prescriptive, distinctively Japanese and nonetheless intentionally constructed by drawing on Western standards of physical beauty. Club management attempts to counter the hegemonic notion of beauty by emphasizing health over appearance are doomed to fail because it is the desire for the right look that drives the majority of club members into the studio. Thus the fitness industry capitalizes on the desire for appropriate appearance, with good health, well-being and exercise serving as the means to achieve good looks. But female consumers shun the hard work of exercise and prefer catered service, quality leisure and ultimately the beauty industries' tricky promises of slimming down or toning up any body part in isolation. Being trapped into the functional chain of consumerism, both members and instructors of aerobics classes find themselves 'shaping up' to an unrealistic ideal, denying them private fulfilment and actual empowerment in the end.

The school as a social institution proves to be incapable of establishing counter-trends to the hegemonic body regime. Cultural discourses on the 'reproductive capabilities' and 'domestic destiny' of the 'fair sex' confront girls with social responsibilities overshadowing the private realm of personal pleasure and physical sensation. Female subordination and male domination are codified at political and administrative levels, exploited in economic relations, symbolically reproduced in popular cultural forms and most pervasively performed in school sport in everyday life.

A closer reading of official curricula and the guidelines for PE teachers reveals the impact of the changing social context on the significance of sport in modern society. While traditional elements of teaching style and pedagogic ideology have proven to be persistent well into the postwar period, contemporary physical education has come a long way from the nationalist and indoctrinating function it had in earlier times. But even today the state continues using its power via the educational institutions to shape the national body, albeit for different reasons and purposes. The following chapters on sport supply, health management and body surveillance in contemporary Japan will introduce a number of additional objectives that have inflated the role of sport in the body politics of the Japanese state.

5 How to Sell a Public Good

The Current State of Sport Supply in Japan[1]

INTRODUCTION

At the beginning of the 21st century, sport has been assigned special importance to counterbalance the widening gap between urban centres and rural peripheries in Japan. The new roles of sport include enhancing quality of life for those living in the regions, boosting their attractiveness for newcomers and financial investors and reducing the financial burden of an aging society in which responsibility for health and fitness is shifted from the public sector to private initiatives. Especially the Basic Plan for the Promotion of Sports (Supōtsu Shinkō Kihon Keikaku), issued in 2000 by the Ministry of Education, Culture, Sports, Science and Technology (Monbukagakushō, MEXT), the establishment of Japan's first professional football league in the early 1990s (Ubukata 1994; Hirose 2004a) and the hosting of half the 2002 Football World Cup Korea/Japan (Horne and Manzenreiter 2002a) have contributed to a policy shift towards public–private partnerships as the core of sport for all opportunities. On a very practical level, the implementation of the basic sport plan related to the new policy aims has to face two impediments. Particularly since the collapse of the asset-inflated economy, industrial corporations stopped doling out money to sports that do not generate profits. At the same time, local governments saw their budgets tightened by decreasing income revenues and mounting debt burdens. But private sector initiatives were badly needed to assist the politicians' visions, as hardly any case study on sport-centred development initiatives provides evidence of the profitable and efficient use of public money. Drawing on major recent trends, with particular reference to the professional football league and field visits in southwest Japan, I will outline the changing role of sport policy and some new faces of public–private partnerships in Japan.

In this chapter, I am going to analyse the framework of Japan's sport for all policy and the conditions that shape the behaviour of the state and regional governments. Japan's integration into the global flow of symbols, images and consumption goods has left its impact on the Japanese economy, polity and culture. The interplay of these fields is giving shape to the future of amateur sport, which is oscillating between public good and market-regulated consumption. Since many Western European societies are exhibiting similar trends in terms of demographic development, economic maturity, value change and the gradual dismantling of the traditional social welfare state, the case of Japan can be of great interest for comparative policy analysis: To what degree are initiatives set by central governments effective and conducive to the goal of promoting mass sport participation?

My analysis will start with short reflections, both theoretical and empirical, on the very basic question of why regional authorities might invest in the promotion of sport. These frequent and general expectations are confronted with practical experiences from hosting sport events and building sport facilities. The following sections establish the links with mass sport promotion. First I will take a look at the distribution channels of public funds; then I will present the implementation of the organizational framework of voluntary sport associations which has been remodelled according to the German model of civil associations (*Vereinswesen*) only recently. This model has been enthusiastically welcomed by local communities as well as professional football teams since the 1990s. Whether and how these actors are successful in forging a partnership, and what impact these initiatives are having on the promotion of mass sport, will be discussed in the following sections. Empirically, my analysis is based on official documents, secondary sources and expert interviews conducted in a number of locations in the southwest of Japan in 2003. Drawing on more recent developments in the field of sport promotion, my final conclusion will reveal a rather critical assessment of the achievements so far and its future potentials.

WHY GOVERNMENTS INVEST IN SPORT

The conceptualization of sport as economic growth generator is indicative of the differentiation process of sport in late modern societies. Characteristic programmes, which include the enlargement of the sport infrastructure, the promotion of national and international sport events or the recreation of regional self-images by exploiting the symbolic value of sport, are designed to stimulate the local economy, to enrich the attractiveness of the region and to foster community bonds. The idea that public investments in sport not only benefit the people's health, but also the economic revitalization of their region by means of direct and indirect returns is comparatively new in Japan. In the US, however, the linkage between public investments in sport and profit expectations is much older, dating back to the establishment of professional leagues and the commercialization of sport since the early 20th century. Sport boosterism achieved additional momentum in the 1980s, when the Reaganomics in Washington shifted towards a drastic austerity policy and conferred the future of regional development to the discretionary power of local administrations. Facing domestic as well as increasingly international competition, local governments opted for new strategies of interregional cooperation and pooled financing, privatization and promotion strategies based on services, tourism and sport. Because the global economy has become increasingly important as a framework in which cities and regions are competing for flows of investments and tourist spending, similar developments were likely to happen in Japan, and in fact they did. Japan's unipolarization and the long-established regional disparities of productivity and prosperity added a particular twist, forcing even small municipalities and rural districts to forge new development strategies. Although the Japanese central government had stopped its unbalanced industrial development policy in the 1970s, peripheral regions that always struggled to keep pace continued to fall behind the metropolitan areas and industrial zones of Central Honshū. Gradual industrial decline and steady migration into the overcrowded capital and other major cities inflicted severe threats upon the vitality of regions confronted with a rapidly aging population and a diminishing tax income base. Within this scenario, leisure- and consumption-oriented development catering to the needs of a post-industrial, service-oriented society marked the economic policy shift of many localities (cf. Funck 1999; Nakayama 2000; Harada 2001, 2002).

During the last decade of the 20th century, sport became a central topic of top-down discourses on urban planning (*toshi keikaku*) or bottom-up conceptions of town development (*machizukuri*) in Japan. Both camps strongly sympathized with the label of 'sport community', which gained considerable attention among administrators, politicians and the media. Until the mid-1990s, 14.4 per cent out of 3,281 local authorities had issued a Sport City Declaration or heralded themselves as Health City (*supōtsu / kenkō toshi sengen*; Nagazumi 2000:291). Within the rhetoric of contemporary city planning, the label of *supōtsu komyuniti* signified the process or product of regional revitalization policy (*chiiki kasseika seisaku*) engendered and realized by large-scale sport development programmes. From the Teshio River Network in Japan's northernmost Hokkaidō (Maeda 1998), the *sakkā taun* Kashima (Koiwai 1994) and the ski resort Nozawa Onsen (Saitō 1994) in Central Honshū to the Ōiwa Aso Racing Park in Kyūshū (Aigaki 1994), all over Japan cities, towns and even villages came to put their hopes and efforts for regional restructuring into the promising prospect of sport promotion. Although the declaration was in most cases merely an event-ridden statement of local community leaders, the numbers of communes that adopted the sport community concept emphasized the appeal of health, fitness and sport for regional governments.

Local policy planners envision two general benefits emerging from the promotion of sport. On the one hand, sport is considered an economic income generator. Being hometown to a professional sport team or staging an international sport event affords public investments into sport facilities and related infrastructures. It is well known that governments usually generate only a tiny fraction of direct return, but their local constituencies are promised that expenditures are regained by indirect returns to the region by way of economic development. On the other hand, sport plays an integral role in the way cities regard themselves. A modern and enlarged sport infrastructure in the region is understood as a powerful symbol and an asset that has a positive impact on the quality of life of the local inhabitants. Similarly, staging world-class sport events, or being the hometown to a sport team competing in a professional league, might provide ample sources of regional pride, thereby fostering feelings of community belonging and local identification. Precisely because of such intangible benefits, even critical observers are reluctant to condemn subsidies for sport facilities as simply a waste of the taxpayers' money.

In fact there is little evidence to suggest that subsidizing professional sport by pumping public money into stadiums, teams and sport competitions affects economic chances at all. Within the growing body of literature on the economy of sport, the claim that staging world-class sport events or having a sport team does not yield any significant benefits for the region (among others, cf. Nunn and Rosentraub 1995; Baade 1996; Rosentraub 1997; Noll and Zymbalist 1997; Schimmel 2001; Nogawa and Mamiya 2002; Siegfried and Zymbalist 2002; Szymanski 2002; Miller 2002; Manzenreiter and Horne 2005) may nowadays find more consent among sport economists and sociologists than a prediction on the outcome of a football match between Brazil and Bhutan. In the US, supporters of the 'growth machine' myth therefore increasingly turned to non-economic justifications in their quest to mobilize public funding for sport-related construction work (Eckstein and Delaney 2002). In other parts of the world, notably in Europe, where sports have been preferably treated as a public good rather than as a commodity, local politicians still tend to advocate the economic multiplier assumption. Most recent examples would include Salzburg's unsuccessful bid for the 2010 and later Winter Olympics, the 2006 Football World Cup in Germany (Rahmann et al. 1998) and the 2008 UEFA Championship co-hosted by Austria and Switzerland (Helmenstein, Kleissner and Moder 2007; Helmenstein and Kleissner 2008; Hachleitner and Manzenreiter 2010). In all of these instances, the bidding committees hastened to present 'hard data' on the economic windfall for the region to the public. The media played a crucial role in disseminating the 'good news' and solidifying the assertions as hard facts: Prior to 2006, the mainstream media hardly ever critically questioned the reliability of the data or its interpretation.

In Japan, similar expectations on economic effects to be triggered by the Nagano Winter Olympics in 1998 and the Football World Cup in 2002 were equally pushed to great heights (Maeda 2001; Harada 2002). While the Nagano Olympics were reported to have generated a surplus income of JPY 2.5 billion and the World Cup a plus of JPY 7.6 billion, it remained largely unreported that in each case profits bypassed national taxpayers. In fact local host cities and prefectures ended up in huge debt and additionally had to provide funds for covering the maintenance costs of the hardly ever fully used stadium infrastructure. What's more, both the Nagano Winter Olympics and the 2002 World Cup failed to repeat the mystical experience of national rebirth and economic growth which their hosts had hoped would emerge as in the case of the Tokyo Olympics, which had come to serve as a cogent signifier within the dominant reading of postwar Japan (Tagsold 2002).

Research into the political mechanism of sport boosterism has provided various explanations for the apparently contradictory phenomenon. The urban regime theory (cf. Andranovich, Burbank and Heying 2001; Schimmel 2001) assigns responsibility for pumping public subsidies into prestigious yet unprofitable hallmark projects to a powerful coalition of local business representatives and politicians who measure the economic and social well-being of their communities in terms of increases in population, jobs, companies, etc. Eckstein and Delaney (2002), among others, alternatively claim that the positive appeal of sport and its premises prompt political leaders striving for re-election to assume a primary role. The successful hosting of a sport event and the infrastructural legacy of sport promotion are highly suggestive symbols representing the politicians' abilities to negotiate with central government, to bring jobs and new business chances into the region, to interact on an equal footing with representatives from powerful transnational sport organizations and their affiliated multinational sponsors and the world of celebrities. Hence even if governments are ready to concede that public investments into sport facilities generate only a tiny fraction of direct return, they promise to their local constituency that expenditures are regained indirectly through economic development. But more often they promise new jobs and direct revenues from sport tourism, as well as indirect revenue streams from new business formation, which usually find unanimous consent among the local electorate. The strong appeal of employment also tends to give direction to the outcome of popular referendums or votes on the construction of large-scale sport facilities (Siegfried and Zymbalist 2002).

In many cases these projects are trumpeted as successful not because of any objective assessment about their benefits to local residents, but because of the symbolic power of the edifices themselves (Schimmel 2001). In considering the situation in Japan, it is important to recognize the extent to which construction and civil engineering have long underpinned its political economy. Japan's *doken kokka*, or 'construction state' (McCormack 2002), is built upon the centrality of construction and public works in Japan's economy, which are the product of the operation of an 'Iron Triangle' of construction industry chiefs, senior bureaucrats and politicians. When the Ministry of Construction merged with the former Ministry of Transport and other planning agencies to form the National Land and Transport Ministry in the wake of the administration reforms carried out in 2001, it became responsible for 80 per cent of tax moneys available for public works. In the late 1990s, Japan's public works were three times the size of that in Britain, the US or Germany, and employed seven million people, or 10 per cent of the Japanese workforce, spending JPY 40–50 trillion per year. The result is that Japan has more dams and roads per unit of land than the continental US. Half the Japanese coastline and most of its rivers are wrapped in concrete. Ninety per cent of its total wetlands have been drained and lost, and its bio-diversity is threatened. Despite cutbacks by the Koizumi administration—in 2004, the fifth consecutive year of annual decline, local governments forecast to spend a total of 14.2 trillion yen on public works, down 700 billion yen from fiscal 2003 (*Nihon Keizai Shinbun*, August 21, 2003)—the ratio of 4 or 5 per cent from GDP still topped most other OECD countries by roughly 100 per cent.

The construction sector also absorbed the largest part of sport-related federal expenses. Between 1987 and 2000, more than JPY 2 trillion had been spent for the construction of slightly less than 150 sport stadiums (Nogawa and Mamiya 2001:203). In 1995, construction consumed 65 per cent and sport event management 32 per cent of the national sport budget; only 2.2 per cent were assigned to sport organizations and 0.8 per cent to the education of sport trainers (SSF 1997:119). About 35 per cent of the national sport budget of JPY 440 billion was immediately assigned to the former Ministry of Construction, while the Ministry of Education (21 per cent) and the Ministry of Health and Welfare (15 per cent) also invested parts of their allocations into facility management. Until the national government reform in 2001, no less than 12 ministries were competing for shares of the sport budget. Throughout the mid-1980s and the administrative reshuffle, sport-related expenses of the central government remained quite stable in relation to GDP (about 0.08 per cent, including local government expenditures 1.7 per cent of GDP), and so was the distribution of the budget among the ministries, which clearly indicates how well the arrangement was established.

Shrinking government budgets in the late 1990s enforced a major turn away from the construction-led policy. In terms of public sport, sport facilities-related expenses of the authorities in charge of social education have continued to contract since 1995, placing downward pressure on the entire sport budget. In 2000, the national sport budget shrank towards JPY 395 billion, yet still 41 per cent was assigned to the Ministry of Construction and 65 per cent to construction projects (Takahashi 2003:9–12). Facility maintenance continued to be the largest burden of governmental spending on sport (57.4 per cent in 2005) even after increasingly dramatic cuts on governmental spending saw the national sport budget further declining to JPY 269 billion in 2005 (54.7 per cent for facilities; Tazaki 2006) and approximately JPY 230 billion at the end of the decade (*MRI Today*, January 7, 2009).

But it is local governments that bear the largest burden of public sport expenditures, despite having hardly any direct income of their own. Thus their construction projects heavily rely on central government subsidies (*chiiki supōtsu shinkō hojokin*) or the issuing of local government obligations (*chihōsai*). As debt service is partially taken into account for the calculation standards of the respective shares of the local allocation tax (*chihō kōfuzei*), they often work as an indirect variant of subsidizing. The composition of the public sport administration budget for 1990 showed central government contributing 43.8 per cent, prefectures 10.3 per cent and local municipalities 45.9 per cent to the aggregated amount of JPY 754.2 billion. In 2005, central government spending on sport was JPY 269 billion, and prefecture governments invested JPY 44.8 billion, but we don't have aggregated data for the level of the municipalities Apparently no one dared to look through the many thousands of local government budgets thereafter (SSF 2008:117). But there are ample reasons to assume that shrinking central government spending has not eased the burden at the local level.

MASS SPORT PROMOTION

The relationship of sport infrastructure building, sport event hosting and public spending on sport apparently is closely connected to the Japanese political economy. As such, it has become a long-standing tradition in Japan, dating back to the early postwar years, when the Occupation Forces actively promoted sport as an educational tool of democratic virtues. Starting in 1946, each year a different prefecture was selected to host the National Athletic Meeting (*kokumin taiiku taikai*, or Kokutai), Japan's greatest amateur sport festival, which drew thousands of participants from all over the country. Until the first circuit was finished in 1992, each prefecture had been provided with at least one large-scale multifunctional sport stadium and other sport-related facilities needed to host major sport events. Another result of building these facilities was Japan's capacity to host major international sporting events, beginning with the judo world championships in 1956 (staged in the newly built Budokan) and the Tokyo Olympic Games of 1964. While these construction projects first of all served the national goals of representing the nation and nurturing the athletic elite, as well as pleasing the construction industry and politicians alike, they largely bypassed the daily needs of the masses for sport participation.

Arguably a strong and centrally administered sport promotion policy was needed to outweigh the self-interests of this powerful alliance. The need for central planning and administrative implementation was particularly strong in the case of Japan, which lacked the historical experience of social struggles which in many European countries gave birth to the idea of sport as a basic human right. For most of the 20th century, sport in Japan was therefore either seen as educational device (school sport), corporate welfare (company sport) or commercial enterprise (professional baseball, sumo and government-controlled racing sport). As a consequence, public access to sport has always been severely restricted and regulated. Whether privately owned or publicly managed, sport facilities were accessible only for those affiliated with an educational institution, a larger corporation or the military. During the second half of the 20th century, almost all of the central government's sport policy research councils paid attendance to this handicap and accordingly addressed the need to encompass government interventions within their proposals. Yet the supply side remained underdeveloped until the early years of the 21st century.

Mass sport promotion started in the early 1960s with the issuance of the Sports Promotion Law (Supōtsu Shinkō Hō) in 1961, just in time for rising national interest in the Olympic Games. Under the influence of European national health and fitness programmes, such as Germany's 'Golden Plan' or 'Trimm Dich' movement, Japan's national and local governments started to include the well-being of the populace into their sport policy. The revised Social Education Law (Shakai Kyōiku Hō) from 1964 officially acknowledged sport as a public good for the first time. Guidelines for the bureaucracy were published to guarantee sport opportunities for all. The National Sport Council (Hoken Taiiku Shingikai), which the law prescribed as the central advisory council in all questions of sport politics, followed in its recommendations of expanding the sport infrastructure in general an internationally acclaimed key strategy for raising sport participation rates. However, the one-sided policy approach based solely on the development of the hardware clearly had its downsides as it was cost-intensive and did not prove to be sufficiently effective. Onimaru (2001:10) critically interpreted the Sports Promotion Law as part of the central bureaucratic strategy to mitigate some of the problems created by the economy policy of the high-growth period, and it never saw its principal objectives of improving the quality of life and raising sport participation rates realized. It was too permissive in nature and lacked the disciplinary power to force local governments to fulfil their share of responsibility.

A Parliamentary Commission for Health and Physical Fitness was established in order to develop concrete programmes adjusted to the needs of the people. According to the final report (*Taiiku, supōtsu no fukyū shinkō ni kansuru kihon hōsaku ni tsuite*) issued in 1972, coping with the lack of public sport facilities continued to be the most urgent task facing local administrations. Under the years of Japan's honeymoon with the welfare state, the sport infrastructure grew considerably. A first survey of 1969 reported 10,193 public sport facilities; this number tripled within the following decade (1980: 29,566) and doubled again until 1990 (62,786; Nagazumi 1999:160). Yet it should be mentioned that the Ministry of Education, which is formally in charge of public sport facilities (*shakai taiiku shisetsu*), operates a fairly broad definition of sport facilities, which may include anything from swimming pools, sport arenas and multiplex stadia, to golf courses, gateball pitches, sport parks (*undō kōen*), martial arts *dōjō* and mountain paths. After peaking in the mid-1990s, the number of public sport facilities started to shrink again, declining to 56,475 in 2002 and 53,732 in 2008 (cf. Figure 5.1). The impact of the collapse of the asset-inflated economy on company-owned sport facilities was quite dramatic.

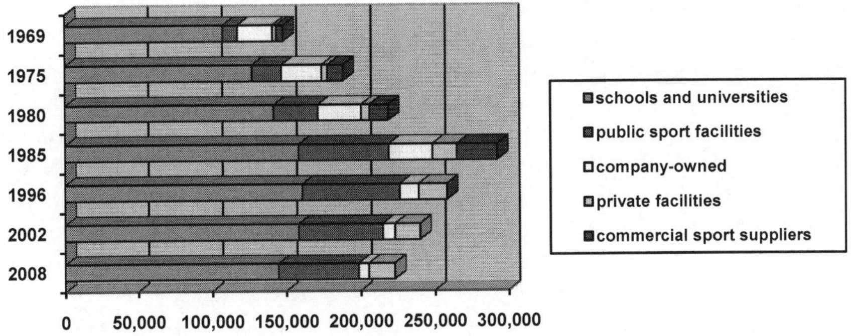

Figure 5.1 Ownership of sport facilities in Japan, 1969–1996.
Note: No numbers available for commercial sport facilities after 1988.
Source: Ministry of Education, Japan: *Waga kuni no taiiku supōtsu shisetsu*, 1996 and various years.

From the 29,332 facilities counted in 1985, only 12,737 were left in 1996 and 6,827 in 2008. Even school sport facilities, which traditionally provided the largest share of all sport facilities, saw a drastic decline due to adjustments of local governments to the shrinking population: More than 15,000 of such facilities have disappeared over the past decade.

Since the late 1970s, school gyms and sport grounds assumed central position in the social education politics of local governments. Opening up these resources after school, in the evening or during the weekend, for the local population was regarded as a comparatively cheap and straightforward strategy to expand the supply side. At the end of the century, the public was principally granted access to 90 per cent of sport facilities at compulsory schools and 50 per cent of those at public high schools. Yet for a number of reasons, including fairly limited opening hours, unresolved questions of insurability and the poor state of many school facilities, they were hardly used by amateur athletes; during the 2000s, less than 8 per cent of sport people polled by a series of nationwide surveys frequented school sport facilities; about every second was practising in public space (streets, parks, riverbanks), and more than a quarter reportedly relied on private sport facilities (SSF 2009:33). The disproportional share of profit-oriented private facilities that comprise less than 10 per cent of the Japanese sport infrastructure supply but meet a quarter of demand apparently is a matter of supply–demand mismatch.

The finally achieved ratio of roughly one public sport facility per 2,000 people seemed to be in line with international standards. Yet a ratio of facilities to population size cannot adequately represent the supply side for three reasons: First, as stated earlier, mountain trails, bicycle lanes and other infrastructure adjustments are also counted by these official statistics; second, regional distribution patterns are largely ignored; and, third, the different capacities of huge sport arenas and tiny swimming pools are not taken into consideration by the average value. Space per capita is a more appropriate indicator. But also the 0.9–1.3 sqm per capita was much lower than Germany's 3–4.5 sqm per capita (Takahashi 2003:14) and far away from the standards proclaimed by the National Sport Council as early as in 1972. Sport funding by the state (0.08 per cent of BIP in 2000) also never had come close to the spending ratio of Germany (0.35 per cent), which has traditionally been Japan's paragon in terms of public sport administration.

This is partly due to policy shifts caused by budgetary deficits and the global rise of neoliberal ideology in the 1980s, which gained approval by some of the counsellors of the Nakasone administration. Hitting the mood of the time, in its attempts to straighten out the budget deficit, the Second Ad Hoc Research Committee on Administrative Reform (Daini Rinchō) aptly suggested the reduction of public investment in sport while encouraging private sector investment as much as possible. Recreation, sport and tourism were explicitly named in the Fourth National Development Plan of 1987 as viable options to expand domestic consumption and to revive the peripheral regions. All these ambitions became most clearly visible in the Comprehensive Resort Region Provision Law (known as the 'Resort Law') passed in 1987. Prefectures were invited to submit development plans for regions to be designated as resort areas. Public input was either meant to come from freeing public assets, especially from privatization and land sales, or from tax incentives, low-interest loans, relaxed land use regulations and supporting development programmes of the surrounding infrastructure. The execution of the construction projects and the management of resort areas and leisure sites were to be left to private businesses or public–private partnerships.[2]

The economic potential of sport also featured prominently in the Ministry of International Trade and Industry (MITI) report *Sports Vision 21*, published in 1990. This report designated sport as a key industry and growth market of the 21st century, but it strongly recommended that the management of it should be left entirely to the private sector. The Ministry of Education, supposed to be the public's advocate for sport participation, also submitted to the logic of the market. The Ministry's *Basic Plan for the Promotion of Sports in the 21st Century* (1989), which was partly born out of the disappointing results of Japanese athletes at the Seoul Olympics in 1988, when they obtained less than half the number of medals achieved in Los Angeles in 1984 and finished 14th overall behind local rivals South Korea and China, was more concerned with questions of quality management of elite sport than with issues of social education. In this regard, the plan attempted to separate the uneven siblings of elite sport and mass sport from each other: A Sports Promotion Fund was established for the financial needs of the former, while the responsibility for sport supply and mass participation opportunities was delegated to the local level. Public governments should secure funding for the basic supply autonomously, and publicly owned facilities were to be administered by local educational boards or non-profit public corporations to be founded for this purpose. And of course, commercial providers should enrich the sport market (Seki 1997:482–487). Municipalities supported the establishment of commercial sport suppliers and even handed over the management and maintenance of sport facilities to private business. Privately owned and profit-oriented sport facilities indeed were the only viable growth segment of the sport infrastructure during the last decades of the 20th century.

FROM SPORT FOR ALL TO SPORT FOR EVERYONE

Taking account of demographic development, social change and the deteriorating economic climate, the government set out to re-evaluate the role of sport once more in the wake of the 21st century. After many hearings and long deliberations, the Council on Sport Issues filed a new mandatory programme for all communal authorities, which the later Ministry of Education, Culture, Sports, Science and Technology (MEXT) enacted in 2000. The Monbukagakushō Basic Plan for the Promotion of Sports (Supōtsu Shinkō Kihon Keikaku) still reflected the approach taken by the Japanese government during the long 'Heisei recession'. Its preamble stated:

> the promotion of sport also produces economic spin-off effects in that it helps expand the sport industry and thereby create employment opportunities. Sport thus contributes to the economic development of our country and is apt to make a major contribution to the maintenance and enhancement of national health both in mind and body. In this sense, it has the potential of saving medical costs. Sport is thus a contributory element to the national economy. (MEXT 2000:I.1.c)

However, the new Basic Plan was not simply a sequel of the neoliberalism-tainted policy from a decade earlier. Rather it took account of sport as a:

> cultural phenomenon affecting both man's physical and mental aspects [that] is essential for the development of a happy and vigorous society and for the attainment of the individual's psychosomatic health. It is therefore of the greatest significance that people should engage in sports throughout their lives [. . .]
>
> . . . it is one of the first and foremost duties of the nation and the local public entities to make an even stronger commitment than ever in the past to the creation and expansion of an infrastructure that will give further impetus to the promotion of sport. (MEXT 2000:I.1)

For this purpose, the Basic Plan aspired to refashion the domestic sport landscape according to the German model of organized sport (*Vereinssport*). Replacing the former focus on 'hardware' development with a new emphasis on 'software', the new sport policy centred on the local community as point of reference for the most imminent social and organizational aspects framing sport participation chances. In many regards, the Ministry's policy shift acknowledged the limited efficiency of former programmes and conceded as legitimate the critical stance of prominent sport sociologists. Nakamura Toshio (1995), Uchiumi Kazuo (2002, 2005) and Seki Harunami (1997) unanimously agreed that the Japanese state had failed to issue an effective regulatory body of laws and administrative measures for the promotion of sport as well as to provide an adequate infrastructure of public sport facilities and a sufficient minimum of publicly employed sport instructors. Attempts to establish the local community as the social centre of sport clubs go back to the regional restructuring policy by the Economic Planning Agency in the 1970s. This strategy showed only modest results. The Ministry itself conceded that in 2000 'the present situation can hardly be described as offering everybody an opportunity to enjoy and engage in sports anywhere, anytime and throughout life regardless of interest and purpose. This is because about 90 per cent of the sport clubs centring on public sport facilities are typically designed for only one particular type of sport and their scope is limited in terms of sex, age and type of sport' (MEXT 2000:II.1.A.2). It should be added that these sport clubs listed an average of less than 30 members and that they commonly faced the aging of club members as a vital threat to their continuity (Kado 1998:98; Manzenreiter 2004c).

The preamble of the Basic Plan paid tribute to the various changes in the social environment which had a lasting impact on lifestyles of the young and the old, including eminent social phenomena such as demographic change, urbanization, the erosion of traditional communal bonds, technology-induced increases in convenience of life and the appreciation of leisure time activities. Facing the rapidly aging society and the decrease of birthrates, but also the decline in fitness and strength among the younger generation, the Ministry acknowledged its responsibility to promote sport by establishing 'sports as a form of culture essential to the Japanese lifestyle' and by encouraging the individual to independently address sport in order to maintain happiness of the individual as well as strength and vigour for the nation as a whole. For the sake of the Japanese nation, the Ministry aspired to achieve 'a society that is active in sport throughout life by giving everybody the opportunity to engage in sport anywhere, anytime and forever, regardless of physical strength, age, capability, interest and purpose' (MEXT 2000:II.1.a). These phrases reflected an interesting change in terminology. While previously the concept of 'Sports for All'—another import from European welfare states—had flourished in the discourse on national sport promotion, it was now replaced by 'Sports for Everyone', which emphasized the diversity of motives, capabilities and objectives of an active sport life.

In marked difference to former programmes, the Basic Sport Promotion Plan specified some concrete target numbers to evaluate policy outcome. First, as soon as possible a level of participation in sport should be achieved whereby one out of every two adults would engage in sport activities at least once a week. Second, any regional authority nationwide was requested to create at least one comprehensive community sports club on the local level (city, town and village), and to create at least one advisory sports centre covering a wide area in each prefecture until 2010 (MEXT 2000:II.1). This was only a mid-term objective as ultimately all local communities should establish comprehensive community sports clubs at the level of each junior high school catchment district, and every city, town and village should have its own sports centre (MEXT 2000:II.1.A.1).

'Comprehensive community sports club' (*sōgō-gata chiiki supōtsu kurabu*) became the key concept for the promotion of lifelong sport in the new decade. This new type of community sport clubs was envisioned to provide a rich diversity of sport available to people of all ages, from children to senior citizens, and of all levels of skill, from beginners to top-level athletes in competitive sport. Run independently by the local communities, the clubs should comprise sport facilities and a clubhouse in order to provide an opportunity for regular and constant participation in sport and social exchange activities as well as instructions to cater to individual sport requirements under the guidance of highly qualified instructors. Complementary to the Sports Promotion Fund, which was established to improve the performance of top athletes in 1990, a football lottery (*toto*) was started in 2001 as a new source of revenue for the promotion of community sport. In order to obtain financial autonomy at large, the Basic Plan also suggested that the future lay with private funding initiatives (PFI) and low-cost projects, i.e. the 'creative usage of all spaces deemed to be suitable for sport or recreation activities'. More than a hundred model clubs were set up. Between 1995 and 2003, the foundation and progress of model clubs in 115 regional communities were closely scrutinized in order to gain data for a concise manual for local bureaucrats in charge of supervising the creation of sport clubs. Guidelines stipulated that any comprehensive community sports club should provide a diversity of sports to people of all ages, from children to senior citizens, and of all levels of skill, from beginners to top-level athletes in competitive sport. The manual also recommended securing a broad range of income sources, including membership fees, event management, sponsorship and funds from maintenance work in charge of the community. Outsourcing of janitor jobs—such as taking care of school sport facilities, public gyms or the maintenance of pitches and sport grounds—would help clubs to cash in additional funds and local authorities to save on personnel expenditure (Nihon Taiiku Supōtsu Keiei Gakkai 2004).

SPORT IN THE HANDS OF THE LOCALS

The initiative towards a sport policy based on comprehensive community sport clubs was paralleled by similar debates on the packaging of football as a new professional sport in Japan. The broader background and key social issues involved in the establishment of the Japanese professional football league, the J.League, have been the subject of my earlier research (Manzenreiter 2002, 2004; Manzenreiter and Horne 2005; see also Horne 1996, 2001). In this section, I consider the impact of professional football on the concepts of sport community and community sport. The J.League was founded with the explicate goal of changing the culture of sport in Japan. The grand design of the incorporated professional football league was indebted both to the European club sport system and the American business model of professional team sport. Prospective member clubs were expected to be closely linked to a local entity, a hometown, and to work as autonomous and economically viable corporations, rather than relying on subsidies and the management decisions of owner companies, as is the case in Japan's professional baseball leagues.

Leading advocates and managers of the professionalization initiative came from a generation of ex-footballers who had been socialized into the sport during the 1960s when the German Dettmar Cramer was involved in coaching the Japanese national team. During their occasional visits to football schools in Germany in the early 1960s, the young Japanese players experienced firsthand the previously unknown quality of training facilities, available for amateur players as well as professionals, and the enthusiastic mass support of the local population. The appealing image of 'Sports for All', which had been the core notion of the German sport policy of the time, in combination with the organizational standards of top-level sport formed a lasting impression in the minds of the aging Japanese football bureaucrats. This is very likely the major reason why Germany's sport and football clubs were explicitly picked out as the main role model for Japan's professional football league, despite the multifaceted problems the European sport club model has faced since then.

A grassroots approach, community service and local roots are the characteristic features of the European sport club model, which turned out to be influential in the promotion of football in Japan. The J.League demanded from any of its member clubs demonstrable evidence that their 'hometown' was willing to support the promotion of football in the region, most clearly by delivering financial guarantees and infrastructure projects like stadiums and other facilities, if needed by the local clubs, and other more direct forms of capital investment. In exchange, J.League member clubs were required to 'unite with the community, familiarize people with the sport-oriented lifestyle and contribute to the physical and mental well-being and pleasure of local society', as the official mission statement declared. Under the slogan of 'Sports Community for All', club team activities should encompass the cooperation with their hometown municipalities and other locals sport organizations in order to create an environment in which all people can participate in sport, and to develop training programmes for sport instructors at local schools.

Key words that intimately resonate with the J.League's corporate community model include the technical term of 'hometown', where all stakeholders are based, its vernacularized version of *oraga machi* ('our town') and *chiiki mitchaku*, which means 'regional adherence', or simply having a very close relationship with the hometown region. These core notions were found in virtually all public statements issued by the J.League concerning its mission. In 1996 when the J.League had lost some of its initial dynamics, it re-emphasized its commitment to the public, particularly the inhabitants of hometown areas, by the public declaration of the 'J.Mission', which is rendered in the original Japanese as 'The Centennial Plan' (*hyakunen kōsō*). The Japanese naming referred back to the 100-year history of European sport clubs and forward to the long-term perspective of contemporary football initiatives in Japan.

Another prominent key word was 'trinity' (*sanmi ittai*), referring to the J.League ideal image of 'football in the community', based on the cooperation of civil society (*shimin*, townspeople) with businesses (*kigyō*) and local authority bureaucrats (*gyōsei*) from the hometown region. The administration should serve as a hub and communication point between the dispersed actors in the region and channel public funds into the football community. Broad popular interest in the local team was therefore of crucial importance for the commercial viability of the team. Spectator turnout fed directly and indirectly into club revenues, since ticket sales were the major source of income and attendance rates a striking argument for sponsorship activities of the corporate community members. Football clubs also catered to the needs of urban redevelopment programmes since they promised to enhance the quality of life of the local inhabitants in the region by providing 'healthy entertainment' (*kenzen-na goraku*) as well as a source of local pride and communal identification, which the cultural and sporting hierarchy of earlier times had largely restricted to the Tokyo conurbation in the East and the area around Ōsaka in Western Japan. It was clearly desired that these and other intangible benefits of the J.League would also be effective in stopping the depopulation of the peripheries, preventing the younger generation from migration into the large cities, and bridging the gap between older residents and newcomers to their neighbourhoods.

According to the J.League community model, football was thus the point of entry into a vibrant community life sustained by actors from the three different fields of business, politics and civil society. While having their own particular interests, needs and potentials, they also provided the three pillars on which the sustainability of football would rest. Football should be added as the fourth and distinctive player within the ideal new community, not least because the managing body of the J.League proposed to establish professional football throughout Japan for purposes far beyond the limits of the game. Its stated mission was 'to foster the development of Japan's sporting culture, to assist in the healthy mental and physical growth of Japanese people and to contribute to international friendship and exchange'. Such statements reveal a functionalist ideology of football; however, they do not show whose interests it ultimately serves.

In the two decades since its inauguration, the Japanese Professional Football League, or J.League, expanded from its original ten member teams to 40 teams that were playing in 2013 in two divisions. Many more clubs have joined the semi-professional or amateur leagues organized below the professional level. Dozens of large stadiums and thousands of pitches have been erected, and both the finals of the FIFA World Cup in men's and women's football have been hosted. In 2010 nearly 30,000 11-member teams were registered with the Japan Football Association, and there were over 1.2 million players and officials—including 900,000 players and 125,000 futsal players. Hundreds of thousands of football fans have come to attend the weekly matches live on a regular basis. Among young kids, boys and girls, football has become the most popular team sport, and no one can truly assess the impact the game has had on communal bonds or regional pride. However, despite the tight control by the J.League, many clubs, which differ greatly in terms of spectator numbers, public support and sponsorship appeal, appeared to be incapable of becoming self-sustained business operations. Larger shares of club income (about 45 per cent) continued to come from the teams' former owner companies, which had turned into their main sponsors and disguised their funding as promotional expenditure. When economic decline forced some of them to withdraw from sponsoring and no alternatives could be secured, public corporations had to jump in to fill the gap. According to the annual balance sheets published by the J.League in 2009, out of 36 professional J1 and J2 teams, 14 noted operating losses for the current season; in eight cases most of the teams' assets were financed through debt rather than equity; and only ten teams had accumulated total profits since their beginning. As a great number of teams were struggling to make ends meet, resources for activities beyond the core business of football were severely limited. It is an open question whether the same corporations that received so much public support throughout their history will ever be able to pay back society by establishing 'such an environment in which anyone could enjoy sport appropriate to their age, physical condition ability and objectives', as the J.Mission declared.

JOINT FORCES OR SEPARATE PROJECTS?

The J.League's 'Mission' and the Basic Plan for Sport Promotion apparently share a number of objectives and strategies to achieve the common goal of a community-based sport culture. While the football league advocates the combined advance of J.League teams, residents and the local business community, the bureaucrats' sport model is based on a slightly different trinity of the community, the administration and local entrepreneurs. The similarity of goals, proposals, actors and role models prompts the assumption that joint efforts would be in the interest of local authorities and the J.League alike. But equally possible is a scenario where one side is exclusively relying on initiatives by the other. Professional football would not have come so far without immense financial support by the public that poured hundreds of billions of yen into the infrastructure needed for the J.League and the FIFA World Cup over the first ten years (Hirose 2004b). The J.League proposal to provide sport to everyone in the community, at least in the long run, could help to appease concerns of those taxpayers, who have no particular interest in football and therefore do not see any direct benefits from the spending of their tax money. Or politicians and bureaucrats of impoverished local governments could hope for the J.League, i.e. local football teams and their main sponsor companies, taking a leading role in the provision of sport opportunities to their constituencies. The interviews I conducted with club managers and local administrators in seven J-League hometowns in Central and Western Japan in 2003 failed to provide a coherent answer to the question, not least because of the lack of a general road map while the communities largely differ in population size, industrial base and sport infrastructure. But it is justified to state that both parties were primarily concerned with tackling their own problems. Only occasionally were there joint programmes between clubs and cities to realize some particular objective. None of the clubs I visited had established itself as a community sport club in the sense of the 'Mission'—in fact at that time only a few football clubs, such as Urawa Reds or Albirex Niigata, offered sport opportunities other than football to the local people, and up to the time of writing not a single club has come close to being justifiably called a comprehensive sports club.

Hence football was the only field where the two actors from my sample met each other. Each municipality fulfilled its responsibility as a hometown, albeit in varying degrees. The most often cited example was subsidizing the clubs' rental fees of the local stadium. In some instances of severely indebted clubs, the city even abstained from charging the club. In exchange, coaches and players regularly appeared at physical education classes of the local compulsory schools or supported as sport instructors occasional community events hosted by the local administration. The J.League, by the way, was awarded JPY 5 million in 2003 exactly for this purpose by the foundation in charge of managing the revenues from the football lottery. Local bureaucrats also helped advertise J.League matches. Hints at match days and ticket sales were featured in public bulletins and distributed to private households and in notifications that appeared in the local newspapers and other mass media channels.

None of the cities I visited was holding shares of the corporation managing the football team; such a comparatively direct form of commitment was known from football strongholds, such as the cities of Urawa, Kashima and Shimizu. Only in the case of Tosu, a largely rural city of roughly 80,000 inhabitants in Northern Kyūshū, had the city been a shareholder of its local team in the past. Tosu's most valuable asset is its location as a key juncture of transportation in Kyūshū. The intersection of highways and railway tracks was prominently depicted on the homepage of the city, together with the football venue prominently located right next to the main railway station. The local football club, Sagan Tosu, was established in 1997 by the initiative of some thousands of local enthusiasts. Staging signature collections and petitions to the local council, they documented the broad support of the local population for football and the building of a brand-new roofed stadium. If fully packed, the 25,000-seat stadium would have offered a place for nearly every third Tosu citizen. Nike and Coca-Cola, two multinational corporations, were attracted as main sponsors. But upon joining the second division in 1999, Sagan Tosu became better known for mismanagement and the first female president ever of a Japanese football club than for success on the pitch. The splendid location in the heart of the city did not safeguard the hapless club against playing in front of a home crowd of merely 2,000 or 3,000 spectators. After only two years of mediocre results, Sagan was facing bankruptcy when the corporate sponsors withdrew.

The restructuring of liabilities and management prevented the club from financial insolvency, but only after the city of Tosu had fully renounced its financial claims. Stadium maintenance was outsourced to a public corporation at an annual price of JPY 178 million. The company was founded for this particular purpose, and while it was also involved in holding sport seminars and managing sport events, its most important client remained the city, which provided 95 per cent of its income. Tosu was no exception as facility-related expenses consumed in all cities are the largest part of the sport expenditure, ranging between 65 and 80 per cent, as in Hiroshima and Ōita, respectively. Among my sample, I also noticed quite similar forms of outsourcing public services to semi-private corporations that actually operate as the prolonged arm of the bureaucracy. In many instances, the company board was staffed with members from the local education council or regional sport associations, which were used to teaming up with local bureaucrats, but hardly commanded over the knowledge how to manage the business of sport facilities. A similar lack of expertise needed to efficiently operate a professional sport club characterized the boards of many football teams. At that time they were mainly run by staff members who had been detached from the clubs' main corporate sponsors or the hometown administrations. In the boardrooms of football clubs in Ōita, Kyōto, Kōbe and Nagoya, I found myself sitting across from slightly aged managers that appeared rather unhappy with their involuntary mid-career assignment. While the sending party usually emphasized the benefits of smoothing information exchange between business, bureaucracy and sport, the employees concerned saw themselves cut off from their accustomed field of responsibilities, habitual working routines, career paths and the daily flow of communication. Instead they were confronted with the insurmountable task of running a loss-making enterprise which made no sense to them. They felt more obliged to protect their employers' financial interest than demand more funding on behalf of the company they were currently working for but had no idea how else to generate revenues. Rather than being unmotivated, they appeared to be frustrated with the lack of clear-cut principles and instructions. The J.League has responded to the situation by offering training and education for club management since 1999, though it took more time until professionalization also entered the boardroom.

As in Tosu, the neighbouring city Ōita had high expectations in football. Ōita is the capital of the prefecture of the same name with a population of about 650,000. For largely geographical reasons, the mountainous terrain impeded the development of industry and the integration of the region into larger communication and trade networks. Ōita was once famous for being the most depopulated prefecture in Japan (Arimoto 2004:68). But Ōita also became famous for the way football was used by local elites to stem rural depopulation and urban migration. The initial impetus to set up a professional team was proclaimed by Ōita governor Hiramatsu Morihiko in front of the local assembly in 1994, making the objective of becoming a World Cup host city most explicit. Since the World Cup was coming to town, the immensely active prefecture government used the opportunity to channel large amounts of public funds into the expanding communication network of motorways and railway tracks connecting the basically rural city with the busier cities in Kyūshū's Northwest and the main island. The greatest part of the total funds to cover the construction costs, for the Big Eye, Ōita's new World Cup stadium, was collected from general obligation bonds issued by Ōita prefecture.

Ōita did not have a semi-professional company team or the financial support of a potent sponsor company. In comparison, Kyushu's largest metropolis, Fukuoka, had more attractive conditions to offer and hence was able to attract a complete team (the amateur predecessor of Avispa Fukuoka) from Shizuoka, where already some popular teams were based. Ōita's team had to be built up from scratch, largely using local talent from high school and university teams. Support was mandatory for all public employees of the prefectural government as they automatically belonged to the team's official fan club. Public sponsorship for the football club thus could be disguised as buying tickets en bloc for the supporter group—a strategy that the City of Kōbe, for example, rejected as a feasible strategy of saving local team Vissel Kōbe from financial collapse in 2003. Ōita clearly was more determined in using football for regional promotion. Government employees were also sent as temporary staff workers to run the club office and manage team affairs. A career track bureaucrat from the former

Ministry of Local Autonomy in Tokyo was officially dispatched as general manager to help establish the club. Without any large corporation available in the home region, the bureaucrats solicited sponsorship fees from numerous small and medium-sized companies in the region and even succeeded in recruiting sponsors from the main island (Kimura 2003). Ōita Trinita, the name of the club, had been deliberately selected to appeal to the trinity of the sponsors from the business world, the local administration and the citizens in the prefectural region. The leading role of public administration is neatly expressed in a leaflet from Ōita City, stating that 'Oita Trinita have total prefectural support, since not only the prefecture of Oita but also enterprises, companies, and all the inhabitants support it'. Research on the fan communities in the city suggests that grassroots football fan groups in fact did not appreciate the promotional role of local elites in running the official supporters club or the involvement of the bureaucracy in management affairs (Yamashita and Saka 2002).

Generally, the willingness to forge close working relations between local bureaucrats and professional football providers has been most prevalent in those areas where no other soft assets, such as cultural property or natural scenery, were available for promoting the local image. This explains the strong commitment of peripheral cities such as Tosu and Ōita. The sheer existence of a professional baseball team as in Fukuoka, Hiroshima, Ōsaka or Nagoya markedly reduced the local politicians' willingness to speak out for the hometown partnership. Similarly, football was of limited value to refurbish the established image of places like Japan's ancient cultural capital Kyōto, the international harbour city of Kōbe and the Peace City of Hiroshima.

CONCLUSION: THE LIMITED EFFICIENCY OF PUBLIC–PRIVATE PARTNERSHIPS IN LOCAL SPORT INITIATIVES

Sport as a tool of town development (*machizukuri*) has been applied by Tosu, among others. But the declaration as sport city Tosu in 1993 did not bring about the aspired positive changes. City documents reveal that the city-sponsored sport facilities and events were attended 45,255 times in the year of the declaration; usage rates increased only for the next two years and declined thereafter, undercutting in 2001 the value from 1993 (TSKJ 2002:53). It is impossible to state that there is a direct connection between the unlucky private–public partnership with the local football club and declining sport participation. Yet the balance sheets reveal that public expenditure on social education decreased from JPY 2.45 billion in 1996 to 1.68 in 2001; slightly larger was the cut in sport-related expenditure, down from JPY 1.29 billion to 731 million (TKI 2002:11–12). At the time of my visit, the Tosu city department was still in the process of planning a model club to be established in 2005. Amateur sport also ranked high on the administrative task list of the cities of Fukuoka and Kōbe. Administrators in Fukuoka proudly hinted at the young average age of its population and the corresponding need for a vital sport infrastructure; however, as in the case of Nagoya or Ōsaka, they were still in the planning process on how to fulfil the Monkashō requirements. The city of Kōbe already commanded a locally coordinated network of sport clubs that had been founded within the catchment districts of its elementary schools. Similarly, Kyōto and Hiroshima possessed an independent net of local sport clubs dating back to times prior to the invention of the comprehensive community sports club. At the time of my visit, they were in the process of adapting the existing sport landscape to the model prescribed by the Ministry.

The general picture in 2003 was less benevolent as only 17.4 per cent of all municipalities had reached the prescribed goal. A major reason for the delay in progress was the scarcity of funds needed to establish the comprehensive community sports clubs. Neither in the chapter on the role of the national government nor in the section dealing with local authorities did the Basic Plan indicate the government's intention to invest fresh money into sport facilities and sport programmes. Next to regular budget allocations and subsidies from the Sports Promotion Fund (Supōtsu Shinkō Shikin), which was established in 1990 with public start capital of JPY 25 billion primarily for the development of world-class athletes, temporarily limited funding was promised under certain conditions from revenues of the newly established football lottery (*toto*). The Sports Promotion Lottery Law was enacted in 1998 after long disputes on the moral effects of public gambling. Its main objective was to help local sport organizations and community sport clubs to operate. Yet in its first year of business, the World Cup host organization swallowed a third of the entire allocation in order to prevent the threatening national disaster of disorganized games. This one-sided distribution sparked the fierce opposition of domestic sport bodies, including the Japanese Olympic Committee and the Japan Amateur Sports Association. In the following years, annual turnover decreased from JPY 60.4 billion to 40.8 billion (2002) and 20.3 billion in 2003 (*Sankei Shinbun*, January 29, 2004), notwithstanding attempts to raise popular interest in *toto* by increasing chances (since 2003, *toto goal* accepted bets on outcome and number of goals per match) and sales points (Lawson has become the first convenience store chain to handle sales). Total subsidies accordingly shrank from JPY 5.9 billion (2002) to 2.7 billion in 2003, when 385 community sport clubs received an average of JPY 1.7 million (NAASH 2003). They continued to decline to JPY 118 million in 2006, when 108 community sport clubs received an average of 800,000 yen.[3]

As the lottery was assigned a primary role in financing public sport, amateur sport associations and sport clubs were forced to search for alternative funds or ways to cut expenses. In line with the recommendations noted in the MEXT manual, all kinds of local resources were employed. Elementary school sport facilities served as sport facilities and clubhouses, and in most cases members of the educational committee, the local branch of the Japan Amateur Sports Association or even the bureaucracy took the lead in the development of managerial structures, even though the Basic Plan had encouraged the local community to manage clubs autonomously. Clubs usually achieved a critical size quickly by simply merging older sport clubs with associations for children's sport or middle school sport clubs. Size mattered if the newly founded clubs wanted to take advantage of the corporate (foundation) status for non-profit organizations (NPOs) 'as a way of making a more effective contribution to public activities, including community sports promotion, and in order to ensure greater permanency and transparency of these organizations' (MEXT 2000).

The introduction of new betting variants of the national football lottery promised to solve the nagging problem of financing mass sport. The introduction of 'BIG', which offered a top prize of JPY 600 million, proved immediately popular and allowed the National Agency for the Advancement of Sport and Health to pay back its debts of nearly 22 billion yen to Resona Bank, its initial partner institution, in 2006. Thanks to the ongoing popularity of BIG, the sports lottery posted record sales reaching JPY 93.7 billion in 2010. In that year, NAASH was enabled to channel funds of JPY 9.6 billion into the promotion of sport, including 3.7 billion for the funding of 180 public sport facilities and 2.2 billion for subsidizing 842 community sports club (NAASH 2010). At the end of this decade, the Ministry of Education recorded that its ambitions of founding at least one comprehensive community sports club had been achieved in 71.4 per cent of cities, towns and villages. Most of the 2,664 clubs in 998 out of 1,750 administrative districts had been founded in the final stage of the ten-year period, and 450 clubs were in the process of establishment in another 252 districts (MEXT 2011). According to a survey from 2009, three out of four clubs had been established in response to bureaucratic initiatives or recommendations from the local bodies of the semi-public sport administration. Thirty-seven per cent were completely new establishments, while the remaining two-third emerged from the merger of formerly independent smaller sport clubs and circles. Of the community sports clubs, 24.4 per cent had a membership of 301 to 1,000, 46.3 per cent between 101 and 300, and 21.7 per cent less than 100. Thirty-seven per cent offered more than ten sport activities to select from, and 32 per cent between 6 and 9 (MEXT 2010).

The lack of a public debate on the morality of funding sports for all or everyone by money generated from gambling is eye-catching but will not discussed here in great detail. To some degree, the money was needed to finalize the bureaucratic ambitions, and with having set up at least one community sport club in three out of every four communities, this was certainly a remarkable achievement deserving acclamation. Yet what seemed to be a success story and a strong argument for a central sport bureaucracy in Japan demanded a more cautious assessment on second thought. First, judging from the age composition of club members (in 2009, 18.4 per cent were of elementary school age, 9.5 per cent of secondary school age and 3.6 per cent even younger), it became clear that the main objective of raising fitness levels, health awareness and sport participation rates among Japanese adults had not been achieved. Accordingly, less than 2 per cent of the adult population were members of a community sports club in 2008, while 70 per cent had never heard about comprehensive community sports clubs (SSF 2008:63–65). At the time of writing this chapter, regular sport participation under the framework of community sport clubs remained a viable option for senior citizens, schoolchildren and housewives only.

Second, bureaucratically articulated sport communities have few characteristics in common with the autonomous kind of (sport) communities that may be defined as a group of people who are socially interdependent, who act together and who share certain practices, norms, values and memories of a history that define the community and, at the same time, are nurtured by it (cf. Heywood 1994:191). This may be another reason for the lack of popularity. As in the case of football, the creation of sport communities was firmly linked to weak traditions of initiatives from the bottom up, while top-down initiatives were widely institutionalized and socially accepted. For the main target of the Basic Sport Promotion Plan, working Japanese adults, it needs more than sport facilities and sport clubs. Without accompanying changes of the culture of work and corporations, which still demand huge personal sacrifices, time and dedication from workers and employees, adults are not likely to fall for the pleasures of a healthy and sportive lifestyle. Those who are too busy and too exhausted for sport activities during the workweek are not likely to get involved in active sport during their sparse free time on the weekend (Yano et al. 1995:109–113, 119–122).

Hence neither the J.League's Mission nor the Ministry's plans of changing the culture of sport in Japan has been achieved so far. While the traditional one-sided reliance on schools and corporations has been mitigated to some degree, this change is largely due to commercial enterprises or private initiatives bypassing the role of the state. Hence the new ten-year plan, called 'Strategies for a State Built on the Foundations of Sports' (*supōtsu rikkoku senryaku*), continues to feature demands for a favourable environment for sport for the benefit of the larger public as well as the elite of top athletes, the shaping of a new public for the efficient utilization of all public and private stakeholders and the reconsideration of the core values of sport. Particular emphasis is put on the tailored supply of sport opportunities in order to match the different demands accrued at specific life stages. The greying of society is among the most severe challenges modern societies have to face these days, and the next chapter will pay attention to the deep and lasting impact of demographic change on the appearance and significance of sport in late modern society.

6 Sport and Challenges of the Aged Society in Japan[1]

INTRODUCTION

Japanese society, as any other society, has developed its own agenda and set of images associated with the body, sport, fitness, health and beauty. Ideas of what sport is, and what sport is good for, are to the same extent socially constructed as the social institutions in which practice and consumption of sport are embedded. These constructs are related to conventions, roles, behaviour and values associated with mainstream society and the capability of dominant ideologies to bear up against contending claims. The notion of sport, based on the outcome of social interaction between various groups of society and their underlying power relations, therefore is fluid, unstable and open to transformation, triggered by shifting constellations of the broader environment. Japan's enforced integration into the world economy in the later 19th century, defeat in World War II, the rise of the consumption-led economy and recent globalization processes have been decisive moments of social change with a major impact upon the role of sport in society. At the outset of the 21st century, it is the greying of society which is leaving the most evident marks on the sport system in Japan. Between 1970 and 1994, when the proportional share of people aged 65 and older increased from 7 to 14 per cent, Japan was one of the fastest 'aging societies'. For the following 13 years, Japan turned into the fastest 'aged society', and since the share of the elderly exceeded the 21 per cent mark of the entire population in 2007 for the first time, Japan became the first nation to pass the line towards a 'hyper-aged society'. Numerous challenges have been associated with these demographic transgressions ever since media reporting about the government's *1.57 shokku* in 1990, when Japan's total fertility rate of 1.57 was far below reproduction rate and had initiated public awareness for the first time.

Changes in the demographic stratification of society affect sport basically at both ends of the age strata. First, the dramatically declining birthrate is curtailing the population share of the young generation. Since sport in Japan has been largely promoted as an educational device and firmly established within the school curriculum, those at the age of attending compulsory education up to tertiary education have traditionally accounted for the largest segment of the active sport population. But the proportion of Japanese youth at compulsory school age including high school (6–18 years of age) decreased from roughly 20 per cent in 1970 to 14 per cent in 2000 and will continue to fall to a level of about 10 per cent in 2030. Second, the prolongation of the average life span is fuelling the growth of old age groups that so far have largely been neglected by public and private sport suppliers. The enactment of the Sports Promotion Law (Supōtsu Shinkō Hō) in 1961 and the revision of the postwar Social Education Law (Shakai Kyōiku Hō) in 1964 officially acknowledged sport as a public good for the first time. Yet sport as a leisure activity remained largely restricted to educational objectives targeting the young, as discussed in the previous chapter, corporate welfare (company sport) or profit-seeking private enterprises. Japanese people aged 60 and older, standing in the shadow of these programmes, accounted for 11 per cent of the entire population in 1970. They accounted for 24 per cent in 2000, and they are forecasted to reach 37 per cent in 2030 (ISSP data, 2006).

Within this scenario, sport and physical activity have recently received a prominent position to counter some of the mounting problems associated with the aging society. This chapter will identify the way sport in Japan is affected by demographic change directly and indirectly. My analysis focuses on the elderly and their sport experience, although, as I will demonstrate, outcomes of this ongoing process of change are of concern for the entire population. First I will sketch out the discussion on the widely claimed benefits gained from rising sport participation rates. Then I will demonstrate how Japanese state authorities have been employing sport to address the challenges of aging and old age in contemporary Japan. The next sections will identify some outstanding aspects of the demographics of sport in greying Japan and the way sport is accommodated by the consumer industry. In the concluding section, I will discuss the most urgent problems associated with Japan's sport policy and, finally, how the notions of sport and age themselves are affected by the changes within the broader social environment.

THE BENEFITS OF SPORT PARTICIPATION IN THE AGING SOCIETY

The close association of sport with physical health, mental sanity and social skills has been at the core of the modern sport ideology ever since it started to spread from English boarding schools throughout the Victorian Empire and the rest of the world. Since its early years, the Olympic Movement has been a powerful agent behind the international dissemination of a sport ideology that too often is taken at face value. Although doping, cheating and hazing have emerged as salient features of sport practice worldwide at the amateur as well as the professional level, these are taken as aberrations deviating from the idealized norm of healthy sport. Half a century of medical research into the physical effects of sport has provided solid evidence of the various benefits deriving from regular physical activity. Sport-medical research into sport and physical activities has provided ample evidence on the benefits of sport for maintaining cardio-respiratory fitness, physical mobility and health in general.

Since Jerry Morris's landmark studies into the importance of physical activity as a cardio-protective factor in 1953, numerous studies have confirmed that regular physical exercising reduces the risk of developing diabetes, high blood pressure and colon cancer, and of dying prematurely (Rejeski and Mihalko 2001; Stathi, Fox and McKenna 2002). Singular voices in Japan occasionally echo concerns about the lack of well-designed and large-scale research in this country because of 'obvious differences in the disease patterns of Japanese and Europeans', as well as in their genetic background and lifestyle routines (Miyachi 2005:3). But the general consent among Japan's gerontologists, physicians and health professionals is represented by Amaha Keisuke (2003:20–35), a specialist in critical care medicine, who quotes the positive impact of physical leisure-time activity on the most widespread age-related symptoms of physical decay, including ischemic heart disease, hyperlipidemia, hypertension, diabetes, obesity, osteoporosis and postmenopausal syndrome.

In fact, not a few studies on health patterns of Japanese elderly provide adequate evidence for such claims. A recently published report on a longitudinal survey among senior citizens indicates that kind and degree of outdoor activities have an immediate impact upon mortality risk (Inoue, Shono and Matsumoto 2006). Concerning osteoporosis, a large-scale research project on aging conducted by the Aging Bio Marker Research Team at the Tokyo Metropolitan Institute of Gerontology came to the conclusion that continuous and devoted practice in sport or physical movement effectively contributes to the maintenance of bone density and thus the prevention of physical immobility among their sample of Japanese senior citizens (Shimizu and Shirasawa 2006:16). A *Nikkei Science* report on the activities of the research team hinted at surprising variations in the pace at which the aging process takes place over the body, its singular parts and functions, indicating that many physiological aspects of aging are still wanting explanation, notwithstanding any differences in genetic or cultural background. Similarly, a cross-sectional study to determine the physical fitness levels of more than 1,000 older Japanese suggests that declines in physical fitness, especially those that are related to mobility and risk for falls, occur with rising age, but not at a uniform rate (Demura et al. 2003).

By comparison, a substantial body of Japanese research into the psychological effects of sport participation supports the assumption that sport and physical activities help fight depression and anxiety (Yoshiuchi et al. 2006) as well as promote psychological well-being (Yaguchi 1988) and thus enhance the subjectively assessed level of quality of life. In a study among

180 independently living senior citizens, the lowest quartiles of participants in physical activities scored lowest in terms of health-related quality of life (Yasunaga 2006). A large-scale longitudinal survey among senior residents in Shizuoka prefecture demonstrated that daily physical activity had an important impact upon maintaining mobility (Kubota, Ishiwata-Takata and Ohta 2005). A smaller-scale study among the elderly in rural Japan (Yasunaga, Yaguchi and Tokunaga 2002) came to the conclusion that regular exercise leads to a higher level of daily life activities and thus enhances both self-rated health and social support, which in turn can influence subjective well-being for elderly adults. Furthermore, Ishizawa (2004) confirmed the positive impact of physical exercise and daily life activities on the life satisfaction of even the older elderly, i.e. senior citizens aged 75 and above.

The close link between physical fitness, life satisfaction and social integration was hinted at as early as the 1980s. A pioneering survey study from 1986 demonstrated that physical activities of the elderly were significant not only for improving their health, but also for maintaining their social relationships. The elderly who had less life satisfaction clearly showed negative attitudes towards physical activities and also had many more complaints about their physical conditions than those who enjoyed the social setting of sport participation (Sugiyama et al. 1986). A more recent survey from 2003 among 1,500 physically active and non-active elderly confirmed the findings since active elderly gave higher ratings to health, physical fitness and their capabilities of coping with everyday activities (KTJZ 2004).

The relationship between physical mobility and life satisfaction may appear self-evident in such societies that highly esteem autonomy and independence of the individual. Thinking about the preference of living in multigenerational households after old age and the well-known essay in psychology on *amae* ('anticipating indulgence', or 'indulgent dependence') as a structuring principle of social relations in Japan (Doi 1973), the Japanese elderly may have quite different ideas of the self in communal life or family relations. Opinion surveys on life after retirement age by the Japanese government do not feature questions on independence, which ranks very high on the agenda of the *Active for Later Life Resource* by the British Heart Foundation, the UK *Game Plan*, *Health Canada* or other health programmes related to senior citizens in the Western world (Cameron 2004). Certainly there is a need to differentiate among physical, mental and emotional kinds of independency. If independence means the physical capacity to get up from bed and walk freely outside the house, then Japanese elderly do not differ much. According to the governmental opinion survey among the elderly in 1998, about two-thirds of the sample felt worried or at least uncertain about life in old age, with most quoting some kind of severe health condition that may require long-term care or medical treatment. When asked during a follow-up survey in 2005 what they would want society to pay attention to, more than five out of ten respondents said health management (*kenkō kanri*), including physical activity (*shintai undō*), while only one out of ten wanted recreational activities, including sport, to be on the political agenda (SCK 1999, 2005a).

The data show a strong correlation between these answers and socio-physical characteristics. People who felt healthy and participated regularly in social affairs gave higher ratings to their capabilities of coping with everyday activities, health and physical fitness (self-assessment) and had a more positive image of physical exercise (KTJZ 2004). They also showed much more interest in the promotion of leisure activities than non-active elderly who favoured health and care issues instead (SCK 2005b). Of course, anxiety about one's health in old age is not limited to the already aged: In the Japanese government's survey on people's lifestyles (NDK 2005), nearly every second adult (47.6) called the future state of health a troubling point of concern in old age (*fuan o kanjite iru*), topped only by financial worries; the older respondents were, the more attention shifted from money to the body. Correspondingly, Japanese adults place their hopes on the positive health effects of sport participation. In a 1988 comparison of Japanese attitudes towards sport participation with findings from a pan-EU survey on consumer attitudes to physical activity, body weight and health, 'maintaining one's health' as the reason for getting into sport scored highest among Japanese respondents. They also mentioned extraordinarily often the motivational power of 'social exchange', while no European nation showed less inclination of falling short to the prospect of 'relaxation', 'getting out under the sky' or 'experiencing one's physical strength' than the Japanese (SSF 2004:31).

The connection among physical health, fitness and finances is a further argument featuring predominantly in debates on the benefits of sport. If sport participation contributes to health promotion, it also helps reduce medical costs. This saving potential is of less concern for the retired whose medical expenses are covered by national health insurance. It may be more important for the young and middle-aged in employment that must bear 30 per cent of medical treatment costs since the reform of the insurance system in 2003. The economic consideration definitely is of interest for public health finances and the macro-economy. Concerning private consumption, a survey in Miyagi prefecture among the local members of the National Health Insurance System aged 40 and older found that those living a healthy life (no smoking, holding adequate weight and taking regular physical exercise) spent 35 per cent less on medical expenses (SSF 2001:21). Health-related expenses in Japan amounted to JPY 30 trillion per year at the beginning of this decade and were projected to reach as much as JPY 81 trillion in 2015 (Iwamoto 2004:225). The average Japanese (without elderly aged 65 and above) generates medical expenses of about JPY 150,000 per year, while four times more (645,000) is spent on the average elderly, and a quarter of all medical expenses (26.3 per cent) on the age group of 75 years and older; both total volume and the distributional imbalance have shown a sharp increase over the past 15 years (KRDK 2003).

Other countries facing a rapidly aging population and a similarly fast increase in lifestyle-related diseases have commissioned research on the economic impact of mass sport participation.[2] According to research findings from Australia, the outcome can be as much as a quarter of GDP if the rate of people participating regularly in sport is raised by 40 per cent (Okada 1999:112). The Canada Fitness Lifestyle Research Institute asserted in 1997 that a reduction of the inactive population share by 1 per cent translates into 10 million Canadian dollars less on expenses for coronary diseases (SSF 2001:21). Even tiny Austria may save 8 billion euro annually if the sport inactive group is convinced to take up regular exercise (Weiss et al. 1999:8). The UNESCO Declaration of Punta del Este, gathering more than 200 ministry officials in charge of physical education from all around the world, also proclaimed in 1998 that 'one dollar invested into physical activity means 3.2 dollars saved on medical costs' (SSF 2001:18).

SPORT POLICY FOR THE AGING SOCIETY

The Japanese state acknowledged the instrumental potentials of sport for public health and community building quite early. Under the influence of European national fitness programmes, such as Germany's 'Golden Plan' from the 1960s, guidelines for the regional bureaucracy were issued in order to guarantee sport opportunities for all, and particularly to those who were denied access to sport facilities due to their lack of formal membership in either school teams or company clubs. Sport participation rates beyond the primary target groups of youth and young adults started to rise modestly when community sport appeared on the agenda of regional politics in the wake of the welfare state in the 1970s, and lifestyle changes established new business opportunities for private sport suppliers in the following decade. Concerning health promotional activities directed toward the enhancement of better nutrition and physical fitness of the elderly, the Ministry of Health and Welfare launched the National Movement for Health Promotion in 1978 and the second instalment, dubbed Active 80 Health Plan, in 1988. A certification system of health trainers was initiated, and fitness clubs having a certain number of qualified health trainers were granted preferred tax treatment and special designation by the government (JPHA 2006:16).

The Ministry of Education, which is basically in charge of sport administration, also noted the rising importance of sport to maintain a healthy and active physical and mental life in the aging society. Acting on suggestions from the November 1989 report of the Health and Physical Education Council entitled 'Strategies for the Promotion of Sports towards the 21st Century', new guidelines were issued to improve the supply side of public sport in 1991. The policy line basically complied with the core points of an earlier report by the Sports Promotion Advisory Council to the prime minister, stipulating the necessity for raising the social evaluation of sport, training and securing sport coaches and leaders, enriching sport facilities and taking measures to fund promotional sport activities (Monbushō 1992). However, the shift in emphasis from 'social education' (*shakai kyōiku*) toward lifelong sport (*shōgai supōtsu*) confined itself primarily to the rhetorical level without eliciting actual change on both supply and demand sides (Kiku 1998:18).

As we have seen in the previous chapter, the Basic Plan for the Promotion of Sport enacted by the Ministry of Education, Culture, Sports, Science and Technology (MEXT) in 2000 aspired to introduce a new organizational concept of comprehensive community sport clubs to combat the mounting problems of the aging society. In marked difference to former programmes, the Basic Sport Promotion Plan specified concrete numerical targets as a guideline for the evaluation of the administrative realization of the national sport policy. Numbers were set up in fields of sport participation rates to be achieved and sport clubs and sport centres to be opened over the first decade of the 20th century. Concise target numbers also appeared within the third instalment of the national health programme in 1998. Covering the period between 2000 and 2010, 'Healthy Japan 21' (Kenkō Nihon 21) identified 70 numerical targets in nine areas, including physical activities and exercise. The basic goal was to promote people's health comprehensively through the extension of the healthy life span, i.e. the period during which people can live without suffering dementia or being bed-ridden (SSF 2001:25). Training physical strength is at the core of all efforts to counter the 'deflationary spiral of health' (Shirai 2000:126), which is fuelled by the susceptibility of fragile health to injury and immobility. The new emphasis on 'primary prevention' replaced traditional efforts having prioritized 'secondary prevention', which aimed at early detection and early treatment. Actions related to physical activity intended to increase the number of persons who intentionally exercise from a base value of 50 per cent to 63 per cent and to increase the number of people who exercise regularly from a base value of 24.6 per cent (women) and 28.6 per cent (men) to a minimum of 35 per cent and 39 per cent, respectively. In addition, the number of walking steps of men and women per day should be raised by roughly 15 per cent (WHO Centre for Health Development 2005:15). As in the case of the Basic Sport Promotion Plan, Healthy Japan 21 took an all-encompassing look at public health in Japanese society, identifying points of concern in all age groups. With regard to pre-school and school-age children, the programme noted the negative impact of reduced playtime in the school yard, the vanishing of open space and an increase in sedentary activities, such as watching TV and playing video games, which all have led to declines in daily physical activity; among the elderly, Healthy Japan 21 hinted at their worrying tendency to remain at home instead of adopting a more physically active lifestyle. Four target values of the national health programme aiming particularly at the elderly thus explicitly referred to regular exercise, extensive walking and participation in social activities outside of the home (WHO Centre for Health Development 2005:24).

Maintaining physical mobility for as long as possible was an essential prerequisite for the government-sponsored ideal of an 'ageless life'. Since 1998, the cabinet office has solicited nominations to showcase practices of an ageless life (*eijiresu raifu jissensha*) every year. Appropriate candidates were defined as persons aged 65 years and above who, irrespective of their age, in self-responsibility and according to their capabilities, lived their life in an unconstrained and spirited way (*nenrei ni torawazu mizukara no sekinin to nōryoku ni oite jiyū de ikiki to shita seikatsu o okuru*; Naikaku-fu 2004b). Among the nominated role models, a considerable number was selected for their remarkable achievements in sport. For example, 72-year-old Midorikawa Shichirō from Iwaki in Fukushima prefecture was nominated for holding six records in track and field at the Asian level. The senior athlete got into track and field at school age but stopped after graduating from high school until the age of 43. Up to the time of his nomination, he continued his daily training, aiming at a future world championship title. Another example featured the marathon runner Momoda Arata, aged 90, from Shimonoseki in Yamaguchi prefecture. He took up long-distance running at the age of 60 and had participated since then in numerous road races in Japan and abroad. Thanks to his physical fitness, the senior runner was proud of never having been to the hospital in all his life. Another nominee from 2004 was Azuma Shōgorō, aged 92, from Yokohama, who got into competitive swimming at the age of 69. Since then, he had won 22 world championship titles and broken 32 Japanese records (Naikaku-fu 2004b). While these senior athletes are far from being representative for their age cohort, their public appraisal served the objective of any role model: to inspire successors and to invite emulation.

PATTERNS OF SPORT PARTICIPATION IN AGING JAPAN

Despite all governmental efforts, international comparisons continued to feature Japanese adults as 'couch potatoes' and inactive in sport until quite recently (cf. SSF 2002). In most international surveys on sport participation rates, Japan ranked low, close to the bottom of the country list (cf. SSF 1997:35; 2001:36). According to the 2001 Survey on Time Use and Leisure Activities (*shakai seikatsu kihon chōsa*), adults on average spent less than 20 minutes a day on sport and physical exercise. The share of active sport participants dedicating more than 90 minutes a week to strenuous exercise in 2002 was 13.2 per cent, roughly a quarter of the quota desired by the MEXT bureaucrats. Despite notable differences in participation rates in advanced sport nations such as Canada, Australia and the UK, time series data on Japanese participation in sport activities undeniably reflected favourable changes in lifestyle behaviour in the recent past. Since 1992, the SSF has conducted biannual surveys on the sport life of the Japanese adult population. According to the SSF surveys, the totally inactive sport population shrank from one out of two Japanese (49.3 per cent) in 1992 to slightly more than one out of four adults (28.1 per cent) in 2008. By contrast, the active sport population, which consists, according to the SSF definition, of those who exercise somewhat hard at least twice a week for a minimum of 30 minutes at a time to maintain and improve health and physical fitness, showed a similarly remarkable progress from 6.5 per cent in 1992 to 17.4 per cent in 2008. The share of those included that take it more easy but nonetheless exercise twice a week or more nearly tripled over the period from 16.2 per cent to 45.5 per cent in 2008 (SSF 2009:23–25).

As Tables 6.1, 6.2 and 6.3 show, rising participation rates have been evident in all age groups until the most recent backdrop among the younger age groups. Generally people stayed away from sport the older they were. According to the SSF survey from 2004, less than a fifth of young adults in their 20s were completely inactive, compared to 20.5 per cent in their 40s, 32.5 per cent in their 60s and 44.8 per cent of the elderly aged 70 and older. This tendency towards age-related abstinence from sport clearly reflects both physical and social processes related to the life course. But in 1992, the respective shares of non-participants among the age groups were at much higher levels, comprising about one-third of young adults, roughly half of the middle-aged and two-thirds of the aged Japanese. This shift indicated a tremendous change having taken place in terms of physical awareness, health consciousness and lifestyle choices over the 1990s. Participation rates of age groups among the serious-minded sportsmen and sportswomen (Table 6.2) showed that sport had become a viable and respectable option for everyday life activities among senior citizens. At the level of regular exercising, the distinction between young and old had become hardly visible. The share among younger adults had shown only moderate increase, while the shares of middle-aged and older Japanese exhibited not only the highest growth rates; they also replaced the young in relative terms as the age groups with the largest share of active sport participants. These data imply that the constraints of career building and setting up a family have a downgrading impact upon regular sport participation. They also demonstrate that demographic change in combination with lifestyle changes lead to a bifurcation in the population: The numbers of both the exercising elderly, who regarded sport as an essential part of their daily life routines, and the non-participants, were growing (see also KTJZ 2004).

We also know from the SSF surveys that sport participation of the elderly is no longer restricted to light gymnastics, which are actively promoted by national broadcasting, or gateball, a Japanese variant of croquet that gained nationwide popularity in the 1980s. Initially, this game was applauded for its easy accessibility; it offered sport novices and the physically impaired the opportunity to meet with like-minded people for the enriching purposes of meaningful leisure, light physical exercise and social contacts (Kalab 1992). At that time, gateball clubs, tournaments and local leagues were established all over Japan, while municipalities rushed to erect specially designated gateball grounds. About two decades later, gateball

Table 6.1 Share of Inactive Sport Population in Age Groups, 1992–2008

	20–29	*30–39*	*40–49*	*50–59*	*60–69*	*70+*
1992	31.5	39.9	46.3	57.7	66.1	73.1
1994	40.3	38.5	44.0	57.8	63.5	71.8
1996	24.2	24.9	29.1	40.5	51.0	60.4
1998	22.4	26.6	26.2	38.1	47.1	61.7
2000	19.3	20.8	26.6	28.0	41.0	48.4
2002	19.8	22.9	30.7	30.8	39.5	51.1
2004	17.2	20.2	20.5	26.2	32.5	44.8
2008	25.8	23.0	22.4	28.2	29.0	44.8

Source: Sasakawa Sports Foundation, *Sport Life Japan*, various years.

Table 6.2 Share of Very Active Sport Population in Age Groups, 1992–2008

	20–29	*30–39*	*40–49*	*50–59*	*60–69*	*70+*
1992	9.1	7.4	5.6	5.8	5.8	5.8
1994	9.2	9.5	7.8	3.9	9.4	4.8
1996	15.0	9.3	10.3	8.2	8.2	1.8
1998	15.2	11.9	12.7	16.0	11.2	9.0
2000	18.4	14.8	21.4	20.2	14.4	13.7
2002	17.4	14.3	11.1	12.3	13.8	11.1
2004	15.7	14.8	16.4	16.4	18.9	13.5
2008	16.3	18.7	17.1	16.0	19.3	16.7

Source: Sasakawa Sports Foundation, *Sport Life Japan*, various years.

Table 6.3 Share of Quite Active Sport Population in Age Groups, 1992–2008

	20–29	*30–39*	*40–49*	*50–59*	*60–69*	*70+*
1992	8.5	8.3	10.6	8.7	11.6	11.5
1996	19.2	19.4	23.4	20.6	17.8	22.5
2000	20.2	21.8	14.7	27.2	26.3	26.7
2004	23.5	20.7	33.2	35.2	32.8	27.4
2008	25.2	24.8	21.5	32.2	36.0	28.5

Note: In SSF categories, quite active refers to levels 2 and 3 (= twice a week of moderate sport).
Source: Sasakawa Sports Foundation, *Sport Life Japan*, various years.

still was played by many thousands, but younger seniors seemed to shun the game because of its reputation as a silver sport. Instead, they preferred to play golf, both at the green or at the driving range, or the simplified version of ground golf, another Japanese invention and contribution to the category of play-like, low-competitive 'new sports'. Strolls, walking and light calisthenics, including the early morning radio or television gymnastics, exhibited participation rates of more than 10 per cent and took the lead among the 15 most often practised sport activities of the seniors. Still among the top 15, yet with notably lower participation rates, were hiking, golf, swimming, cycling and workouts in the gym (SSF 2004:25).

Various tournaments and sport festivals are opened every year for those who continue competitive or social sport throughout their life. Sports Masters Japan is an annual all-Japan tournament for high-aspiring athletes aged 35 and older. Held for the first time in 2001, the event features competitions in track and field, bowling, golf, badminton, tennis, bicycle racing, swimming, football, volleyball and softball. Competitions are organized according to age groups of the participants, numbering about 6,000 a year. Age-specific competitions have also been added to the programme of the annual National Athletic Meeting (Kokutai). On a more playful level, the broader public in general and the elderly more specifically are encouraged to participate at sport events such as the Nenlympics (Nenrinpikku, literally Tree-ring Olympics), the All Japan Sports and Recreation Festival (Zennihon Supo Reku Matsuri) or the Challenge Day. Particularly the first, which has been held every year since the 50th anniversary of the Ministry of Welfare in 1988, aims to maintain and improve public health, social participation and zest for life among senior citizens so that they may enjoy an extended life in a vibrant community (Ikeda, Yamaguchi and Chogahara 2001:32). As the National Health and Welfare Festival for the Elderly, the tournament features traditional sports as well as new sports suitable for sport participation at old age as well as an 'energetic long-life-time society' (ibid.) The All Japan Sports and Recreation Festival has also been held annually since 1988 under the auspices of the Ministry of Education, regional authorities and the Nihon Rekuriēshon Kyōkai. The nationwide event regularly attracts some 100,000 participants. The main programmes contains a number of non- or low-competitive 'new sports' such as petanque, indiaka, touch rugby, *sport chanbara*, folk dance and walking and attempts to convince people of all ages of the joy and pleasures of sport. The Challenge Day is a unique event of Canadian origin: Municipalities of a similar population size compete against each other during the last Wednesday of May in order to assemble the highest number of participants at simultaneously staged tournaments. In case of defeat, the flag of the winning municipality flies from the main pole of the winning town hall for a full week. Japan participated at this international event for the first time in 1993; over the first eight years, more than two million people took part at the annual Challenge Days. Since 2001, the tournament drew an average of about one million participants throughout Japan year after year. Other events targeting the elderly include walking events such as the Japan Three-Day Walk March (Nihon Surii Dē Māchi), staged every year around the first Sunday in November since 1978 and attracting up to 100,000 participants; 'new sport' festivals; and the traditional local sport days (*undōkai*). All of these mass sport events are putting more emphasis on the social merits than on the competitive aspect of sport involvement. Such a re-engineering of the notion of sport makes perfect sense since senior citizens typically are less inclined to get into serious sport training than into some kind of light physical exercise, social integration or entertainment. And it seems they are willing to spend on it.

THE SILVER BUSINESS OF SPORT IN THE GREYING CONSUMER INDUSTRY

Amidst the upswing of Japan's economy in the first decade of the 21st century, the consumer industry was facing the first wave of the *dankai jidai*, Japan's baby boomers of the immediate postwar years hitting retirement age in 2007. In media reports, this new generation of seniors was heralded for its financial power and big impact on consumer markets due to its population size. Since the average retiree was expected to receive JPY 20.5 million in severance pay upon retirement, consumer industries eagerly awaited the unprecedented total spending power of JPY 75 trillion over the second half of the decade (METI 2006). According to a government report, the entire silver market was having annual growth potentials of 4 to 5 per cent. Care and welfare related expenses were expected to compose about one-tenth of the entire silver market and medical expenses between two- and three-tenths, with the overwhelming rest fuelling final consumption (SKS 2000:60). Fuji Chimera Research Institute estimated in 2002 that sport consumption contributed 5.6 per cent to the total health and welfare market. Already a decade earlier, both sport industries and the silver market were identified as key markets of the 21st century. Stimulated by the golf and resort boom during the affluent years of the bubble economy, the Ministry of International Trade and Industry published in 1990 its report *Sports Vision 21*, predicting a JPY 15 trillion market to come in 2000 (Seki 1997:491). For the same year, a report from the insurance company Asahi Seimei expected the silver market to reach a volume of JPY 124 trillion (Matsunaka 2001:333). However, these forecasts failed to materialize in the recessive climate. While the sport market peaked in the early 1990s and decreased subsequently to a size of JPY 4.9 trillion (SKSH 2003:99), the silver market stopped short with a volume of JPY 40 trillion in 2000 (SKS 2000:60).

Of course, marketers of leisure- and sport-related goods and services have begun customizing their products for the aging population and particularly those 70 to 80 per cent that report no health problems. Outdoor recreational activities, particularly hiking and mountaineering, were among the pioneering sectors of the leisure industry foreshadowing the demographic change. When during the 1980s the average age of mountain hikers and organized mountain climbers suddenly leaped to heights previously unheard of, the sport industry responded with the development of hiking shoes, special journals and book publications and commercial tour packages geared to the middle-aged. With the greying of the protagonists of the mountaineering boom, walking and hiking also became prominent leisure activities of the elderly (Manzenreiter 2000:214–217). Major apparel producers such as Asics or Mizuno established R&D departments on senior sport and contributed actively to the promotion of new sport programmes for health-conscious middle-aged and older customers. Among these new sports, walking appealed particularly to the elderly, who comprised the bulk of participants at walking courses and tournaments. When the walking boom hit Japan in the late 1990s, Mizuno utilized its own dense network of local shops to offer all-encompassing packages of goods and services related to the new fashion. Special corners geared at the middle-aged were opened in more than 100 Mizuno shops. Shifting the shop concept from the traditional sport shop that sells goods for competitive sport to health shops offering diverse goods and services to the middle-aged is a long-term strategy of small-sized retailers to survive under the pressure of large retailers and sport shop chains (Matsunaka 2001:338).

Since the most often practised sport activities hardly require access to facilities and regular training partners, most of the elderly exercise either at home or somewhere in public, in the streets, parks or along the riverside (SSF 2004:35). Only a minority of 17 per cent has enrolled in a sport club, usually a community sports club. Occasionally the elderly, more women than men, join a commercial sport club (SSF 2004:156–157). But the fitness industry is setting high expectations in the silver sport market. Health and fitness clubs suffered heavily from the recession as belt-tightening forced many to limit leisure spending. Only when the rising medical costs generated a national concern with health, did memberships begin to rise again, particularly among the middle-aged and postretirement population that emerged as the fastest-growing group of new members at health clubs recently (Spielvogel 2003:3; SCSK 2002:11).[3] Renaissance, the third largest fitness club chain in Japan, operates about 80 stores throughout the country with a membership of 260,000. In-house data show that the proportional share of senior members nearly doubled over the years from 1998 to 2006 to reach nearly 20 per cent. Growth rates characterized also the share of the middle-aged, while the relative contribution of younger age groups declined. The prospective market also attracts foreign competitors. Curves, the largest US-based fitness franchise in the world, opened its first outlet in Japan in 2005. During its first year of operation, Curves Japan opened 30 clubs targeting seniors in their 50s and 60s and aspired to establish 2,000 fitness clubs by the end of the decade (METI 2006).

Marketing specialists hint at the necessity of understanding the psychosocial needs in the 50-plus members. The senior generation is not a homogeneous group of hard-to-please consumers but is differentiated into lifestyle groups as any other segment of society (Carrigan 1998). Product development for life-stage segments, centred on chronological age groups, also commonly fail since disposable income, health perception and social independence are more important variables for the explanation of fitness motivation. How to get senior clients to come into the gym is the first problem marketers have to solve; how to keep them coming is the second. More than age-specific norms of behaviour, negative attitudes towards one's own physical capabilities have been identified as a major impediment preventing Japanese seniors from getting engaged in sport (Yaguchi 1988). For the average senior, the prospects of training side by side with much younger customers is as embarrassing as the category of senior sport annoys the physically fit, ambitious senior athlete. In correspondence with their target groups and local conditions, health clubs and fitness gyms addressed these problems by redesigning the image of fitness clubs.

Since Japanese seniors are rather intrigued by the course leader's social competence to help them modify their health behaviour than by licensed qualifications (Tanaka et al. 2002:16–17), instructors were re-educated as animators, health counsellors and service providers paying heightened attention to the expectations and needs of their clients. While larger facilities can afford to rely on the mass market approach, including the expansion of age-appropriate sport programmes such as yoga, t'ai chi or gymnastics, and fee reductions for off-peak visits, smaller clubs have to be more aware of local needs. One sport club in the rural part of Chiba prefecture sent its staff around to visit every household within a radius of three kilometres, asking the residents for their needs and wishes. Another company operating six clubs in the suburbs of Tokyo realized the importance its senior members attached to social life. Holding culture classes, cooking courses and lectures on dietary and health issues, the chain tried to establish the gym as a kind of local meeting place. Providing sport medical advice and health checks have been identified as another best practice of Japanese fitness club operators targeting the elderly (CKSJ 2001).

Since it is easier to work with existing participation to keep people involved, rather than re-engage them or introduce them to entirely new activities (cf. Long 2004:34), 'catching them young' is the key solution to enhance participation rates among the society of lifelong sport. A large panel survey among Japanese aged 65 and older showed that socially active seniors differed from less active seniors insofar as they had participated in more hobbies during middle age, had higher levels of education and had had a more varied diet between the ages of 30 and 50. In other words, maintaining general health habits and lifestyles from middle age on are the foundations for successful aging and high social activity in old age (Ohno et al. 2000). But the process of successful sport socialization starts at a much younger age. Looking at sport participation patterns of the middle-aged, Kiku (1996) found that the experience of sport during school age was a major determinant in explaining the level and the kind of sport activities of adult athletes. Therefore, sport and health politics in the aging society should adopt an all-encompassing approach stretching over the entire life course.

CONCLUDING OBSERVATIONS

In this chapter I have shown how public and private actors in contemporary Japan have impacted upon the position of sport in the aging society. Sport certainly has been adopted as a valuable resource to navigate through the three successive phases of the 'aging shock' at ages 50, 60 and 70 because of its supportive qualities for the 'eventide dowry' of the three Ks: *kenkō* (health), *keizai* (economics) and *kokoro no hari* (determination or spirit).[4] However, the link between age and sport activities is still very weak since the share of non-active adults shows a disproportionate increase among the old, and, within the older age groups, there is a preponderance of women, who are consistently less likely to fall for the appeal of sport. While Japanese elderly nowadays have command over fairly good health conditions in international comparison, this seems to be a cohort effect and should not be the cause for overt optimism. Rather it is likely that a future breed of older people will not evidence the same robust health conditions as contemporary seniors who were born and raised under harsher conditions and lived a much less sedentary, comfortable life. Observations on the present elderly population do not allow reliable predictions about the future shape of their lifestyles as future generations of seniors are certainly as susceptible to lifestyle diseases as the present generation. Particularly the prolongation of old-old age is likely to aggravate the 'double dichotomy of aging': We may expect a growing number of physically active and health-conscious seniors in correspondence to what Höpflinger (2005) called the 'socio-cultural juvenescence of age', but the group of non-active seniors will concurrently increase at a much faster pace. No 'ageless living' campaign is ultimately able to annihilate the risks of age-related disease and disability in the later stages of old age.

I have also argued that the discussion of sport and demographic change cannot be reduced to the role of sport for the aged but must cover all age groups since sport-related lifestyles before retirement and the experiences of sport during school age strongly correlate with fitness level and sport motivation in old age. The current rhetoric of sport and health politics clearly shows that the state has acknowledged the significance of sport for all Japanese. Over the past 15 years, remarkable changes in lifestyle behaviour have equally contributed to raising sport participation rates among all age cohorts (and the increasing involvement of the elderly in sport volunteering and sport-related consumption). In terms of growth rates, Japan is doing fairly well and has narrowed the gap with the more advanced sport nations. But Japan started from a very low level, and all postindustrial societies are facing similar problems of obesity and lifestyle-related atrophy among the young generations. Since the late 1980s, the measured level of physical fitness and athletic ability in Japanese children has dramatically decreased, which the Ministry of Education related to the common neglect of the importance of sport, a lack of factors needed to be involved in sport (time, space and friends) and a disorderly lifestyle. The ideological link between healthy body and sound mind has not been limited to the bureaucracy. Instead the moral panic has echoed through the media. A commentary to the *Yomiuri Shinbun* (August 9, 2002), for example, compared the decline of children's physical strength to a 'reflection of the decline of Japanese society'. It seemed that during the so-called 'lost decade' of the 1990s, when Japan's industries lost much of their competitiveness, its financial system went haywire and the political establishment failed to solve the mounting social, political and economic problems, the nation also lost its children's physical strength. In 2009 the *Asahi Shinbun* (January 22) reported on interpretations of the continuing decline that saw a direct association, if not correlation, between physical strength and intellectual performance.

There is one more reason left to feel concerned. The SSF surveys suggest that the preliminary goal of the Japanese government of achieving a sport participation level of 50 per cent of all adults doing sport at least once a week seems to have been realized within the first five years of the Basic Plan. However, in its mid-term revision of the Basic Plan,[5] the Ministry of Education quoted a lower participation rate of 38.5 per cent, which was based on the governmental opinion survey on physical strength from 2004 (Naikaku-fu 2004b). Given that in 2004 only one out of six adults was fulfilling the appropriate training schedule regarded as necessary for gaining health benefits ('active sport population'), the results achieved so far are far below the level ultimately desired by the Ministry. Progress is also wanting in the case of the establishment of comprehensive community sport clubs. According to the mid-term revision, the goal of opening at least one such sport club in all cities, towns and villages until 2010 was realized only in 33 per cent of all designated districts: At halftime, a total of 2,155 clubs were registered in 783 municipalities (Naikaku-fu 2006:79). Hence the majority of local communities still were lacking a single community-type sport club, while progress in new establishments cooled down. Particularly smaller and rural municipalities were struggling to fulfil their task. Research on the implementation of central government health politics at the local level indicates that the progress of the establishment of Healthy Japan 21 programmes in rural and small communities was lagging far behind the results metropolitan and large municipalities had achieved so far (Katanoda, Hirota and Matsumura 2005). Of course, stagnancy and delay may have also been due to slack demand since just 10 per cent of adults have enrolled in such a public sport club. Opinion polls usually yield results depicting strong interest in sport club membership. But the total share of club enrolment (public and private combined) among Japanese adults (2004: 19.2 per cent) did not change at all over the past 12 years. That indicates that the number of sport club members increased with the same speed as the overall expansion of sport participation and the ratio of non-affiliated sport participants. Asked for the reason why people abstained from joining a club, most answered because of time constraints, financial concerns and the lack of sport buddies (SSF 2004:42).

Hence poor public funding and lack of other resources are very likely to have been a major cause for the slow progress. Public expenditure in general has been drastically curtailed in recent years. In the case of sport, despite all promotional programmes, sport-related spending by the central government shrank from JPY 453 billion in the peak year of 1996 to JPY 269 billion in 2005 (Shibuya 2005).[6] Funding dedicated explicitly to mass sport promotion has fallen from JPY 3.3 billion in 2002 to 166 million in 2005. This decrease has been largely caused by the dramatic loss of income generated from public gambling. Revenues from *keirin* (cycling races) and horse racing to the Japan Amateur Sports Association went down from JPY 760 million in 1998 to 315 million in 2004. A severe shock for the Basic Plan has been the lukewarm reception of the new football lottery *toto*, which the Ministry of Education particularly created for the purpose of financing public sport.

The decrease in revenues for the promotion of public sport is a potential threat to the prospects of the lifelong sport society. Data from the national household survey (*kakei chōsa*; see STK 2000, 2005) clearly indicate that the willingness—or capability—to spend on sport has decreased in general during the long recession and particularly among lower-income groups. Their sport budget comprises an increasingly smaller share of total household spending than the sport budget of higher-income groups, and the gap has been widening. Disposable income also correlates strongly with active sport involvement. The 2001 Survey on Time Use and Leisure Activities (STK 2001) reveals that higher-income groups have higher participation rates and spend in average more time on sport per day than lower-income groups. Hence public sport supply fulfils the important task of securing the less wealthy against the deprivation of equal health chances (concerning the downgrading effect of socioeconomic disadvantages on health expectancy and longevity of older Japanese in urban areas, cf. Fukuda, Nakamura and Takano 2005).

But the central government seems to be torn between contemporary financial constraints and public interventions for the sake of future benefits. Shifting the responsibility for health and physical fitness to local communities and ultimately to the individual is a notable concession to the lurking spirit of neoliberalism which has left its impact on Japan's sport politics since the late 1980s (Uchiumi 2005:220). Sport and health promotion politics nowadays are characterized by a previously unknown style of accountability and controllability expressed by the numerical targets for action by public bodies as well as physical bodies. The meaning of sport, in the context of public management, has expanded; it still is a disciplinary tool, a business and a source of individual pleasure, and now also an instrument of social engineering. The biological component certainly is still of importance for determining who are the old. But social components, crafted by the individual in their interactions with the social world, mediated through the body and linked to sociability, autonomy and self-perception, are increasingly gaining in significance for the new old. In the culture of accountability, aging is not a natural process but something that can and should be managed. Recent developments in the field of health politics have delivered a very similar message. The introduction of the Special Health Check-Up in 2009 signalled a major shift in Japan's health policy away from a high-risk approach to a population approach based on the epidemiological probability of contracting a disease. Far from being an objective risk, obesity emerged within the government's approach to health monitoring as a social construct and a major apparatus of neoliberal politics through which individuals were encouraged to engage in self-regulation. The next chapter will place the Japanese government's new concern with mapping obesity into its long-standing interest in surveying the national physique and sociological debates on risk in late modernity.

7 Health, Lifestyle Risks and the Japanese Obesity Crisis[1]

INTRODUCTION

The body has taken on a central role in many of the emergent debates about managing life risks in late modern society. Individuals are increasingly expected to take responsibility for the care of their health and to monitor the state of their body. 'Health work', consisting of a balanced diet, regular fitness activities, proper sleep and medical check-ups, is seen as crucial, if not essential, for good citizenship, particularly in societies under neoliberal rule that champion individual freedom against collective responsibilities and therefore propagate voluntary self-discipline rather than state interventions. The body itself is the primary means of communicating biological states of health and illness, or moral qualities of appropriate and inappropriate, both to the individual concerned and to other bodies. However, and this is of utmost importance for the following discussion, such messages are far from being matter-of-fact or value-neutral. The meaning and implications of body messages emanating, for example, from a straight back, accurately angled knees, a slack handshake, a courteous bow or the bulky frame of a yukata-clad sumo wrestler; the slim silhouette of a styled aesthetician; and the nimbus of bodies in uniform are deeply interwoven in a complex web of cultural and social relations. Fine arts, consumption habits, education, communal life and political economy are most noteworthy among the institutions through which the powers of society act upon the human body and its regulation.

Within the dialectics of modernity, bodies in varying manifestations of size, aesthetics, agility, purity or ethnic origin have been utilized as markers for conditions and qualities encompassing young–old, healthy–unhealthy, productive–non-productive, fit–unfit, useful–useless, capable–incapable and desired–despised, to name but a few. Since the body is the interface between self and society, such markers continue to be powerful points of reference wielded by discursive regimes to demand reflection, adjustment and discipline from each and every body. Bodies are constantly targeted, measured, assessed, categorized and evaluated in accordance with the dominant discourses of the time by the institutional powers that represent governments and laws, the disciplinary power at work in economic relations and the discretionary power displayed by consumption habits and media representation. Hence, a great variety of agents and institutions, from both private and public sectors at different levels of national, international and local governance, are involved in the political process of mapping bodies and defining hazards to physical health.

The corpulent body is a prominent case in point. Traditional societies knew about the impact of nutrition on the state of well-being, but they were not concerned with the medicalization of obesity. For the greater part of human history, mankind has rated the peril of malnutrition as the more pressing problem—a problem which, seen globally, has remained unsolved until today. In contrast to the emaciated and severely undernourished bodies signalling the imminent threat of starvation, overweight and massive bodies were hardly ever seen as seriously jeopardized. Occasionally they were ridiculed or even bullied by contemporaries, but stout and bulky body frames were more often appreciated as status markers of wealth and well-being.[2] It is only in recent decades that (excessive) overweight has been labelled as a terrifying threat of pandemic proportions by medical specialists, dietarians, politicians and health insurers alike. Obesity, or adiposis (synonym medical terms for the condition of excess body fat accumulating to a degree that may adversely affect health), is perceived today to be one of the most pressing health issues faced by society. This assessment is caused by epiphenomena of obesity ranging from premature death to severe chronic diseases that curtail the overall quality of life. Obesity-related illnesses include cardiovascular and diet-related chronic diseases such as type 2 diabetes, hypertension and stroke and some forms of cancer, which are the most common serious chronic diseases in industrialized countries. Alerted by these interdependencies, the World Health Organization (WHO) warns of 'globesity', a globally emerging phenomenon of obesity that affects the lives of more than one billion adults and children today—not just in industrialized countries, but also in emerging nations and, to an alarming degree, in developing countries.

According to the WHO online database, Japan is among those countries blessed with a very low ratio of obese (3.1 per cent) and overweight adults (23.4 per cent). These comforting data are based on results from the 2004 National Health and Nutrition Survey (*Heisei 16-nen kokumin kenkō eiyō chōsa*; see MHLW 2007) and are in remarkable contrast to the startling numbers that signalled the emergence of a Japanese obesity crisis shortly thereafter. In numerous newspaper articles, government reports and publicized statements from medical associations, every second male and one out of five women in this country were identified as seriously threatened by the risk of being overweight. These alarming figures made headlines in connection with the controversial Special Health Check-Up (*tokutei kenkō shinsa*) enacted by the Japanese government in April 2008. The exceptionally large-scale project, targeting 57 million adults 40 to 74 years of age, or roughly 45 per cent of Japan's total population, has been popularized as *metabo kenshin* (*metabo* health check-up). As the nickname indicates—*metabo* is short for metabolic syndrome, a medical term referring to a cluster of well-known heart disease risk factors—the new health promotion strategy focuses on the metabolism of the body, weight conditions and lifestyle habits in order to counteract what the International Diabetes Federation dubbed in 2001 'the cardiovascular disease time bomb'.

However, the nationwide physical examination which is at the centre of the national combat against obesity is not just a continuation of the Japanese central government's long-standing interest in surveying the national physical body, but rather a response to larger transformations reaching far beyond health policy and the organizational logic of health care. Over the past two decades, Japan's economy has struggled with unprecedented difficulties in adjusting to global change, worsening labour market conditions, a dysfunctional financial sector suffering from huge bad loans, hapless monetary politics, mushrooming public debt and price deflation, all the while limping along at a very slow growth rate. In its attempt to respond to these crises, the state increasingly employed the core strategies of neoliberal rule: privatization, deregulation and liberalization. In this chapter I will place the government's newly emerged concern with mapping adipose bodies into the context of sociological debates on risk, reflexivity and governance in late modernity. In doing so, I will focus on four major issues emanating from the risk society theory and the governmentality perspective on risk: the notion that risk is a pervasive concept shaping social life in late modernity; the fabricated nature of risk in contemporary society; the significance of risk for contemporary forms of governance; and the interrelation of risks and the individualization process. As I will show, Japan's obesity crisis is as much a consequence of social change as it is a social construction and a continuous point of contention. My argument is based principally upon primary sources distributed by the Ministry of Health, Labour and Welfare; academic and popular secondary sources on health promotion; media accounts; and records of Diet sessions and parliamentary committee meetings retrieved from the Online Database of Proceedings on the National Diet of Japan (*Kokkai kaigiroku kensaku shisutemu*). This chapter continues with a short introduction to the main precepts of the sociology of risk, focusing on the particular directions or schools that are usually associated with reflexive sociology and the governmentality perspective. The next section presents an overview of the anthropometric tradition in Japan's health policy, followed by two sections which detail some of the long-term changes in the average Japanese physique. The empirical case study outlines the making of the obesity crisis, its major actors and their interests, and analyses its ramifications for contemporary forms of governance and the changing relationship between state and society in late modern Japan. Throughout the final discussion, I will also examine the degree to which the current debate on health and obesity in Japan has been tainted by neoliberal politics.

HAZARDS, RISKS AND THE RISK SOCIETY[3]

In his book *Risk Society,* written more than 20 years ago, the sociologist Ulrich Beck (1986) proposed an alternative means of theorizing modernization. He focused his analysis on the production of 'social bads', in contrast to the proliferation of 'social goods', which was at the centre of most social theories on progress and development in modern society. For theorists like Marx, Weber or Habermas and their Hegelian worldview, social history was powered by struggles over the entitlement to the labour surplus. The call for a fair or at least appropriate redistribution of wealth was at the core of socialist dreams and capitalist ideologies in which the promise of a better future legitimized present sacrifices. In the long run, technological innovations and industrialization contributed greatly towards the fulfilment of modernist aspirations. However, in Beck's perspective, secondary effects like the lurking or already materialized perils of environmental pollution, climate change, terrorist threats and other man-made catastrophes had acquired a fatal momentum of their own.

The sociologist suggested that late modern societies were faced with multiple risks accrued by human invention and political will. Risks such as the destruction of biological diversity in the rain forest, nuclear fall-out or the deglaciation of the Alps arose because of societal decisions leading to the deforestation of the Amazon, the impossibility of controlling the armories of failed states and the decades-long unwillingness to impose stricter carbon emissions thresholds upon industries and private households. Risks are not the same as hazards, which Beck acknowledges as factual; risks can potentially be constructed. Tuberculosis, for example, may become a life-threatening danger of epidemic dimensions, as it has been in the past. But knowledge regarding the transmission principles of the mycobacterium and on the curative potential of antibiotics has greatly limited the perils of the infectious disease. Hence, contracting tuberculosis has become a risk, dependant on knowledge and rational calculation. Beck argues that traditional societies were not familiar with this specific concept of risk. They accepted hazards as natural and matter-of–fact, and supernatural forces were often summoned to explain the horrors of war, plague or drought.

Modern society promised to develop the expertise for taming nature and its dangers. The residual risk, or the likelihood of an adverse occurrence against all odds, was to be rationally assessed, limited through intervention and calculated by insurers. Yet the principle of insurance, of protection against the worst case, was suspended by scientific exploration into uncontrollable terrain, such as nuclear and genetic technologies, coupled with capitalist greed and politics with no accountability. When the illusions of scientific neutrality, engineers being in charge of control and rational decision making were debunked at the end of the 20th century, modernity was confronted with itself, with the negative consequences as the reverse face of its achievements. The threats of the risk society have acquired dimensions so immense that no class or status group is ultimately privileged enough to be protected from their effects. When class consciousness is replaced by the common awareness of living in a risk environment, class struggles are displaced by uncertainty as a catalyst of major social transformation.

Reflexivity is a prominent feature of the later period of modernity, designating the risk and inevitable occurrence of unexpected and unscheduled threats as a collateral of arrogance and over-confidence in the wonders of technological progress. For the sociologist Giddens (1990), reflexivity is a trait particular to post-traditional society with which individuals respond to the loss of the certainty once established by customs, traditions and superstitions. By the end of the 20th century, social structures had lost much of their determinative power; yet freedom from social control also implies the loss of assurance. As a consequence of the individualization process, individuals perceive their selves and their relationships as requiring constant improvement and work; they are increasingly compelled to make decisions on their own. Self-making is no longer a collective but an individual action. Being confronted with multiple risks, they are forced to seek information on the options available to enable them to take personal responsibility for their private lives and the broader consequences of modernity. Experts are of crucial significance for assessing threats, informing state politics and devising guidelines for appropriate risk avoidance strategies. In line with the predicaments of modern rationality, these experts conceive of risks as factual, calculable and ultimately manageable. Expert knowledge is providing the norms or benchmarks whereby individuals and individual behaviour are assessed, categorized and put into comparative positions.

Yet it is one of the paradoxes of a risk society that the proliferation of knowledge undermines trust in expert knowledge and in the political institutions in charge of implementing societal decisions. As Foucault and his followers have demonstrated, knowledge is contingent on power, and risk strategies therefore are subjected to the negotiation of truths. The Foucauldian governmentality perspective on risk echoes the sociologists' understanding of risk as a central concept emerging from the modernization process. While the latter are focusing their analysis on the interconnectivity of the emergence of risk and broader macro-social trends such as modernization and globalization, writers in the Foucauldian tradition attend to the way governments are strategically employing knowledge in general and risk discourses in particular as a disciplinary power. Hence instead of analysing risk as an unwanted but unavoidable after-effect in the backwash of modernity, they are interested in deconstructing the functionality of risk discourses for the maintenance of the social order. Lupton (2006a:87) suggests that in terms of the governmentality approach, 'risk may be understood as a regulatory power by which populations and individuals are monitored and managed through the goals of neo-liberalism'.

Foucault argued that modern societies replaced overtly oppressive forms of regulation with softened and more subtle forms of disciplinary power which encourage individuals to submit to certain norms and adopt appropriate forms of behaviour voluntarily. As knowing how to act properly is assumed to be a prerequisite for 'good citizenship', power and knowledge directly imply each other. A dense network of institutions and apparatuses is concerned with the construction, proliferation and mediation of knowledges that govern social life; give meaning to social institutions; and provide the basis on which power relations are constituted. Risk, however, is detrimental to the social order. The responsibility for adjusting to an environment of 'known unknowns' and 'unknown knowns' has been diverted away from collectives and organizations and displaced upon the individual, particularly with the ascendance of neoliberal governments and the post-Keynesian political economy.

Neoliberal governmentality presumes that the macro-technologies, by which states exert power upon populations, equally enable the state to govern individuals 'at a distance,' as individuals translate and incorporate the rationalities of political rule into their own micro-technologies for conducting themselves (Binkley 2007). While risk discourses on the surface are often highly committed to rationality and scientism, many if not all are actually tainted by moral underpinnings: Risk avoidance is conceived as a moral enterprise relating to issues of self-control, self-knowledge and self-improvement. Individuals that fail to comply with the norms run the risk of being stigmatized or even ostracized. In order to avoid moral condemnation, they are prone to adjust their behaviour and employ the necessary strategies of self-control and self-regulation (Lupton 2006b). As 'good citizens', they are willing to exercise and stop smoking in order to avoid the risk of poor health. Public health is no longer taken as the domain of the welfare state and understood as a policy problem. Instead, individuals are summoned to minimize the risks of getting sick by adopting routines and rationalities aimed at the cultivation of the correct disposition in their regular behaviour (Binkley 2009:95).

Views on health and illness serve as a fine case study to illustrate the shifting of socially constructed perspectives on health within the modernization process. Within societies, different layers of knowledge have accumulated over the ages to constitute respective images of the body, its working and its malfunctions at different times. Our understanding of the world also forms our understanding of health and illness, meaning that these are inevitable social constructs that depend on a privileged form of knowledge, recognized expertise and commonly accepted standards. Traditional societies linked physical harm with destiny, divine will or magic spells; convalescence was often sought after with the assistance of supernatural powers. In modern society, Western medical knowledge has become the most powerful repository for explaining the well-being or malfunctioning of bodies. Yet, despite the progress achieved during the long process from early anatomical experiments to the deciphering of the human genome, knowledge about the biochemical conditions of physical health, not to mention mental health, is still limited, of a preliminary nature, compartmentalized at best and therefore contested. Many of the most pressing threats to health have now been linked to the unintended consequences of technological development and human interventions. Within this environment of risk, maintaining health and fitness has become the task of each individual, even though the proper way to realize this goal, or even the boundary between healthy and unhealthy, still remains uncertain.

THE ANTHROPOMETRIC TRADITION

The instrumental use of experts and expert knowledges in managing and monitoring the Japanese people refers back to a well-established tradition of rule by bureaucratic rationality and numbers fetishism closely associated with anthropometric surveys. The Japanese state has been a leading principal and agent in the production of knowledge about national health and population quality since the late 19th century. Harsh living conditions among poor farming and urban proletariat populations endangered the success of the modernization project, which maintained a constant demand for fertile, productive and martial bodies. The politico-economic objective of increasing the population, especially the workforce and the military, as well as new knowledge based on Western medicine about germs and transmission paths of infectious diseases were powerful incentives for the government to conduct a large-scale survey of the health and physical condition of the Japanese people. Initial experiments were conducted on behalf of the Physical Education Training College (Taisō Denshūsho) as early as 1878. These experiments focused on mapping the body and its functions in order to validate the effectiveness of different physical exercise training methods. In 1888, the vitality survey (*katsuryoku chōsa*), which measured height, weight, chest girth, grip power, physical strength, lung capacity and eyesight, was carried out in all educational institutions under direct control of the central government (Yamamoto 1999:33–34). A revision was implemented by the Ministry of Education in 1897; the 'ordinance concerning the physical examination of students and pupils' (Gakusei seito shintai kensa kitei, 1898) made the annual heath examination mandatory in all schools. From 1900 to the present, Japan's schoolchildren and students have been measured and weighed every spring and the records noted on a personal spreadsheet kept in the school archive.

In postwar Japan, Article 13 of the School Health Law (Gakkō hoken hō, 1958; revised in 2008 School Health and Safety Law, Gakkō hoken anzen hō) mandates that schools conduct annual health examinations of students and teachers (*kenkō shindan*). The focus of the exam has changed slightly but still emphasizes the need to prevent the spread of communicable disease and the early detection of physical deficiencies. Therefore, the records continue to document body height, weight and proportions as well as the state of nutrition among all age groups. The government's continued interest in mapping the physique of the nation was also manifested in the Nutrition Improvement Law (Eiyō kaizen hō) enacted in 1952. Fifty years after the enactment, this law was replaced in 2002 by the Health Promotion Act (Kenkō zōshin hō). As in the past, the law stipulates a National Health and Nutrition Survey (*kokumin kenkō eiyō chōsa*), which registers anthropometric data such as height and weight together with data on nutritional habits, lifestyle and biomedical phenomena, including blood pressure, blood biomarkers and medication. This survey uses a randomly selected sample of approximately 5,000 households and 15,000 individuals from 300 separate locations to chart the health of the nation.

A second set of data on the state of the young body was added in the aftermath of the 1964 Tokyo Olympics, when the immediate confrontation of athletic bodies from Japan and abroad spurred the Ministry of Education's ambitions of raising the athletic performance of Japan's youth as well as the country's Olympic medal output. The Annual Survey of Physical Fitness and Athletic Ability (*tairyoku undō nōryoku chōsa*) was implemented in 1964 for fifth and sixth grade elementary schoolchildren. In 1967, the survey was extended to include junior high school students and adults up to the age of 29, and a physical fitness test for adults of 30 to 60 years of age was added (Noi and Masaki 2002:148). Since the 1980s, the survey has also covered the younger grades of elementary school. In addition to the basic parameters of body composition, the survey gathers data on muscle strength in the trunk and limbs as well as on speed, endurance and coordination in athletic competition. In contrast to the census model of school health examinations, the fitness tests are based on a random sample of up to 70,000 children and adults.

Other early surveys charting the national body were authored on behalf of the conscription army and bureaucrats in charge of labour conditions before 1945. Draft examination data provide quite an accurate impression of the physical health of young males aged 20 for the period between the declaration of the Conscription Act (Chōhei rei, January 1873) and the end of World War II in 1945. After the passage of the Factory Act (Kōjō hō) in 1911, employers of large enterprises, such as the spinning mills or coal mines, were occasionally summoned to conduct health surveys of their workforce (Mosk 1996). With the enactment of the Labour Safety and Health Law (Rōdō anzen eisei hō, article 66) in 1972, annual health examinations became mandatory for all regular employees. As with the health check-ups in schools, the law was intended to regulate workplace sanitation and the physical well-being of workers in general. Therefore, the checklist emphasizes work-related health problems as well as the surveillance of the biological consequences of the aging process.

In the 1960s, general health examinations for the senior population were introduced which aimed at countering some of the medical problems related to demographic change. A decade earlier, some medical experts had already begun to advocate comprehensive health screenings for all adults. This particular procedure has been nicknamed *ningen dokku* (literally human dockyard) because it conveniently offers a battery of standard medical tests in one single visit. Nowadays, the Ningen Dokku Gakkai, a medical association promoting health screenings and certifying clinics and hospitals, recommends this examination for adults 20 years and older. Insurance companies usually refuse to wholly accept expenses, based on the grounds that most of the tests are identical with the health check-ups offered to students, employees and their family members. However, due to a general shift towards preventive medical care, insurers have started offering partial compensation for adults within certain age groups, particularly at five-year intervals after the age of 40. Initiatives like the 1978 First National Movement for Health Promotion, which was succeeded by the Active 80 Health Plan in 1988, laid the infrastructure for health promotion activities and municipal health centres became the focal point for health check-ups at the community level. Revisions of the Health and Medical Welfare Law for the Elderly (Rōjin hoken hō, 1982) also encouraged middle-aged Japanese to undergo basic health check-ups (*kihon kenkō shinsa*) on a regular basis. After the most recent revision of health and medical care laws in 2007, adults 40 years of age and older are more aggressively encouraged to participate in the 'special health examination' (*tokutei kenshin*). The largest part of expenses is covered by insurance companies, employers or local governments. Some cities, like Ōsaka or Saitama, who are in charge of administering the local needs of the National Health Insurance (*kokumin kenkō hoken*), and some insurance companies provide the service for free to their residents and clients; others charge a small fee of approximately 500 to 3,000 yen. The exact amount of the required co-payment depends on the type of insurance held, place of residence, income, age and range of medical tests. Private clinics and hospitals also offer equivalent health examinations for a fee of about 6,500 yen. Insurers are required to enter results in a government-designated Excel file, keep the records and supply them for statistical purposes upon request.

THE NATIONAL BODY IN NUMBERS

Demographic data indicate that in terms of population management, the state of Japan's modernization project has been more than successful. Over the past century, Japan's population increased from slightly more than 50 million to over 125 million. The Japanese government successfully lowered the national infant mortality rate from 160 per 1,000 births in 1910 to 2.3 per 1,000 in 2006. Improvements in hygiene and medical standards were significant factors in the extension of average life expectancy from less than 50 years of age in prewar Japan to 82 years by 2007. However, economic prosperity, technological progress and the development of mass media and communication technologies not only impacted population growth and longevity; they also sparked changes in lifestyle, values, attitudes and behaviour. The affluence of the mass consumer society, a Westernized diet and the habituation of sedentary lifestyles left their mark scattered across the human body. Survey data illustrate that over the past century, Japanese bodies have become taller and heavier—though not necessarily stronger, a fact clearly shown by developments charted in the Physical Fitness and Athletic Ability Tests carried out since the 1980s (Noi and Masaki 2002; MEXT 2007).

Historical surveys and international comparisons of industrialized and developing countries have demonstrated a high degree of correlation between stature and standard of living (Komlos 1994; Steckel 1997). Anthropometric history suggests understanding height as a biological proxy for factors such as the state of health care, the quality of nutrition and the level of income distribution, which all contribute to the standard of living. This connection will come as no surprise to anthropologists, who have been examining the impact of the environment on body size since Franz Boas's classical study *Changes in the Bodily Form of Descendants of Immigrants* from 1911 (Degler 1989). Based on anthropometric surveys of thousands of migrants from various parts of Europe to the US, the founder of American anthropology argued in favour of the shaping influence of culture and refuted the predominant beliefs of his contemporaries about race and racial heredity. Notwithstanding widespread doubt regarding the scientific framework of Boas's study, there remains ample evidence to show that genetic differences account for variations within populations while variations between populations tend to decrease with equal levels of socioeconomic development.

A comparison of American and Japanese data supports this general observation. At the end of the 19th century, the average American male stood at about 170 cm, towering above the average Japanese. While Japanese males averaged about 155 cm, women were approximately 10 cm smaller in size. The height of both sexes was virtually unchanged from their Muromachi era ancestors in the 16th century (Komiya 1997:2). However, only a century later, the difference between Americans and Japanese has shrunk to a third of what it previously was. While the stature of Americans seems to have stagnated at 175 cm in recent decades (Steckel 1997:1919), the Japanese continued to grow. This is particularly true for the latter half of the 20th century, when average heights of 171.9 cm for men and 158.4 cm for women were reached in 2006 (MHLW 2007). Earlier research has focused on the link between increased height during the former half of the 20th century and the supply and quality of health services and nutrition (Mosk 1996), and income development (Bassino 2006). However, a comparison of pre- and postwar human growth suggests that caloric intake and the composition of food is probably of even greater significance. The average height of males in their 20s increased by approximately 0.9 cm per decade between 1896 (156.7 cm) and 1937 (160.3 cm; see Shay 1994), and stagnated until the end of the immediate postwar period. Statures then began to increase at a faster pace, roughly 2 cm per decade, until well into the beginning of the 21st century—most probably due to the increased animal protein intake of Western-style cuisine.

Changes in nutrition and lifestyle are also reflected by body proportions and the composition of body parts. For example, while Asian people in general tend to have relatively short legs in comparison to torso length, changes throughout the 20th century showed a trend towards European physical proportions. In 1930, an 18-year-old Japanese reached a height of 162.9 cm while standing and 88.9 cm while sitting; in 1960, standing height was 167.7 cm and sitting height 90.3 cm; in 2000 the respective values were 170.8 cm and 91.3 cm. The difference between total length and trunk length changed from 74 to 77.4 and 79.5 cm (Mosk 1996:20; MIC, Statistics Bureau 2008:671). Satisfactory explanations for this change are still wanting, although there are voices mentioning everything from co-evolution (Mosk 1996), the impact of Western furniture and a decreased need for leg strength due to changes in the labour market (Arai, Naito und Morita 1988:12–13). A second change refers to the proportion of fat tissue to overall weight, which has also increased, particularly during the second half of the 20th century (Komiya 1997:6).

BMI, WAIST CIRCUMFERENCE AND LIFESTYLE-RELATED DISEASES

In fact, over the course of the life spans of consecutive generations, changes in nutrition and dietary habits had a much more profound impact on weight than on height, at least for Japanese males. During the first half of the 20th century, members of both sexes in their 20s had seen average weights rising by 3.7 kg for men and 3.3 kg for women. After 1950, women only gained 1.3 kg more, reaching 51.7 kg by 2006, whereas a man's average weight rose from 55 kg to 67.4 kg during the same period (Komiya 1997; MIC, Statistics Bureau 2008:672). This gender-specific difference is particularly pronounced because of a countertrend sustained by younger women. For the past half century, women under the age of 40 have recorded decreasing body mass index (BMI) values. The BMI index is commonly used in identifying overweight and adiposity in adult populations and is defined as the weight in kilograms divided by the square of the height in meters (kg/m2). According to a study of young Japanese women, this index is regarded as the most important factor for the self-appreciation of body weight (Tanaka, Itō and Hattori 2002), even though it is sharply criticized for its inaccuracy: Because of the high correlation of muscle mass to fat mass, athletes are often classified as overweight, while others with above-average fattiness are identified as having a normal weight. Since one out of two young women are reported to have unsuccessfully and repeatedly dieted, the BMI curve powerfully illustrates the devastating impact of media and peer groups defining slimness as a cultural norm and common desirable objective.

Despite their rapid increase in body weight, Japanese men fare pretty well in direct comparison with other nations. The overwhelmingly positive weight-to-height ratio is attested to by the low body mass index values recorded by Japanese adults. According to the WHO in 2005, men (23.7) and women (21.8) scored mean values well below the critical cut-off point of 25, which defines overweight. Obesity is defined as a BMI equal to or more than 30. Notwithstanding the positive ranking placing Japanese men and women well ahead of other OECD nations like the US, the United Kingdom, France and Germany, there is still some reason for unease and concern. First, according to the WHO (2002:60), there is evidence that risk of chronic disease in populations increases progressively from a BMI of 21, which is below most national averages, including Japan's. Second, these mean values should be seen foremost as a benchmark for quick assessment—they neither inform the individual about his or her personal state of health nor accurately map the exposure of populations to the most critical medical challenges of the 21st century. Third, other measures such as the waist-hip-ratio (WHR) or the circumference of the waist, which have been proven by medical sources to be more reliable predictors of individual susceptibility for the diseases and physical malfunctions prompted by changed lifestyles patterns, are attesting to a less benign state of health in Japan, particularly for Japanese men (Komiya 1997; Matsuzawa 2006).

Over the past two decades, medical experts in Japan have become aware of the annual growth rates of patients suffering from diabetes, hypertension, hyperlipidemia, coronary diseases and cerebral apoplexy and the deaths caused by these diseases. Traditionally, these diseases were grouped as 'adult disease' (*seijinbyō*) because of their prevailing occurrence among adults and the elderly. In 1996, following a proposal by the Council on Public Health, the term was replaced by the new expression 'lifestyle-related disease' (*seikatsu shūkan byō*) because, instead of age and maturity, lifestyle habits such as diet, exercise, smoking and drinking were identified as the major source of their symptomatic appearance and progression. Statistical surveys, such as the National Health and Nutrition Survey, demonstrated the correlation between excessive body weight and diabetes, which the Annual Report on Health and Welfare 1998–1999 identified as one of the most serious health problems—possibly affecting up to one out of seven adults in Japan. Alarmed by the concomitant annual increases in national health expenditure, the government initiated a task force of experts and officials to redraft the national health plan for the first decade of the 21st century. For nearly two years, the task force discussed policies and action plans to cope with new financial and medical challenges. Dubbed *Kenkō Nihon 21* (Healthy Japan 21), the new framework emphasized 'primary prevention', including the promotion of healthy living, prevention of incidence and coordination of the various implementing bodies, thereby replacing traditional efforts that prioritized 'secondary prevention' aimed at early detection followed by early treatment. Based on these principles, 70 specific goals were established in nine focus areas, of which the first six are related to lifestyle and the remaining three to disease: (1) nutrition and diet, (2) physical activity and exercise, (3) rest and mental health, (4) tobacco, (5) alcohol, (6) dental health, (7) diabetes, (8) cardiovascular diseases and (9) cancer (Sakurai 2003). As in the case of the Basic Plan for the Promotion of Sports, which was implemented in 2000, Healthy Japan 21 took an all-encompassing look at public health in Japanese society and identified points of concern for all age groups, including the primary task of tackling obesity (WHO 2005:24).

A mid-term evaluation of the programme revealed that the increase in the proportion of obese individuals, defined as those with a BMI of 25 and above (note that the Japanese threshold is significantly lower than the BMI of 30 as suggested by the WHO), has slowed down in comparison to the 25 years prior to its enactment. The ratio of obese women aged 40 to 69 has moderately decreased from 25.2 per cent in 2000 to 24.6 per cent, approaching the level of 20 per cent targeted under the 'Healthy Japan 21' initiative. Yet for men aged 20 to 69 years, the percentage has alarmingly increased from the baseline value of 24.3 per cent in 2000 to 29.0 per cent in 2005, nearly twice as much as the target level of 15 per cent or less. The report also noted decreasing intakes of vegetables, soybeans and milk. Reflecting upon worsening trends in dietary habits, health consciousness and weight control, the interim report argued in favour of a new strategy of non-communicable disease prevention—cancer, heart disease and stroke—focusing on the control of the metabolic syndrome (Udagawa, Miyoshi and Yoshiike 2008).

JAPAN'S OBESITY PANIC AND THE METABO KENSHIN

Progress in microbiological research has shed new light on cell metabolism and thereby established a new foundation for linking virtually any lifestyle-related disease with obesity. Developments in X-ray and CT scan technology, which play a prominent role in Japan's medical care system, also helped raise awareness of the metabolic differences between subcutaneous fat tissue and visceral fat inside the abdomen, which is said to be the primary source of health anomalies (Matsuzawa 2006:9). These observations have been bolstered by epidemiological surveys that suggest the close correlation of excessive overweight and diabetes, cardiovascular disease, heart attack, stroke and certain kinds of cancer. However, since the metabolic syndrome, which literally refers to a cluster of symptoms related to abnormalities of metabolism, is no disease in the proper sense of the term, there are no symptoms specifically and exclusively associated with it. There is also no precise definition of the metabolic syndrome, and medical experts do not agree about its causes. An attempt to formulate a global consensus has been put forward by the International Diabetes Federation. Its definition acknowledges first of all the concurrence of multiple heart attack risk factors such as diabetes and raised fasting plasma glucose, abdominal obesity, high cholesterol and high blood pressure (IDF 2006:4). It is noteworthy that the official criteria for each and any of these symptoms can vary from country to country and from medical association to medical association.

In general, people are classified as suffering from metabolic syndrome if they are diagnosed with central obesity and a combination of symptoms related to insulin resistance (like diabetes mellitus) deterring the body from lowering glucose and triglyceride levels in an efficient manner. As a result of consistently high levels of insulin, glucose and triglycerides, people become more susceptible to contracting damage to the coronary and other arteries, malfunctioning of the kidneys, type 2 diabetes and blood clot formation, among other complications. The concurring diseases are putting a major burden on public health systems worldwide. In Japan, 7.4 million people are estimated to be suffering from diabetes, 31 million from high blood pressure and 30 million from hyperlipidemia, leading to 130,000 stroke-related and 50,000 heart attack-related fatalities per year (Yamamoto 2008:4). The Ministry of Health, Labour and Welfare officially states that the treatment of lifestyle-related diseases accounts for about a third of all medical spending in Japan, with rising tendencies which could amount to 2 trillion yen by 2025. 'Fighting *metabo*' thus became a convenient key for Japan's health administration to curtail exploding health care expenses.

The introduction of the '*metabo* health check-up' constituted a major shift in Japan's health policy away from a high-risk approach focusing on people who fell seriously ill, to a population approach based on the epidemiological probability of contracting a disease. Starting in April 2008, the Ministry of Health, Labour and Welfare began requiring insurers to screen all their members aged 40 to 74 for metabolic syndrome and provide subsequent health counselling for those identified as being overweight or suffering from a combination of coronary risk factors or prone to developing the metabolic syndrome in the future. With the exception of waistline measurement, the newly proscribed 'Special Health Check-Up' (*tokutei kenshin*) basically followed outline and content of the general health examination (*kihon kenshin, jūmin kenshin*) previously provided either by employer-based health insurers or the National Health Insurance. Yet, because the waistline measurement gained prominent coverage in media reports on the introduction of the new public health programme, the medical examination was instantly dubbed as *metabo kenshin* (an abbreviation of *metaborikku shōkōkun kenkō shinsa*). According to the guidelines adopted by the Ministry of Health, Labour and Welfare in April 2007, any man with a waistline circumference of 85 cm or more and women with 90 cm or more were categorized as *metabo* if they had any combination of the following factors:

high blood sugar levels, high blood pressure, high levels of lipid and current smoking record.[4] People with a narrower waistline but a BMI of over 25 combined with a combination of three risk factors were also categorized as *metabo*, requiring immediate intervention (*sekkyokuteki shien*). The acute support programme consists of consultations with health specialists, establishing diet plans and exercise programmes and follow-up sessions to monitor progress over a period of six months. Motivating support (*dōkizuke shien*) was made mandatory for the so-called '*metabo* standby' (*metabo yobigun*), which includes all those who failed the waistline criterion but recorded metabolic abnormalities in only one field (Yamamoto 2008:5). Pre-emptive measures including early identification of risk, a balanced diet, healthy lifestyle habits and regular physical exercise hence became the key to controlling the obesity epidemic.

During the first year following the implementation of the revised Act on Assurance of Medical Care for Elderly People (Kōreisha no iryō no kakuho ni kansuru hōritsu) in 2008, about 57 million middle-aged and older adults were summoned to a health check-up, either by their employer or the local government. National law actually does not oblige individuals to participate in the examination, since it is assumed that without voluntary consent changes in diet, exercise habits or quitting smoking are rather unlikely to occur (Yamamoto 2008:5). Instead, a stick-and-carrot system targeting the insurers is used. Their contribution to the newly established health care fund for the old-old-aged (75 years and older), which will provide health care for the senior elderly of 75 and more years of age from 2012 on, has been set at a preliminary value of 40 per cent. Yet, depending on the reach and ultimately the results of their health programmes, the government may either reduce or increase its own subsidies by 10 per cent. If insurers fail to reach targets, they would face additional burdens and would be compelled to collect additional premiums to fund the new scheme. Three parameters will be used in evaluating success or failure: the percentage of insurants participating in the annual health examination, the percentage of counselling successfully completed for those in need and the overall impact on the reduction of the metabolic syndrome (Yamamoto 2008:6). To avoid financial penalties, insurers are inclined to reach as many of their clients as possible. According to the July 2009 online newsletter by the Japan Preventive Association of Lifestyle-Related Diseases (Nihon Seikatsu Shūkanbyō Yobō Kyōkai), Kenpōren (Kenkō Hoken Kumiai), with a membership of 30 million, set their target value for 2012 at 80 per cent and the National Health Insurance (membership 36 million) at 65 per cent.

During the first year of implementation, only a fraction of insured persons followed the call. The *Nishi Nihon Shinbun* reported on July 3, 2009, that Kenpōren, the National Federation of Health Insurance Societies providing health care to companies with a workforce of 300 and more employees, succeeded in reaching 59.8 per cent of its insurants. Kyōkai Kenpo (Zenkoku Kenkō Hoken Kyōkai Rengōkai), which combines health insurance programmes for employees of small and medium enterprises, reported a result of 35.9 per cent. The quota of employer-based insurers was particularly lowered by the reluctance of co-insured family members who in the past had obtained health examinations at the municipal health centre. Under the new programme, this public service is limited to people under public health care. Of the 23.9 million persons aged 40–74 who were covered by public health care, only 6.77 million (28.3 per cent) obtained the new health check-up, according to the *Yomiuri Shinbun* from July 22, 2009. A poll by the *Mainichi Shinbun* (August 20, 2009) revealed that, in comparison to the general health examination from the previous year, screening coverage had declined in 63.7 per cent of the surveyed municipalities.

EXPERTS, EVIDENCE AND COUNTER-EVIDENCE

Opposition to the new health survey has been voiced by many of the actors involved. Insurers felt worried by the need to either employ additional medical staff, nurses and health counsellors or depend on the availability of appropriate outsourcing facilities (Nozaki 2007:279). Municipalities complained about early cancer diagnosis tests being dropped, which had previously been part of the general health examination but were now subjected to extra billing and appointment. People surveyed lamented that standards were far too strict (Shoji 2009)—in fact, Japan's waistline standards were the strictest for men worldwide. Some said they shunned the examination in order to avoid governmental interference in their living routines and dieting habits (Onishi 2008). Medical experts also questioned the validity of the data on which the definitions of the metabolic syndrome and the underlying symptoms were based. Ōgushi Yōichi, professor at the medical school at Tōkai University, was quoted by the *Yomiuri Shinbun* in October 2006 as estimating that 98 per cent of men and 92 per cent of women would be considered as being in poor health because of overly stringent definitions. Ōgushi's book *Metabo no wana* (The *metabo* Trap, 2007) argued that more than 30 million people were likely to be diagnosed with some problem at the health check-up and thereafter encouraged to go to hospital for further clarification. His claim was made on the basis of a comparison of some 50,000 medical cases who had taken all the items as prescribed by the new health check-up. In consequence of the new procedure, he predicted that medical expenses would rise by approximately 5 trillion yen per year, causing an adverse effect on public finances.

The controversy over benefits versus expenditures also fuelled a political debate on the introduction of the new health promotion scheme. In committee meetings and plenary diet sessions, opposition parties questioned the validity of threshold values applied to singular symptoms.[5] They charged the government with ignoring international standards as well as studies providing counter-evidence,[6] and they cast doubt on the usefulness of the metabolic syndrome for preventive purposes at all.[7] Based on such studies, they refuted the plausibility of the financial scenario drafted by the government,[8] and refuted its claim that the new procedures were effectively capable of curbing medical expenses.[9] The government was criticized for having used its parliamentary majority to muscle in a bill drafted by the cabinet without taking the necessary time for accurate deliberation and democratic debate.[10] During the most heated phase, prior to the ballot in the Lower House, the opposition accused the ministry of 'hyping a fabricated disease' (*metaborikku shindorōmu no kyokōsei*)[11] invented by Japan's medical doctors,[12] and of intimidating the population with unsubstantiated data on the future financial burden of public health care. According to the opposition parties, the year this bill was enacted would aptly be named 'year one of the era of health care destruction' (*iryō hōkai gannen*).[13]

After the bill passed the Lower House with a simple majority on May 18, 2006, the debate continued in the Upper House. It largely echoed topics and patterns of the earlier debate, battled out between attacking politicians from the Democratic Party, the Social Democratic Party and the Communist Party and defensive representatives from the government and the bureaucracy. A medical doctor from Kyōto University Hospital, speaking on behalf of the Democrats, disqualified the new health programme as *kanja-gari*, a hunt for patients, which exclusively benefited the pharmaceutical industry and commercial health service providers.[14] Others presented study reports from abroad to question the scientific basis of the health promotion bill;[15] uttered their concern about consequences on the quality of health care for the oldest elderly;[16] and condemned the commercialization, outsourcing and privatization of health care services.[17] Yet, due to the coalition government parties' firm majority, the bill was never endangered and passed the Upper House on June 13, 2006, only few weeks after its passage in the Lower House.

Minutes of the deliberation process reveal the degree to which political decision making has become dependent on externally hired expertise. Both the administration officials of the government and politicians from the opposition built their cases on the premises of medical competence and scientific reason. The government's definition of the metabolic syndrome followed recommendations put forth by a consortium of eight national medical associations in April 2005. For a year, representatives from professional associations concerned with arteriosclerosis, adipositas, diabetes, circulatory organ system, hypertension, nephrology, thrombosis and internal medicine had debated on setting the diagnostic symptoms and corresponding threshold values of the metabolic syndrome. The final report was published a week prior to the global consensus developed by the International Diabetes Federation (Matsuzawa 2006:4). While the symptoms comprised by the metabolic syndrome are basically identical in the Japanese definition, the IDF global consensus and a number of other definitions developed by the WHO or the National Cholesterol Education Program (US), some of the values proscribed by the Japanese consortium were remarkably different. With regard to the measurement of obesity, the IDF global consensus acknowledges genetic differences in people of different ethnic origin and therefore uses specific waistline values for people of Asian or European descent. Based on large-scale surveys of Chinese and Southeast Asian populations, the IDF values were set at 90 cm for men and 80 cm for women (IDF 2006:11). However, the Japanese definition of 85 cm for men and 90 cm for women undercut the recommendation for males and generously expanded the tolerable range for females to an extent that ultimately reversed the globally adopted practice of permitting men a higher threshold value than women. According to the head of the Department of Health Affairs at the Ministry of Health, Labour and Welfare, the domestic standard is based on evidence gained from computer scans, a screening device much more often prescribed in Japan's hospitals than in any other national health system.[18] As one advocate of the Japanese standard explained, waistline thresholds were determined as an approximation for a total fat tissue surface of 100 square centimetres. Since the visceral fat hidden inside the abdomen was of ultimate concern for the origination of the metabolic syndrome, women, who in general have a larger proportion of subcutaneous fat tissue, were conceded higher values than men (Matsuzawa 2006:10).

The critics presented epidemiological surveys, both from Japan and from abroad, that failed to show any association between the metabolic syndrome and obesity, and ultimately between obesity and mortality risks.[19] Grouping single risk factors would not necessarily create a stronger predictor but fabricate a new disease to be listed on individuals' medical records (*karute*, or *shinryōroku*).[20] Since the evidence presented by the ministry was exposed as untenable, the whole strategy was dismissed as a 'castle built on sand' (*sajō no rōkaku igai nanimono de mo nai*).[21] Yet, in a stand-off between competing truths, the ministry was less inclined to reflect on the counter-evidence provided by the opposition. Instead, its speakers routinely warded off factual questions by referring to their trust in the consortium which had assisted in drafting the bill,[22] or the matter-of-factness of controversial disputes existing within medical professions.[23] By shifting back and forth between 'what we used to know', 'what we know by now' and 'what we will know in the future', administrative officials adopted a 'truth trick' characteristic in the risk discourse (Wheatley 2005). Medical knowledge was depicted as the outcome of successive discoveries; however, the concurring struggles about disease definition were downplayed.

The debate also showed that collusion of interest was not a major ethical issue for the government. When a DPJ politician confronted the ministry with an advertisement for a commercial diabetes product that verbatim featured the major slogan of the ministry's still unpublished promotion strategy: 'first exercise, second diet, strictly no smoking, and finally medicine' (*ichi ni undō, ni ni shokuji, shikkari kinen, saigo ni kusuri*), it became evident that some of the experts serving on the ministry's advisory board were also on the payroll of pharmaceutical corporations. Ninety per cent of all medical doctors at national universities involved in the clinical testing of hypertonic or *metabo* drugs were reported to receive funding from pharmaceutical corporations.[24] Ethical concerns were not only linked to the suspicion of collusion and bias, if not corruption, but also to struggles about influence and acknowledgment within medical sciences. One of the advisors, singled out as having received more than half a billion yen of industry funding between 2000 and 2003,[25] was also identified as a regular media commentator, a core member of various medical organizations involved in curing lifestyle-related diseases and as a leading expert in fat science, who also had co-authored the global consensus. The establishment of this subfield of clinical research in fat metabolism has been actively promoted by Japanese researchers—even the name 'adiposcience' originated in Japan (Matsuzawa 2006:13). Having clinical guidelines set as strictly as possible is thus in the interest of the pharmaceutical industry as tighter threshold values would account for more prescribed medical drugs (and body fat CT scans). Medical associations would also benefit, since an increase in the numbers of persons defined as ill would demonstrate the importance of their particular agenda, research and methods of treatment, which in turn would channel more research funds into their field. For these reasons, the Japanese definition of the metabolic syndrome was critically assessed as a by-product of the *sankangaku* triangle. The close collaboration of eight medical associations generated a compromise, which was to the mutual benefit of the industry (*san*), the administration (*kan*) and the sciences (*gaku*), albeit at the expenses of the well-being of the public.[26]

RISK TALKS: THE MAKING OF AN EPIDEMIC

In terms of raising crisis awareness, the Ministry's strategy of deliberately centring its health promotion initiative on the metabolic syndrome, as the head of the Department for Health Affairs in the MHLW conceded, apparently was a full success.[27] A search of the Yomiuri Database found no mention of the term prior to 2005; hence when the parliamentary debate started in 2006, the Minister of Health, Labour and Welfare emphasized the necessity of making the term familiar to at least 80 per cent of the population.[28] Just two years later almost everyone was familiar with the term, according to a poll by the Nippon Research Council, and three out of four adults were quite well informed about the particularities of the new health check-up.[29] As early as 2007, parliamentarians were surprised that there was constant talk about *metabo, metabo*, particularly among middle-aged men.[30] Another member of the Diet marvelled about how the word had become so widespread (*seken ippan ni ninchi*),[31] and only one year later everyone, even junior high school students, was said to make frequent use of the word to a degree that it likely would be awarded the prize for the buzzword of the year.[32] In fact, a Wikipedia list of popular Japanese terms (*ryūkōgo*) featured *metaborikku shindorōmu* among the buzzwords of 2006, while *shintai kensa* (physical examination) was one of the nominees in 2007.

The media played a crucial role in disseminating the term and its abbreviated form. In 2005, eight articles in the *Yomiuri Shinbun* featured the medical term—which also made its first-ever appearance in the Proceedings on the National Diet this year on the occasion of a hearing of a nutrition specialist in front of an Upper House committee deliberating the new Basic Law for Food Education (Shokuiku kihon hō) in June 2005.[33] Over the following years, the number of *Yomiuri* newspaper articles on the metabolic syndrome rose to 89 in 2006, 192 in 2007 and 353 in 2008 (cf. Figure 7.1). A similarly increasing curve characterizes the appearance of the word in Parliament meeting minutes. The inflationary usage of the term was not sparked by the political debate alone, which reached its climax in the month of the enactment of the new Special Health Check-Up, but also by its pictorial appeal to the opposition. After the revised law on securing the health care of the elderly had passed through the Diet, metabolic syndrome and its popularized abbreviation, *metabo*, were often used in a metaphorical sense, referring either to a state of invisible crisis (e.g. *gyōsei no metaborikku-ka*, the inflation of bureaucracy),[34] or a real disaster occurring through an aggregation of various symptoms (e.g. global warming),[35] or a pretentious claim (e.g. *metabo intā*, a pun on *sumāto intā* and the purported cost-saving effect of electronic toll collecting devices on highway interchanges).[36]

In common speech, however, *metabo* soon became synonymous with *fat* (*himan*), and the new health policy became incrementally associated with weight control. Leaving questions of scientific evidence and fiscal efficiency aside, as crucial as they are in accounting for health care politics, the *metabo* check-up has left a definite impact on general health consciousness. While many deemed the threshold too low, two out of three respondents to an opinion poll on health management, conducted by the *Yomiuri Shinbun* in spring

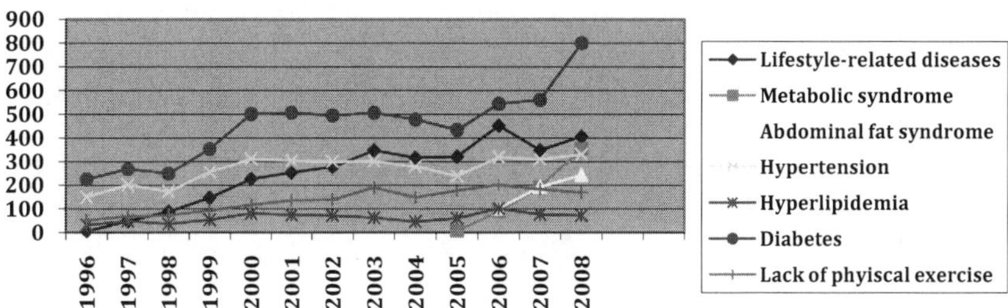

Figure 7.1 Number of health-related articles in the *Yomiuri Shinbun*, 1996–2008.
Source: Yomiuri Shinbun Database (retrieved April 10, 2009).

2008, believed that the *metabo* campaign was contributing to the improvement of the health of the Japanese people.[37] Every second respondent admitted that the *metabo* debate had given rise to concern about his or her state of health. Comparisons with previous polls showed that the portion of people who do not consciously and actively care for a healthy lifestyle had sharply declined from 26 per cent in 1981 to 22 per cent in 2001 and 17 per cent in 2008. Worries about body weight control, eating right and living healthily fuelled the growth of a market for *metabo*-related goods and services. According to the Family Income and Expenditure Survey in 2004, spending on dietary supplements had grown by 227 per cent over the previous ten years. By April 2008, more than 850 products had been acknowledged by the Ministry of Health, Labour and Welfare as Food for Specified Health Use (FOSHU, *tokutei hokenyō shokuhin*). In 2007, the market for industrially processed health food (called *tokuho*) was estimated at 680 billion yen. During the previous year, paralleling the *metabo* debate, demand for 'neutral fat' products (*chūsei shibō*) had soared with an annual growth rate of 75 per cent (JETRO 2008:1–2). According to the *Japan Food Newspaper*,[38] *metabo*-related products accounted for 229.7 billion yen in 2008, roughly 30 per cent of a *tokuho* market that was otherwise suffering from the sluggish economy and sinking sales prices. Business opportunities were not restricted to neutral fat oil or health drinks advertising the burning of hidden visceral fat. Drinking glasses or food containers with mechanized calculators for the visualization of caloric intake appeared in shops, along with pedometers to count steps and track of energy consumption and a new generation of game consoles like Nintendo's Wii brought sport games and physical exercise simulations into the living room.

CONCLUSION: HEALTH CARE RISKS, CORPORATIST WELFARE AND NEOLIBERAL POLITICS

The meaningfulness of the metabolic syndrome as a risk predictor is disputable, but the implementation of a health promotion strategy based on its presuppositions has contributed to the heightened state of crisis awareness in contemporary Japan. It is not the purpose of this chapter to evaluate the efficiency of Japan's new health promotion policy. Rather it is my intention to demonstrate how the notion of risk has pervaded the foundations of social life in late modern Japan and how the issue of fighting obesity and maintaining health has redefined the relationships between the state and society. In addition, the *metabo kenshin* serves as an excellent case study to show how late modern societies are prone to the fabrication of risks and that risk discourses are employed as a disciplinary device in neoliberal politics. Risk governance in fields beyond the competence of the politicians drafting bills and the officials administrating the law increases their dependency on experts, who are not democratically confirmed in office, and inevitably involves the risk of selecting appropriate political advisors. As the 'truth wars' on the benefits and costs of the population approach have shown, medical experts and professional interest groups, backed by the economic power of the health services and goods industry, have hijacked health politics for the accomplishment of their particular agendas. The proliferation of risk factors underlying the health prevention programme has been spurred by technological developments and advancements in medical knowledge giving birth to new medical disciplines and experts. The perpetuating process of updating professional knowledge is itself a source of uncertainty, as new knowledge and technologies introduce new areas of untamed uncertainty. If the definition of the metabolic syndrome changes, which is likely to happen, the efficacy of the new health examination and the financing of the insurance of the oldest elderly will come under even greater debate.

Epidemiology in the service of risk governance does not just indicate risks, but also produces them, and in the particular case of the metabolic syndrome, does this to such an extent that a large number of people without physical symptoms are identified either as ill or 'at risk', as they are potentially exposed to future illness. The emerging 'surveillance medicine' (Armstrong 1995) has dissolved established distinctions between ill and healthy people by rearranging the temporal cycle of contraction, illness, cure and prevention. As prevention has become the focal point of health policy, it is not the illness as such but rather the probability linked to potential risk factors that attract medical attention. Under surveillance medicine, as Armstrong (1995:400) has argued, the body is seen as a compound of predictive risk factors related to individual behaviour. In the case of the metabolic syndrome, which conflates symptoms, signs and diseases into an infinite chain of risks in which each risk factor can be understood as a risk for something else, bodies are in a permanent state of imminent crisis. When symptoms and signs are equated with a disease that only medical experts and technologies are able to detect, 'every body' becomes subjugated to the permanent threat of health risk. Anyone whose health is at risk is placed in a liminal category of wellness, being neither actually ill (yet) nor fully well. As the *metabo* health check-up records certain lifestyle habits as risk factors threatening the future financial stability of the public health care system, lifestyle choices and their consequences become visibly politicized and habitual practices turn into a field of political intervention.

Neoliberal policies emphasize the responsibility of the individual while promoting the privatization of health services and the reduction of public expenditure. Takeda (2009) described the preferred 'object/subject' of biopolitical governing under neoliberal rule as an autonomous, competent, responsible and enterprising individual who appreciates goods and services offered by professionals. 'Health-literate' (Enomoto 2003) citizens are expected to maintain command over the capacities needed to improve their health by soliciting widespread cooperation and support from various administrative bodies, private associations and commercial suppliers (Sakurai 2003:47). Self-healing, mature clients and consumer choice are key words of Japan's new health policies opening up various opportunities for profit making, as over-the-counter sales of functional health food in recent years have shown. The idea of prevention and lifestyle monitoring is, in fact, decidedly individualistic, since it draws on lifestyle choices as the source of, and solution to, personal health risks (Wheatley 2005:199). Self-motivated individuals are actively involved in managing their own health and quality of life. Individuals are held responsible for the consequences of their behaviour, which therefore needs monitoring, guidance and correction. The new health policy heralds a culture of individual accountability and rational subjectivity as the maintenance of the body becomes the sole responsibility of an emancipated individual meant to enter an entrepreneurial partnership with society. By means of a health insurance membership, individuals are incorporated into the welfare state; as entrepreneurial selves they are encouraged to maximize their own advantages by following the guidelines proscribed by the state—and perhaps enforced by the insurer. State power is mediated through the insurers, which are legally compelled to decrease the number of people with cardiac disease risks; companies may feel the temptation to use discriminating measures against overweight workers in order to reach their target numbers.

Risk is inextricably interwoven with new forms of organizational logic underlying how health care services are managed, provided and consumed (Fine 2005). As responsibility and blame are shifted to insurers and municipalities, and indirectly towards (hopefully) 'health-literate' citizens, Japan's health policies have developed the characteristics of a corporatist variant of neoliberal politics. The preventive health promotion strategy based on the metabolic syndrome establishes a 'bio-political correctness' of standardized bodies, body ideals and appropriate ways of living. The issuing of personal health records and the public circulation of target values and national averages enable the individual to reflect about progress and stagnation, or effort and slackness, and to find its place either inside or outside of the politically desired boundaries. However, effects on longevity and mortality risk are likely to remain negligible. Insofar as the indices being used to define the metabolic syndrome naturally rise with age, the health risk discourse denaturalizes aging and puts 'bio-politically incorrect' bodies under technocratic surveillance. Since the health indices, particularly waist circumference and BMI, are not capable of identifying people eating right, exercising or following healthy lifestyles, but are primarily indicators of aging, genetics and social disadvantage, they are in fact discriminatory. In Japan, neoliberal politics, albeit under the disguise of corporate welfarism, have ultimately shifted responsibility for health to the individual, whose individuality, tellingly, is completely blanked out by the population approach forming health politics.

8 The World Cup Comes to Town

Critical Investigation of the Political Economy of Sport Mega-Events[1]

INTRODUCTION: WHY INVEST IN HALLMARK SPORTING EVENTS?

This chapter ties in with the previous chapters insofar as the connection between sport infrastructure building, social politics and the rationale of contemporary policy makers is addressed once more. The case under investigation is a single one, albeit a very special and distinctive one which is outstanding because of its symbolic and material dimensions: It examines Japan's experience in hosting (half) the 2002 FIFA World Cup. In particular this case study addresses the very practical questions about the kind of benefits hosting authorities anticipated from the sport mega-event, what kind of policy and implementation measures were used to achieve the goals and how actualized outcomes matched with expectations. Drawing on macroeconomic data from official sources and a secondary analysis of an ex post survey among local bureaucrats in charge of Japan's ten World Cup cities, this case study gives fresh insight into the political economy of sport mega-events. By highlighting both the business of sport events and the politics of hosting, the chapter seeks to fulfil three objectives. First, it integrates the so far largely neglected Asian experience into social scientific debates on sport mega-events. Second, it provides evidence on the nature of the commonly purported, yet hardly ever realized economic benefits of hosting by contrasting national with regional economic indicators. Third, it illuminates the variety of motivations and aspirations causing regional authorities to bid for such actually costly endeavours. Bringing the World Cup finals to Japan (and South Korea) was part of a larger programme initiated in the late 1980s by the Japan Football Association in cooperation with major players from the domestic political scene and the global 'sport industrial complex'. For FIFA and its corporate partners, the general aim of popularizing football in Japan and the broader Asian region meant getting a foot into a largely underdeveloped market on the continent with the largest population share and the most dynamic economic growth rates (Manzenreiter and Horne 2007). For the local politicians, the World Cup was a welcome opportunity to put the names of their cities onto the map.

The FIFA 2002 Football World Cup then was the first to be hosted on Asian soil and by more than one single nation. It was also the first time that public discourse openly associated the world's largest single sport event with overtly mundane expectations for economic growth, place marketing and cultural promotion. Over the previous two decades, the FIFA World Cup stood mostly in the shadows of the Summer Olympic Games while these were maturing into the flagship of commercialized world sport. But the deregulation of national media markets and labour laws, together with the ongoing sophistication of global broadcasting technology and capital markets, opened access to new and sheer inexhaustible income sources for football clubs and their associates. Players, agents, national and international associations, tournament managers, sport apparel producers, media corporations and other interest brokers joined hands in turning football into big business (Sugden and Tomlinson 1998:chap. 4).

Numerous regional development studies have highlighted the significance of hallmark events and re-imaging strategies for urban growth. Cities and regions in highly developed economies increasingly operate in a global economy. Particularly in the US, and to a similar extent in European and Asian countries, too, the neoliberal advance since the 1970s triggered cuts in tax allocations and a general tendency of the central state to withdraw from regional policy. Local governments responded to the challenge of an increasingly global competition (for jobs, enterprises, tax income, etc.) by crafting new development strategies, increasing cooperation, pooling financing and establishing public–private partnerships (Andranovich, Burbank and Heying 2001). Although there is little evidence to suggest that subsidizing professional sport teams or sport events affects economic chances at all, as stated in Chapter 5, political actors in all late capitalist societies have adopted similar development strategies capitalizing on the attraction of first-class sport events. However, the distribution of revenue streams is far from being transparent, and profits are much too often unequally distributed between actors from private and public sectors.

So far research on the political economy of hosting sport events has been limited to case studies from the US, where the myth of sport as an 'urban growth machine' has been most prevalent, and Western European countries, which only recently conceded sport as a public good for the sake of commercial interests. Japan as a testing field has been largely overlooked, even though the country has its own distinctive history of sport-related development politics and hosting of large-scale sport events (Harada 2002; Manzenreiter and Horne 2005). Because Japan is woven into dynamics and structures of the global economy to no less an extent than late capitalist societies of the West, leisure- and consumption-oriented development since the 1990s has also marked the economic policy shift prompting numerous localities to invest in theme parks, marine or golf resorts, or to forge partnerships with owner companies of football teams and to present themselves eventually as potential host cities for the Football World Cup. In front of these observations I hypothesize that anticipations of economic gains and prospering have been core arguments throughout the bidding process and preparatory stage of the World Cup, while the actual economic impact has been minimal or even negative. These claims are easily verified if high-rising economic expectations played a leading role in official statements about the objectives of World Cup hosting, on the one hand, and if Japan's economic performance in the World Cup year 2002 failed to differ significantly from other years. The impact of hosting will also be questioned by a comparison of regional with national economic indicators.

HOSTING HALF THE 2002 FIFA WORLD CUP: TALKING BUSINESS

Public debates on the business of hosting sport mega-events usually fail to differentiate neatly between the costs associated with managing the event and expenditures related to the larger infrastructure. Large-scale sport arenas, which are a common basic prerequisite for host cities, usually do not burden the operational budget of organizing committees because they are either extant or, if newly built, will remain to be used by their owners for many years to come. Long-term-oriented investments into communication and transport are for the same reasons excluded from the balance, since expenditure on new airports, railroad connections and roads put strain on public households while sparing the riches of the organizing committees. Partially for this reason, the Japan World Cup Organizing Committee (JAWOC 2003) was finally able to report a surplus income of JPY 12 billion from the staging of the tournament.[2] According to the final JAWOC report (cf. Table 8.1), issued half a year after the finals, managing the World Cup cost JPY 61 billion. But in order to be a proper host nation, Japan's taxpayers subsidized the tournament by a JPY 338 billion investment in ten state-of-the-art World Cup stadiums and other infrastructure projects (Naikaku-fu 2003:42).[3] The actualized profit thus was far from matching the accumulated expenditures of JPY 570 billion or the current costs of maintaining the prestigious but oversized 'white elephants' with seating capacities exceeding average J.League demand by roughly 200 per cent (cf. Table 8.2).[4]

Even without taking the infrastructure expenditure into account, political support and public subsidies were necessary for the JAWOC budget to break even. Revenues from a FIFA grant of USD 100 million and ticket sales amounted to just 60 per cent of the foreshadowed operational costs (cf. Table 8.1).[5] News on sluggish ticket sales abroad threatened to cut up to 75 per cent of the second most important financial pillar of the JAWOC business plan (*Hōchi Shinbun*, January 29, 2002). JAWOC thus had to secure supplementary sources, such as corporate sponsorship, revenues from World Cup memorial stamp sales and national funds withdrawn from

Table 8.1 Staging (Half) the World Cup: The JAWOC Budget

Expenses (in million yen)		*Revenues (in million yen)*	
Office management JAWOC	15,422	Fifa grant	11,709
International Media Centre related	4,068	Official sponsorship	6,800
Broadcasting	3,710	Host cities support	9,022
PR advertising	2,121	Operating asset contributions	1,900
Events	1,128	Ticket sales	21,800
Marketing	1,525	Contributions and subsidies	7,070
Ticketing	2,810	Business revenues	2,395
Security	2,780	Other	22
Communications	2,573		
Tournament support	10,046		
Venue management	10,975		
Tournament management	1,408		
Reserve for unexpected issues	2,152		
Total	**60,718**	**Total**	**60,718**

Source: JAWOC (2003:54).

the newly established football lottery *toto*. With the recession biting into corporate gains, only JPY 700 million out of an expected JPY 4.1 billion of sponsoring grants were grossed in early 2002.[6] Under the threat of imminent crisis, JAWOC persuaded the ten host cities in 2001 for additional support funds of approximately JPY 10 billion (*Yomiuri Shinbun*, December 26, 2002; JAWOC 2003:54). This donation was merely the tip of the iceberg since local government budgets had been continuously encumbered with contributions to the bidding campaign and subsidies in the run-up to the tournament. Over the years, local government accounts accumulated World Cup-related expenses of JPY 26.3 billion (cf. Table 8.3). It is important to note that these numbers do not take into account the salaries of public administration staff loaned out to the local organizing committees or the expenditures on infrastructure mentioned above.

Seventy per cent of total construction costs of all World Cup stadiums were secured through public bond issues to be paid back by the taxpayers over the coming decades. The Niigata 'Big Swan' Stadium, for example, was mainly financed by the prefecture (82.5 per cent) with the remaining 17.5 per cent coming from the city budget. More than half of the JPY 25 billion required to build the Oita 'Big Eye' Stadium was collected from general obligation bonds issued by Oita prefecture. Usually local referendums were required to gain approval for publicly financing the World Cup stadiums. Since local governments promised their electorate the soon-to-come benefits from the huge investments, such as the creation of new jobs, new revenue streams for local companies and increasing wealth for the greater

Table 8.2 World Cup Impact on Spectator Turnout at J. League Match Days

Name of Stadium	*Estimated Annual Income (million yen)*	*Estimated Annual Balance (million yen)*	*Capacity Crowd*	*Home or Would-Be Home Team*	*Avg. Home Attendance Prior to World Cup 2002*[2]	*Avg. Home Attendance after World Cup 2002*[2]
Sapporo Dome 'Hiroba'	2,300	100	42,300	Consadole Sapporo	10,520	23,980
Miyagi Stadium	30	-340	49,133	Vegalta Sendai	22,230	19,390
Ibaraki Prefectural Kashima Soccer Stadium	270	break even	41,800	Kashima Antlers	25,490	24,610
Niigata 'Big Swan' Stadium	no estimate	no estimate	42,300	Albirex Niigata[1]	18,480	28,890
Saitama Stadium 2002	300	-400	63,700	Urawa Reds	26,040	28,090
International Stadium Yokohama	435	-600	72,370	Yokohama F Marinos	33,230	26,560
Shizuoka Stadium 'Ecopa'	no estimate	deficit	51,349	Shimizu S-pulse	14,300	14,920
Nagai Stadium	79	-620	50,000	Cerezo Osaka[1]	4,850	8,780
Kobe Wing Stadium	250	deficit	42,000	Vissel Kobe	13,245	9,270
Oita 'Big Eye' Stadium	50	-250	43,000	Oita Trinita[1]	6,870	14,610
Total			497,952		175,255	199,100

[1]J.League Division 2 (J2) in 2002: eight home matches before and ten after the World Cup.
[2]J1 visitors count only for the initial seven matches of the 2002 season (March 2 to April 21). The first leg was stopped thereafter due to the World Cup and resumed for the remaining eight encounters on July 13 (until August 17).

Source: Financial balance sheet figures from Nogawa and Mamiya (2002). Averages are own calculations, based on crowd numbers according to official J.League home page (http://www.j-league.or.jp).

Table 8.3 Regional Economic Burden of Hosting World Cup Matches

Awarding Authority of Construction Project	*Construction Cost (million yen)*	*Capacity Crowd*	*Population (million)*	*Burden per Capita*	*World Cup–Related Budget (million yen)*
Sapporo City 'Sapporo Dome Hiroba'	42,200	42,300	1.82	23,190	3,492
Miyagi Prefecture Miyagi Stadium	27,000	49,133	2.36	11,440	2,890
Niigata Prefecture 'Big Swan'	31,000	42,300	2.48	12,500	2,550
Ibaraki Prefecture Kashima Soccer Stadium[1,2]	23,600	41,800	2.99	7,890	2,713
Saitama Prefecture Saitama Stadium 2002[1]	35,600	63,700	6.98	5,100	2,822
Yokohama City International Stadium Yokohama	60,000	72,370	3.35	17,910	1,370
Shizuoka Prefecture 'Ecopa'	30,000	51,349	3.74	8,020	1,965
Ōsaka City Nagai Stadium[2]	40,100	50,000	2.61	15,360	4,739
Kobe City Kobe Wing Stadium	23,100	42,000	1.51	15,300	1,571
Oita Prefecture 'Big Eye'	25,100	43,000	1.22	20,570	2,141
Total	337,700	497,952	29.06	11,620	26,252

[1]Football-only stadium.

[2]Including renovation costs for World Cup purposes.

Source: Population size at year end of 2001 according to prefectural data; construction costs according to *Nihon Keizai Shinbun*, April 8, 2002; operational expenses according to Hirose (2003:137); own calculations for per capita debit.

public, approval rates ranged between 80 and 95 per cent. Japan's politicians and citizens are largely accustomed to pork-barrel politics (cf. Manzenreiter and Horne 2005), and most people throughout the country were willing to believe in the myth of sport as a 'growth machine'.

WORLD CUP ECONOMICS (PART I): THE NATIONAL ECONOMY

Public opinion polls conducted in January 2002 revealed that over 80 per cent of Koreans and 60 per cent of Japanese believed that the World Cup would provide a significant boost to their economies (*Far Eastern Economic Review*, March 7, 2002). An online survey among 25,000 respondents by NTT-X and Mitsubishi Sōken showed that most people in Japan indeed expected some positive (64 per cent) or even a strong impact (12 per cent), while only 7 per cent feared a negative economic impact and 15 per cent expected none at all (Goo Research 2002). The widespread belief in the growth myth was most prominently articulated by Prime Minister Koizumi Junichirō's address to the National Diet on February 4, 2002:

> This year, the Football World Cup will take place. During the event, the attention of the world will focus on Japan, and a great many visitors will come. This is a nonrecurring opportunity to raise interest in Japan and understanding of Japan. We are planning to introduce the cultural traditions and rich tourism resources of our country to the world, to increase the number of visitors from abroad and to activate the regions by these means. It is our strong hope that this tournament, including its economic spill-over effects, will turn into the chance for Japan and the Japanese to return to vitality. (Source: online database on minutes from parliamentary sessions)

The media played a crucial role in disseminating the image of the economic income generator. Prior to the World Cup, a number of highly optimistic forecasts on the benefits of hosting circulated through the national papers and were echoed by public discourse. The NEC Research Institute pegged the total economic benefit of the core event at JPY 141.7 billion, equal to 0.1 per cent of GDP (Amagai 2002:1), while the Dai-ichi Life Research Institute estimated an economic impact of JPY 370 billion pushing the GDP up by 0.3 percentage point (*Nihon Keizai Shinbun*, April 2, 2002). The most ostentatious figures forecasting an impact of up to JPY 3.6 trillion were provided by a joint research unit of the Institute of Social Engineering and Dentsu Institute of Human Studies (Nomura 2002), the research unit of the advertising agency Dentsu that had played a leading role in the promotion of world football (Manzenreiter and Horne 2002:10). This would have represented an enormous boost from the playing of 32 football matches, considering that Japanese economic growth averaged only 1.1 per cent per year over the previous decade. Public Management Minister Katayama Toranosuke speculated that, in the wake of Japan's 1.4 per cent one-quarter GDP spurt, the World Cup could accelerate growth that quarter to 2 per cent (Mallard 2002).

Not least because estimating the economic windfall of sport mega-events itself has become a viable business, think tanks and research institutes often succumb to the danger of delivering the messages their customers want to hear. For obvious reasons, forecasts are much more abundant than ex post analyses and many of these make cardinal errors. Basically all studies factor in direct effects generated by investments prior to the event and consumer spending during the event, as well as indirect effects which are created by the stimulus to economic activities induced by the direct effects. But much too often the dimension of these economic multipliers is based on sheer speculation. Studies also err in ignoring substitution effects of direct and indirect expenses that only substitute consumption and business activities in other fields. Equally difficult to quantify are crowding-out effects: Tournaments tend to supplant rather than supplement the regular tourist economy because host cities are often attractive travel destinations. A further problem is related to the inherent difficulties of separating World Cup effects from the usual cyclical experience. Sport economist Stefan Szymanski (2002:173–176) calculated an economic multiplier effect of 1.47 at the largest for Japan, but a comparison with long-time averages, cyclical norms and equivalent figures for similar economies at the same stage of the business cycle made him reduce his forecasts to a very minor and negligible impact. His reservation is supported by other researchers and my own calculations trying to verify some of the boosters' claims.

For example, Chang Se-Moon (2002), who had reviewed the growth rates in all the previous 12 World Cup host countries for the years before and after the event, predicted a stronger economy after the World Cup finals.[7] In most cases, growth was stronger in post–World Cup years than in those years prior to the Finals. The average growth rate for post–World Cup years was 3.1 per cent, compared to 2.2 per cent of growth for pre–World Cup years. Now when we look at the corresponding OECD figures, Japan replicated the general trend pattern with growth rates of minus 0.4 per cent in 2001 (to 2002) and 2.7 per cent in 2002 (to 2003). But in South Korea the pattern reversed from 6.3 per cent growth in 2001 to 2.6 per cent in 2002 (OECD 2004:14–15), which at least invites a critical reassessment of the growth hypothesis.[8]

Stock markets, too, have been used as an indicator to argue that football is a major coincident or at least a slightly leading indicator of economic activity. A report by HSBC analysts foreshadowed a typical inverse-u-pattern, since host nation's stock markets tend to rally in the months leading up to the competition, but sell off as the event starts (*Financial Times*, December 21, 2001). A look at the Japanese stock market confirms this observation since the Nikkei index clearly matched this pattern. During the first five months of 2002, the Nikkei showed a steady rise from 10,542 to 11,764, which was followed by a sharp decline to the lowest year end close in 20 years (8,579). In South Korea, too, the Korean Composite Stock Price Index steadily climbed up from 698 points to 855 and plummeted down to 633 at the end of the year. Since stock markets tend to reflect moods and attitudes rather than real economic trends, these patterns show the high expectations in the World Cup kick-starting the economy followed by widespread disenchantment in both countries.

Given that the only lasting real estate legacy from the World Cup showed a remarkable absence of specific and viable, longer-term business operations, the research unit of the hotel investment services group Jones Lang Lasalle was surprised by the high-rising expectations on economic regeneration (Sanderson, Webb and Hobkinson 2002:10–11). In fact, Dentsu's bold forecast was largely built on the premises of all infrastructure investments of the past six years, amounting to a total of JPY 1.44 trillion in this study, while the remaining piece of the cake would have to rely on notoriously volatile consumer spending.[9] Yet when Sumitomo Life Research Institute examined Japan's historical experiences in hosting large-scale cultural events, including Tokyo's 1964 Summer Olympics, which public opinion in Japan usually considers as proof of economic benefits of mega-event hosting (e.g. Makabe 2002; Harada 2002), they found out that out of ten events none of the sport events and only the Ōsaka World Expo from 1970 had a considerable impact on consumer spending (Yamamoto 2002:3). For the World Cup year 2002, I examined the data from the Family Income and Expenditure Survey (*zenkoku shōhi jittai chōsa*) and the national household survey (*kakei chōsa*) (TKK 2003). The average monthly living expenditure of all private households in 2002 was JPY 268,787, down from JPY 271,759 in 2001 (0.3 per cent decrease) with particularly low figures during the second quarter of the year.[10] Rising consumer sentiments of 0.3 per cent in 2002 showed a moderate recovery from a minus 1.5 per cent decline in 2001; yet broken up in quarters, the highest growth was procured prior to the World Cup (1.5 per cent), followed by shrinking growth rates of 0.9 per cent during the World Cup period and 0.3 per cent immediately after the World Cup. Negative growth of minus 1.5 per cent during the last quarter almost offset the annual growth effect (ESRI 2003).[11]

WORLD CUP ECONOMICS (PART II): THE REGIONAL ECONOMY

The discussion so far has shown that the Japanese economy and private consumption showed inconsistent signs of recovery and stagnation in 2002. To get more precise information on World Cup benefits, the level of analysis has to be scaled down from the national to the regional level, where the growth machine myth has been most influential. Studies on the economic effect for the regional economy were commissioned by most local authorities ahead of the tournament. Figures largely differed, due to differences in methodology, the time frame of the analysed period, the depth of diffusion effects and the composition of the regional economic structure. But in general, the regional think tanks usually replicated the over-estimates of the nationwide surveys introduced above. For Niigata, the local branch of the Bank of Japan calculated effects of up to JPY 100 billion; Ōita estimated direct effects of JPY 6 billion and Yokohama of JPY 26 billion (Naikaku-fu 2003:42); Ibaraki expected a total impact of JPY 77 billion (Ide 2002) and Sapporo of JPY 7 billion (HIFA 2002).

Since hallmark events attract large numbers of visitors and the number of spectator admissions correlates highly with the economic impact attributable to the event (Gratton, Shabli and Coleman 2006:51), tourism-related spending is used as a major standard variable in all models. The Ministry of Land, Infrastructure and Transport, and the Sumitomo Life think tank expected between 360,000 to 400,000 World Cup tourists from abroad alone. The expenditure of the aggregated 1.44 million spectators to the matches and of many thousands others who were involved in making the games (such as players, sport officials and those working for the teams, the tournament and the media) thus can be rendered as the most obvious net inflow of foreign capital into the local economy. Since 'foreign' bears the meaning of both from abroad and other parts of the country, the local economy should benefit more than the overall economy from the World Cup. But the figures for tourist entries in 2002 reveal that the anticipated tourist (and thus financial) flows were over-optimistic and that the World Cup actually impacted negatively on the growth of tourist entries. According to the Ministry of Justice (online database), 441,000 foreigners entered Japan between May 31 and June 30, 2002. This marked an increase of 37,000 people over the same period for the previous year. The year-by-year growth of foreign visitors to Japan during the World Cup month of June (19.4 per cent) outperformed the annual growth rate (8.4). But so did February (55.7 per cent), May (21.4 per cent), August (16.2 per cent), October (23.0 per cent) and November (21.3 per cent), culminating in the highest annual number of visitors from abroad ever (5.77 million in 2002). Any visible impact of the World Cup proper tends to fade out in the monthly arrival statistics provided by the Japan National Tourist Association (JNTO 2004). The year-by-year increase of tourists (as a sub-category of foreign visitors) coming to Japan during the month of the tournament (9.3 per cent) was outperformed by the annual growth rate of 9.8 per cent and the second half of the year in particular (11.6 per cent).

The spending of World Cup visitors from abroad had only a minor impact on the growth of Japan's inland travel market by 3.3 percentage points.[12] According to annual industry surveys on the tourist market by the Ministry of Land, Infrastructure and Transport, two-thirds of annual growth in 2002 was fuelled by day trip–related spending by Japanese tourists, with the remaining one-third equally coming from domestic overnight travel and expenditure by foreign visitors. Since the share of foreign visitors comprises far less than 10 per cent of Japan's domestic travel market, growth within the tourist market (16.5 per cent) rebounded strongly with the recovery of domestic overnight travel in the year following the World Cup. A growth of 30.4 per cent within this segment more than offset the retarding revenues from day trip spending and foreign travellers to Japan.

These data reveal some core aspects of the crowding-out effects accompanying large-scale events: First, the expectation of rising prices due to the event, the anticipated danger of football hooliganism and other unwanted side effects of sport mega-events ousted the regular type of visitor. Entry data by nationality indicate that tourists from neighbouring Korea, China, Hong Kong and Taipei in particular forwent travelling to Japan throughout the World Cup period, countering the generally strong rise of East Asian inbound tourism during the first years of the decade. Second, if there was any event-related increase in domestic travel and tourist consumption, it was countered by austerity in other fields of tourist activities. In fact, JATA (Japan Association of Tourist Agents) reported an exceptionally strong slack in domestic tourism sales over the second quarter of 2002. Small retailers as well as wholesalers particularly suffered from the negative impact of the World Cup in June when demand for all kind of domestic tourist products conspicuously cooled down (JATA 2002).

Because football spectators did not necessarily spend more time in the World Cup cities than match-time, access and departure afforded, regional data on the flow of people (cf. Table 8.4) do not show a consistent growth pattern related to the World Cup. Among the ten regions, Saitama (2.2 per cent), Kanagawa (1.5 per cent), Miyagi (1.5 per cent) and Ōita (1.0 per cent) recorded annual growth rates of Japanese and foreign visitors alike, while the respective numbers decreased in all the remaining host regions. Macroeconomic indicators of regional growth also fail to reveal a clear pattern of World Cup effects (cf. Table 8.4). Japan's GNP growth of 1.2 per cent in 2002 was outperformed by the prefectures of Shizuoka (2.9 per cent) and Hyōgo (1.6 per cent); growth rates were smaller in Ibaraki and Ōsaka (both 0.3 per cent) and negative in all other regions. Year-on-year growth of per capita distribution of regional income stagnated in Ibaraki and decreased within all the remaining prefectures with the notable exception of Shizuoka (1.7 per cent) and Hyōgo (0.5 per cent). Somehow surprising is the relation between debt at the regional level and national average, given that public debt has financed the World Cup arenas. With the exception of Sapporo, Ōita and Niigata, which became infamously renowned for over-excessive spending on public infrastructure projects in the past, indebtedness per head stayed in all other regions below the national average of JPY 585,000. The increase of public debt accelerated over the World Cup year in Sapporo (6.4 per cent) and Niigata (4.6 per cent), as well as in Ibaraki (5.7 per cent) and in Saitama (5.4 per cent). However, the average annual growth

Table 8.4 The Local Economy in the World Cup Host Regions, 2002

	Regional GDP 2002 (real)	*Regional Income per Head in 2002 (million yen)*	*Change (y/y)*	*Outstanding Local Government Debt per Head in 2002 (1,000 yen)*	*Change (y/y)*	*Change of Foreign and Domestic Visitors (y/y)*	*Unemployment in 2002*	*Change of Unemployment (y/y)*
All Japan	1.2	2.843	-1.5	585	3.8	—	5.4	8.0
Hokkaidō[1]	-1.0	2.563	-2.8	868	6.4	-0.6	6.1	5.2
Miyagi	-0.9	2.576	-3.7	557	0.9	1.5	6.2	17.0
Ibaraki	0.3	2.902	0.0	498	5.7	-2.6	4.8	4.3
Saitama	-0.5	2.657	-4.0	392	5.4	2.2	5.8	9.4
Kanagawa	-0.3	3.061	-1.0	287	2.5	1.5	5.1	10.9
Niigata	-0.8	2.713	-2.0	789	4.6	-3.1	4.5	4.7
Shizuoka	2.9	3.221	1.7	529	2.1	-3.7	4.0	5.3
Ōsaka[2]	0.3	3.030	-0.6	469	2.0	-1.6	7.7	6.9
Hyōgo[3]	1.6	2.647	0.5	553	3.6	-1.7	6.6	6.5
Ōita	-4.2	2.585	-2.3	794	1.4	1.0	4.9	-10.9

[1] Prefecture surrounding Sapporo.
[2] Ōsaka prefecture.
[3] Prefecture surrounding Kōbe.
Source: All data from the statistical bureaus of regional governments and government-related websites.

within the World Cup regions (3.4 per cent) turned out to be lower than the national average of 3.8 per cent.

Employment turned out to be one economy-related field in which host regions came off better than the national average. While the growth rate of unemployed exceeded the national increase of 8.0 per cent in Miyagi (17 per cent), Kanagawa (10.9 per cent) and Saitama (9.4 per cent), unemployment grew slower than the national average in all other regions with the exception of Ōita, where the total number of persons in employment actually increased. However, it is difficult to gauge any positive impact on employment just by referring to labour statistics, particularly since there is strong suspicion that most of the new jobs actually were low paid and only temporary. Previous research into the employment effect of sport mega-events have raised critical issues about the quality and duration of jobs created. Case studies from the Olympics Games in Montreal, Barcelona and other sites have clearly shown that the majority of new jobs actually opened within the tourist industry and related service industries, which are notoriously known for unstable and insecure labour conditions. Hence hosting mega-events may enhance employment opportunities of unskilled workers at best, but not the creation of value-added jobs from which the quality of local employment would improve (Whitson and Horne 2006:79–80).

POLICY OBJECTIVES, ACTIONS AND RESULTS

My overall exploration of losers and winners among the World Cup host cities does not stop in front of the predicted—and predictable—gap between political rhetoric and actual outcome. The following discussion of hosting politics is set within my broader concern with the motivations and aspirations of regional governments. As the expected economic benefits failed to materialize, how did local governments reflect on the experience? Had they actually pursued objectives other than economic gains, and if yes, what specific goals did they strive for? Were they satisfied with their overall performance, and in which regard were they disappointed? In order to assess the degree of accountability of local authorities in charge of managing public affairs, Hirose (2003) conducted an ex post evaluation survey of the business performance among the ten authorities in charge of hosting the 2002 World Cup. Data of the comprehensive survey were gathered by sending questionnaires to the respective municipalities and prefectural governments as well as by oral or written interviews of governors or other top-level bureaucrats of the host regions. Respondents were invited to check the applicability of 25 policy objectives identified during a preliminary research project on sport and regional development commissioned by local governments, the Japan Centre for Regional Development and the predecessor of the current Ministry of Internal Affairs and Communications in 1998. The post–World Cup questionnaire asked regional officials to identify and evaluate the significance of the respective items at three different stages of political action: at the level of policy vision, as target figures and as outcome. Respondents were asked first to specify which of the 25 items actually matched their specific expectations of hosting the World Cup (policy vision). Second, they were asked to confirm whether specific policies had been installed for the realization of these objectives (target figures). Finally, in order to assess the outcome of their implementations, they were asked to assign a value of 1 (no effect), 2 (hardly any effect), 3 (effect), 4 (quite an effect) or 5 (great effect) to the respective items.[13]

For the purpose of comparability, I regrouped the originally unsorted and ungraded categories from the questionnaire into four distinctive policy fields: identity politics, local development, infrastructure building and the promotion of outward relations. Identity politics refer to intangible benefits such as local pride, social cohesion and branding of the local image. Development politics include various methods of raising revenue streams into the local economy and the promotion of sport in the local community. Infrastructure building comprises of material and immaterial legacies for the host region, i.e. transport, cityscape, environment and volunteer organizations; outward relations include all objectives contributing to international-mindedness and exchange programmes. The left column of the table in Table 8.5 identifies the 25 objectives in detail as well as their distribution among ten subgroups and the four general topics outlined in the preceding.

While politicians and bureaucrats in all host regions evaluated the event as largely successful (see the three outermost columns on the right end of Table 8.5), the comparison of their respective policy objectives, implementation of target figures and actual outcome reveals a more complex and markedly differing picture. The aggregated survey data reveal considerable differences both in number and kind of objectives (n/po) and measures (n/pm) pursued by the ten local governments (cf. Table 8.6). While Miyagi, Saitama and Ōita laid claim to each of the 25 objectives, and Yokohama, Shizuoka and Ibaraki still to more than 20, Sapporo and Ōsaka selected only 15 and 13 targets, respectively. The spread of policy performance increased between host cities at the next stage of implementing concrete tasks to achieve the objectives associated with hosting. Again the three prefectures of Miyagi, Shizuoka and Ōita purported to have issued some kind of tasks and target figures in each of the 25 categories they had identified as policy objectives. Ibaraki (23), Yokohama (23), Saitama (18), Kōbe (15) and Niigata (14) introduced special programmes in nearly each of their selected fields; Sapporo (9) and Ōsaka (5) even abstained from implementing congruent measures in six or eight of their self-selected policy fields. The apparent differences in engagement were often directly linked with differences in the way outcomes were evaluated. In general, prefectures that had issued more policy goals and implemented more tasks to achieve them expressed a higher degree of satisfaction with the outcome. The prefecture

Table 8.5 Local Governments' World Cup Policies, Implementation and Self-Assessment Results

Policy (pt)	*Policy Field (pf)*	*n/po*[1]	*n/pm*[2]	*Policy Objectives (po)*	**pts*[3]	*pts*[4]	*Ø pts*	*Ø pm*	*Ø pt*
1 identity politics	1.1 regional identity	8	8	1.1.1 unify local consciousness	24	25	2.8	3.1	3.0
		8	8	1.1.2 create sense of unity	23	25	2.8		
		8	8	1.1.3 enhance self-esteem	29	29	3.6		
	1.2 regional image	4	4	1.2.1 reconsider the local flavour	12	17	2.4	2.9	
		9	9	1.2.2 maximize media exposure	31	31	3.4		
2 development politics	2.1 economic revitalization	10	9	2.1.1 increase tourist flows	21	21	2.3	2.1	2.7
		9	7	2.1.2 vitalize shopping districts	16	17	1.9		
		10	6	2.1.3 diffusion effects for the regional economy	20	20	2.2		
	2.2 sport promotion	9	9	2.2.1 provision of large-scale sport facilities	31	32	3.2	2.9	
		8	5	2.2.2 activate usage of public sport facilities	18	19	2.7		
		10	6	2.2.3 vitalize sport system in the region	16	16	2.7		
		10	6	2.2.4 enhance sport participation rate	11	11	2.8		
		9	9	2.2.5 gain knowledge on sport event marketing	30	31	3.1		
		9	7	2.2.6 increase regional popularity of football	28	29	2.9		
3 infrastructure building	3.1 transportation	7	7	3.1.1 improve road and traffic conditions	22	22	2.4	2.3	2.7
		5	5	3.1.2 improve railway network	16	20	2.2		
	3.2 cityscape	7	8	3.2.1 redesign the inner city	18	23	2.6	2.6	
	3.3 environment	5	6	3.3.1 contribute to environmental concern	15	16	2.3	2.3	

(continued)

Table 8.5 (continued)

Policy (pt)	*Policy Field (pf)*	*n/po*[1]	*n/pm*[2]	*Policy Objectives (po)*	**pts*[3]	*pts*[4]	*Ø pts*	*Ø pm*	*Ø pt*
	3.4 civil society	10	10	3.4.1 encourage volunteer participation	34	34	3.4	3.1	
		7	5	3.4.2 encourage establishment of new NGOs	23	29	3.2		
		7	7	3.4.3 citizens' participating in city refurbishing	23	28	2.8		
4 outward relations	4.1 international-ization	10	9	4.1.1 level up international consciousness	26	26	2.9	2.9	3.0
		10	10	4.1.2 foster international exchange	29	29	2.9		
		10	9	4.1.3 social and international education of youth	29	29	2.9		
Ōita	4.2 hospitality	10	10	4.2.1 level up regional hospitality	31	1.0	4.9	3.1	

[1]n/po = number of host regions that envisioned policy objectives for the respective item.
[2]n/pm = number of host regions that developed special measures for realizing the respective item..
[3]*pts = total score of outcome according to self-assessment, only for those items that matched policy objectives of the regions.
[4]pts = total score of outcome according to self-assessment.

Source: All data from the statistical bureaus of regional governments and government-related websites.

Table 8.6 Ranking of Local Government: Policies, Implementation and Results

Policy Objectives[1]	*Target Figures*[2]	*Total Score*[3]	*Average Score*[4]	*Index 1*[5]	*Index 2*[6]
1 Miyagi (25)	1 Miyagi (25)	1 Ōita (90)	1 Ōita (3.6)	1 Ōita (0.90)	1 Ōita (0.9)
1 Saitama (25)	1 Shizuoka (25)	2 Shizuoka (86)	2 Shizuoka (3.4)	2 Shizuoka (0.88)	2 Shizuoka (0.86)
1 Ōita (25	1 Ōita (25)	3 Saitama (69)	3 Saitama (3.3)	3 Ibaraki (0.84)	3 Saitama (0.82)
4 Yokohama (24)	4 Ibaraki (23)	4 Ibaraki (68)	4 Ibaraki (3.0)	4 Saitama (0.82)	4 Ibaraki (0.81)
4 Shizuoka (24)	4 Yokohama (23)	5 Miyagi (66)	5 Miyagi (2.8)	5 Kobe (0.70)	5 Kobe (0.73)
6 Ibaraki (22)	6 Saitama (18)	6 Yokohama (61)	6 Sapporo (2.6)	5 Sapporo (0.69)	6 Osaka (0.70)
7 Niigata (19)	7 Kobe (15)	7 Niigata (55)	7 Yokohama (2.4)	7 Miyagi (0.67)	7 Sapporo (0.69)
8 Kobe (17)	8 Niigata (14)	8 Kobe (45)	7 Niigata (2.4)	8 Niigata (0.64)	8 Miyagi (0.67)
9 Sapporo (15)	9 Sapporo (9)	9 Sapporo (37)	9 Kobe (2.0)	9 Yokohama (0.60)	9 Niigata (0.66)
10 Osaka (13)	10 Osaka (5)	10 Osaka (33)	10 Osaka (1.7)	9 Osaka (0.60)	10 Yokohama (0.59)

Explanations: Position in the column and numbers in parentheses indicate ranking and value of

[1] Number of policy objectives related to World Cup hosting .

[2] Number of policy objectives for which special measures were enacted.

[3] Total score of evaluation of outcome (1 = hardly any effect; 2 = some effect; 3 = quite effective; 4 = very effective, per policy objective).

[4] Average score of evaluation of outcome, weighted according to number of policy objectives.

[5] Index 1: Total score of outcome in fields that were identified as policy objectives, divided by the maximum possible score of outcome for all those fields.

[6] Index 2: Total score of outcome in fields in which policy measures were implemented, divided by the maximum possible outcome for these fields.

of Ōita registered the highest score (90 out of a possible maximum of 100), followed by Shizuoka (86), Saitama (69) and Ibaraki (68). At the opposite end of the spectrum, Kōbe (45), Sapporo (37) and Ōsaka (33) represent the bottom of the chart. If it is assumed that scores of the self-assessment test are only valid for those fields in which initiative was indicated either tentatively by developing policy visions or more concretely by implementing politics, the ranking hardly changes at the top. Rearrangements in midfield and at the lower ranks are greatly affected by the less-determined municipalities as they tended to rate the outcome higher in the limited fields on which they had concentrated their efforts.

In terms of policy themes, non-tangible effects on regional identity and civil society recorded the highest degree of acknowledgment of outcome (3.1 each; cf. Table 8.5). There was general consent that the event had fostered identification with the region among locals, creating a sense of unity and local pride. The governor of Ōita openly expressed his deep satisfaction with the fact that even peripheral cities can master the requirements for staging a global event such as the World Cup. Shizuoka's governor observed that the foreign visitors' appraisal of the successfully managed event reinforced awareness of traditional Japanese virtues among the Japanese themselves. During the World Cup local colour and traditions were displayed at all venue cities that staged cultural festivals and other sideshows for their visitors. Youth organizations and women's associations were integrated into the regional programmes, and many thousands volunteered either to work as official JAWOC volunteers or to join the activities of other organizations under the control of local authorities. Officials from Ōsaka City, which at that time was bidding both for the 2008 Summer Olympics and the 2007 Track and Field World Championship, said that the 2002 FIFA World Cup had further promoted the interest in volunteering, which would be an important resource in the case of future international events.[14]

On average, regions were least interested in using the World Cup as a kick-starter to re-brand the regional image (4), to redesign the cityscape (7), to expand the transportation networks of roads (7) and railways (5) and to spread environmental concerns (5). But all host cities awarded high significance to the policy objectives of strengthening outward relations and promoting economic development. Each of the ten regions expected that their contribution to the World Cup would raise the international-mindedness of their inhabitants. Related objectives such as increase of tourist flows (10) and maximizing media exposure (9) also received nearly unanimous assent. For the purpose of presenting themselves as hospitable, economically viable and culturally distinctive locality, host cities scheduled several activities. Taking the nationalities of teams scheduled to play at their venues into account, all host cities organized special welcome events for the foreign supporters, decorated shopping districts and roads with the visitors' national flags and issued leaflets and brochures in the respective national languages. Elementary schools in the vicinity of the stadiums in Kōbe and other cities changed their regular teaching courses in order to instruct the local schoolchildren in history, culture and tradition of the particular guest teams; their pupils were given free access to the World Cup games, where they were seen vividly supporting the visiting team. The outcome of internationalization politics received the second highest score (2.9) in the bureaucrats' self-evaluation, which is in marked contrast to the evaluation of development programmes (2.7). This category would have even scored lower if the six items of sport promotion (2.9) had not been included. Policy objectives such as the provision of sport facilities (9), expanding mass sport participation (10), knowledge on sports event marketing (9) or rising regional interest in football (9) were commonly quoted. However, actual measures and, probably in consequence, results were far lower for those fields of sport promotion which were not directly linked to football or the World Cup in general.

The low score given to economic promotion (2.1), which had been ranked high at the level of policy vision, attests to the general failure of this particular goal. Virtually all governments had hoped for the cash flow generated by Japanese and foreign tourists (10), the stimulation of trade and services at the local level (9) and wider diffusion effects for the regional economy (10). Hirose's survey quotes the governor of Shizuoka saying that 'in a matured advanced economy as Japan, there are large opportunities that sport and culture in general become important pillars of the economy'. Both the governors of Shizuoka and Ibaraki reported an estimated 1.5-fold return on all expenses made by their governments, whereas responses from all other representatives were less enthusiastic. Looking at the level of policy implementation, only lukewarm efforts were devoted to local economy promotion, as only nine, seven and six regional governments installed target figures for the respective policy fields. In contrast, virtually all host cities had started several initiatives for the internationalization target.

ASSESSING WINNERS AND LOSERS OF THE WORLD CUP

Reviewing each regional case in isolation, differences in expectations, implementation and performance evaluation draw a quite complex and contradictory picture. According to Hirose, responses from the local governments differed widely depending on how they perceived the World Cup. The most conspicuous gaps were observed in the degree of significance they attached to the 'meaning of hosting the World Cup'. Ōita stood out in its strategic approach. From the viewpoint of the continuity of administration, the prefecture demonstrated outstanding coherence in its strategic intention prior to the event, actual policy measures implemented and the utilization of the performance results after the event. In the course of long-term policy planning, the mainly rural prefecture of Ōita was equipped with new transportation facilities that linked the province with the economic centre of Kyushu and the main island of Honshū. The media exposure during the World Cup, which was fairly amplified by the enthusiastic treatment of the Cameroon team in the neighbouring tiny village of Nakatsue, reflected positively upon the formerly widely held perception of 'provincial backwardness' and put Ōita onto the national map. Even though the expected economic windfall did not materialize and despite the actually declining regional economy, the government showed utmost satisfaction with the result. The long-term effects of public encumbrance, the downside of Ōita's strategy, were downplayed in the bureaucracy's self-assessment.

Regions that ranked highest in the evaluation of the outcome were either peripheral areas like Ōita or Miyagi, that used the World Cup event as an occasion for a more integrated development policy, or traditional strongholds of football, such as Shizuoka, Saitama and, to a lesser degree, Ibaraki. In Ibaraki, taxpayers' funding for the World Cup and the post-event utilization of the stadiums were less likely to arouse local resistance. As football has become a core commodity for the regional image over the past decade, the once-in-a-lifetime chance of being host to football's most important public event was wholeheartedly embraced to further enhance this image and encouraged the officials to herald the event as successful. While total running operations of the World Cup stadiums amounted to annual deficits of more than JPY 2.5 billion during the first two post–World Cup years (*Yomirui Shinbun*, May 5, 2003), chances to break even are fairly better in the self-declared 'football kingdom Shizuoka' and other football centres.

The comparison of survey data with economic figures does not establish a direct relation between actual outcome and the degree of involvement of regional authorities. Even though the business year closed fairly well in Ōsaka or Kōbe, preparations for the event and its effects received relatively low marks. In contrast, Ōita scored high on the self-assessment scale even though the economy showed no sign of recovery. Miyagi in northern Japan also continued to suffer from the economic crisis, but outcomes were assessed in comparably negative terms although—or perhaps because—the local authorities had been thrilled by the chance of reviving the city, as seen by the large number of policy visions and target figures. Generally speaking, major Japanese cities (Sapporo, Yokohama, Kōbe and Ōsaka) treated the World Cup as just one of many major events hosted on a regular base. The regional economy might be too big, the cultural supply too rich and the locals' demand too diverse for paying particular attention to the World Cup event. Ōsaka is a telling example for this conclusion as the survey revealed both the lack of a policy vision and insufficiency of concrete actions pursued by the world city. Having been home town to professional baseball teams for many decades, Ōsaka (as well as Yokohama) clearly envisioned less necessity to reinforce its regional image by exploiting the cultural appeal of the World Cup.

CONCLUSION: THE BENEFITS OF HOSTING

To summarize this discussion of the political economy of hosting sport mega-events, it is evident that the logic of sport boosterism has also left its marks on politics in Japan. But promises of easy returns on public investments for the football event ranked high in debates prior to the World Cup. Both at the national and the regional levels, 'evidence' on the economic windfall to come was put forth by mostly private research institutes, catering to the need of politicians and bureaucrats, who, via the media, disseminated the 'facts' as well as other figures showing the potential benefits to the greater public. Since no one opposes the creation of new jobs or rising wealth of the locality, the population in turn approved public expenditure on projects related to the World Cup. But little had been done to actualize economic gains and those tangible benefits that featured prominently among the prime objectives of hosting the World Cup.

Concerning the variety of objectives and implementations to achieve political goals, this chapter has shown the significance of environment and conditions surrounding the host locality. Depending on cultural riches and other resources, local governments placed very different expectations on the World Cup and initiated supporting programmes to a varying degree. Regions with a greater variety of soft assets attached less value to the tournament; these host regions could not afford allocating too many resources to one outstanding event when they have to organize a number of reoccurring events. In general, policy fields that required additional allocation of public funds (such as transportation infrastructure and city rebuilding) received distinctively lower scores in the self-assessment, whereas objectives which were hard to quantify, and those that did not require especial implementation, were marked as comparatively successful.

In terms of the economic impact of sport mega-events, Japan is no exception to the rule and complies with all serious and independent ex post studies on the economic impact of hosting. Notwithstanding the crucial difficulties in actually numbering the scale of negative and positive effects, this chapter demonstrates that the 2002 World Cup had no significant effect either on the regional or on the national economy of the co-hosting nation.[15] As the analyses of forecast data and statistical information on the national and the regional economy have shown, the business of hosting was a success for the organizing body but a sacrifice for the hosting authorities. It is interesting to note that the survey among local governments failed to show any significant linkage between economic performance and the marks that the local governments gave themselves in the self-assessment reports. What the study author Hirose has interpreted as a clear expression of lack of accountability is to me rather a function of size—as in mature economies the business of global mega-events can only have very limited impact on productivity and economic growth—and one more case in support of the urban regime theory. Even if economic benefits are unequally distributed and hardly keep the regional economy in good stead, figureheads and power brokers from the area avail themselves of the complex opportunities provided by the mega-event. Countries therefore should stop inventing economic benefits from sporting events and simply treat them as expenses, or investments, in national promotion and cultural supply. As the comparison of winners and losers in Japan suggests, host regions would be better advised to concentrate their efforts on the promotion of cultural life within the region and the strengthening of links between the regional administration and the local population in order to develop civil society. Host regions are recommended to utilize sport mega-events for the promotion of non-tangible yet lasting effects. This could also include attempts to stand to benefit from the symbolic value of sport for the purpose of place marketing, a strategy which Japan's national government has so far neglected. However, some rather recent phenomena indicate a new awareness among its diplomats on the usability of sport in the interest of Japan's foreign policy. This is an issue that the next chapter will discuss.

Part III

Global Dimensions

Sport and Geo-Politics of the Body

9 The Global Game in the Service of Japan's Foreign Diplomacy[1]

INTRODUCTION

Since Japan and South Africa have been host of the Men's Football World Cup, the incorporation of their continents into the world of football has been accomplished. With an estimated 250 million active players around the globe (this is the gross outcome of FIFA's 'Big Count' at the beginning of the 21st century), which today would be roughly 1 out of every 28 people in the world, football truly deserves to be called the global game. The sport's governing organization, FIFA, never tires of emphasizing the fact that the number of its national member organizations (208 in June 2011) actually exceeds the number of states with membership in the United Nations Organization (n = 194). Because of its reach, FIFA, like the International Olympic Committee, is granted semi-official ambassador status, allowing its directors and board members to mingle on an equal footing with the world's most powerful and influential elite. The symbolic weight of football in the political arena is also evident in the case of goodwill programmes such as Football for Peace, a values-based project for Arab and Jewish children in Israel, or Football for Development, which seeks to use the power of the game to positively transform communities in Third World countries. Because of football's ostensible ability to traverse all cultural boundaries and unite the world's citizens, the 'beautiful game' was even nominated for the Nobel Peace Prize in 2001 (*International Herald Tribune*, January 24, 2001).

However, the global history of the game consists of numerous controversial incidents portraying quite a different image of football as a battlefield and breeding ground of aggression, violence, racism, xenophobia and homophobia. Hooliganism and jingoism are common challenges to any pretence of football's unifying experience, as regular incidents of verbal abuse and physical violence reveal to the observer in many European and South American football stadiums. Given the global reach of football and the power of its administrators and corporate sponsors, the persistence of racist defamation and chauvinist hostility in football becomes a political issue, notwithstanding FIFA's attempts to frame itself and the sport of football as politically disinterested. Leaving the purported 'football war' between Honduras and El Salvador in 1969 aside,[2] from the moment that national representation and the antagonism of modern team sports were articulated, the game has lent itself to political usages. In re-occurring four-year cycles the sport's pre-eminent event, the FIFA World Cup, reminds the world of the fact that the tournament and the appearance of national teams in the 'theatre of the great'[3] also serve as a showcase for the display of nationalism and nation-state achievement. Thus, not least because of their impact on public opinion, sporting competitions can become an instrument of international policy.

It has been argued that the representational power of the nation-state in sports has been waning under current influences of globalization (Sassen 1998; Held 2000). Concurring with Sassen's hypothesis of the Global City, metropolitan clubs, benefiting from the growth of valuable sponsorship contracts and broadcasting rights sales, should turn into the major focal point of fan loyalty (Miller et al. 2001:22). While such a claim is partially supported by sociologists' observation of the deterritorialization of identity due to greater individual mobility (Jacobson 1996) and the global flow of images (Castells 1996), socio-psychological demand for the representational qualities of the state continues to flourish in the 21st century (Bairner 2001). As the huge media investment and viewing rates in the FIFA World Cup and other international sporting events clearly demonstrate, the concept of the nation-state has been too eagerly dismissed. Nation-states continue to serve as an integral part of the world economy as well as key agents of regional integration.

Regionalization, which has unfolded on a worldwide scale over the past decade, is a prominent undercurrent of the contemporary stage of globalization. In Europe, the European Union (EU) continues to expand, while North and South American states have crafted the North American Free Trade Agreement (NAFTA) and the Mercado Comun del Cono Sur (MERCOSUR). The institutionalization of regional integration in Asia is represented by multilateral organizations such as the Association of Southeast Asian Nations (ASEAN) or the Asian Pacific Economic Cooperation Conference (APEC). The increasing degree of economic integration, which has been identified as a key factor in the current rise of the Asian region as the world's most prolific economic centre, conspicuously contrasts with the apparent lack of political integration. Difficulties are further reinforced by the direct competition between Japan and China for economic superiority, along with the historical legacy of the Cold War and Japan's colonial project and military suppression of the Asian subcontinent during the first half of the 20th century.

This chapter examines regional integration and postcolonial nation-building as the two cornerstones between which discussions of the political meaning and usage of football in contemporary East Asia are oscillating. In order to identify the vexed relationships between football and foreign policy and the conditions under which these are formed, I will trace the historical roots of football in the relationships between Japan and its geographically closest neighbours. In turn, I will present some characteristic features of football in the foreign policy arena, using the 2002 World Cup, the 2004 Asian Cup and the second qualifying round of the Asian Football Confederation for the 2006 World Cup as prominent case studies. We will see that in the North Pacific, different state actors have utilized football as a vehicle (albeit a weak one) for the acquisition of power and the expression of status in the international community. It will become evident that football diplomacy in the North Pacific constitutes a field that can be exploited and mobilized for specific policy goals in international relations as well as in domestic affairs. As a tool in international relations, football can serve the strengthening of official ties and the promotion of semi-official exchange programmes as well as the articulation of otherwise suppressed partisan interests.

FOOTBALL IN THE NEW REGIONAL ORDER: POLITICAL AND ECONOMIC HISTORIES OF INTERNATIONAL RELATIONS

The spread of football throughout East Asia is deeply interwoven with larger issues of globalization. Due to the shifting geopolitics of power in the history of global football, in East Asia the sport has always been situated at the periphery, largely disconnected from dynamics and developments within the European and South American centres of the people's game (Manzenreiter and Horne 2002:6). To understand East Asia's marginal position as well as its current progress into the semi-periphery (of the global football system as well as the global economy) requires placing the political notion of the spread of Western culture into the long-term perspective of capitalist expansion as the driving force of globalization, which corresponds with the basic argument of world system theory (cf. Wallerstein 1974; Arrighi 1994). Football was first introduced to the region in the late 19th century by members of the military forces and commercial communities that safeguarded, administered and financed the British Empire. The formation of the first Asian football associations took place in two of Britain's colonies—Singapore, where the game was a popular way of socializing among rival business houses, and India, where the game proved a popular alternative to cricket with the infantry regiments of the occupying forces. In 1873 in Japan, Lieutenant Archibald L. Douglas of the Imperial British Royal Navy taught the rules of the game—after the essentials of naval warfare—to his students at the later naval academy in Tsukiji. In Korea, British sailors introduced the game to the Korean cities of Inchon and Seoul during the 1880s. In Hong Kong, the British residents organized football matches from the 1890s onward.[4] As the period of introduction concurred with the final chapter of European colonialism and the growing

US American influence in the North Pacific, football was easily overpowered by spectator sports of American origin, most notably by baseball. Even after World War II, when defeated Imperial Japan democratized, its former colony Korea was liberated (and subsequently devastated by civil war), and mainland China fell under Communist rule, football remained in the shadows of the overwhelming popular support for baseball. For that reason, football in East Asian never acquired the kind of over-determinist meaning for the redefinition of postcolonial relations between peripheries and Western centres as in many other well-documented cases of nation-building in Africa (Darby 2002), South America (Giulianotti 2002) or Eastern Europe (Foer 2004).

However, since Japan had meticulously copied the model of Western colonization, sporting rivalries in the North Pacific became significant for the symbolic representation of the relations between Japan and its formerly colonized neighbours from the North Pacific. The annexation of Korea, the usurpation of Manchuria, the military foray into China and the expansion of the so-called Greater East Asian Sphere of Co-Prosperity were all attempts by the Japanese state to generate or inflate economic surplus from colonization. Cooperation with the colonized people was initiated through a carrot-and-stick policy that promoted the integration of political elites and brutally oppressed any resistance. Research into the role of sports within Japanese colonialism remains limited, but it seems that the colonial state followed the Western example at least to some extent. Teams from the colonies were selected to participate at national tournaments such as the All Japan Football Championship, in which Hansong (present-day Seoul), but known as 'Keijo' by the Japanese, became the first Korean football team to take part in the tournament and proceeded to win it in 1935 (Sakaue 1998; Date 2000). While the Japanese military was showing few inclinations towards either Japanese or Western sports as a tool of colonial education, there is ample evidence that from the 1920s onwards the Japanese state developed a growing interest in sports for obtaining international acclamation as well as for forging internal cohesion. In order to realize these imperialistic goals, in 1940 teams from Japan's colonies or satellite states were invited to participate at the Oriental Games hosted by Japan for the celebration of 2,600 years of imperial rule. The colonial state also exploited human resources from the colonies that were forced into Japanese delegations to international tournaments. The most famous indentured athletes of Korean origin were the marathon runners who won gold and bronze for Japan at the 1936 Berlin Olympics. While the imperial state was joyfully celebrating the victory of its colonial children, a Korean daily newspaper featured a retouched photograph showing the victorious athletes without the characteristic Japanese flag *hinomaru* on the athletes' jerseys. This act of repatriation was immediately penalized by the colonial authorities, who temporarily shut down the newspaper. Less well known is the contribution of Korean footballers to the 'Miracle of Berlin', a legendary turnaround victory against Sweden at the Berlin Olympics which was secured despite Japan trailing by two goals at halftime.

For many Koreans, football enjoyed a special position as a sport at which they regularly sustained some national prestige by defeating Japan (Lee 1997). A Korean newspaper report from December 1928 indicates the intensity of feeling generated by football competition during the occupation period:

> On the day before departure an enthusiastic crowd of students, seniors and students from other universities came to say goodbye to the football team of Seoul University, wishing them all the best for the victory. The gathered students asked the players to win the cup. . . . and to triumph, even when injured. Ah, what is behind that? It is not just football fever but rather the objective of beating the Japanese perfectly. Our blood is running so fast and getting hot . . . We attach great importance to this journey. (Jung 1996:167)

After Japan's defeat in war and the restoration of Korean independence, football continued to serve this prominent function for Korea. Playing the game against the former oppressor offered the postcolonial subjects and the former wartime opponents from China, at least ritually, a chance to demolish the claims of cultural superiority or political supremacy through which imperial rule and military expansion had been rationalized. In this regard, sport has been aptly described as a ritualized combat, matching only war in its ability to channel national passions. Those passions are tied to an almost mythic connection fans make between their team and their national narrative—for example, when facing Germany, English fans routinely chant lines like: 'Two World Wars and one World Cup', thereby linking England's defeats of Germany on the battlefield with victory on the football field (*Asia Times*, June 10, 2006).

When Japan joined the newly formed Asian Football Confederation (AFC) in 1954, and entered the FIFA World Cup qualifying competition for the first time, the national team only had to play against the Republic of Korea. But public opinion in South Korea, as well as President Rhee Syng-Man, would not permit a visit by a Japanese team to Korea and so both matches were played in Tokyo. Winning the first and drawing the second match, the South Korean players wisely followed the presidential advice of either returning as winners or else drowning themselves in the sea between the countries (Podoler 2006). South Korea also eliminated Japan from the qualifiers for the football tournament to be held at the 1960 Rome Olympics as well as from the qualifiers for the 1962 World Cup. These matches were played in Seoul in November 1961 and marked the first ever visit to the Republic of Korea by any sports team from Japan. Although there was no success on the pitch for Japan, it can be argued that football played a minor role on the diplomatic floor by fostering links between the two countries at a time when few other channels existed. It should be noted that losing against Korea was fairly acceptable for most Japanese, as long as they could continue to beat them in baseball.

Records from the Japan Football Association (JFA) show that continuous defeats at the hands—or, more accurately, feet—of the Koreans were at the root of their decision to install a fully professionalized football league in the early 1990s. As a national project, the set-up of the professional league required the close cooperation of local administrators, business elite and the citizens and the financial back-up of private sponsors and public households. Raising the playing level of the national team was one explicit core objective behind the launch of the J.League, besides attracting the World Cup finals to Japan and popularizing football throughout the country. What the JFA was essentially seeking was the advancement of Japanese football to a level worthy of its economic power and overall achievements after 40 years of postwar peace and prosperity. What its corporate sponsors wanted was the exploration of a new fad and promising market (Watts 1998; Hirose 2004a).

The initiative leading towards the launch of the J.League coincided with the enormous accumulation of wealth in Japan during the late 1980s. The huge increase in value of real estate and assets listed on the Tokyo stock market provided Japanese corporations with the wealth for sponsoring the new sport as well as for buying into the heart of American industry. The concomitant end of the Cold War heralded a new global world order arising on the premise of economic rather than military power. Riding high on the waves of economic success, Japan's leaders articulated a new sense of national self-consciousness, for example, by asking for a permanent seat in the UN Security Council and a stronger military involvement in defence and regional security issues. Throughout the 1990s, several laws and ordinances were issued allowing the Japanese Self-Defence Forces to expand their scope and actual area of activity. But Article Nine of the Japanese Constitution, in which the right of waging war was renounced, denied Japan normal state status ever since autonomy had been restored in 1952. Constitutional pacifism, which constituted the core feature of the collective self-image in democratized Japan, came under increasing challenge when hawks and conservative nationalists among Japanese politicians demanded constitutional reform. Since their aspirations were even echoed by more liberal-minded voices and the general media, abandoning Article Nine was a crucial element of the provisions for revising the constitution delivered by a parliamentary council in 2005.

Any Japanese aspiration for regional leadership has met with strong resistance from neighbouring Korea and China, where recollections of colonial suppression under the Japanese Empire have remained vividly in the collective memory. The dispatch of Japanese troops—first under UN mandate to Cambodia and Somalia and later as part of the US-led so-called 'alliance against terror' into the Indian Ocean and Southern Iraq—raised suspicions about the actual objectives of constitutional reform and Japan's quest for 'normal state' status. Japan's inherent difficulties coming to terms with the past further undermined any official attempts at restoring trust. In 1995 at the occasion of the 50th anniversary of the end of World War II, the cabinet of social democrat Prime Minister Murayama Tomiichi elicited an apologetic statement that went beyond all previous declarations. But inflammatory remarks on the validity and benefits of the Japanese occupation of Korea that were made by some Liberal-Democratic Party members offset any positive effect. High-profile visits to the war-tainted Yasukuni Shrine (which is dedicated to Japan's war dead but also honours 14 Class A war criminals) by former Prime Minister Koizumi Junichirō and other government representatives, the controversial depiction of Japan's aggressive role in the Pacific War and the omission of wartime atrocities conducted by the Japanese army in history textbooks continued to obstruct any progress towards regional integration. Territorial disputes on a number of uninhabitable islands are another legacy of the Pacific War straining the relations between Japan, South Korea and China. The issues at stake are not only of symbolic significance, but also of political and economic relevance, since the territorial question is directly connected with fishing rights, the grip on natural resources and the delineation of maritime security zones. The reluctance to acknowledge a more powerful role of Japan in any kind of multilateral framework in the region is further enhanced by China's own aspirations for regional leadership, a role that many Chinese support in light of the country's growing economic weight as much as for historical reasons.

The political meaning of football in East Asia is thus linked to the remnants of Japan's imperial past, on the one hand, and to the current colonial project of neoliberal ideology, on the other hand. The shift from saturated markets towards new territories, consumer segments and modes of consumption was triggered by the crisis of over-accumulation that hampered the profitability of US manufacturers in the 1960s and destabilized the Fordist production system. According to David Harvey (1989:147), the post-Fordist regime of flexible accumulation is characterized by 'the emergence of entirely new sectors of production, new ways of providing financial services, new markets, and, above all, greatly intensified rates of commercial, technological, and organizational innovation'. Over the past decades, changes in communication infrastructures and technologies, as well as the deregulation of national media markets, spurred the transnational concentration of capital ownership and control over the cultural industries. Within the global cultural economy, international television broadcasts of football opened up access to giant consumer markets, providing media corporations, media rights brokers, football clubs and players with unprecedented revenue streams.

Awarding the 2002 World Cup finals to Asia clearly served the strategic interests of FIFA authorities and the global aspirations of its corporate associates aiming at a region that within a few years would be home to the second and third most powerful economies in the world. Prior to the event, all East Asian countries witnessed the establishment of professional home leagues, often with the support of football and marketing intelligence from the centres and football talent and labour imports from the periphery of the football world system. The successful integration of the former East Asian 'football periphery' into global commodity markets as well as changing relations of consumption in areas, where football previously was close to non-existent, has also impacted upon the way the game nowadays is associated with national prowess, both by national populaces and their official representatives. During the 2002 World Cup, viewing rates in Asia skyrocketed due to the close geographic proximity and the participation of all three football powerhouses from the Far East. More than 14 million people, or 56 per cent of the potential television audience in South Korea, tuned in to watch the first game of their national team against Poland. In Japan, 66.1 per cent of households watched Japan's 1–0 victory over Russia, thereby setting a Japanese record for a football match and the second highest for any sports event. According to a global comparison by Nielsen Media research, Thailand took the top spot with a combined total of 269 million World Cup viewers for the entire tournament, narrowly beating South Korea (266 million viewers) and China (263 million viewers) for the largest total audience for all World Cup matches in a single country. As these numbers are in marked contrast to the very low viewing rates of domestic league games; they arguably indicate the huge interest in seeing the national team symbolically playing out questions of status and power in the international arena.

However, a simplified dichotomy of centre and peripheries can be misleading: Japanese capital, inter-corporate networks and marketing know-how have always been at centre stage of the commercial exploitation of world sport. This began in the early 1980s, when Japan's largest advertisement agency, Dentsu, started to negotiate sponsorship and broadcasting deals for the Olympic Games or the Football World Cup or the interests of ISL, the sport marketing arm of Adidas, the leading sport apparel producer based in Germany (Horne and Manzenreiter 2002b:199).

JAPAN, KOREA AND THE 2002 WORLD CUP

The first World Cup on Asian soil in 2002 delivered a very pronounced example for the strategic use of football for political ambitions beyond nation-building. Colonial history as well as contemporary aspirations added a particular twist to the way the World Cup entered the agenda of foreign politics in the eventual host countries, Japan and South Korea. Japan, having led the region economically for a long time, consequently wanted to lead Asia into hosting the first World Cup in Asia. For South Korea, the stronger contender at least on the pitch, this was hardly acceptable, not least because football had been 'a means of resistance to Japanese rule' during the occupation. South Korea's partial success can ultimately be traced back to a very strong political streak running through its entire bidding campaign. A vice prime minister, a party leader, foreign ministry officials, army generals and leaders from the business world joined forces in the campaign which heavily played on politically positioning the World Cup as a 'catalyst for peace' on the Korean peninsula. The unification ideal apparently was an attempt to woo FIFA with the temptation of potential diplomatic powers and the FIFA president's desire for the Nobel Peace Prize. The Korean bid obtained immediate government approval leveraged by a highly persuasive president, who met the executive members of FIFA and went jogging with a '2002 World Cup' T-shirt (Butler 2002; Sugden and Tomlinson 1998). By contrast, Japan's bidding committee was mainly staffed by executives from the football association and, partly in response to the political heavyweights in Korea, by former prime minister Miyazawa Kiichi, who served as honorary chairman. Despite requests for government approval as early as 1992, Japan received it just a week before the deadline for submitting in February 1995.

While the Japan bid was counting on the weight of FIFA strongman Joao Havelange's promise of delivering the World Cup, South Korean football administrators were slicker and positioned themselves immediately within the networks of power. Hence South Korea was better prepared to canvass support when the bidding campaign was high-jacked by two fractions rivalling for leadership within FIFA in a post-Havelange era. The 'Solomonian' decision of awarding the World Cup finals to both Japan and South Korea was largely motivated by a power stalemate between the two camps and revealed a remarkable lack of historical knowledge and sensitivity towards international relations in the Far East. The negotiating power and experience of the political members of the bidding committees were instrumental in pressuring their respective national bodies towards consenting to the co-hosting arrangement. In a secret meeting between Miyazawa and his South Korean counterpart, former prime minister Lee Hong-Koo, and the honorary chairman of the South Korean bidding committee, the deal was sealed in late May 1996, just before the decisive FIFA congress in Bangkok.

The experience of co-hosting caused the formation of a fragile, yet gradually viable, alliance between the two states and their people. Occasional frictions showed that both parties, and South Korea in particular, understood that there was an opportunity to make effective use of the World Cup as moral leverage in diplomatic relations. For example, Korean lawmakers questioned the co-hosting of the World Cup when the Japanese Ministry of Education gave approval to a history textbook that ignored the atrocities by the Japanese army in Asia during the Pacific War. But in general both sides were keen to play down the disputes, separating politics from the hosting of the football event. Bilateral relations also improved when South Korean president Kim Dae-Jung's 'sunshine policy' helped warm general relations with Japan. South Korea gradually opened its doors to Japanese popular culture, and both countries sported a successful rapprochement policy at the diplomatic level. For Japan, 'co-hosting presented a means of re-orienting Japan's relations with South Korea toward the future without having to make the apologies and compensation that South Korea demanded as a prerequisite to such a development' (Butler 2002:52).

Political involvement at such an occasion is hardly surprising given that large-scale mega-events make governmental cooperation essential. FIFA statutes in fact demand government approval, back-up for bids and guarantees that sometimes even supersede national law. Managing World Cup logistics required Seoul and Tokyo to improve ties long before the finals took place. The anticipated increase in travel, money transfer and communication exchange between Japan and South Korea by teams, supporters and media representatives from all over the world required governmental cooperation on security, visas, flight schedules and telecommunications. Regular meetings between the two local organizing committees—featuring many bureaucrats as well as public figures in both countries—were held to discuss common issues. On the sub-state level, governors and mayors from the host regions met on several occasions. On the local political level, city partnerships were forged and numerous youth sport exchange programmes and goodwill projects were launched.

The undisputed success of the World Cup is probably most important for staying in public memory as a symbol for the turnaround in the relations between the host nations. After the final game, South Korean President Kim and Japan's Prime Minister Koizumi issued a joint communiqué in which the two leaders declared their determination to develop cooperative relations between Japan and the ROK to an even higher dimension in light of the successful co-hosting experience. Official declarations on the state of bilateral relations, such as Koizumi's policy statement during the opening session of the Japanese Diet in January 2003, prominently featured the World Cup as the key factor in good political and economic relations with South Korea. Opinion polls showed that cultural proximity and mutual understanding between the two people had reached unprecedented heights. Korean food, movies, fashion and language became immensely popular among Japanese (women); the number of travellers from any of the two countries to each other increased to all-time highs. A joint statement by the local organizing committees issued immediately prior to the finals on June 29, 2002, indicated that on the cultural level, in particular, the nations had grown together:

> Both Korea and Japan, more than merely representing the countries of Asia in hosting the FIFA World Cup, have been able to fulfill their responsibilities and produce results as the host countries. These results are something that will remain in Asia as a whole and will, without doubt, provide a significant incentive for other Asian countries to participate actively in future FIFA World Cup tournaments. We are proud to be members of Asia.

For Japan, viewing itself as being a part of Asia was quite an accomplishment, given that 'Out of Asia' has been a key term for Japan's modernization strategies since the 19th century. Adopting an Asian identity in a public event certainly enhanced, if not strengthened, Japan's options for negotiating its position among the states of the East Asian region.

FOOTBALL DIPLOMACY: CAPTAIN MAJED AND BALLS FOR IRAQ

The worldwide appeal of football is one reasonable explanation for the growing share of football-related activities in Japan's cultural diplomacy. In general Japan's government used to bank on the appeal of tradition and heritage in the field of cultural diplomacy, thereby ignoring the immense market value and marketing power of its popular culture industries. Only for the past few years has the work of Japan's creative industries, including *manga* (comics) and *anime* (animated cartoon), received heightened attention for the promotion of the official image of the country (Manzenreiter 2007b). In March 2006, the Ministry of Foreign Affairs announced in cooperation with the Japan Foundation and Animation International Middle East that it provided the costs of airing the cartoon series *Captain Tsubasa* in Iraq. The enormously popular animated cartoon is based on the equally appealing comics by Takahashi Yoichi. Since its first appearance in 1981, both comics and cartoon series have been translated in many languages and broadcast on all continents under localized titles such as *Super Campeones* (South America), *Flash Kicker* (US) or *Olive et Tom* (France). According to the Ministry's announcement, *Captain Tsubasa* appeared in memoirs of players all over the world as one key factor that brought them into football; probably the most famous example cited was Zinedine Zidane, three-time World Footballer of the Year. Focusing on the adventures of a Japanese youth football team and its captain, named Ōzora Tsubasa, the story line reveals a highly idealized image of football and the way core values of Japanese society (cooperation, collective orientation, determination and persistence) are linked to the world of football. The Japanese government expected that the Arabic-language-dubbed version of *Captain Majed* would strengthen goodwill toward Japan in Iraq, where about 1,200 Japanese ground forces were stationed in the Southern town of Samawah. Stickers depicting the football star were also placed on water supply trucks provided by Japan to the waterworks in Iraq from the time the troops had been dispatched (MOFA 2005). In this instance, the virtual football player was used as a globally recognizable proxy for Japan in order to make its assistance activities widely known among Iraqi people.

Securing a peaceful environment for the Japanese troops in Iraq was most certainly a central motive for the export promotion of the football cartoon and the sponsorship of football-related events within the Middle East. In November 2003, only a few days before the announcement of the dispatch of

Japanese troops, the JFA collected football equipment from all over Japan for donations to Iraq. On a later occasion, when the ground forces were already in Iraq, the Department of Youth and Sports in the Governorate of Al-Muthanna received more balls, shirts and inflators, which were explicitly donated for Southern Iraq. Japan's Self-Defence Forces provided transportation for the football equipment to Baghdad and further on to Samawah, where the handover ceremony took place, together with a mini-tournament between three local football clubs and a team from the Self-Defence Forces. For the Japanese government, this was a welcome and highly publicized opportunity to refashion the image of the Iraq mission, which many in Japan saw as unconstitutional and a breach of international law.

The Ministry of Foreign Affairs also backed international friendship matches between Iraq and Japan, inviting the team players to fly into Japan and offering live television coverage of the friendly match from Tokyo to Baghdad. It also dispatched former national team midfielder Kitazawa Tsuyoshi on behalf of JICA (Japan International Cooperation Agency) as celebrity football trainer to places in Asia, Africa and the Middle East. Founded in 1974, JICA is a central component of Japan's official development assistance. The implementation agency is responsible for technical assistance, focusing on institution building, organization strengthening and human resources development in developing countries. Kitazawa, who became the first JFA ambassador after ending his playing career in 2002, and well-known tennis player Date Kimiko officially supported the objectives of Japan's official development assistance among which sports and physical education issues have gained in prominence. JICA began conducting sports programmes for the purpose of health promotion and alleviating the mental and physical living conditions of people living in disaster-stricken areas.

Territorial disputes between divided nations provided another field for the Ministry's attempts to gain clout in foreign diplomacy. In May 2004, Japan's Ministry of Foreign Affairs (MOFA) hosted the Ministerial Conference on Peace Consolidation and Economic Development of the Western Balkans, which closed with the signing of a 'peace ball' by Koizumi and other heads of state of the five Western Balkan States to express their commitment to peace. The keynote was spoken by Goodwill Ambassador 'Pixie' Dragan Stojkovic, a Serbian football star who enjoys a very high reputation in Japan in part because of his years with Nagoya Grampus Eight during the late 1990s, but also for his passionate playing style, which resonates with Japanese core values such as initiative and perseverance. Contemplating the chances of ethnic reconciliation through sports, Stojkovic opened his address with a personal reflection about 20 years of service in professional football:

> The word 'football' is a common word that every one of us can understand. And ethnic groups, religions, borders and languages do not matter when we speak of football. Football teams around the world are

> made up of players from each and every nationality, race, religion and language. Every player takes this situation for granted; I myself was never aware of the nationality or the ethnicity of my team mates. As a matter of fact, my team mates who have shared joys and sorrows with me are from various Western Balkan countries. [. . .] Truly, football itself is the bridge that can cross over national, ethnic and language barriers.[5]

As part of its attempts to bridge gaps, MOFA also frequently invited Israeli and Palestinian youth players to participate in training camps in Japan and to meet each other in direct competition. The *Blue Book of Diplomacy* from 2003 and later shows a steady increase in the number of football-related events sponsored by the government and often executed by the JFA, for example, during the Japan–ASEAN Exchange Year 2003 or the Japan–Korea Friendship Year in 2005.

At the occasion of the latter, two former national team captains from Japan and South Korea were nominated as Goodwill Ambassadors of Football. By coincidence they happened to enter the diplomatic pitch as substitutes for football players from Japan's and South Korea's Parliaments that had played against each other on several occasions since 1998. Established as a group of Diet members interested in securing the success of the World Cup, the Japanese branch of the network was rebranded as the Association of Parliamentarians for the Promotion of Football Diplomacy in 2002. One Japanese participant remembered the dead-serious attitude of the South Koreans, 'who played without compromise'. Japan had to concede a defeat at this first encounter, even though their team was strengthened by Upper House member Kamamoto Kunishige, who had been the leading scorer at the Mexico Olympics 1968, and a former pro-wrestler whose hard tackling actually broke the leg of a Korean delegate. The scores slightly improved after Japan's parliamentarians hired a Brazilian trainer and intensified the training schedule, including winter camps.

Over the years, the groups visited each other for six friendly matches, which probably helped to establish new channels of communication between the countries. Japan's football diplomats also played against visiting parliamentarians from England and Russia or abroad against Slovenia and Hungary. In 2005, the Year of Africa, they played against a selection of representatives from 17 African countries that defeated the Japanese team 5–0. However, the links established by means of football were too weak to cope with newly arising tensions. In 2005, the annual match against South Korea had to be rescheduled when the Japanese team rejected South Korea's request for a list of those parliamentarians who had accompanied Prime Minister Koizumi on his visit to the Yasukuni Shrine in April. They failed to understand why the South Koreans did not want to play against anyone having worshipped the war dead enshrined at the national monument. The match was cancelled after the Japanese prefecture of Shimane, which faces Korea via the Japan Sea, symbolically annexed the 'Takeshima Islands'.

This act provoked harsh reactions from Korea, who also claims ownership of the 'Dokdo Islands', as they are known to the Koreans. Since then talks about resuming the match series seem to have faded out. The underlying incommensurability of positions is nicely portrayed by Etō Seiichirō, a key figure in the diplomatic usage of football. The former vice-minister of Foreign Affairs was chiefly involved in founding the parliamentarians' football team and establishing the links with South Korea's team. But he also happened to be a board member of the Association for the Joint Visit of All Parliamentarians to the Yasukuni-Shrine. As the representative from Ōita prefecture also acted prominently on a committee of support measures for Iraq, this position may help to explain some of the previously mentioned uses of football in Japan's foreign policy in the Middle East. But in general, the experiences from 2005 rather showed the limited capabilities of active football diplomacy.

REACTIVE FORMS OF FOOTBALL DIPLOMACY

With respect to regional integration in the North Pacific, football often served to influence diplomatic engagement that was more reactive in nature. Prior to the middle of the decade, foreign policy issues came to the fore during several encounters between the Japanese national team and opponents from North Korea or China. During the 2004 Asian Cup, hosted by the People's Republic of China, Japan's national side faced hostile crowds in all their matches. Chinese spectators heckled Japanese players, booed the national anthem and displayed banners reading, 'Look into history and apologize to the Asian people', or 'Return the Diaoyu (Senkaku) Islands!' (*Asia Times*, August 7, 2004). When Japan beat Thailand, Chinese fans in Xinan Province converged on the Japan team bus, which was forced to depart earlier than scheduled, leaving two players behind. At the semi-finals against Jordan in Chongqing, Chinese fans reportedly insulted their opponents, hurled garbage and stormed a bus carrying Japanese fans. The worst case threatened when Japan was set to face China in the finals. The Japanese embassy advised fans not to wear the national team jersey, to enter the stadium early, to leave quickly and to avoid celebrating in case of victory. Expectations were heightened to such an extent that one Shanghai TV commentator forecasted: 'It's going to be a war' (*The Observer*, August 8, 2004).

What had started on the pitch caused the Japanese embassy in China as well as Foreign Ministry officials in Japan to formally protest against what they perceived as an abusive treatment of the Japanese fans and symbols of Japanese dignity. Foreign Ministry Kawaguchi Yoriko, appearing before a committee in the Diet, said: 'I want Chinese soccer fans to think a little more about their anti-Japanese actions. It is deplorable. It has no positive impact on advancing Japan-China relations'. Japan Vice Foreign Minister Takeuchi Yukio met with Wu Dawei, China's ambassador to Japan, to urge him to stop Chinese fans from abusing the national anthem. China was formally requested three times to control its fans and ensure the security of Japanese players and fans. Chief Cabinet Secretary Hosoda Hiroyuki stated: 'We want China to firmly deal with it as Japanese spectators are likely to go there. No trouble or violence should take place'. Prime Minister Koizumi insisted: 'It's a sport event. Why can't we just enjoy it?' Yabunaka Mitoji, director general from the Foreign Ministry's Asian and Oceanian Affairs Bureau, threatened a boycott of the 2008 Olympics unless China proved its ability to control its people (all quotes from Sugita 2004).

Despite all diplomatic interventions and a massive deployment of 6,000 security forces, Chinese football supporters clashed with riot police outside the Beijing Workers Stadium after China was defeated 3–1. During the match, bottles and other objects were reportedly thrown at Japanese fans. Obscenities as well as anti-Japanese songs from the war of liberation from colonial rule roared through the arena. After the match, which Chinese fans criticized due to a number of dubious referee decisions, they burnt Japanese flags and surrounded the Japanese team bus, which was pelted with fireworks and forced to return to the stadium. A diplomat's car had its window smashed. Japanese fans had to wait for an hour after the game inside the stadium until enough buses were provided for their safe escape from the stadium. Compared to some European or Southern American experiences of hooliganism, these were rather minor incidents. However, they were not trivial for the Japanese media, who arguably grossly exaggerated the actions of a few hundred among the many thousands at the 60,000-seat stadium.

Another incident laying proof to the media's capability of amplifying international dissonance was provided by the second round of qualification games for the 2006 World Cup. Japan had to face North Korea, with which official relations had turned ever more hostile since North Korea had withdrawn into isolation. The home game in autumn 2005 was played under enhanced security conditions. The JFA stocked up the number of security guards in Saitama to 1,400 that joined a 2,000-strong police force. Fans of the two teams were channelled into the stadium by separate entrances, and a buffer of 1,000 seats prevented the 5,000 North Korean fans—virtually all members of the Korean community in Japan—from coming into contact with the Japanese fans. The match ended with an uncontested victory for Japan and no sensation for the media. The return match in Pyongyang would have generated the largest presence of Japanese on North Korean territory since liberation from colonial oppression in 1945. Because of the hostile relations on the state level, the Japanese Ministry of Foreign Affairs was planning special measures like the opening of a temporary consulate in Pyongyang to guarantee the protection of Japanese visitors. But due to massive spectator riots in Pyongyang that followed an earlier group game against Iran, FIFA relocated the match to a neutral venue in Bangkok without any crowd. In the ghost stadium of Bangkok, Japan also won the second match and a ticket to the World Cup in Germany, whereas North Korea saw itself discriminated against twice: first, by a biased Syrian referee, who caused the upheaval in Pyongyang, then by FIFA, whose decision deprived it from the chance to play Japan under more favourable conditions at Kim Il Sung Stadium.

Appeals to fair play and equal opportunities are common to sports as well as to an idealist conception of international relations. Chinese fans remember the finals of the Asian Cup as an unfair game in which bad refereeing robbed China from a chance to gain the Cup title, whereas Japanese officials recall the game as a very uncomfortable display of hostility based on a distorted historical memory. Clinging to the international norm of fairness at both the levels of sport and foreign relations simultaneously, however, imposes irreconcilable problems on the side of the host nation. But what seemed to have been caused by the ghostly shadows of Japan's colonial past acquired quite different meanings when put into context with contemporary domestic and international politics.

From a Chinese perspective, their fans acted in a way commonly observed abroad and thus it was rather a problem created by the Japanese media that exaggerated the incidents and linked sports with politics. In what could be interpreted as a reference to the ideologically loaded demand of keeping sport and politics apart, China's Foreign Ministry spokesman, Kong Quan, expressed his regrets that Japanese politicians and media had established such links. Conversely, for the Japanese, it was China that had brought politics into football. Not only were the Chinese fans held accountable, but also their government since neither had demonstrated any control and both acted inappropriately during the Asian Cup affair. Negative responses to Japan were not seen in relation to a past that continued to inform the present, but rather as a cause of nationalistic education used by the power elite to forge national cohesion and cover the increasing gaps among the Chinese people. Stirring up anti-Japanese sentiments enabled the government to divert criticism of its own policies and monopolize power by directing the anger of its people towards its closest competitor, Japan. But if the government was interested in utilizing anti-Japanese demonstrations as a safety valve, it might better seek to pre-empt or co-opt it. Otherwise, as the writers Shimada Yasuhiko and Tamaki Masayuki noted in comparing North Korea to the Romanian Ceausescu regime, the agitated atmosphere at football internationals might rapidly turn the people against the oppressive system.[6]

From the people's point of view, both in China and North Korea, the football stadium is the only safe place for critical articulations that are otherwise censored or prohibited. Japanese wartime atrocities are constitutive of the official state history of PR China and North Korea, much more than the millions of tragedies experienced during the Great Leap, the Cultural Revolution or the uncountable casualties that were lost during these periods and famines. In North Korea, the dominant historical narrative of Japanese aggression leaves little scope for events and figures that are not related to the 'Great Leader' Kim Il-Sung and his family. Since the state is limited in its legitimacy and opportunities to suppress anti-Japanese demonstrations in the public arena, the football spectators in China and North Korea could easily transform the sport stadium into their court of international appeal. Hence the cases of fair play in football, and of anti-Japanese sentiment, became sites for testing out new forms of civil society engagement, or for criticizing censorship, the lack of political participation rights and other domestic issues related to the anti-democratic state.

CONCLUSION

This discussion of football in the North Pacific confirms the claim that football, and sport in general, can be easily integrated into foreign policy goals as well as put onto the agenda in specific circumstances (Arnaud 1988:7). To be clear, the power of football in foreign policy is relatively weak and its influence should not be overrated. Yet its influence should not be underappreciated. As I have argued, throughout the region, state actors have utilized football as a vehicle for the acquisition of status and the expression of authority in the international community. As an actively implemented tool in international relations, football served the strengthening of official ties and the promotion of semi-official exchange programmes as well as the articulation of special interests, such as the claim to leadership or the self-display as peaceful and supportive member of the world community. Particularly during the preparations for the 2002 World Cup, football was consciously employed as a foreign policy tool by South Korea and Japan for the enhancement of national prestige and the improvement of bilateral ties. In general, Japan, and to a lesser extent other East Asian states, regarded the worldwide appeal of football as an opportunity to gain credibility as a state actor conforming or appealing to international norms.

But football more often enters the agenda of foreign policy in response to the critical state of international relations. Football continues to be interwoven in larger issues of postcolonialism and regional integration in the North Pacific, where bilateral as well as multilateral relations are continually held hostage by opportunistic politicians beating the drum of nationalism for their own purposes. While the World Cup may have made this more difficult in South Korea, the 'history card' is played out by South Korean political actors no less frequently than in North Korea or China. The colonial past, which indirectly caused the formation of Japan's 'fatalist pacifism', continues to hamper any aspirations of Japan for a stronger role in multilateral frameworks of the region. Since pacifism and denial of war responsibilities are two sides of the same coin (Asai 2004), Japan is denied the desired normal state status and sees itself being forced under the military security umbrella of the US. The self-imposed dependence on the US tears the country away from a closer leaning towards China and limits Japan's choices of opening up alternative ways to institutionalized frameworks of regional integration. Such 'issues of the past and the present' probably haunt Japan's foreign policy makers more than the playmakers on the pitch, though they show their faces inside the football arenas, too.

10 Sport, Spectacles and Subalternity

Positioning East Asia in World Sports[1]

INTRODUCTION

A number of chapters of this study have already argued that sport has always provided a useful mechanism for reminding people and nations precisely where they stand in relation to one another. The close association of sporting prowess with national progress is not by chance, given that the modern sporting form developed its central ideologies and modes of governance in line with the formation of the nation-state and industrial capitalism. The global dissemination of sport followed the trails of trade, empire and Christian mission. Not surprisingly, the Olympic Movement emerged at the height of the age of colonialism and has proven to outlast all the great transformations of the world system during the 20th century. Like the capitalist 'quest for accumulation', it has constantly widened its sphere of influence, searching for new markets and additional programming. Its flagship event, the Olympic Games, has become a significant component of global culture, reaching out to many millions spectators simultaneously. Hardly any other cultural spectacle of contemporary times is of greater appeal,[2] with the possible exception of the Men's Football World Cup.

The Beijing Summer Olympics in 2008 was only the third occasion at which the attention of the entire sport world was drawn to the Far Eastern subcontinent. Since Japan's first successful bid for the ultimately 'missing Games' of 1940, East Asia had hosted the Summer Olympic Games twice (Tokyo 1964, Seoul 1988). By comparison, the Olympic Games took place 15 times in Europe, six times in North America and twice in Australia. The regional bias clearly indicates subtle status differences assigned to the countries of the respective regions by the principal rights owners of this sport spectacle. But it is a matter of fact that East Asia has witnessed quite a number of other impressive large-scale sport events of international and even global significance reaching the region, such as the FIFA World Cup (Japan/Korea 2002), the Olympic Winter Games (Sapporo 1972, Nagano 1998) or the IAAF World Championships (Tokyo 1991; Ōsaka 2007) and IAAF World Junior Championships (Seoul 1992, Beijing 2006) in athletics as well as the Women's Football World Cup (China 1991 and 2007). Recent times also witnessed how the region became firmly entrenched within the annual travel circuit of major sport event serials, such as the Formula 1 races, the tennis ATP world tour or PGA tours in golf. Notwithstanding the far-reaching appeal and importance these sport events have for athletes and fans alike, they inevitably pale in significance when compared with the more spectacular sport 'mega-events'.

Only these sport spectacles effectively focus the world's awareness of a particular place and nation and the success thereof, in either hosting or performing well in the event. With such concentrated media attention on the hosting nation, it would be surprising if the nation in question did not take advantage of this opportunity to assert its identity and to promote its international aspirations. The promises of gaining currency from the symbolic display of national accomplishment and cultural authority on an international stage repeatedly prompted East Asian bids for the Olympic Games and eventually for the Football World Cup. Studies of East Asian experiences with hosting the flagship events of contemporary global sport culture provide ample evidence of the significance sport mega-events,[3] situated at the crossing of the universal and the particular, have acquired for 'official' versions of public culture in this region of the world. Yet because of the sense of ambiguity about the costs and benefits of such state-run projects, the conventional equation of hosting mega-events with forging national cohesion and gaining clout in the international arena cannot go unquestioned.

EAST ASIA, SUBALTERNITY AND THE WORLD SYSTEM OF SPORT

Global flows and global movements have played a significant role in disseminating the notion of sport. Appadurai has shown how flows of people, goods, technology, finance, media and ideas have undermined the power of the nation-state, as the world became multicentric. These flows are linked with the emergence and transmutation of five interrelated landscapes or '-scapes' that constitute the global condition. I suggest adding 'sportscapes' as a sixth one to his well-known dimensions of globalization, i.e. ethnoscapes, technoscapes, financescapes, mediascapes and ideoscapes (Appadurai 1996), in order to emphasize the significance of sport as another landscape of global dimensions and its autonomy. Sportscapes are characterized by the transnational flows of physical culture, ideologies and practices centring on the body. Globally branded apparel and sporting goods, which are making use of the new international division of labour and transnational commodity chains; fan allegiances crossing the globe; live broadcasts from the other side of the world; international non-governmental organizations exerting global governance on sport and tournaments; sport tourists travelling to the Olympics; and similar phenomena have contributed to the raising of a common awareness of One World. The phenomena of sport constitute not just an object of globalization, but also a driving force of globalization; both a metric and a motor of it, as Giulianotti and Robertson (2007) suggest.

Any exploration of global flows in the mutual interactions between East Asia and the Olympics will provide a number of protruding and troubling paradoxes at the backbone of the Olympic sports movement. For much of the 100 years that have passed since the Olympic Movement reached out to the Far East for the first time, the subcontinent has been a pivotal testing ground for the internationalist pretensions of the Olympic ideology, which aspires to universal values, despite its very particularistic origins in Western society. At the same time, Olympic sports have had a deep and lasting impact upon vernacular body cultures, transforming and erasing traditional games, contests and philosophies of the body of which the East Asian region has been abundant. Within the context of international relations, the Olympic Games have left a high impact on representations of self and otherness via the dominant West. Power relationships between Western and Eastern nations, between developed and late developing states and between the centre of world sport and its peripheries are far from being static and stable. Here I consciously employ the concept of subalternity in the sense of Spivak's more generous interpretation that encompasses 'everything that has limited or no access to the cultural imperialism' (1985:121), because it provides the ability to read East Asia into ideologies of difference and otherness simultaneously. Subaltern actors are situated in a 'space of difference' that enables them to subvert the authority of those having hegemonic power (Bhabha 1996). Dipesh Chakrabarty (1985:376) defines subalternity as 'composite culture of resistance to and acceptance of domination and hierarchy'. While dominated, the subaltern is not entirely obliterated and retains values, ideas and modes of action that are not prescribed by the dominant and which can draw upon beliefs and experiences exclusive to the acting subject.

These asymmetric power relations between centres and peripheries of the Olympic globality model are characteristic modes of representation by the subaltern facing the dominant West. Subalternity in sport events is not only generated by the social levelling off-effect of fair play and equality that Mills (2006) observed in South Asian sport. It is also created by disruptions of the social order and the suspension of the rules of everyday life. Celebrators turn the competition for superiority and dominance into a shared moment of collective bonding; spectators, lacking the stakes of the celebrating mass, turn the event into a spectacle. But as Spivak (1985) made clear, the voice of the subaltern does not achieve the dialogic level of utterance; talk of the subaltern does not become part of 'a transaction between speaker and listener'. If sporting activities or the hosting thereof incite subalternity, then they will also act as mechanisms by which subaltern groups are oppressed and through which dominant groups assert their power. Reflecting upon past and present encounters of East Asia with the Olympic spectacle, this chapter will show how the voices of Asian nations hosting sport mega-events have been raised quite successfully to transmit messages of high relevance for their domestic audiences, while attempts to address issues of fair representation by the universal meta-languages of signifying, representing and imagining whilst hosting Olympics Games have largely been in vain.

OLYMPIC SPORTS INTO THE FAR EAST, FAR EASTERN SPORTS INTO THE OLYMPICS

Colonial empires and missionary regimes were at the background of the early stage of the global spread of sport. Later generations of writers therefore critically assessed sport as a colonial tool. Postcolonial writers identified the modern conceptions of sport, games and physical education as elaborated ideologies and techniques of subjugating and assimilating the colonial subject. Sport in the colonial mind worked upon indigenous bodies, dissected its parts and functions and reassembled them after having replaced autochthonous parts by Western ideas of the rationality of physical exercise, the rule-bound ethics of contest and competition and modernist inscriptions of the state on the colonial subject's skin and muscles. In Japan, the modern nation-state actively promoted sport within the confines of public education, the conscription system and mass youth organizations. In Korea and China, missionary movements like the YMCA or the YWCA played a crucial role in subverting established body ideologies privileging mind over physique prior to the phases of republican or colonial rule. Like its Western role model, the Japanese colonial state used modern sport, gymnastics, games and athletics for the education of its subjects abroad (Manzenreiter 2008).

The 'Ys' have not been the only global movements actively involved in forming the athletic body in the East. Of more importance for the great somatic transformation has been the Olympic Movement. With its particular form of dialectical play between national and transnational allegiances, it has been described as 'the largest modern example of a movement born in the context of European concerns with world peace . . . [and] the most spectacular among a series of sites and formations on which the future of the nation-state will turn in the post-colonial world' (Appadurai 1993:419–420). The invitation was motivated by the expansionary mission of the International Olympic Committee (IOC) seeking to promote Olympism as 'a way of life based on the joy of effort, the educational value of good example and respect for universal fundamental ethical principles' (Olympic Charter). It is debatable to what degree the fundamental principles of Olympism, encompassing international goodwill, peace and equality, resonated with the worldview of ruling elites abroad.[4] Yet as a new and modern kind of body culture, sport in general was decidedly marked as positive and beneficiary for the transmogrifying process from feudal to modern civil society. Rather than placing 'sport at the service of the harmonious development of man, with a view to promoting a peaceful society concerned with the preservation of human dignity' (Olympic Charter), East Asia's advocates of modernization championed a conception of sport and physical education according to social Darwinist ideas, which were highly in vogue in the age of imperialism. Herbert Spencer's idea of the 'survival of the fittest' provided the intellectual framework for a somatic view of society, in which the valorization of physical strength and competitiveness was directly linked with state power and imperial rule.

East Asia's embracement by the Olympic Movement began with the formal invitation to Imperial Japan, which spearheaded the path to modernity among the nations of the region, to solicit a suitable representative of Japan at the IOC in January 1909. This was certainly not an early attempt by the Olympic Movement to validate its pretensions as patron of universal humanist principles. Rather it was a 'noble gesture' bestowed upon the new emerging Far Eastern power that recently had defeated China and Russia in two wars and had muscled its way among the exclusive club of colonial powers, after having annexed Taiwan and Korea. China, a later target of Japan's expansionist desires, joined the Olympic Movement considerably later in 1922, and a first delegation, consisting of a lonely short track runner, was participating at the 1932 Olympics in Los Angeles. Koreans had to wait for national acclamation by the IOC until independence from Japanese colonial rule was restored after 1945. Shortly thereafter the Korean Olympic Committee became a member of the IOC and was invited to send delegations to the London Olympic Summer Games and the Winter Games in St. Moritz in 1948. Even after the Korean War, athletes from the South and the North continued to participate as representatives of a Korea until Cold War hostilities and the postcolonial struggle for autonomy and identity reached its early heights in the years running up to the 1964 Tokyo Olympics. Seoul was hosting the second Asian Olympic Games in 1988 prior to the sudden end of the Cold War System. China's first aspirations date back to the bid for the Olympics 1952, but these dreams had to be postponed for more than half a century.[5]

Hosting the Games is the highest but not the ultimate aspiration of states and nations struggling for recognition by the IOC member states. Adding one's own body culture to the Olympic canon is probably ranked highest in the gradual process which sees nations and states becoming integrated into the world sport system. At the first and lowest level, nations desire the right to participate; second, they hope to win any medals; third, they hope to rank high in the medal list; fourth, they bid for hosting the Games; and, finally, if they have command over a distinctive competitive body culture, they aspire to gaining acknowledgment of their own tradition. It is easy to show how these steps have repeatedly occurred in line with the modernization process of East Asian states and their positioning within the world system. The most exclusive prices, and therefore the achievements most desired for, are based on premises of adapting to Western models of hosting and to Western notions of sport.

Modern ideas of body, subject and nation impacted upon the 'invention of judo' (Inoue 1992) in the late 19th century. Kanō Jigorō, founder of the *kōdōkan jūdō* and Japan's first representative at the IOC, reassessed traditional fighting techniques to refine and reassemble these movements for his new martial art. His pedagogic key concepts of 'maximal efficiency' and 'mutual welfare and benefit' closely resonated with rationalism and modernist societal visions that saw the individual integrated into a larger group of like-minded subjects, performing for the good of the nation. Kanō's tireless campaigning for the promotion of judo abroad was finally crowned when the IOC accepted judo as a new Olympic sport in 1964. Adding Taekwondo to the Olympics did not take that long but afforded more straightforward initiative-taking. After a decade of intensive lobbying all over the world, the Korean martial art was admitted as a demonstration sport at the Seoul Olympics in 1988; it took some more Olympiads and further lobbying by the Korean-run World Federation of Taekwondo to convince IOC officials to list Taekwondo as a competitor sport in Sidney 2000. China's similar ambitions of seeing its national wushu on display at the 2008 Beijing Games did not materialize: Having scrutinized the international spread and appeal of China's martial art, the IOC declined China's request and even prohibited wushu athletes from showing their skills at any official event related to the Olympic Games. This decision left many Chinese disappointed since they had taken it for granted that their country, similar to Japan and Korea, would get the honour of being represented with a native sport at the Olympic Games.[6]

The border-crossing diffusion of indigenous body practices was initiated by Orientalist curiosity and accelerated by the increasing mobility of people, texts and images. In the course of their ultimately global career, Asian martial arts underwent a process of rationalization and reorganization according to major didactic and ideological principles taken from the competitive body cultures of the dominant West. Judo and Taekwondo, as well as karate and wushu, were separated from their cultural origins. Their purpose was streamlined to match with the logic of competitive sport, and organizational structures were transformed to reproduce the hierarchical structures of local organizations, national associations and international federations. However, the structures and functions of bureaucratic rationality are often in contrast to and conflict with authority derived from blood relationships with charismatic founding figures, hierarchical and interpersonal relationships and dyadic genealogies that are commonly observed among and within many martial art schools in East Asia. The internationalization of the local body cultures received a huge promotional thrust when the custodians of the heritage officially transferred their control rights to bureaucratic domestic associations and international sport federations.

OLYMPIC GOLD: THE BUSINESS OF SPORT

Global spectacles such as the Summer Olympic Games have been explained as occasions in which cultures or societies reflect upon and define themselves, dramatize their collective myths and history, present themselves with alternatives and eventually change in some ways while remaining the same in others (MacAloon 1984:1). Such a functional appraisal, however, over-emphasizes the effectiveness of one master-script and it downplays interests and the influence of transnational actors such as the IOC itself, but also multinational corporations sponsoring the spectacle and the media that have largely gained in significance over the years. Back in the 1960s, hardly anyone would have seriously considered the flagship event of global sport as business. As a matter of fact, the IOC repeatedly expressed its annoyance with commercial interests entering into the Games, the rising grandezza of hosting and the no-nonsense seriousness of competitiveness dividing the camps of the Cold War system. The Seoul Olympics, however, were staged in an environment that had radically changed since the 'Hollywood Games' of Los Angeles 1984 had shown for the first time that privatizing the hosting of mega-events could produce an economic surplus.

The privatization of broadcasting services and new developments in mass communication technologies were the most important factors contributing to the rising demand for sport events. Print media, television and nowadays the internet establish the imagined communities of geographically distant, yet interested and engaged ephemeral communities, united in their shared interest in sport or the event. In the age of global mass communication technologies, viewing rates have become more important than live spectatorship to demonstrate the size and significance of the event via sponsors and the media. Official event reports usually quote aggregates of television viewers in a size of a multiple of the actual world population, which is a blunt hint at both the significance of the event as well as the assertiveness of its principal rights holders. Tokyo 1964 was the first Olympic Games to have employed satellite technology for overseas live broadcasting, while Seoul 1988 was riding high on the lucrative wave of deregulating national media markets and the inroad of big sponsorship money into television sport, which is another factor changing the meaning of sport spectacles. According to the demand of the economy and in line with the logic of the commodity form, sport and sport events, particularly as media content, chiefly fulfil the function of linking the manufacturers of consumer products with their customers. The alliance of sport and television is of crucial importance for targeting ever larger audiences, and the capability of sport to reach transnational customer markets is particularly appealing (Horne and Manzenreiter 2002b). The IOC has been able to cash in twice both by selling exclusive broadcasting rights to media agencies that resell the rights or net in their investment by selling advertisement time, and by trading sponsorship rights with its official partners, who in return are granted global media exposure and the positive association with the sport event.

Broadcasting rights for the 1964 'Media Olympics' in Tokyo generated comparatively modest revenues of USD 1.6 million. But the price for the Summer Games registered a thousand-fold increase over the following 44 years (2008 Olympic Games: USD 1.74 billion). The steepest increase occurred during the 1980s, securing USD 402.6 million for the Seoul Olympics in 1988, which was still four times less than the result to be grossed 20 years later. The increase in revenue streams was paralleled by the global reach: The 'satellite games' of Tokyo 1964 were broadcast to 40 countries; in 1988, 160 countries tuned in, and the Beijing Olympics was aired in 220 territories. Sales of broadcasting rights continue to be the most important single revenue source to the IOC, though partnership programmes have gained in significance. The Olympic Partners (TOP) programme was first launched for the quadrennium 1985 to 1988, generating revenues of USD 96 million from nine partners; the last one running up to the Beijing Olympics contracted 12 partners paying a total of USD 886 million for exclusive association with the Games. In addition, domestic sponsorship programmes were introduced in 1996 to support the staging of the Games. At the Beijing Games, 51 domestic partners provided a stunning USD 1.2 billion to the operational needs of BOCOG in revenue, goods and services (IOC 2009:19).

It should be noted that these giant flows of funds largely bypass the local host society but fill the books of the 'sport industrial complex', a triangle of transnational media corporations, international sport organizations and multinational corporations. The state and its local representatives are part of the new global political economy of sport in as far as they are increasingly forced into underwriting the private risks of hosting by investing public funds into the required infrastructure and management of the events while largely giving up control over the images generated by the new network of institutional powers governing the narratives of the events (Horne and Manzenreiter 2004).

THE DIFFICULTIES OF REPRESENTATION

Sport mega-events have always provided a stage for the symbolic contestation of modernity between elites and the masses, as well as between different models of development. As the Cold War rivalry between the Soviet bloc and the 'Free World' has shown both in sport competitions and in hosting them, sport spectacles acquired high significance for 'official' versions of public culture and point of reference for the collective orientation of national societies toward international audiences. As showcase events for domestic as well as global consumption, previous East Asian spectacles laid proof to the level of socioeconomic development and they demonstrated the political reliability of their hosts to their international partners. At the same time, holding up a mirror reflecting the tangible merits of labour, thrift and dutifulness to their local audiences, the Games were also a politically motivated event meant to reconcile the former antagonistic blocs within their own populations.

The symbolic contest between nations seems to have a particular appeal in East Asia where the first 'Far Eastern Championship Games' took place in 1913. These were the first out of a series of ten multi-sport competitions held between 1913 and 1934, albeit under a different name, as the IOC had no intention of accepting this early infliction of its property rights. Originally called the Far Eastern Olympic Games, the tournament was initiated in 1912 by the American YMCA representative E. S. Brown in Manila, where the first tournament took place in 1913. The six-nation tournament, which included the Philippines, China, Japan, British East India, Thailand and Hong Kong, has been next to the Olympics the only other early instance of a regular series of international multi-sport competitions. Many of these tournaments were overshadowed by political tensions between the participating states. Struggles between China and Japan over the question of granting membership status to the athletes from Manchukuo, which allegedly was a Japanese puppet state governed by politicians without a popular mandate, finally dissolved the Far Eastern Athletic Association (Date 2000).

Inspired by the political clout it gained from the 1932 Los Angeles Olympic Games, Japan aggressively pushed to host the 1940 Olympics. The successful backdoor dealings and negotiations with head of states and politicians required more diplomacy in political corridors than the IOC was usually willing to accept. Yet Tokyo gained the Games when Mussolini withdrew in 1936. However, together with the planned Winter Olympic Games in Sapporo, the 1940 Tokyo Olympic Games were foreclosed by the outbreak of the war with China in 1937, which caused city officials to renounce the bid in 1938. In the short period between acceptance of the bid and withdrawal, the imperial state was determined to use the Games as key ideological apparatus to display its unique national essence (Collins 2007:101). Particularly challenging, however, was the task of adjusting the Olympic protocol to the ceremonial procedures deemed to be suitable for Emperor Hirohito, head of state and living god. Furthermore, foreshadowing the mass attendance of foreigners in the vicinity of the sacred precincts of the Meiji Shrine next to the National Sports Grounds prompted delays in planning and construction work. Twenty-four years later, preparations for the 1964 Tokyo Olympic Games followed a very different script that signified the changed relationships between Japan and the West within a global hierarchy of nation-states and regions.

In 1964 references to traditional elements of Japanese culture were understated, since the producers of the spectacle were more concerned with demonstrating a new and largely Westernized variant of Japan. Japan fully embraced the opportunity to put onstage its return to the international community of nation-states and to celebrate its rebirth as a peace-loving nation and economically successful industrial state. This complex message was highlighted by the state-of-the-art stadium infrastructure and the normalization strategy behind the display of contested symbols of the state, like the national flag, the anthem and the emperor. Its climatic moment was delivered by the final scene of a torch run that had seen the Olympic flame carried through some of Japan's previous war victims and throughout all regions of Japan, including the American protectorate of Okinawa where the fire actually entered Japanese territory for the first time. At last the sacred flame was brought to light the cauldron towering above the National Stadium by the hands of Sakai Yoshinori, a 19-year-old athlete from Hiroshima who had seen the light of the world on the day when the atomic bomb devastated his home city. The public presentation of the emperor as symbol of the state, who fulfilled the honorary role of opening the Games, and the mass display of the controversial symbols *kimigayo* and *hinomaru*, the national anthem and flag, simultaneously pleased conservative nationalism and provided a sense of unity to the Japanese spectators (cf. Tagsold 2002). The official logo of the Tokyo Olympics was consciously designed to symbolize the country, thereby transcending the space of the host city. Featuring the red sun of Japan's national flag, it left no doubt that these were actually Japanese Games, and not just the Tokyo Olympics.

In a similar fashion, the ceremonial opening of the Seoul Olympics in 1988 offered the South Koreans an opportunity to come to terms with a tragic past of colonial oppression under Japanese imperial rule, a bloody civil war and years of military dictatorship in a divided country. The Olympic fire was lit by a young female athlete who had received the torch from the gold medal winner of the 1936 Olympic marathon, Sohn Kee-chung. The Korean runner participated at the 1936 Olympics as a subject of the Japanese Empire (and under the Japanized name of Son Kitei) and thus was forced to endure the moment of his greatest triumph under a different flag and to the tune of a different anthem. These climatic moments of the Opening Ceremony powerfully condensed various sets of relations between East and West, past and present and present and future, senior and junior, male and female, colonized and liberated, and suffering and rejoicing. For the organizers, the Games offered a way to display Korea as distinct not just from the West, but from Japan as well. Hundreds of scholars and artists had been involved in writing the script of the ceremonies that would introduce Korea to the world and raise appreciation of forgotten cultural traditions at home (Kang 1987, 1991). The Opening Ceremony therefore featured a colourful array of choreographed scenes of dance, music, costumes and folklore, evoking images of traditional Korean culture. Referencing a history of 5,000 years, South Korea emphasized its cultural autonomy from the considerably younger cultures of China (3,000 years) and Japan (2,600 years, according to nationalist historians).

Sandra Collins (2008:185) has pointed out that the East–West dichotomy is a common trope to be found in many of the ceremonial scripts of

East Asian Olympics. While Western host cities tend to present themselves as world-class cities, Asian host cities subscribe to a narrative of modern hybridism, uniting cutting-edge high technology conjoined with rich cultural heritage and exotic civilization. This convention, which seems to be rooted in lingering anxieties of participating in the Western hegemony of the Olympics, can alternatively be read as a careful suggestion that modernization is not synonymous with Westernization or as a more assertive claim for the moral right of hosting the Games to prove the global spread and universalism of the Olympic Games (Collins 2008:186). Much more than Japan and South Korea, which used the Games to secure recognition by the international community, China was self-consciously prone to reinterpret the fundamental Olympic principles in order 'to promote the harmonization of world civilizations' from a non-Western perspective (Girginov 2008:899).

BRANDING CHINA: THE ROLE OF THE OLYMPIC GAMES IN NATION-BRANDING

Like many other commentators, Kevin Caffrey (2008) characterized the 'spectacle as politics by other means' as a two-front communicative ritual operation aimed both inwardly at the Chinese populace and outwardly at an international audience of global neighbour-states. To a considerable degree, the opportunities of the organizers to use the Beijing Games for advertising a coherent and positive image throughout the world were limited by a number of general problems. Branding a nation is notoriously difficult to achieve for three major reasons: First, the brand image of a nation tends to be complex and diffuse; second, a single image or message is inherently difficult to communicate to different audiences in different countries—it even may appear 'foreign' to the domestic audience; and, thirdly, long-standing stereotypes and cultural associations, which are often not very favourable, are a significant impediment for the development of the national brand (Fan 2006:9–10). With regard to China's abilities in selling its products in global markets and achieving other foreign policy goals, three commonly held views of China that were such obstacles were the poor human rights records, the low quality of its manufacture on behalf of other countries' industries and the lack of environmental awareness. These image problems were—consciously or not—tackled by the local organizers' key concepts: People's Olympics, High-Tech Olympics and Green Olympics (Berkowitz et al. 2007:171–172).

Arguably these messages were equally or primarily meant to engage the Chinese people. For Susan Brownell, one of the most knowledgeable researchers of Chinese sport, any one-sided debate about the Olympics as public diplomacy tool completely misjudges the intentions of the local organizers and by extension, the Chinese government. While it was widely agreed that the Beijing Games offered an excellent opportunity to promote China to the world, there was less consent with regard to the way this could have been achieved. From earlier Olympic Games, the organizers had drawn two main lessons: First, avoiding at all costs problems like delays in venue completion, terrorist acts, transportation problems and media glitches that had provoked negative media reports; second, as research has shown that culture constitutes the core of national image, placing the idea of 'Cultural China' into the centre of the dialogue with international audiences in Olympic discourse. Hardly any attention was paid to the danger of negative images, and no recommendations were made with regard to spinning the media and public opinion abroad (Brownell 2008, 2009).

China's political structure, the lack of a clear communication strategy and scarcity of resources to forge such a one therefore suggest that most of the attention and effort were deliberately focusing on the domestic audience. Such a reading echoes the traditional conviction that the moral education of the people has always been regarded as a function of good government in China (De Kloet et al. 2008:12). A critical review of visual media of Olympic propaganda displayed in the Chinese capital also revealed something more complex behind the slogans than simply attracting public support. The analysis disclosed the instrumentalization of the Games for larger political objectives like the education of a populace fit for the 21st century, the maintenance of the nation-state and urban planning, since the 'celebration of Chineseness' was shaped by deep-running concerns with the modern civilized subject, issues of harmonious coexistence and Beijing 'going global'.

The slogan of 'People's Olympics' (*renwen aoyun*), obviously most unclear in meaning among the concepts, was not a promise to the international community about improving human rights, as understood by many abroad. Depending on the interpretation of *renwen*, it either referred to the Games as an opportunity for training the Chinese people for a globalizing world, or the blending of Chinese and Western culture for their mutual benefit. The latter message was also enshrined in the official Olympic slogan 'One World, One Dream' (*tong yige shijie, tong yige mengxiang*), which resonated well with both the universalistic aspiration of the Olympic Movement and the government's efforts in harmonizing its multiethnic population. The other two concepts of 'Green Olympics' and 'High-Tech Olympics' similarly paired international concerns with domestic politics. Staging 'Green Olympics' delivered a promise not to dismiss the international criticism of China's pollution problems, which had become a significant irritant in its external relations. Olympic officials who had adopted the environment as an official Olympic theme in the 1990s also repeatedly expressed their concern for the well-being of athletes (DeLisle 2009:188). By effectively facing environmental challenges, China showed its capability to respond to international expectations, and the government proved to its people its abilities of improving their quality of life.

Striving for a 'High-Tech Olympics' signalled China's ambitions to utilize the Beijing Games as a window to showcase the city's high-tech achievements and its innovative strength. A further slogan 'New Beijing, New Olympics' (*Xin Beijing, Xin Aoyun*) celebrated progress and change and intrinsically connected the city with the global, which became particularly visible in the city's new hallmark architecture. At an estimated expense of USD 41 billion, Beijing residents were bestowed with the world's largest airport terminal, subway lines, roads and rail links to the airport. The physical backdrop for the Games, most explicitly in the shape of Herzog and de Meuron's Bird's Nest and the Water Cube by Australian PTW Architects, were strikingly cosmopolitan and designed to impress. More foreign star architects left their footprints on the cityscape. Outstanding facilities like the National Theatre (Paul Andreu) or CCTV headquarters (Rem Koolhas), while having no discernible connection to the Games, were equally regarded as legacies of the Olympic construction boom (DeLisle 2009:184).

Similarly as the Tokyo Olympics served as a showcase for made-in-Japan modern architecture and high technology, the Seoul Olympics and Beijing Olympics were vested into larger urban planning initiatives in order to demonstrate modernity and advanced development. The sport stadiums, highly suggestive edifices themselves, were only the pinnacle extruding from larger redevelopment sites that, on the one hand, featured the iconic architecture that powerfully signifies the privileged position of dominant actors and ideologies within the social order, and, on the other hand, forcefully evicted many thousands of people out of their previous residential areas to make way for the construction projects. In all these incidents, old residents or homeless people were either expelled from the area or even taken into custody by city authorities since they were least likely to contribute to the positive responses the organizers were striving for. The ideological charging of place in accordance with the politics of place-marketing and investment was enforced by the redefinition of moral probity and the state-controlled reinforcement of appropriate behaviour in the public. The ruling elites therefore used the event as an occasion to educate their people in standards of behaviour that comply with norms imported from abroad.[7]

The Opening Ceremony, followed by 91,000 spectators in the packed Bird's Nest and a worldwide TV audience of billions, repackaged all these key topics in a great spectacle choreographed by the internationally acclaimed filmmaker Zhang Yimou. The narrative of the Opening Ceremony exhibited the plurality of China, its vast historical riches and traditional craft. The display of China's ethnic minorities, as well as the design of the mascots, delivered a harmonious message acknowledging their differences as much as their shared happiness under Communist Party rule. The outward message of East meets West, represented in the visual juxtaposition of Eastern and Western cultures, also showed how the Games were perceived of as facilitating the combination of two albeit essentialized cultural traditions among the Chinese today. Combining old and new, East and West, tradition and modern, the world as well as the Chinese people were instructed how much world history and Western modernization were indebted to Chinese civilization. They were taught in a historical tour de force that ancient China had once commanded technological, material and military resources that could have enabled them to explore the world beyond the four oceans; yet it decided against external expansion and instead sought to secure internal growth, as well as aesthetic, intellectual and cultural refinement. By implication, the art of navigation, gun powder and printing, among others, enabled the West to embark on its own specific path to modernity, which resulted in the suppression and exploitation of large parts of the non-Western world. China's tragic colonial past and its contested contemporary history were suspiciously absent from the elaborated show of 'Disney-China'.

Traditionally such a spectacular demonstration might have been sufficient to legitimize the ruling elites' claim for power; it still can be argued that the Olympic Games enabled the Chinese government to convince its people of a distinctive way of state development and party rule, which is in no way subordinate to the Western model of modernization and democratic governance. If the Beijing Games indeed were a celebration of an alternative modernity, in which not the rights of the individual but the interests of the collective are to be secured, or in which freedom rights of the individual must not be valued higher than the functionality and robustness of the collective, the familiar narrative of Asian hybridism encompassing cutting-edge high technology conjoined with rich cultural heritage and exotic civilization (Collins 2008:186) has obtained a new chapter in the fusion of China's state authoritarianism and Western liberal capitalism. In this sense the Beijing Summer Olympics has the potential of becoming in retrospect a Chinese *lieu de mémoire* (Nora 1989) for the purpose of remembering China's rise to economic power, global leadership—or the end of such aspirations—in the future.[8]

CHALLENGES TO THE PRIMARY DEFINER

As an extensive body of media research demonstrates, hosting in general produces little new knowledge about the place in question; however, the mediated correlation of a place with a significant event promotes lasting impressions and associations that audiences make with cities and nations (Rivenburgh 2004). My study of the impact of the Beijing Olympics on the Western perception of China (Manzenreiter 2010) reveals that the usage of sport spectacles for achieving foreign policy goals does not necessarily yield the desired or foreshadowed results. Neither has China's image been changed for the better nor has China gained more international acclamation as a global power. This is partly explained by the transformation of the sport festival into a global spectacle of mediated consumption which amplified the reliance of their principal agents on financial and technological assistance by multinational corporations. Pursuing their own interests, these agents devised the 'domesticating techniques' of the media which deliver customer-tailored media productions of the global event to national audiences and localized consumer markets. Since sport has turned into a leading content for globalizing media markets, sport mega-events are employed not only by political elites, but also by global capital and quite different lobbyists for their particular needs.

New forces, such as multinational corporations, civic movements and partisan interest groups that challenge political and economic elites, have joined the circle of forces competing for access to the network of 'primary definers', whose material and ideological relevance to the sport mega-events has a direct bearing on the shaping of narratives as well as the production of the events and their regulation. In the case of the Beijing Olympics, an unprecedented number of global movements used the opportunity to attract attention for their particular concerns. Amnesty International rallied against China's human rights infringements; a coalition of labour unions and non-governmental organizations, including Oxfam, Clean Clothes Campaign and Global Unions, making the links of China's garment industry with global sport brands and the Olympics explicit, advocated China's enhanced compliance with basic labour rights and core ILO conventions; Reporters Without Borders demanded the right for freedom of the press; and the Save Darfur Coalition mobilized against China's backing of the totalitarian regime in Sudan: Actress Mia Farrow, the public face of the campaign and goodwill ambassador of the UN Children's Fund, lobbied against the 'Genocide Games' among the celebrities of Hollywood and pressed the acclaimed director Steven Spielberg to withdraw from his role as artistic advisor to the Olympic ceremony as he risked becoming the 'Leni Riefenstahl' of the Games.[9] The Olympic torch relay, the longest ever, was meant to draw sympathies from people all over the world to China; yet as it turned out, it rather attracted the attention of contenders like the Free Tibet Movement, Greenpeace and other organizations opposing the politics of the Chinese government. Internet bloggers rallied against the torch relay and opened a public space for criticizing China as well as the IOC. Disturbing images were broadcast live from all the continents where the torch was presented; the lasting impressions of occasionally violent clashes between protesters and supporters turned the charm offensive into a public relations disaster of such an extent that the IOC openly questioned the future of the torch relay. Such controversies received widespread media attention prior to the Games; they were largely downplayed by the sport spectacle and its official media coverage, but returned afterwards once more, leaving many doubts about China's progress (see Horne and Whannel 2010).

CONCLUSION

This discussion has shown how global forces and movements have contributed to the transformation of sport spectacles on the global stage. The increasing diversity of actors involved in the process of signifying is one of the primary reasons for the multivocality of sport spectacles and their susceptibility to be used for extrinsic purposes, such as forging national cohesion, educating the public, moral campaigning, place-marketing, selling goods to ever-increasing markets or rejecting such objectives. As a result, streamlining and controlling the message they are about has become inherently difficult, particularly under the constraints of a sign system stemming from the world system of the late 19th century. Eurocentric notions of self and others are as much responsible for the failure of representational power as the diversity of interests that sport spectacles have come to serve. The dialectics between the two corner poles of Western hegemony and East Asian subalternity have been effectively shaped by the repercussions of a global political economy, which saw China, Japan and Korea, albeit with differing degrees, positioned at the fringes of a world order dominated by the West. Even though in the course of this historical epoch both the relationships between East Asia and the West as well as the role and usage of the Olympic Games within global public culture have considerably changed, a commonly accepted or anticipated belief in Western superiority—in economic as well as in political terms, in moral as well as in cultural dimensions—has continued to mar the relations between centres and peripheries as well as the image of East Asia. Its power of representation is hampered by the limited repository of signs and signifiers to be employed for the presentation of the self vis-à-vis the Western gaze. Even though the history of intraregional relations was much more of significance for the constructions of collective identities in past and present Asia, the use of a script-play, stage technologies and an apparatus of signifiers that correspond to the reading abilities of the Western audience and the reoccurrence of the binary codes of old and new, tradition and modernity, rural and urban, spiritual and technological clearly hint at the geopolitical location of the main audiences their producers were having in mind.

Questions about what, how and to whom it is represented at sport spectacles are ultimately bound to the geography of social relations that constitute the world system of sport. In this regard, markers of advanced and advancing, or developed and under-developed, have been of major significance for the relational positioning of the nation. Within this expanded spatial context, which has proven to be of stubborn resistance against change, the under- and misrepresentation of East Asian notions of body culture and humanist thought are enhanced by an arguably antiquated institutional design of the international non-governmental organizations in charge of sport. Both of its main pillars have become increasingly problematic over the course of time. On the one hand, the power of representation, in the guise of membership rights, is based on the axiomatic equation of place, state and culture and the people exclusively associated with both the spatial representation of culture and the cultural appropriation of the space. This reference to the idealized notion of the nation-state and state sovereignty is rooted in the political landscape of the late 19th century as well as the retro-futuristic design of the sport spectacle. These conditions of representation have accompanied more than a century of world sport without any changes that would have assigned agency, voice and representation to ethnic or cultural minorities or stateless nations.

On the other hand, the attraction of internationalism and universal humanism at the heart of the Olympic philosophy has largely contributed to the worldwide spread of Olympic sports. Particularly the insistence on morality, which is readily derived from a reading of the sport ritual as 'idealized make-believe versions of the real world' (Cheska 1979:61), and the self-acclaimed transcendence from the politics of the day continue to have a persisting hold on the worldwide imagination. Yet the claim of universalism and moral superiority has been challenged by the paradoxical ease with which the Olympic Movement has found itself co-opted by authoritarian regimes and paired with exploitative capitalist corporations. As in the case of its membership regulations, the illusion of separating itself from the profanity of power is another symbolic relict from the political context of 19th-century Europe, while the Olympist universalism is actually deeply entrenched within Eurocentric appropriations of fundamental human rights. All these inherent contradictions, which have further been aggravated by the hypocritical politics of some Western states, have undermined much of the moral legitimacy of the Olympic Movement to speak on behalf of universal human rights issues. Since the particular internationalism of the Olympic spirit is not based on the mutual exchange of particular versions of body cultures and cultural traditions but effectively a one-sided force impacting upon the signification processes of bodies, athletes and nations within the peripheries, the Olympic philosophy holds on and actually consolidates the privileges and prerogatives of those agents that have taken a leading role in developing its agendas (Radhakrishnan 2001). As Friedman observed, 'ethnic and cultural fragmentation and modernist homogenization are not two arguments, two opposing views of what is happening in the world today, but two constitutive trends of global reality. The dualist centralized world of the double East-West hegemony is fragmenting, politically, and culturally, but the homogeneity of capitalism remains as intact and as systematic as ever' (1990:311).

11 Japan, Asia and the New International Division of Sport Apparel Labour[1]

The previous chapter closed with an argument that acknowledged the concomitant effects of the levelling power of capitalism and the fragmentation of the world along the lines of cultural diversity. This view corresponds with the world system approach that in general concedes the relative autonomy of culture but emphasizes the determining weight of economic relations giving shape to the position states and nations have in relation with each other. This chapter will put this generalized assumption into perspective. It examines the position of Japan and East Asia within global sport apparel manufacturing, which provides an excellent case for the critical evaluation of the developmental aspects of border-crossing production networks, industrial upgrading and the varieties of capitalism. While the homogenizing effects of the capitalist mode of production can be taken for granted to some instant, the power of culture to oppose streamlining and standardizing effects cannot go unnoticed.

Due to the great influence that powerful brand name companies such as Nike and Adidas wield over the production and procurement processes as well as distribution structures of oligopolistic consumer markets, the sporting goods industry apparently embodies the quintessential example of a consumer-driven supply chain (Korzeniewicz 1994; Gereffi 2002). However, the sporting goods sector is in fact highly diversified and supplies a heterogeneous industry that can be divided into three main categories: sport equipment, athletic apparel and sport shoes. Production processes can be subdivided into five core sectors: supply of raw materials, such as natural or synthetic fibres; production of basic elements, such as thread, fabrics and other components; final fabrication or assembly of apparel, shoes and equipment; export; and marketing to the end consumer. Throughout each segment of the production chain capital demand, technological input, price calculation and the distribution of added value considerably differ in accordance with the final product's degree of specialization.

My analysis of the international division of labour in the sporting goods industry is based upon the Global Production Networks Approach (Henderson et al. 2002; Hess 2009), which specifically emphasizes the non-linearity and complexity of the relationships involved in transnational production, marketing and consumption of goods. Global production networks are constructs joining a multitude of production units in various countries with one another. Thereby, the components, materials, and non-material resources necessary to manufacture a specific product are all made available. This approach follows the notion that development cannot be seen as an autonomous process occurring within the borders of a nation, a concept shared with alternative theories such as the global commodity chains or global value-added chains approach. Instead, development must be seen in context with the systematic forces of interdependence that cannot be attributed to governmental and political power balances alone. The network approach differs from the global commodity chains approach in that it takes into consideration the fact that the differences and hierarchies of power and the control over value creation cannot be traced back to the endogenous automatism of any one specific organizational pattern (see Gereffi 1996, 2002). As will be shown using the example of sporting goods production, the dichotomy of buyer-driven and producer-driven product chains does not sufficiently explain the variety of production networks that are currently operating in East Asia. Also, it ignores the multifaceted myriad relationships that can run vertically, horizontally and multidirectionally within a given production network. The network approach diverges from the global value-added chains approach by maintaining reservations regarding over-eagerly equating value creation and industrial upgrading with improved social conditions (Bair 2005).

The empirical part of the study focuses on Japanese and other Asian companies of the athletic apparel and sport shoe sectors, which make up well over half of the global market for sporting goods. Because of their highly labour-intensive production, the textile and clothing sectors have played, and continue to play, a key role in the development of many emerging economies throughout the region. To demonstrate the significance of the global political economy, I will first outline the regional context of the ongoing economic integration of Asia in recent decades before introducing the global sporting goods market. Using key data combined with case studies of global sporting goods brands positioned centrally in production networks, I will demonstrate the significance Asian economies are having for the global production of sporting goods and particularly for consumer-driven supply chains as exemplified by the globally well-known brand name companies of Nike and Adidas. I refer to macroeconomic data on international trade to plot the trajectory of production sites shifting throughout the region. Further case studies of Asian companies that have come increasingly to dominate the production process argue in favour of a greater variability of production systems than usually assumed. The final section addresses the concerns of international solidarity organizations bringing the sweatshop conditions of many sporting goods manufacturers to the attention of consumers in the north. Here I will approach the controversial assessment of the implications that such production networks may have for social and economic development opportunities in the Global South.

ASIA AND THE GLOBAL ECONOMY

At the start of the 21st century, Asia emerged as the new epicentre of the world economy. In this phase of economic globalization, no other world region displayed such a strong dynamic of growth or could demonstrate so many examples of successful development improvement. For many years, Japan was considered to be the only instance of successful modernization outside of the Western centres. Meanwhile, however, two of the three greatest global economic powers, Japan and China, are at home in the Asian region. In East Asia, Hong Kong, Singapore, South Korea and Taiwan have also successfully completed the transition from emerging market to industrialized nation. Malaysia, Thailand, Indonesia and the Philippines followed in their footsteps in the 1990s, creating a second generation of Asian 'Tigers' and enormous economic development. The third generation of tigers includes China, Vietnam and India. It is possible that Cambodia, Sri Lanka and Laos could also adopt the typical development pattern of import substitution and export-oriented growth in decades to come. These fourth-generation nations are already partially incorporated into sourcing strategies and location politics of transnationally operating corporations. Asia now accounts for up to one-quarter of total global economic output and one-third of the total world trade. The segment accounted for by Asian emerging markets alone has tripled since 1980 and China's share has increased tenfold (Ross 2008). The apparel sector plays a paramount, and therefore typical, role in this process of late development (see Table 11.1).

Asia's ascent goes hand in hand with a fundamental structural transformation: In the past two to three decades, intraregional production networks have expanded to integrate a multitude of companies, including many of those not in the textile and garment industry. Never before has economic interdependence in the East Asian region been as high as today (Oikawa 2008:1). Intraregional goods flow has increased fivefold since 1980, twice as much as trade with the rest of the world. The Terms of Trade attest to the sustained industrial development and increasing interlocking of economies in the region: 50 per cent of exports remain in the region; intermediate and semi-finished goods disproportionately represent 65 per cent of all merchandise traffic. From 1990 to 1996, intraregional trade increased ninefold; intraindustrial trade within Asia made up 33 per cent of total exports in 1992, a figure which grew to 47 per cent by 2005 (IMF 2007:42–45).

The International Monetary Fund traces the division of labour, trade and development in the region back to the comparative advantages of the factor endowment of Asian national economies and the effects of free market forces. This corresponds to the Ricardian tradition of classical economic theory. However, this assumption contradicts empirical findings indicating that despite the many differences in economic development, governments played a central role in the steering of business and trade in almost all cases in East Asia. Protectionism and the regulation of domestic markets

Table 11.1 Asian Exports to the World Market

	1980		1990		1998		2008	
	Total	*Clothes*	*Total*	*Clothes*	*Total*	*Clothes*	*Total*	*Clothes*
Northeast Asia								
PR China	19	8.6%	65	15.7%	191	16.4%	1,431	8.4%
Hong Kong	21	25.4%	84	18.7%	176	12.7%	370	7.5%
Japan	130	0.4%	287	0.2%	388	0.1%	781	0.1%
South Korea	18	17.0%	66	12.4%	140	3.4%	422	0.4%
Taipei China	21	12.3%	71	5.8%	135	2.5%	256	0.5%
Southeast Asia								
Indonesia	24	2.4%	28	10.3%	52	8.6%	137	4.6%
Thailand	7	4.2%	24	12.2%	62	5.5%	176	2.4%
Malaysia	14	1.2%	31	4.5%	75	3.2%	199	2.0%
Philippines	6	4.9%	8	8.4%	30	8.0%	49	4.1%
Vietnam	0	7.3%	1	5.0%	9	14.7%	49[1]	17.9%
South Asia								
Bangladesh	1	10.0%	1	60.0%	5	78.0%	12	80.3%
India	8	7.5%	19	13.7%	41	11.7%	182	6.0%
Sri Lanka	1	10.0%	2	35.0%	4	57.5%	9	40.0%
Pakistan	3	3.3%	6	18.3%	9	22.2%	20	19.2%

Unit: volume in USD billion; export share of the apparel sector in per cent.

[1]Angaben für 2007.

Source: 1980–1998 Gereffi 2006; 2008 UN Comtrade Database.

boosted the development of competitive industries. In many instances, the state acted as the investor, contractor and even as the entrepreneur. Already in the 1930s, Japanese economist Akamatsu Kaname put the responsibility of the state to ensure conditions conducive to development growth at the centre of his alternative explanation of industrial development in emerging economies. Based on his detailed observation of the textile industry in Japan's early phases of industrialization, he drafted his 'Flying Geese Paradigm of Development' (*gankō keitai hatten ron*; see Akamatsu 1935, 1962; Korhonen 1994; Schröppel and Nakajima 2002). His original contribution to developmental economics anticipated the transfer of technology, capital, and goods production from advancing companies, industrial sectors and nations to the following generations of businesses, industries, and countries safely ripening in their lee (cf. Figure 11.1).

Cumings (1984) connected Akamatsu's product cycle pattern with the world systems approach, illustrating 20th-century East Asian development as the continual result of a cyclic process taking place throughout four stages: import substitution, the development of competitive industries, improvement of a domestic demand market and the export of investment goods. Korea and Taiwan became the new homes of declining Japanese industries. First the apparel and textile industries relocated, followed by heavy and chemical

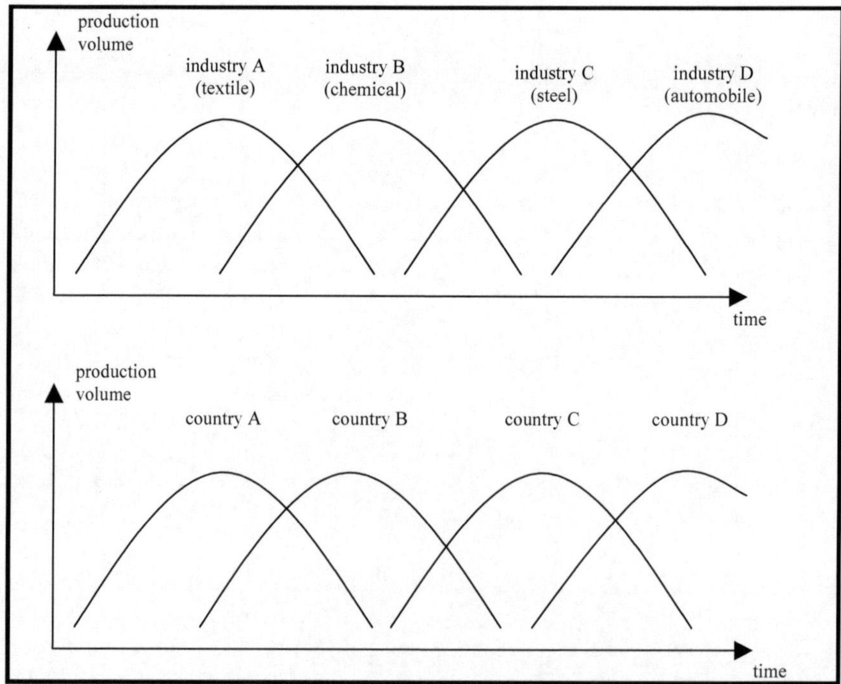

Figure 11.1 Intraindustrial and international dimensions of the Flying Geese Model.

industries and finally the electronics and automobile industries. Though, as later critics emphasized, a complete exodus of entire manufacturing sectors did not take place—Japanese companies preferred to outsource less technologically intensive and unprofitable production phases, while maintaining control of manufacturing processes and product development in the country of origin. Until now, neither Taiwan nor Korea, not to mention China, has imitated Japan's production structures to the degree predicted by the Flying Geese Paradigm (Bernard and Ravenhill 1995:184). With mounting production complexity, higher technological input and the increasing speed with which new products appear on the market, possibilities for imitation became more limited. Instead, local knowledge as well as site-specific institutions and traditions impacted the way production processes were organized. The partial diffusion of technology has led to a regional hierarchy defined by asymmetrical profit distribution. In sum, it must be noted that the Japanese variation of the product cycle theory duly gave the regional perspective the recognition it deserved; however, it does not thoroughly encompass the full complexity of regional political economies (see Bernard and Ravenhill 1995). This is above all true for the increasingly modularly organized production processes of the global consumer goods industry, particularly in the manufacturing of sporting goods.

THE GLOBAL SPORTING GOODS MARKET

The sheer complexity of the sport industry and its entwinement with other economic sectors means that the true magnitude of the sport business can only be estimated. It is, however, clear that the market is not small, and that it is growing and increasingly spreading into the peripheries. About 2 per cent of the total economic performance of Western industrial nations is tightly tied to the sport phenomenon. In European Union countries, 1.3 per cent of all employees are employed in sport and/or gain income through sport. In 2005, the global sport television rights market totalled about USD 50 billion. Approximately USD 20 billion are moved annually by athletics sponsoring, a number that has continued to increase over the years and through the decades (Andreff and Szymanski 2006:5–6). Average annual growth rates of 5 per cent caused the total revenue of the sporting goods industry to grow to USD 125.5 billion between 1994 and 2004. About 40 per cent of the market is supported by the sport equipment and athletic apparel sectors; a fifth is generated by athletic shoe sales (see Figures 11.2a, 11.2b). With a volume of approximately USD 50 billion, the sale of skis, exercise machines, tennis racquets, soccer balls, bicycles and related merchandise of an athletic lifestyle makes up 0.5 to 1 per cent of total world trade (Andreff and Andreff 2009:267). The total volume of the worldwide athletic shoe and sportswear markets is even greater, estimated at USD 74 billion at the end of 2005 (MSN 2008:17).

The total sport equipment and sportswear market is estimated as high as USD 280 billion by the American market research company NPD (2008), one of the reasons being the fluid transition between functional athletic apparel and fashionable lifestyle. The sporting goods industry owes at least one-third of its global trade to the use of their products for fashion and lifestyle. If sport equipment was removed from the overall calculation, only about half of total turnover could be attributed to purely sport-related purposes (including wellness and fitness).

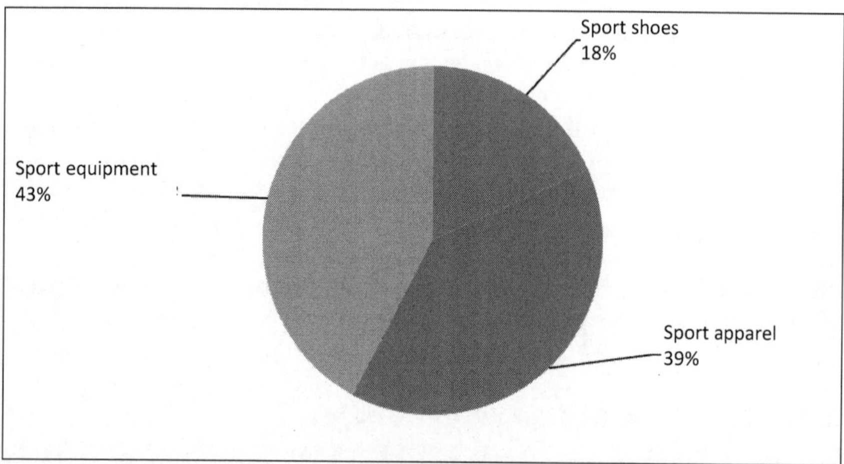

Figure 11.2a World market for sporting goods, 2005 (by products).

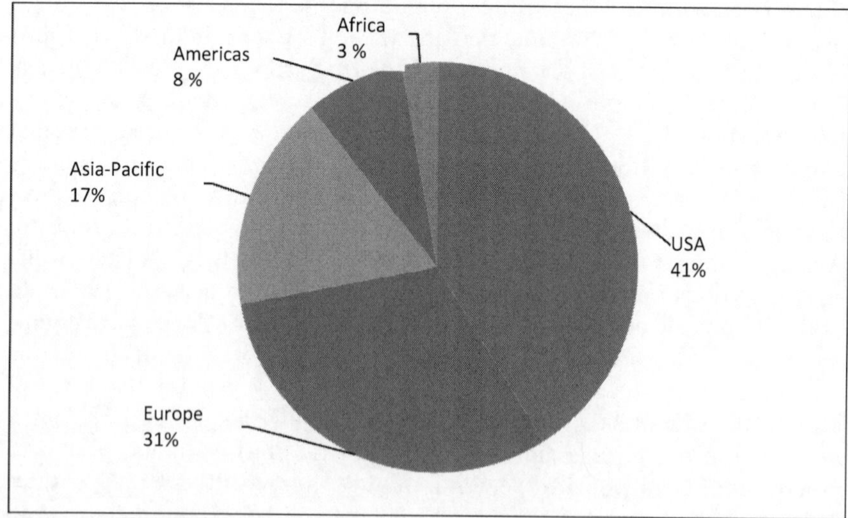

Figure 11.2b World market for sporting goods, 2005 (by regions).

The Asian economic region is centrally important to the sporting goods industry for two main reasons. First, Asia is emerging as an increasingly important sales market for the global sporting goods industry. Global brands in the sector, such as Adidas, Reebok and Nike supply the aspiring middle classes of the region with a relatively inexpensive means of dousing themselves with a breath of luxury, thereby presenting themselves as future-oriented and modern. In the athletic apparel and sport shoes sector, the US and Europe continue to be the key selling markets—in 2002, almost 80 per cent of revenue was generated in these areas, 16 per cent in Asia and 6 per cent in the rest of the world (Merk 2005:9). While Western markets are largely considered to be saturated, especially due to the demographic developments and lifestyle changes threatening to lower the rate of athletic participation, the growth potential for Asia and Latin America is considered to be almost unlimited. The market research institute NPD reported an annual growth rate of almost 15 per cent for the sport trade in China in 2007, and a market of almost USD eight billion (NPD 2008). The dependency of sporting goods production upon the core markets of the developed north is sinking if one takes into consideration the sport equipment market: Somewhat less than 30 per cent of global revenue is generated outside of North America and Europe (see Figure 11.2b).

However, Asia's role in supplying sporting goods to the global athletics market is even more significant than its demand. Currently, 90 per cent of all athletic shoes are manufactured in four nations: China, Vietnam, Indonesia and Thailand. China's production alone constitutes 58 per cent of all sport shoes (MSN 2008:18). The majority of athletic apparel is also produced in Asia, although the geographical distribution of manufacturing locations is considerably more widespread. The leading sport brands, Adidas and Nike, dominate 60 per cent of the athletic shoe market and about a fifth of the global athletic apparel market. They procure their products through a worldwide network of hundreds of independent suppliers. Most of these supplying companies, especially those with high numbers of employees, are located in Asia. The other global brand names of the athletic industry have also shifted their supply chains towards Asia. Puma, Mizuno and Umbro, to name just a few, have their wares produced in the numerous textile and clothing factories spread from Indonesia to India. Nonetheless, Asia's role in the global sporting goods market is not limited to the comparatively labour-intensive, yet low-capital, apparel and shoe production sectors. Asia's share of exports of sporting goods, athletic apparel and sporting goods has risen from 46.2 per cent in 1990 to 57.8 per cent in 2010 (see Table 11.2); the rise was even more pronounced for the sport equipment sector (from 46.1 to 61.2 per cent). Factories in Asia produce almost any type of sport equipment for the world market, from skis, surfboards and golf clubs to tennis racquets, soccer balls and gym equipment (Andreff and Andreff 2009:270, 279).

Table 11.2 Asian Trade in Sportswear, Sporting Goods and Sport Shoes with the World, 1990–2010

Export 1990, 2000, 2010	*Total 1990*	*Total 2000*	*Total 2010*
PR China	n.a.	5,598.7	14,611.7
Hong Kong	n.a.	2,297.8	1,907.7
Macao	6.4	34.7	1.9
Japan	348.8	450.8	733.2
South Korea	1,167.3	517.4	252.4
Taipei	1,803.5	1,627.3	1,252.6
Indonesia	389.1	1,425.3	1,768.4
Thailand	536.3	787.4	671.0
Singapore	112.8	191.0	309.7
Malaysia	83.0	119.3	249.3
Philippines	n.a.	179.6	134.5
Vietnam	n.a.	1,322.3	1,723.4
Cambodia	n.a.	1.5	5.8
Bangladesh	4.5	60.1	118.1
India	65.8	171.5	379.1
Sri Lanka	26.5	88.4	32.4
Pakistan	120.1	282.3	373.3
Asia17	4,664.2	15,155.3	24,524.6
World+TW	10,088.3	26,180.1	42,355.1
share of global trade (incl. Taiwan, %)	*46.23*	*57.89*	*57.90*

Unit: USD million. SITC Classification 6211; 8947 (Taiwan: 9506), 8512 (Taiwan: 640411).
Source: UN COMTRADE; Bureau of Foreign Trade, Taiwan.

REGIONALIZATION OF THE SPORTING GOODS INDUSTRY

During the mid-1960's, Asia was incorporated into the once locally organized and now increasingly global operations of the sporting goods industry. However, the full bloom of the 'New International Division of Labour' (Harvey and Saint-Germain 2001) in sporting goods production didn't emerge until consumer habits in Europe and the US changed during the 1970s, bringing about a high demand for sport and leisure time. It is generally accepted that collaboration between Japanese athletic shoe manufacturer Onitsuka (today Asics) and the American sport dealership Blue Ribbon Sports, which became the brand Nike in 1978, was the starting point for the globalization of sporting goods production. Nike founders Bowerman and Knight's business model was based less upon the accepted quality of Japanese production than upon the effective distribution of costs enabled by directly importing from the emerging nation Japan. After the

Onitsuka partnership came to an end, the company continued to have its own designs produced by Japanese shoe manufacturers for several years. Yet by the mid-1970s the newly industrialized nation Japan was no longer profitable, since during the course of Japan's 'catching up', real salaries had more than doubled. In addition, the termination of the Bretton Woods System meant the end of an artificially undervalued Yen and the volatile price hikes of Japanese exports. Nike began shifting segments of its production towards South Korea, Thailand and Taiwan; two factories were even opened in the US. By the early 1980s, after the South Korean government implemented aggressive financial incentives for the foundation of shoe factories, 82 per cent of Nike shoes came from South Korea and Taiwan (Locke 2003:46). When labour disputes and wage increases caused these nations to likewise become unprofitable, Nike coerced their main supply sources to relocate factories to countries in the region with lower labour costs. Order guarantees minimized financial risk, and on-site Nike representatives maintained the organization of the manufacturer's production processes and ensured quality control. In the 1990s, Thailand, Indonesia, the Philippines and Vietnam joined China as the most important locations of a production network encompassing all of Southeast Asia. In 1996, 34 per cent of Nike's products came from China, 36 per cent from Indonesia, 12 per cent from South Korea, 10 per cent from Thailand, 5 per cent from Taiwan and 2 per cent from Vietnam (Diefenbach 1997).

Today, more than a million workers in 930 factories located in 50 countries manufacture half a million different Nike products. Nike's 2011 manufacturing disclosure listed among a total of 896 contract factories 291 in China, 67 in Vietnam, 40 in Indonesia, 39 in Thailand, 28 in India and 26 each in Japan and Korea. Factories in Vietnam, China and Indonesia manufactured approximately 41 per cent, 32 per cent and 25 per cent of its entire branded footwear (Nike 2012). In 1980, the Nike shoe collection consisted of just 175 models; in the spring of 1990, it came up with 772. Another 10 years later, Nike presented almost 1,200 different models (Locke 2003:43). Controlling a third of the world market for athletic and leisure shoes, Nike became the undisputed number one at the beginning of the 2010s. Nike also vied successfully for the position of market leader in the athletic apparel sector, and placed at number six in the sports equipment sector in 2005 (Schmid and Kotulla 2007). In 2011, Nike turned over more than USD 20 billion of revenue, the best result in its history (USD 11.5 billion in the shoe sector, 5.5 billion for apparel; see also Table 11.1). Knocked down to second place, the German corporation Adidas followed with annual revenues of USD 13.3 billion (approximately 60 per cent in apparel and 5 per cent in footwear; see Adidas 2012a). Beginning as a sport equipment producer and expanding to a global sport and lifestyle brand in the 1990s, the former family business got off to a late start. Even though Adidas still holds some of its own production, it has basically long since become a branded trade corporation. The majority of manufacturing has been shifted to low labour cost countries to better remain competitive as a supplier. Adidas's takeover of the sport brand Reebok in 2005 also served the strategic business goal of attaining economies of scale to maximize their bargaining power over Asia producers.

Like Nike, Adidas employs a workforce of its own (around 40,000 in each case), most of them in wholesale and retail. Prior to the expansion of its flagship stores, Nike had only 5,500 employees, most of them in the US working in design and marketing. The two US factories, in Maine and New Hampshire, have long since closed. The German headquarters still holds a tiny share of its own production, but the core business of both 'sporting goods manufacturers without factories' consists of research, development, design, marketing and management of the production cycles of a continually broadening product palette. Sixty-seven per cent of Adidas's suppliers operated in Asia as of 2011 (833 of 1,232; Adidas 2012b); Nike's percentage was slightly higher at 71 per cent (663 of 930; Nike 2012). The majority of suppliers—28 per cent of Adidas's and 36 per cent of Nike's suppliers—and some of their largest factories are based in China, the 'world's sewing machine'. Among the 62 countries of the Adidas network in 2011, China was hosting the bulk of Adidas's production sites with 349 factories. The five biggest locations also included India (84 factories), Indonesia (80), Vietnam (77) and Japan (60) (Adidas 2012b:44). In 2011, Adidas sourced 97 per cent of its footwear volume from Asia (China: 35 per cent), 83 per cent (China: 35 per cent) of apparel and 98 per cent (China: 64 per cent) of branded sports hardware (Adidas 2012a:93–94).

The decision to relocate production to low-labour-cost nations in Asia followed an already established model for the apparel and consumer goods industry. A tendency towards the creation of oligopolies marked the American sporting goods industry early on. The few remaining bulk producers attempted to maximize returns by relocating or threatening to close locations, thereby avoiding labour rights and laws, security standards and environmental protection standards. This lowered production costs and raised the profit margin. The dynamic that was triggered by this logic has been criticized from many sides as a 'race to the bottom' that is still under way today. Rawlings Sporting Goods, a sporting goods and apparel manufacturer mainly for baseball, basketball, and American football with headquarters in Saint Louis, began its journey of repeated production headquarters relocation in 1953, first within the state of Missouri, allowing it to get rid of the company union. In 1964, tax incentives enticed a move to Puerto Rico; five years later the company reached the coast of Haiti, where not only were the poorest people in the Western Hemisphere willing to work for the paltriest wages, but strikes were also forbidden by law. Later, unstable political conditions instigated a relocation to Costa Rica (Sage 2000:272). The low-wage countries of Central America and the Caribbean continue to play an important role in sporting goods production for the American market; similar to the way Eastern Europe, North Africa and Turkey profit from their proximity to European sales markets. Reduced transportation and communication costs, faster reaction times to demand trends and quota agreements are the main reasons for the development of these types of regionally specific trade relationships. For the same reasons, neighbouring regions have become the preferred targets for direct investments by sporting goods manufacturers, which pass on contracts, raw materials and production components to their local suppliers and manufacturing plants before finally re-importing goods into the target market (Gereffi 2002; Andreff and Andreff 2009).

INDUSTRIAL UPGRADING AND DIVERSIFICATION

Asia's rise within the sporting goods industry is tightly tied to the transformation of the textile and garment sector, a fact which can be attributed in part to the partial overlapping of product palettes. Since the early 20th century, these branches have undergone a series of cross-border relocations throughout several countries, most located in Asia (see Table 11.1). This is a development that was directly and actively promoted by governments. National industry politics played a key role in early industrialization, the relegation of industrial sectors which had lost their competitiveness and the building up of designated future industries. First, the heavyweights were shifted from North America and Europe to Japan, whose industrialization phase had already started, under state directive, with the production of natural fibres and the development of an export-driven textile industry. Ten per cent of national economic output and one-third of export revenue were generated by this sector in the 1930s (Park and Anderson 1991:535). After the war, the Japanese textile industry began to lose successively global market shares. The Ministry for Trade and the Economy banded together with the Industrial Association, suppliers, labour unions, trading companies and retailers to restructure the sector (McNamara 1995). The concerted promotion of synthetic fibre technologies helped cushion the decline of the textile industry. While Japan became a net exporter of synthetic threads and fabrics, more labour-intensive processes shifted to Hong Kong, Taiwan and South Korea, which proceeded to dominate global export markets for textiles and apparel in the 1970s and 1980s.

The two largest Japanese manufacturers of sporting goods, Asics and Mizuno, both joined this trend and began outsourcing segments of their footwear production to the newly industrialized nations of East Asia in the 1970s. Asics first foreign production site was in Taiwan; rising production costs prompted a transfer to South Korea and then, finally, to China. By 1988, half of all Asics products were produced abroad. Asics steadily continued to expand its foreign activities; its revenue growth can be attributed above all to foreign sales levels in the running and sport shoe sectors since 2005 (Asics 2009). Nowadays the Asics group comprises a total of 55 companies with 3,593 employees in Japan and 2,313 outside Japan. Its products are manufactured by 157 subcontracted factories in 20 countries around the world, and recent revenue growth can be attributed above all to sales levels in foreign markets, particularly in running and sports shoe sectors. In 2011, sports shoes sales accounted for 74 per cent (2006: 66 per cent) of total turnover, sportswear for 19 per cent (24 per cent) and sports equipment for 7 per cent (10 per cent). East Asia recently became a market of growing significance (2011: 6 per cent), though the bulk of sales still falls onto the domestic market. Japan is the largest market for all Asics products with a share of 42 per cent (2006: 49 per cent), followed by Europe (23 per cent; down from 29 per cent) and the Americas (23 per cent; up from 18 per cent; Asics 2012a, 2012b).

In contrast, Asics's main competitor, Mizuno, continues to make 60 to 70 per cent of its turnover from the domestic market. Mizuno follows a strategy somewhat different from Asics, opening branch companies in low-wage nations in the Asian region and in key nearby sales markets. In 1970, Mizuno laid the cornerstone for its cross-border expansion with the foundation of a subsidiary company Mizuno Taiwan Corporation. In 1975, its first shoe factory was opened in South Korea; in 1989 a joint venture with a Thai textile manufacturer began. Mizuno subsidiaries were then founded in Hong Kong (1992) and Shanghai (1994) as well as the US, Canada and Europe (Mizuno 2009). The decision to relocate to these regions was made with the rising exchange rate of the yen, among other factors, in mind. In 1985, leading economic powers in the Plaza Accord had decided to control influences on monetary exchange rates to counteract the US trade balance deficit, which had become an ongoing source of friction.

In Taiwan and Korea, the initial successors of the Japanese textile industry, the textile sector also followed the classic path of export-based growth. The production of natural fibres began in the 1950s with the keen participation of the Taiwanese government. Rising exports in the 1960s brought with them an expansion of the production of synthetic fibres and their further processing in garment factories. The apex was reached in the 1980s when, for a short time, Taiwan was the leading exporter of apparel to the American market and second only to the US in the production of synthetics. However, after the end of the decade, rising wages, higher regulation of labour and the introduction of environmental standards by the government, coupled with exchange rate losses, undermined Taiwan's competitive advantages in the labour-intensive areas of the sector (Thun 2001:3). In South Korea, the government issued a series of five-year plans in the early 1960s, in which textile exports played a central role. Import restrictions, government loans and the coordinated allocation of raw materials boosted designated growth areas into the 1970s, when attention was shifted to the chemical industry and the production of synthetics (Amsden 1989:64–68). With the decline of the textile sector in these Newly Industrialized Economies, the second generation of Southeast Asian 'Tiger' nations entered the scene. Malaysia, Thailand, Indonesia and the Philippines were followed by the People's Republic of China and then the South Asian nations.

Table 11.3 World Market Shares of Asian Textile and Apparel Industries, 2004–2008

	Clothes		*Yarns, Textures*		*Export Shares 2008*	
	2004	2008	2004	2008	*Clothes*	*Textiles*
Northeast Asia						
PR China	25.58	34.22	17.58	27.41	8.4%	5%
Japan	0.25	0.17	3.75	3.08	0.1%	1%
South Korea	1.4	0.43	5.7	3.26	0.4%	2%
Taipei China	0.81	0.34	5.28	3.87	0.5%	4%
Southeast Asia						
Indonesia	1.84	1.79	1.66	1.54	4.6%	3%
Thailand	1.65	1.21	1.35	1.35	2.4%	2%
Malaysia	0.97	1.03	0.64	0.65	2.0%	1%
Philippines	0.89	0.56	1.14	0.08	4.1%	0%
Vietnam	1.76	2.70	0.34	0.50	17.9%	2%
South Asia						
Bangladesh	2.60	3.70	0.31	0.37	80.3%	6%
India	2.74	3.13	3.69	4.36	6.0%	6%
Sri Lanka	1.15	0.99	0.08	0.08	40.0%	2%
Pakistan	1.25	1.11	3.22	3.02	19.2%	35%

Source: UN Comtrade database. Taipei government.

The development of more investment and the technology-intensive synthetics industry combined with increased trade with higher-value products within the Asian region provided a political and economic opportunity to compensate competitive disadvantages compared to other societies in development (see Table 11.3). The necessary investment capital initially came from government savings funds. In Japan, South Korea, Taiwan and Singapore, domestic textile manufacturer's associations, business networks, banks and the state were the main investors. In the later phases of development during the 1990s, the rapid development progress of the four tiger nations and China was fuelled mainly by the direct investment of neighbouring countries (Hiratsuka 2005:20). Until the early 1990s, almost all textile companies in Malaysia's Special Economic Zone were founded with foreign capital, most of which came from Japan (Singleton 1997:44). Differences in the price per ton of exported and imported thread are indicative of the qualitative differences that internally structure trade within the branch: Companies in developing nations produce textiles of a simple quality; more advanced nations manufacture higher-quality wares. In 2002, South Korea and Taiwan became the world's two largest exporters of synthetic thread. Taiwan exported low-priced thread and imported high-quality thread; South Korea exported thread in the mid-range price segment and imported high-quality thread. Indonesia, Malaysia and Thailand were all net exporters of thread and fabric, exporting low-quality thread and importing mid- to high-quality fibres. Japan was the largest net exporter of thread and fabric in the upper price echelons (Hiratsuka 2005:15). Looking at intraregional input and output interconnections, it becomes clear that Asia's textile industry has shifted their former dependency on Japan, Taiwan and the US to China (Kuwamori and Okamori 2007:16). Taiwan's chemical corporations, for example, have been dependent upon textile branch demand from the Chinese mainland since the year 2000, while their own textile sector has continuously expanded business relations with textile, chemical and other Chinese production industries (Kuwamori and Okamori 2007:27).

Relocation decisions essentially were made based upon factors such as labour productivity, capital and technological availability, government investment incentives, labour regulations and environmental standards. In many cases, governments occupied a key function, whether this was the establishment of export production zones in Malaysia or special economic zones in China, where foreign investors are offered exclusive conditions or changes in taxation, quotas or tariffs. When its government enacted policies to stimulate export-driven growth in the 1980s, it was Indonesia's turn to become a hub of the global garments industry. Import taxes and other restriction were lifted for foreign investors, as long as at least 85 per cent of their manufactured products were exported. This was the starting signal for the foundation of a large textile and footwear production cluster, owned for the most part by producers from Hong Kong, Korea and Taiwan. Exports were shipped directly to their target markets in the West, which were hermetically sealed to the first generation of newly industrialized nations through tariffs and quotas (Lowder 1999:55–56; Hassler 2003).

The institutional framework of the international political economy is often a key step in the industrial development of emerging nations, especially in the apparel sector, where market entry barriers are comparatively low. Early on, the textile trade sector was regulated by intergovernmental agreements, most-favoured-nation clauses and bilateral import tariffs. Regional trade associations such as the EU or NAFTA then liberalized trade among their members, which had a significant influence upon the purchasing policies of producers. The 1974 Multi Fibre Agreement, which was based upon the cotton agreement of 1961 but included synthetics and garments, had the most enduring influence on the global flow of commodities. Under this multilateral regulatory regime, import nations had the right to implement bilateral quota limitations for specific textiles or articles of clothing. In order to meet deliveries falling under these limitations, exporters had to purchase quota shares from their governments. What was originally intended as a protective measure for domestic industries against low-wage competition from developing countries now stimulated the development of the apparel sector in many low-wage nations and the expansion of triangular manufacturing relations. When the agreement expired in 2004, these guidelines had already had extensive consequences upon production structuring, since in many cases quotas for textiles varied from nation to nation. China's exports to the US and EU rose drastically in the categories that were phased out step-by-step after 2001. In Japan, where the apparel industry is not worth mentioning, the implementation of quotas was forgone and Chinese exports already made up 55 per cent by 1998 (2009, about 80 per cent; Gereffi 2002:15). In general, it is expected that the expiration of the Multi Fibre Agreement will lead to consolidation in the textile industry and therefore to concentration processes similar to those found in the footwear sector, whose quota limits for world trade already fell in the 1980s.

VARIATIONS IN ASIAN PRODUCTION NETWORKS

Particularly in the sport and lifestyle sectors of the global consumer commodities industry, market share competition is based upon brands and the marketing that goes along with them. The brand name companies are also dubbed 'flagship companies' because of their lead position in the chain which has, at least until recently, dominated the crossroads of outsourced production processes, distribution and final consumption. In recent years, sporting goods manufacturers and distributors operating in Asia have reorganized their buying processes and production networks to correspond to shifting patterns of regional integration and local as well as global regulatory conditions of trade and production. These businesses organize the entire process for their clients—from purchasing and production to distribution and marketing—and have created their own development strategies in the process. Companies from the Newly Industrialized Economies, i.e. Taiwan, Korea and Hong Kong, and recently also China, followed the path of their predecessors and moved upwards along the value chain by offering customers integrated value-added services: from CMT (cut make and trim) to OEM (package contractor of original equipment manufacturing), ODM (full package design), OBM (branding) and retailing. Once highly specialized companies, which had gathered technological expertise when supplying global brand name corporations, built up their own supply relations and founded manufacturing plants in special export zones or in mainland China, or contracted out production orders to China or other parts of Asia, Latin America and Africa as a response to rising production costs. In the shadow of the well-known global brands, various new forms of production networks have emerged, leading to new sourcing strategies and relationships between intermediaries, buyers and sellers. Most recently, Asian brands and retailers have started to enter the lucrative markets in the Global North. They thereby entered a new field of action with the control of their own global supply chains. Such developments caused the categorical borders between manufacturer, trader and retailer to become more and more blurred. The following examples introduce a few of the production networks organized by leading Asian corporations. Corporate data as in Table 11.4 indicate the growth value of their operations in comparison with the renown sports brands from the Global North.

Table 11.4 Revenues of the Sporting Goods Industries, 2002–2011

	2002	*2003*	*2004*	*2005*	*2006*	*2007*	*2008*	*2009*	*2010*	*2011*	*CAGR (%)*
Nike	9,893	10,697	12,253	13,740	14,955	16,326	18,627	19,176	19,014	20,862	8.64
Adidas	6,523	6,267	5,860	6,636	10,084	10,299	10,799	10,381	11,990	13,344	8.28
Puma	1,380	1,692	2,017	2,387	2,755	2,738	2,768	2,608	2,862	3,173	9.69
Asics	1,130	1,325	1,371	1,462	1,648	2,262	2,469	2,413	2,836	3,022	11.55
Mizuno	1,166	1,332	1,339	1,296	1,369	1,737	1,650	1,598	1,804	1,887	5.49
Li Ning	116	154	227	304	407	596	983	1,224	1,441	1,420	32.09
Li & Fung	4,780	5,465	6,048	7,130	8,719	11,854	14,195	13,395	15,912	20,030	17.26
Yue Yuen	1,939	2,509	2,720	3,155	3,657	4,114	4,920	5,017	5,788	7,045	15.41

Unit: USD million

Source: Own compilation and calculation of Compound Annual Growth Rate 2002–2001 (CAGR), according to annual corporate reports.

A characteristic example of a highly vertically integrated production network encompassing all the steps between sourcing, production, distribution and marketing is the Esquel corporation in Hong Kong. The company is a leading producer of cotton clothing; its clientele include global brands such as Nike, Lacoste, Esprit and Tommy Hilfiger. Esquel's production process starts in the province of Xingjian in northwest China, where the corporation's own cotton plantations are located. A large part of subsequent processing is concentrated in Guangdong, where four of Esquel's seven Chinese spinning and weaving mills are stationed. Garments are finished not only in China, but also in Vietnam, Malaysia, Sri Lanka and Mauritius. In 2002, the company also founded its own fashion label, Pye, and the retail chain outlet Shirt Stop. Despite such diversification, Esquel remains first and foremost a manufacturer producing mainly for other brands and trading companies (Appelbaum 2009:68–69).

The Yue Yuen corporation's (also registered in Hong Kong) transformation from manufacturer to retailer is more clearly visible. With an annual sales volume of USD 7 billion (2011), Yue Yuen is one of the world's three largest corporations in the sporting goods sector. The name of the 100 per cent subsidiary of the Taiwanese corporation Pou Chen is almost entirely unknown outside of the sector; nonetheless, the company is involved in the production of one out of every six pairs of athletic shoes worn in the world. In 2011, the company's 460,000 employees (up 150,000 since 2008) produced a total of 326.6 million shoes for well-known brands like Nike, Adidas, Asics, Puma, Fila and New Converse. About 40 per cent of total revenues are coming from its two major customers, Nike and Adidas (Yue Yuen 2012:13). Other Taiwanese companies catering to global sports shoe brands are Stella International, which operates six factories in China, and Feng Tay with production units in China, Vietnam and India. With 255 out of 537 production lines, the geographical distribution of Yue Yuen's production is concentrated in China, where Yue Yen has owned factories since 1988. In Indonesia, 140 plants are operating (since 1993), and there are 140 in Vietnam (since 1995; Yue Yuen 2009:210–212). The majority of production takes place in Guangdong Province, where in its heyday Yue Yuen once employed 110,000 people. Numerous factories have sprung up in the direct proximity, delivering basic components such as leather and adhesives (MSN 2008:43). Business and brand clusters also structure the Nikomas Gemilang business complex near Jakarta, where approximately 43,000 workers (85 per cent of whom are female) manufacture shoes for the athletic world, separated into buildings according to brand and contractor. In addition to producing for the export market, Yue Yuen has also built up a rapidly expanding distribution network of wholesalers and retail stores for brand name sporting goods and athletic apparel. In 2006, this constituted 5.6 per cent of company turnover. Only five years later, 20 per cent of sales turnover arose from the retail sales of 3,055 directly operated stores or counters and 3,357 sub-distributors within its Greater China retail network principally operating in the first-, second- and third-tier cities (Appelbaum 2009:73; Yue Yuen 2012:12). Yue Yuen has also become involved in outsourced production phases, such as the supply of raw materials, the manufacturing of shoe soles and specialized machines for production processes. Yue Yuen purchased shares in 76 different companies in 2006, all of which are active in the business sectors listed earlier. In terms of distribution, Yue Yuen collaborates with a global logistics provider to develop computer-assisted management systems that abbreviate reference times and chart more efficient distribution channels. As a global corporation, Yue Yuen nowadays generates 40 per cent of its annual turnover in Asia, about 30 per cent in the US and 20 per cent in Europe (Yue Yuen 2012).

A similar production network variation is clustered around clothing dealers that manage an entire service package for their clients ranging from supply and manufacturing to distribution. Some of such companies also develop designs for their customers, carry out market surveys and ensure quality control. A representative example of a wholesaler with a production manager function is the Hong Kong–based Fung Holding and its subsidiary Li & Fung group. Li & Fung has become a leading supply chain managing company on the premises of a business strategy of sourcing goods in Asia for consumption in developed nations of the Global North. Asia represents about 90 per cent of Li & Fung's total sourcing activities, spanning 20 economies in the region, including China, Vietnam, Indonesia, India, Cambodia, Thailand and the Philippines. In an interview, the company's former CEO Victor Fung described the international division of labour of its production network, using a large-scale contract as an example: Fabric was ordered from Korea and coloured in Taiwan; buttons and zippers were ordered from China, and everything was shipped to Thailand for assembly (Appelbaum 2009:71). The multinational corporation manages all aspects of the global supply chain on behalf of its global customers, relying on an extensive network of more than 300 offices and distribution centres accessing a network of 15,000 suppliers in more than 40 economies. About 4,500 of the group's own 30,000 employees are stationed in Hong Kong. From 2002 to 2011, its pre-tax profits quintupled and turnover grew to more than USD 20 billion; 81 per cent of its sales come from the US and Europe, and about 12 per cent from Asia, including 6 per cent in China. Trading is responsible for 70 per cent of total revenues; distribution and logistics represented 28 and 2 per cent respectively (Li & Fung 2012). Li & Fung has also been involved in retail sales through its subsidiary Li & Fung Retailing Ltd (Li & Fung 2009). Acknowledging domestic consumption increases throughout Asia and new business prospects in the retailing sector, this business has recently been transferred to an independent group operating under the Fung holding. In 2012, Fung Retailing was operating one of the largest menswear retail networks in Greater China with 461 retail stores in greater China (and 379 in mainland China), and further retail stores in South Korea, Malaysia, Singapore and Thailand.

Luen Thai, a leader of the apparel sector, is another example of wholesalers providing their customers with a whole palette of production processes ranging from design and sourcing to supply and distribution is. Luen Thai Holdings is Hong Kong's largest listed garment firm, holding an international customer base that includes Adidas, Banana Republic, Esprit, Polo Ralph Lauren and Fast Retailing, owner of the Japanese brand Uniqlo. The holding's 34,000 employees produced over 80 million garments in 2011, as well as footwear and bags worth of around USD 1 billion from production bases in China, the Philippines, Indonesia, India, Bangladesh and Cambodia. Like many others, Luen Thai has reacted to the expiration of the Multi Fibre Agreement and the rising importance of China as a centre of global consumption by concentrating its assembly lines in the country. In the holding's own 'Supply Chain City' in Dongguan, product development centres, employee living quarters, entertainment facilities and a large hotel can be found next door to the production warehouses. This concentration upon one site permits designers and Luen Thai's international customers alike to directly contact factory engineers to more efficiently plan production.

Chinese corporation Li Ning is to China what brand name companies like Nike and retail giants like Wal-Mart are to the world, only under one roof. Founded in 1990 by former floor gymnast Li Ning, today the eponymous company has become China's most recognized domestic athletic brand. Ten years after founding the company, Li Ning had already cornered a 30 per cent market share in China. Today the brand, whose products sell for 30 to 40 per cent less than equivalent items by global brands Nike and Adidas, is at third place behind the latter on the market. Although Li Ning still manufactures parts of its increasing collection, it is considerably more active in marketing and sales. Its production network is dominated by a flagship enterprise that cannot be definitively classified as a retail business or as a manufacturer. Li Ning profits above all from its dense network of franchises and retail stores, reaching deep into the provincial towns of backcountry China, where its global competitors have just barely managed to gain a foothold. Alone in the year of the 2008 Olympics, Li Ning opened 1,012 new franchises (one every eight to nine hours). At the end of the year, the distribution network consisted of 7,000 outlets, 6,245 of which were part the Li Ning chain (Li Ning 2008). In 2012, the distribution network consisted of 7,500 outlets (Li Ning 2012). This aggressive expansion strategy is visible on the company balance sheet: No other major company in the sporting goods branch has come even close to achieving such hefty profit increases in the last ten or five years (see Table 11.4). As a Chinese brand—98 per cent of Li Ning's profits are reaped in China—the plummeting demand on European and US markets after the Lehman shock had almost no effect on the company's plans for expansion. Immediately upon the crisis, exports in the sporting goods branch as a whole had declined by 26.3 per cent. The drop was even steeper in the core provinces of the textiles industry Jiangsu,

Guangdong, Shandong and Fujian, where the majority of sporting goods manufacturers is located.

With wages in the Pearl River Delta rising by up to 30 per cent in recent times, the region is no longer the low-cost centre of years past. Companies such as Yue Yuen or Li & Fung are therefore moving operations offshore towards Bangladesh, Vietnam and Cambodia as well as western and northern China for sourcing and manufacturing. A survey by Hong Kong's Trade Development Council of 2,400 manufacturers found a quarter would choose to set up new factories in inland China, twice that of those who would opt for cheaper alternatives in Asia, and around half would stay in China's coastal hubs in what were once special economic zones. Keeping operations onshore is more efficient as the supply chain relies on a disciplined workforce as much as on a spatially fixed production technology and transportation infrastructure. Li Ning has also shifted its production westward into the inland. The decision to move to the City of Jingmen in Hubei Province went along with the general trend away from the increasingly expensive production sites along the coast. About USD 300 million have been invested in the construction of the Li Ning industrial park in Jingmen, which became the largest of its kind in the sporting goods branch in 2012. Through the concentration of design, research and development, finishing and distribution all in one place, commodities manufacturing was more tightly coupled to fluctuations in demand, since overall production was streamlined, supply routes and times were shortened and storage costs were drastically reduced. Tailor-made software solutions diminished the necessity of backroom storage in the Li Ning shops as Point-of-Sale data were flowing directly from the sales register to the manufacturers, who monitored the sales quantities of models, sizes and colours to ensure split-second reactions to shifts in demand. When the industrial park is fully functioning, 50,000 people will manufacture half of Li Ning's total goods within a space of two square kilometres (CSGF 2008).

SWEATSHOPS AND THE GLOBALIZATION DEBATE

Profit maximization through the exhaustion of wage expenditure advantages and highly compensated advertising contracts with global sport icons are complementary components of business strategies in the global production networks of the sporting goods industry. Glamour, luxury and the celebrity status of contracted star athletes are the anchors of brand vending, contrasting starkly with the poverty and exploitative conditions under which the products themselves are produced. Since the 1990s, an alliance of trade unions, solidarity networks, critical journalists and development aid organizations has repeatedly drawn attention to the disastrous living and working conditions of textiles industry labourers. Protest against so-called 'sweatshops' established itself as one of the earliest fields of activity of the anti-globalization movement (Klein 1999). Slogans like 'race to the bottom' or 'Fair Wear' have been borrowed from the sport world by the critical globalization movement to denounce the corporate strategy of attaining maximum profit by excessively exploiting labourers in the least developed regions of the world. Activists criticized wages which neither met legal minimums nor ensured humane living conditions; excessively long working hours with no breaks or days off; repetitive assembly tasking; forced unpaid overtime; and the immediate discharge of workers attempting to unionize in any way (Frenkel 2001). However, what marred brand name images the most was the globally outlawed—at least in theory—use of child labour and production in prison camps. Protests on US universities led to the cancellation of millions of dollars of contracts for sport programmes and marketing by institutions of higher learning and left behind an enduring impression on consumer awareness.

Global brands such as Nike saw their profits recede towards the end of the 1990s. Under pressure from consumers, the global brand name began to rethink their management strategies and control over their production networks and were forced to recognize the employment practices of their suppliers as an aspect of their own corporate accountability. Many major sport brand names have in the meantime become members of the Fair Labor Association (FLA), an association founded in 1999 by businesses, universities and NGOs. Members of the FLA commit to protect worker's rights to free assembly and to evaluate their business practices, including the disclosure of their value chains and wage criteria (MSN 2008:24–25). The Code of Conduct, which brand name companies pass on to their suppliers as a provision of their procurement policies, has at least helped alleviate the most extreme types of exploitation in sweatshops. For example, a gradual transition from authoritarian employment relationships to formalized, contractually regulated practices has been observed in the athletic shoe industry in China. In Vietnam, Taiwanese subsidiaries provided better working conditions than companies not involved in transnational supply liaisons in terms of wage level, work hours and labour safety (Frenkel 2001; Wang 2005). In contrast to this positive evaluation, many labour and human rights organizations assess the Corporate Social Responsibility Programs of brand name companies as being mainly nothing more than an image campaign and a fig leaf intended to conceal primary commercial interests beholden to rational financial calculations. The effectiveness of such primarily voluntary behavioural guidelines is indeed limited by the contradictions arising between corporate profit maximization goals, a commitment to social responsibility, harsh market competition and insufficient governmental labour laws. Brand name companies may stipulate compliance with the guidelines, but they don't contribute a cent to the cost increases tied to them, as Yu (2008:526) confirmed for the south China factories of Thai suppliers for Reebok. In the production networks of other brand name companies, contracts were withdrawn from suppliers after unions had organized in their factories (MSN 2008).

In addition to this, the FLA Code of Conduct is often also criticized for its lack of specifications about living wage minimums, regulation of working hours and protection of the right to collective bargaining. Two basic problems dominate the current situation: ILO (International Labour Organization) principles such as the Right to Freedom of Association are not recognized in countries like China and Vietnam, meaning that even when unions can be organized, in many cases they are simply the long arm of management or, in China, made up of party stooges. In the best of cases, these worker collectives support the company's management in matters of personnel administration or company charity. In the worst cases, these collectives actively assist the exploitation of workers (Wang 2005:49). Where tariff agreements are not active, wages and work hours remain an effective means of leverage by companies over their workforce. Employers and contractors face no collective negotiation partner: The International Federation of Sporting Goods Manufacturers refuses to act as a branch representative for its members as a whole and bindingly negotiate a Fair Labor Agreement with other stakeholders. A second problem is the increase of atypical employment conditions and abuse of temporary labour contracts arising from dependency upon the global economy and Northern Hemisphere sales markets (MSN 2008:28).

CONCLUDING REMARKS: THE FUTURE OF ASIAN PRODUCTION NETWORKS

The past three decades have evoked considerable changes which will continue with the development of bilateral relations and the possible formation of an Asian economic area. The shifts in the production networks of the global sporting goods industry seen until now indicate a new process of consolidation and diversification. This process is a reaction by Asian companies to the changing political economy of liberalized world trade and the economic integration of the Asian business region. It is becoming increasingly clear that the consolidation of the consumer commodities industries replicates a vertical integration. This increased production integration and distribution between large retail chains and large intermediaries is similar to the type of vertical integration that once characterized Fordist production. The race to the bottom triggered by buyer-driven commodity chains and their intermediaries in the last quarter of the 20th century seems to finally be slowing. The geo-strategy implemented to squeeze the last drops of added value from labour by competing locations against each other and threatening to close factories can still be observed in production networks, but it is no longer as extreme. For example, the number of companies and supply regions embedded in Nike's commodities chains has receded in recent years, despite a simultaneous increase in overall employment and product output. This reorientation can be traced back to the expiration of the quota regulations mandated by the Multi Fibre Agreement, and also to a newfound trend towards complex production clusters supported by the corporations. These fully integrated networks are especially well positioned in China, where the labour force is inexhaustible and able to react efficiently to continually shortening product cycles and the volatile demand cycles of 'fast retailing'.

Another strategy used by Asian businesses is 'industrial upgrading'. By using new production technologies, manufacturers in long-industrialized East Asian nations can enter higher-value market segments and outsource the simpler work processes. Also, producers and wholesalers alike have developed new business fields, such as direct sales, product development and the marketing of proprietary brands. These fields have become more lucrative as the buying power of local populations has increased. The internet in also an important factor in the improvement of communications within networks—the exchange of information flows faster, clients find contractors more quickly, orders are delivered according to industry standards and product specifications. The standardization of software supported coordination programmes not only increases productivity; is also draws networks tighter and creates longer-term delivery and trade relationships among companies. However, in the case of the developing nations of the fourth generation, chances for industrial upgrading have, as of yet, remained limited.

The chapter has shown that the development of Asian production networks has been affected by local initiatives, regional actors and established institutions. In this phase of globalization, the role played by governments was as significant as in earlier times (Amsden 1989; Hassler 2003). Managements, especially those at neuralgic network intersections, were often staffed according to ethnic or familial criteria, or at least an imitation of familial relations (Carney 2005). Unions, whose role is seen sceptically in their motherland, have also not been successfully established in overseas locations (Wang 2005). On the other hand, global initiatives, actors and institutions were no less important: Despite a plethora of liberalization rhetoric, the deregulation of world trade has brought workers at the lowest echelons of production processes little or no improvements in their welfare. Instead, a united coalition of critical consumers and international solidarity networks proved that the power of a brand is not unlimited and that the responsibility for production site conditions is directly tied to consumer choices in countries of the Northern Hemisphere.

The question remains: Is it possible to speak of a sustainable development process in the case of the regional integration of production networks? Seen from the perspective of the workers involved, even sweatshop conditions can represent a social upgrade releasing them from a feudalistic dependency upon agriculture or cultural patriarchy. Empirical research supports the assumption that exploitative working conditions are characteristic of the early phases of industrialization and that, in the long term, they are replaced by more humane forms of labour relations. Today, the high level of dependency upon demand from industrialized nations was recently made clear by export developments in the year following the global economic crisis. This represents an acute key question in the sector, in addition to the technological dependency of catch-up development, as suggested by the production hierarchy model. Another weak point is the enormous power of brand names and chain stores. From the electronics to the automobile sector, the high dependency upon transnational corporations leads to significant value transfer within production networks. In the sporting goods branch, profit margins for Nike and Adidas, or for Asics and Mizuno, are significantly higher than those of local producers and wholesalers, at least at this point in time. However, it is probable that the burgeoning buying power of the Chinese population will lastingly change the structure of the world market. The rise of Asian sporting goods manufacturers and the concentration of their production processes will strengthen their bargaining power over imported brand names, thereby weakening their dominance. In the mid-term, the interplay of the various political, union and consumer influences will determine if the tectonic changes in the branch also lead to a balanced distribution of welfare improvements to all societal groups of the region, above all to workers in the sporting goods industry.

Epilogue
Japanese Sport and Global Body Culture

How do we explain the Japanese government's increasing interest in gauging and assessing the value of sport? How do we make sense of the fact that the Japanese have come to link physical education, as well as team sport and ball games, with moral guidance and spiritual development? Or that gambling on sport has been promoted as the main revenue source for the financing of recreational sports? Why is it that sports mega-events have acquired such a high symbolic significance that within little more than a decade the Japanese Olympic Committee has issued bids three times to host the Olympic Games? And why has the construction sector been the biggest recipient of federal funding for the execution of sports policy? All of these questions relate to a cultural phenomenon that is of global relevance and prevalence. Its manifestations in Japan are inseparably linked to the political economy of modernity, which must be taken into account when studying the global body culture of sport in any particular nation. I thus share with Tomlinson (1999:70) the view that 'the core idea of global modernity as the social and cultural condition that proceeds from an epochal shift in the social organization of time-space' remains 'a highly compelling way of understanding our present complex connectivity'.

Because the appearances and meanings of sport in a global world are under constant transformation, sport in Japan, too, has become both a motor and a metric of transnational change. Translating the historical timeline of Japan's sport development into a matrix that relates Japan's positioning in the world to global hegemony evokes debates both on continuity and discontinuity and on connectivity and disconnectivity at the same time. Freed from the containment by nation-states and national cultures, this study of sport in the light of globalization was able to analyse social, economic and cultural relations in sport on a transnational level. In such a configuration, social rather than geographical hierarchies (as in traditional developmental trajectories of West versus East) have come to structure the global field of sport, its consumption as well as its production.

Observation of current trends in Japanese sport clearly indicates that the meaning of 'Japanese' in this context itself has become blurred. Transnationalism in sport (ownership, citizenship and consumption) has led to the penetration of the double helix of culture and 'race' with the consequence that the notion of culture implies difference as well as it emphasizing sameness. Under the impact of globalization, there is a shift happening from culture being seen as some kind of inert local substance to more volatile forms of difference. Culture is increasingly inappropriate for the production of taxonomic difference. Rather it now acquires interactive and refractive characteristics. Not long ago Houlihan (2003:358) noted that sport had become a 'vehicle for the demonstration of differences' in a globalizing world. But when difference is no longer geographically represented, arguably the 'other' is interwoven with the 'us' (Lithman 2004:18). In this regard, the 'Japanese' of Japanese sport does not so much only have indexing, but also relating, qualities.

This book has focused on the role of sport and sport-related body practices in regulating the social relations between subject and society in Japan. It has been particularly interested in the agenda of state actors and other players related to the sport industrial complex of the media, sport industries and non-governmental sport organizations, and how their articulations of body politics have been impacted by local, global and transnational forces. In addition, it tried to demonstrate the consequences of their connections, collusions and competitions for sporting opportunities and practices of the body in general. Case studies analysed in this monograph have focused on structures and institutions as well as meanings. One might say, critically, that this emphasis has been at the expense of sport practices and consumption styles, which is peculiar since Japan's most prominent spectator sports—baseball, sumo and football—would certainly have added weight to my argument. Yet I feel that any attempt at linking the rich universe of sport with a politics aimed at the body has to concentrate on sport practices and opportunities that are of practical relevance for each and every body. The deliberate focus on amateur sport is one distinctive feature of this study. The other is its broad and multidisciplinary approach that has been theoretically informed by a heterodox fusion of praxeology with discourse analysis. Searching for commonalities and congruencies among the various approaches and findings of the individual chapters, this epilogue turns once more to the implications of bringing together the fields of body culture, political economy and cultural globalization.

What can we conclude from the discussion of sport in Japan for the meaning of sport and body culture in modern and late modern Japan? Both notions were problematized in the introduction, and the discussion of data and case studies provided ample evidence of their fluidity and malleability throughout the 20th century. The starting point of this book was the assumption that corporeality and play are central features of human experience. The introduction showed how ritualized practices of the body, which are shaped by mutually shared systems of belief and morality and substantiated in social institutions of a community, are enacted in distinctive body cultures and how these entanglements have contributed to their emergence and continuance. I also argued that sport should be understood as a social phenomenon, which is integral to the social fabric in which it is embedded and therefore helps to construct that social fabric. Yet in a globalizing world practices, meanings and structures are no longer exclusively constituted by cross-referencing within the boundaries of a territory or a social aggregation. Instead they are subject to border-crossing, if not also global, impacts that shape meanings, institutions and practices of the body. In Japan, too, the transition from traditional to post-traditional society has been accompanied by a substitution of folk games and ritualized body practices by modern sport, while vernacular forms that proved to be successful in resisting their displacement—such as martial arts—have been subjected to a process of sportification. I suggested understanding these concomitant forces in terms of the twofold appearance of cultural globalization, i.e. the spread of global culture and the change of local culture due to global impacts.

Combining the three axes of cultural globalization, body culture and political economy provided an analytical tool to explore the field of sports as a net of interdependencies. In order to understand how sport and politics of the body impact the social fabric of individual and society, and how this relation is shaped by globalization, I suggested thinking of body culture in terms of a web of correspondences that regulate the interplay of practices of the body, institutions, structures and meanings. These relations constitute a social field and cultural sphere with fuzzy, flexible and osmotic boundaries allowing interactions and exchanges with forces from outside and neighboring fields. Core questions that derived from this model addressed its three key components of: (1) meanings, the objectives of sporting practices, the purposes of body politics and the agenda of state and non-state actors; (2) the institutions and structures enacting the disciplinary techniques of state and society; and (3) corporeal practices emerging as their consequences for sporting opportunities and performances of the body in general.

Making use of multiple case studies and methodologies, diverse empirical questions and theoretical models, this study has been designed to analyse and understand those structures and processes which provided the background of the manifold manifestations, attributions of meaning and functions of sport in modern and contemporary Japan from a great variety of angles. Taking into account the consequential impact of the interplay of such diverse but interwoven structures and institutions like the mechanisms of social inclusion and exclusion, the regulation of public space, the pricing of sport, physiological and medical knowledge, political needs and priorities and standards of body conduct according to the demands of the education system, the military or the production system, it became evident that the meaning of sport differed considerably for Japanese people experiencing the dawn of industrialization in late Meiji Japan, the imperialist-colonial expansion, the democratization of postwar society or the proliferation of consumerism in late modernity. It seems that the high contingency of sport makes it vulnerable to claims and expectations raised by multiple actors and stakeholders that are not always directly involved in sporting matters.

The emerging picture clearly differs from a taken-for-granted notion of sport as a cultural universal that is implicitly or explicitly sustained by the claims and ideologies of international sport organizations and hardly ever questioned by the modern mass media. All the chapters have confirmed what historians, sociologists and anthropologists of sport have been at pains to show in their earlier work (e.g. Guttmann 1994; Hargreaves 1986; MacAloon 1981; van Bottenburg 2001): the historical rootedness of the modern sport ideology; the socioeconomic conditions underlying the worldwide dissemination of cultural practices that originated at a particular time and at a distinctive place for very specific reasons and purposes; and the continuous transformation of sport and related body cultures over time. It must be added that the meanings of sport and ideas about sport not only differ over time, but also in time for populations and locations. Because accessibility, costs and profits have been and continue to be unequally distributed, there is a great variability of sports between countries and social configurations within a country. After all, sport mostly is a conservative social institution, and interest and participation in sport largely differ in line with variance of gender, age, capital ownership and social status. In Japan, too, habitual practices of the body, varying in line with achieved group membership and ascriptive factors such as age and gender, emerged and became more set among generational cohorts and changed again in accordance with commonly accepted ways of life and lifestyle choices. As my review of mass sport participation in late modern Japan suggests, the willingness—or capability—to spend on sport is connected with larger macroeconomic trends, which make lower income groups particularly vulnerable in recessionary times. Since disposable income correlates with active sport involvement, the sport budget of lower-income groups and individuals has shrunk over the past decades of economic crisis in comparison with total household spending and the parallel development among higher-income groups. In terms of social segregation and habitual differentiation, Japan is thus no different from what theory or empirical comparative national studies suggest. Yet while sport contributes to the reproduction of social inequalities, it can also provide a cultural sphere largely independent of political and economic forces, allowing for the emergence of new possibilities in society.

Political economy, in the Foucauldian sense as the guiding principle of control, efficiency and rationalization, has left its imprint on body culture, body practices and body politics for more than a century. Pursuing national goals of nation-building, popular mobilization and productivity gains, the Japanese state has been the leading actor of the political economy of the body. The comparative case study in the first chapter demonstrated how the cultural import of Western sport impacted the perception and disposition of individual and collective bodies. Sport in Japan appealed first and most to those social circles that accepted the Western imperatives of self-governance and body control as beneficial for their own interests and the nation at large. Since the institutionalization of modern governance structures started in Meiji Japan, state institutions saw to it that sport in Japan did not branch out into autonomous organizational structures but remained confined within the social framework of larger organizational units, most notably the educational system within which sport contributed to the moulding of the modern Japanese subject. The close interconnection with the national education system as the foremost channel of sport diffusion not only provided the basis for the dominant perception of sport as an educational tool geared at the young and maturing body. It also contributed to the demographically segregated landscape of sport participation with very different levels of activity according to age and membership status. Linking physical education with moral education, including spirit-building, solidarity, loyalty with the in-group, national identity, the firm and nearly exclusive placement of sport within curricula and the social boundaries of the school system, increased the susceptibility of sports to be used instrumentally for purposes not directly or even necessarily related to sports.

This and the subsequent chapters demonstrated how sports have acquired ever-new and changing meanings for different audiences and participants over time. To the present day the state continues to use its power via educational institutions and mandatory curricula to shape the national body, albeit for different pedagogic purposes that have emerged in line with new ideas about society and the individual and in response to new perceptions of gender relations and gender roles. There has also been a significant change in the targeting of new groups of after-hours athletes and weekend sports people beyond the school populations. Sport as a tool of social education for adults emerged in response to Japan's ascendancy within international society and the concomitant need for a broad social welfare strategy. However, mass sports have always struggled with the contradictory messages of budgetary restraints that never reached the amount of public spending needed for true 'sport for all' policies; the dominant ethics of diligence and hard work that cut down the spare time for sports activities to close to zero; and corporatist politics that assigned agency and responsibility for public health management to enterprises, regional bodies and other corporatist segments of society. The firm grip of the state on the collective body of the nation was one factor that enabled basically the same set of body movements to be understood and used for such divergent purposes as moral campaigning, nationalist indoctrination, regional revitalization or quality of life and health issues, but the lessening of control opened the field to new protagonists, new programmes and new purposes.

Of course, the effects of globalization have countered and partially undermined the power and significance of the state, not just in the fields of sport and body politics, but in many other areas as well. Changes within Japanese sport to be noted since the 1990s have been clearly impacted by the three most significant developments of the global economy: the rise of finance in the global economy; the political shift to neoliberalism; and the increasing emphasis on consumption as an engine of economic growth. The rise of neoliberalism as a dominant ideology has severely undercut the influence of national governments and obfuscated their intentions. National politics influenced by neoliberal ideology has led to the market being perceived as the dominant model for the representation and achievement of commonly accepted standards of rationality and efficiency. Neoliberal body politics meanwhile emphasizes the responsibility of the individual while promoting the privatization of health services and the reduction of public expenditure. Sport and health promotion politics under such an episteme have acquired meanings and techniques previously unheard of in Japan. Accountability and controllability became guiding principles that allowed public health and the national body to be measured, assessed and planned in quantifiable and numerical terms by sport and health bureaucrats. The meaning of sport, in the context of public management, expanded from being a disciplinary tool, a business and a source of individual pleasure to social engineering, ultimately requesting the individual to be in charge of their own fitness, health and well-being. The underlying ideology no longer required the state apparatus and institutions to reach people's minds, as their consumption activities integrated them as participants into the market. Yet we have seen how state interventions continue to manipulate and impose emergent cultural trends. Despite global market forces and cultural trends, top-down approaches initiated by governments continue to be of significance, as they are widely institutionalized and socially accepted, particularly in comparison with the weak traditions of initiatives from the bottom up.

This book has also shown that commercial interests in sport and entrepreneurial activities capitalizing on sport in Japan have a long-standing history dating back into the first half of the 20th century. However, it has been only in the past three decades that processes of commercialization and commodification found broad access and profoundly changed the field of sport, which once had been mainly the preserve of the public sector. Bourdieu noted that the autonomy of such a field from 'the rule of money and interest' has become threatened 'by the intrusion of commercial logic at every stage of the production and circulation of cultural goods' (Bourdieu 2003:67). As actions of the Japanese state, like politics and policy in any one country, are increasingly conditioned, if not determined, by global economic forces, non-market spheres of life such as sport and culture have turned into targets for global capital lobbying for the dismantling of state regulations that so far have closed off non-market spheres to commodification and profit-making. The consequences of these developments include a growth in the economic effects and impacts of sport; an ongoing increase in the value of genuinely global sport properties, including brands, teams and tournaments; and the convergence of economic power in sport ownership, such as the vertical and horizontal integration of Asian apparel and sport equipment producers, distributors and vendors. Economic power and symbolic power have been equally harnessed to the selling of commercialized culture, as my discussion of

Japan's embracing of global sports spectacles and their significance for global sports commodity chains have underlined.

These developments have contributed to the further expansion of the multivocality of sports and their susceptibility to being used for new functions and meanings, such as place-marketing, entertaining the masses, gaining influence and expressing authority in international relations, selling goods to ever-increasing markets or even rejecting such objectives. I have demonstrated how sports have occasionally been integrated into foreign policy goals and put onto the agenda in specific circumstances to strengthen official ties, to demonstrate goodwill in international relations and to display positive images of the self to the world community. The opaqueness of what sport is about is only partially responsible for the limited success of the implementation of sport as a public diplomacy tool; partially it is due to the repercussions of a global sports order that developed on the premises of a taken-for-granted Western superiority that assigned Japan, as well as other Asian nations, to a subordinate position within supranational sport organizations or among competing body cultures until recent times.

As a result of cultural globalization, the mainstreaming and controlling of the message about what sports are actually all about has become inherently difficult, if not impossible in Japan. With the ongoing integration and consolidation of sport, leisure, recreation, television, film and tourism into elements of the entertainment industry, the boundaries between sport and entertainment are dissolving. Further aspects of the blurring of boundaries include diverse processes of sportification (for example, marathon dancing; the sport-like obsession with charts and ranks; virtual games and e-sports; sporting symbols in advertisement; company profiles and political rhetoric) and the de-sportification of sports (for example, staged contests of American professional wrestling; cage fights unrestrained by rules; the fight against doping and all kinds of cheating). As these processes press hard on what were believed to be the essential values of modern sport, they cause cultural change. As a consequence, the relational arrangement of sports has started to change again. Body practices in structural compliance with Olympic sports still provide the hegemonic sports model. But there is an increasing variety of alternative sports constituting a dynamic and differentiated field of everyday practices of the body. Typical alternative sports of the urban consumer society include inline skating, skateboarding, streetball, indoor climbing and free running (parkour). In Japan, too, skaters and breakdancers as part of a glocal hip-hop scene have been seen reclaiming urban space. These lifestyle sports result from the fusion of mass and elite sports, on the one hand, with pop music and fashion, on the other hand, and they celebrate the spectacular performance of the body in a way clearly different from the production society with its emphasis on accomplishment and success. The productive body continues to be of significance, but the consumptive body has become increasingly salient—or even emblematic—in the political economy of late modernity.

Notes

NOTES TO CHAPTER 1

1. Parts of the arguments discussed in this chapter were presented at the JAWS Conference, Senri Ethnological Museum (Minpaku), Ōsaka, March 10–14, 1999; the international symposium on 'Leisure and Work in Edo/Tokyo and Vienna during the 19th Century', Meiji University, Tokyo, January 25–26, 2001; and the First World Congress of Sport Sociology, Seoul, July 20–24, 2001. Edited papers were published subsequently in 1999 as 'Some considerations on the institutionalization of modern sport in Japan'. In: *Romanian Journal of Japanese Studies* 1, 139–150; in 2001 as 'Tokai-gata shintai no yōsei—Tōkyō to Uiin no kindai ni okeru supōtsu no yakuwari ni tsuite'. In: Meiji Daigaku Bungakubu, ed.: *Jūkyū seiki ni okeru nichijō to asobi no sekai—Edo Tōkyō to Uiin.* Tokyo: Meiji Daigaku Bungakubu, 88–97; in 2001 as 'Early sportscapes in late nation-states: Modern bodies in the capital territory of Vienna and Tokyo'. In: Koh Eunha et al., eds.: *Sociology of sport and new global order: Bridging perspectives and crossing boundaries.* Seoul: Organizing Committee for the 1st World Congress of Sociology of Sport, 491–506; and in 2001 as 'Moderne Körper, moderne Orte. Sport und Nationalstaat in Japan und Österreich 1850-1900'. In: *Minikomi—Informationen des Akademischen Arbeitskreis Japan* 2, 14–21.

NOTES TO CHAPTER 2

1. The core argument of this chapter was first presented to the panel 'Sporting Cultures and Nation Cultures in Asia', International Convention of Asia Scholars (ICAS) 2 at Free University Berlin, August 10–12, 2001.

NOTES TO CHAPTER 3

1. Parts of the arguments discussed in this chapter were presented at the international symposium on 'Leisure and work in Tokyo and Vienna during the 1930s and 1940s', University of Vienna, January 8–9, 2005, and the symposium on 'Militarisme et societe. Esthétique et contrôle social dans le Japon des années 1930', Université Paris 7—Denis Diderot, Paris, May 18–20, 2006. Earlier versions were published in 2007 as 'Die Faschisierung des Körpers: Sport in totalitären Systemen. Wien und Tokyo im Vergleich 1930 bis 1945'. In: Roland Domenig and Sepp Linhart, eds.: *Wien und Tokyo, 1930–1945.*

Alltag, Kultur, Konsum. Vienna: Abteilung für Japanologie, Institut für Ostasienwissenschaften, Universität Wien, 33–54; in 2007 as 'Sport et politique du corps dans le Japon totalitaire'. In: Jean-Jacques Tschudin and Claude Hamon, eds.: *La société Japonaise devant la montée du Militarisme. Culture populaire et contrôle social dans le Japon des années 1930*. Arles Cedex: Éditions Philippe Picquier, 71–90 ; in 2008 as 'Sports, body control and national discipline in prewar and wartime Japan'. In: *Leidschrift* 23/3, 63–83.

NOTES TO CHAPTER 4

1. Parts of the arguments discussed in the following chapter were presented at the Annual VSJF Conference, Vereinigung für sozialwissenschaftliche Japanforschung, Japanisch-Deutsches Zentrum Berlin, Berlin, November 19–21, 2004; for the panel on 'Masculinities and femininities in East Asia: Constructions of gender in school and education'. An earlier version has been published in 2007 as 'Physical education and the curriculum of gender reproduction'. In: Claudia Derichs and Susanne Kreitz-Sandberg, eds.: *Gender dynamics and globalization. Perspectives on Japan within Asia*. Berlin: LIT Verlag, 123–142.
2. In 1914 Nishikubo Hiromichi published a series of articles arguing that the Japanese martial arts should be called *budō* ('martial way') rather than *bujutsu* ('martial techniques'). The police official recommended the martial way as an effective tool to teach schoolchildren to be willing to sacrifice their lives for the emperor. When Nishikubo became head of the martial arts college of the Dai Nippon Butokukai in 1919, he ordered its name changed from Bujutsu Senmon Gakkō to Budō Senmon Gakkō. The Dai Nippon Butokukai adopted the new phrase in its publications and the Ministry of Education followed suit in 1926. Since 1931, the word *budō* began to refer to compulsory instruction in the Japanese public schools. The Dai Nippon Butokukai was established at the occasion of the foundation of the Butokuden, a consecrated shrine for martial arts at Heian Jingū in Kyōto in 1895. The Butokukai was patronized by the Royal family. The organization aimed to revive *bushidō* to 'promote *bujutsu* to future military men,' and to make Japan 'a nation of military prowess'. Enjoying rapid growth, branches in 42 prefectures reported about 1.3 million members by 1906. As the most forceful, influential and chauvinistic sport-governing body, it was dissolved by the Allied Occupation Forces in September 1946. For more on this topic, see Nakamura (1994b).
3. The reduction of compulsory subjects is in line with the general shift of emphasis towards a society of lifelong learning (*shōgai kyōiku shakai*) in which individual interests, rather than institutional coercion, are meant to build the platform of self-cultivation.
4. See the online minutes of the council's discussion in its fourth and fifth meeting on August 9 and 27, 2001, at http://www.mext.go.jp/b_menu/shingi/12/hoken/.
5. The survey is a sampling survey covering pupils and students attending public elementary, lower secondary and upper secondary schools, national technical colleges, public and private junior colleges and national colleges and universities as well as working adult of 20–64 years old and elderly persons 65–79 years old. Pupils and students are surveyed annually in May to October through schools, and others by the local boards of education. The 2001 survey covered about 75,000 persons.

NOTES TO CHAPTER 5

1. Parts of the arguments discussed in this chapter were presented at the Geographic Society of Hiroshima and the Department of Geography, Hiroshima University, Hiroshima, March 10, 2003; the Section on Geography and Urban Studies, the 12th Conference of the European Association of Japanese Studies, Warsaw, August 27–30, 2003; and the Centre for East Asia, British Columbia University, Vancouver, February 15, 2004. A preliminary version was published in 2004 under the title 'Sport zwischen Markt und öffentlicher Dienstleistung. Zur Zukunft des Breitensports in Japan'. In: *SWS-Rundschau (Journal für Sozialforschung)* 44/2, 227–251.
2. The Resort Law not only triggered a scramble for 'resort area' status by towns, villages and prefectures, but also a construction boom extending over the whole archipelago. By the end of 1989 more than 850 applications for designated resort projects had been submitted that would have seen nearly 20 per cent of the Japanese landscape rebuilt and refashioned for the leisure industry (Satō 1990:98). In fact, although most of the projects were approved within a short time, many were never realized. Few schemes ever went beyond the level of planning as the bursting of the bubble economy, which had also been inflated by mounting land prices, destroyed these assets and crushed the dreams of many speculators. The devaluation of the assets that served as collateral to the credit-financed projects threatened to crush banks under the burden of non-performing loans. This made many companies bankrupt or forced them to withdraw from their partnerships, and local governments had to explain to their electorate where all the taxpayers' money had gone (Funck 1999:336ff.).
3. The remaining 30 per cent was spent on the promotion of top sport. All data according to the annual reports by the National Agency for the Advancement of Sport and Health, published on the agency's website http://www.naash.go.jp/sinko/happyou.html.

NOTES TO CHAPTER 6

1. Parts of the arguments discussed in this chapter were presented at the World Congress of Sport Sociology, Copenhagen, Denmark, July 31–August 5, 2007, and the 14th Conference of the European Association of Japanese Studies, Lecce, September 20–23, 2008. A shortened version has been published under the title 'Sport and demographic change in Japan'. In: Florian Coulmas, Harald Conrad, Annette Schad-Seifert and Ralph Lützeler, eds.: *The demographic challenge. A handbook about Japan*. Leiden: Brill Academic Publishers 2008, 613–632.
2. The term 'lifestyle-related disease' was introduced in response to a proposal by the Council on Public Health in 1996, replacing the traditional name of 'adult disease'. This new term represents a concept of 'a group of diseases whose symptomatic appearance and progress are affected by living practices including eating, exercising, rest, smoking, and drinking' (Kōseishō 1999:269).
3. Japan's fitness market had an annual turnover of JPY 323 billion; about 3.4 million members were affiliated with more than 2,000 private fitness clubs. While Japan was leading the Asia Pacific in terms of turnover, total number of clubs and memberships, its penetration rate (share of entire population) of 2.7 per cent was lagging far behind New Zealand (10.4), Australia (9.0), Singapore (7.1), Hong Kong (4.7) and Korea (3.0); by comparison, the US

penetration rate was 15.7 per cent, Canada's 14.6 per cent and the average of the EU 25 nations was 8.1 per cent (IHRSA 2006).

4. Cf. Emi's aptly named booklet *Oiru shokku* (2005) on the three phases of aging, beginning with presbyopia and wrinkling at age 50, the rising probability of cancer or hypertrophy at the second stage about a decade later and the increasing dependency on artificial devices such as dentures or hearing aids at the third stage.
5. Revisions were added to the Basic Plan for the Promotion of Sports following a public hearing on July 29, 2006. The updated version, including some reference material on the current progress, was at the time of writing only available from the e-government online database (http://search.e-gov.go.jp/servlet/Public?ANKEN_TYPE=2; refer to project no. 185000217).
6. As discussed in the previous chapter, local government expenditure hardly exceeded the share of the national budget in the past. In 2000, when the national budget was already down at 380 billion, local governments still spent JPY 480 billion on sports. Facility maintenance and public building projects consume the largest proportion (cf. Manzenreiter 2004c).

NOTES TO CHAPTER 7

1. Parts of the arguments discussed in this chapter were presented to the Graduate School on Health and Sport Management, Juntendo University, Tokyo, December 12, 2009, and the DIJ Forum, German Institute for Japanese Studies, Tokyo, April 1, 2010. An earlier version was published in 2011 under the title 'Monitoring health and the body: Anthropometry, lifestyle risks and the Japanese obesity crisis'. In: *Journal of Japanese Studies* 38/1, 55–84.
2. For an introduction to sociological and anthropological aspects of fatness in time and space, see de Garine and Pollock 1995, which also features a chapter on Japan by Ishige Naomichi. See also Gard and Wright 2005.
3. It is not my intention to provide a systematic review of the risk society theory. For a critical review including references to alternative conceptions, advancements of the argument into different disciplines and major shortcomings of the original theses, see, among others, Ekberg 2007; Elliot 2002; Lupton 1999.
4. Threshold values used for the diagnosis of the metabolic syndrome as implemented by the Japanese government in 2008: diabetes mellitus: raised fasting plasma glucose, (FPG) ≥ 100 mg/dL (5.6 mmol/L), or previously diagnosed type 2 diabetes; hyperlipidia: raised triglycerides ≥ 150 mg/dL (1.7 mmol/L) or specific treatment for this lipid abnormality; hypercholesterolemia: reduced HDL cholesterol < 40 mg/dL (1.03 mmol/L) in males or < 50 mg/dL (1.29 mmol/L) in females, or specific treatment for this lipid abnormality; hypertension: raised blood pressure, systolic BP ≥ 130 or diastolic BP ≥ 85 mm Hg, or treatment of previously diagnosed hypertension.
5. 164-LH-budget 5–1–127. References for statements in Parliament are indexed as follows: diet session no.; chamber; committee; meeting no.; speaker no. All statements published in the Proceedings of the National Diet of Japan can be retrieved online from kokkai.ndl.go.jp.
6. 164-LH-health-21–103.
7. 164-LH-health-21–116.
8. 164-LH-health-14–58.
9. 164-LH-health-15–251.
10. 164-LH-plenary-31- 49.
11. 164-LH-health-20–51.
12. 164-LH-health-21–97.

13. 164-LH-plenary-31–14+16.
14. 164-UH-health-24–197.
15. 164-UH-health-21–116.
16. 164-UH-health-27–302.
17. 164-UH-health-27–389.
18. 164-LH-health-21–119.
19. 164-LH-health-20–57; 164-LH-health-21–103. To mention just a few more recent examples that shed a critical light on the usefulness of the metabolic syndrome as a risk predicator: In 2008, the medical journal *Lancet* published the results of two broad prospective clinical trials searching for associations between the metabolic syndrome and risks for cardiovascular disease and diabetes among the elderly. Since both studies failed to find statistically significant differences for waist size or other symptoms related to the metabolic syndrome, they came to the identical conclusion of rejecting the benefits of the metabolic syndrome in clinical medicine. For a digest of the studies, see the June 2008 issue of junkfoodscience.blogspot.com.
20. 164-LH-health-21–99.
21. 164-UH-health-21–150.
22. 164-LH-health-19–34.
23. 164-LH-health-21–119.
24. 169-UH-health-4–145.
25. 169-UH-health-4–145.
26. 164-LH-health-21–103.
27. 163-LH-health-2–39.
28. 164-UH-cabinet-4–221.
29. A summary of the online survey was published online at whatjapanthinks.com.
30. 166-LH-controlling-2–71.
31. 166-LH-controlling-2–104.
32. 169-LH-health-8–187.
33. 162-UH-cabinet-12–5.
34. 166-UH-cabinet-21–14.
35. 168-UH-environment-2–70.
36. 169-LH-transport-7–53.
37. *Yomiuri Shinbun*, online, July 1, 2008. Accessed July, 2, 2008
38. *Japan Food Newspaper*, online, June 3, 2009. Accessed December 4, 2009.

NOTES TO CHAPTER 8

1. Parts of the arguments discussed in this chapter was presented at the International Asia-Europe Workshop 'Hosting Major International Sports Events: Comparing Asia and Europe', University of Edinburgh, Edinburgh, March 11–12, 2005, and the workshop on 'Sports Mega-Event Research', Heilbronn Business School, April 27, 2007. A previous version was published in 2008 as 'The "benefits" of hosting: Japanese experiences from the 2002 Football World Cup'. In: *Asian Business and Management* 7/2, 201–224.
2. Japan also benefited from the favourable development of currency exchange rates. FIFA calculations were based on the US dollar, which plummeted 10 per cent against the yen between 1996 and 2002. At the time of the 2002 FIFA World Cup, 100 JPY was approximately worth 0.85 euro and 0.84 US dollar.
3. In addition to the ten host cities, 84 municipal governments offered themselves as candidates for base camp venues in Japan. As the Japanese press noted,

many municipal governments went to great lengths and expense to host World Cup teams, hoping the investment would prop up their economies. Although FIFA covered transportation and accommodation expenses for the finalists, some local governments spent more than JPY 100 million to host the base camps, including direct payments and indirect fringe benefits to the foreign guests. Most camp cities had excessive expectations of the benefits of hosting a national team. In the end, the majority received little financial return on their investments, and many faced losses. In Iwata, Shizuoka prefecture, a state-of-the-art stadium costing almost JPY 2 billion was built for Japan's national team. Yet the team shunned the new Yumeria field, presumably for secrecy reasons, in favour of Iwata Stadium, a football pitch that had been used by the city for years (*Mainichi Shinbun*, June 8, 2002). According to local newspapers, Toyama City reported a loss of JPY 10 million, primarily due to a hefty entry fee for their Croatian guests meeting a prefectural selection (*Kahoku Shinpō*, August 6, 2002). Fujieda City in Shizuoka prefecture noted a minus of JPY 1.14 million. The city received notorious media attention after the exhausted official in charge of training camp arrangements with Senegal committed suicide in May 2002 (*Shizuoka Shinbun*, August 22, 2002).

4. Operating the prestigious Sapporo Dome cost a minimum of JPY 2.6 billion per year and a very dense calendar of events to cover the burden. Except for this multifunctional state-of-the-art leisure complex, no other arena was able to provide a reasonably balanced plan of operation. Nogawa and Mamiya (2002) highlighted the negative picture of public facility management, showing that many, if not all, of the World Cup stadiums would remain as heavy burdens on local taxpayers and a negative legacy of the 2002 World Cup. The per capita burden of construction costs ranged between JPY 5,000 and 25,000 for every single inhabitant of the host regions.
5. FIFA's lump sum payment was the (unintended) equivalence of what both bidders reportedly had spent on their campaign (*Asahi Shinbun*, May 18, 2002). Because of the surprising decision by FIFA to give the World Cup equally to South Korea and Japan, total costs surged immediately due to the requirements of staging two simultaneous World Cup finals, while income opportunities and chances to promote a particular and undistorted image of the hosting nation became severely limited. According to the *Asahi Shinbun* (from October 2, 1996), a leading Japanese newspaper and later an 'Official Supplier of the 2002 FIFA World Cup Korea/Japan', Japan would stand to lose as much as JPY 50 billion due to the roughly 50 per cent decrease in estimated income. To compensate for the dwindling earnings, FIFA assigned each host country the right to keep proceeds from respective ticket sales of their share of the 64 matches.
6. Finally, six Japanese firms, including the broker Nomura Securities, insurance companies Nissay and Tokyo Marine, food processor Nissin, electric power supplier Tepco and the publisher Asahi Shinbun, were recruited to safeguard the national project. The companies reportedly paid approximately JPY 1 billion for the privilege of becoming official local suppliers (*Asahi Shinbun*, April 4, 2002).
7. The names of the host countries with the date of hosting as well as economic growth rates for pre–and post–World Cup years in parentheses are as follows: Switzerland (1954; 4.0 per cent and 5.5 per cent); Sweden (1958; 1.9 per cent and 4.0 per cent); Chile (1962; 3.2 per cent and 1.8 per cent); Great Britain (1966; 1.4 per cent and 3.0 per cent); Mexico (1970; 2.9 per cent and 5.2 per cent); Germany (1974; 9.5 per cent and 4.7 per cent); Argentina (1978; 0.0 per cent and 5.6 per cent); Spain (1982; -0.6 per cent and 0.5 per cent); Mexico (1986; -2.2 per cent and 0.6 per cent); Italy (1990; 2.4 per cent

and 0.9 per cent); US (1994; 2.4 per cent and 2.3 per cent); and France (1998; 1.9 per cent and 2.9 per cent).

8. The overall picture on growth induced by the World Cup is even more mixed when the traditionally volatile Latin American countries are excluded from the calculation. Under this condition, hosts witnessed a GDP drop by a relative 0.4 per cent in both the year before and the year after the tournament. Apparently England's dismal economic performance in 1966 and West Germany's slow growth in the mid-1970s distort the growth dynamics. But even after stripping both England and West Germany out of the equation, any impact from the World Cup on growth tended to be relatively small and petered out after the first 12 months.
9. Showing perhaps more economic savvy than team spirit, Japan's Economy Minister Takenaka Heizō conceded that it was 'tough to gauge the economic impact since consumers may be cutting back their expenses in other areas' (Mallard 2002).
10. Figures for 2002 quarters I–IV (change from same period in previous year): Q1 267,143 (-1.0), Q2 264,002 (0.2 per cent); Q3 267,970 (1.9 per cent), Q4 278,965 (-0.3 per cent). Data are taken from the monthly Survey of the Household Economy (*kakei chōsa*) by the Statistics Bureau, Ministry of Public Management. Historical as well as recent data can be downloaded from http://www.stat.go.jp/data/soutan/1.htm.
11. Data are taken from the quarterly Survey on Trends in Consumption (*shōhi dōkō chōsa*) by the Economic and Social Research Institute (ESRI), Cabinet Office, Government of Japan. Historical as well as recent data are available online at http://www.esri.cao.go.jp/jp/stat/menu.html#shohi-z.
12. Calculations of the Japanese travel market exclude the domestically spent share of expenditures on overseas travel which roughly balanced the total consumption of foreign visitors to Japan in the years 2001–2003. Cf. the Ministry's research reports 'Ryokō kankō sangyō no keizai kokka ni kan suru chōsa kenkyū', published by Kokudo Kōtsū-shō Kankō-bu (various years). Online available at www.mlit.go.jp.
13. The explanations that respondents added to the evaluative quantification of regional policy appeared to rely on arbitrary interpretations of random observations or non-quantifiable occurrences. Another weakness of the research design stems from the non-linear scale of the evaluation scheme, which hardly allows the computation of data and meaningful comparisons between hosting politics and evaluation of outcome. For statistical purposes, all item scores were reduced by one since a value of 1 for 'no effect' would distort the information of averages and indices.
14. However, volunteering in the Japanese context implies a strong element of administrative control and governmental guidance, which is somehow at odds with the general concept of volunteering and civil society. Nogawa (2004) even accused the local organizers of having exploited the goodwill of the volunteers who received little or nothing in exchange for unburdening local budgets.
15. Not surprisingly, exactly the same message has been provided by the German Institute of Economic Research that surveyed the impact of the 2006 World Cup on the German economy (Brenke and Wagner 2007).

NOTES TO CHAPTER 9

1. Parts of the arguments discussed in this chapter were presented at the 2006 Otago Foreign Policy School on 'Sport and Foreign Policy in a Globalizing

World', University of Otago, Dunedin, New Zealand, June 23–26, 2006; at the East Asian Studies Council, Yale University, New Haven, April 2, 2007; and at the conference 'Catching the Wave. Connecting East Asia through Soft Power' at the University of California, Berkeley, October 5–6, 2007. An earlier version was published in 2008 under the title 'Football diplomacy, postcolonialism and Japan's quest for normal state status'. In: *Sport in Society* 11/4, 414–428. Online available at the Journal's web site: http://www.tandfonline.com/doi/full/10.1080/17430430802019359.

2. This incident actually caused the death of some hundred soldiers and civilians. Yet the outbreak of combat was not triggered by football, as the myth goes, but by frictions rooted in unequal development (Eisenbürger 2006).
3. 'Theatre of the great' was originally coined by E. P. Thompson, but it was John Hargreaves (1988) who used this term to refer to the incorporation of football into political rituals.
4. For a cursory overview of the history of football in Asia, cf. Butler 2001; for a critical commentary on the current popularization, cf. Manzenreiter and Horne 2007. For largely descriptive or narrative chronicles of national football histories for Japan, see Horne and Bleakley 2002; for Korea, cf. Lee 2002; and for China, cf. Jones 2004; Fan and Tan 2003.
5. For the full text, go to the website of the Ministry of Foreign Affairs, Japan: www.mofa.go.jp/region/europe/balkan/speech0404–2.html.
6. The interview was published by the bi-weekly *Sport Yeah* in February 2006 (no.111). Extracts are featured on Tamaki's home page at http://www.tamakimasayuki.com/sport_bn_41.htm.

NOTES TO CHAPTER 10

1. Parts of the argument presented in this chapter were discussed with participants at the International Conferences on 'The Olympics in East Asia. Nationalism, regionalism and globalism on the center stage of world sports', hosted by Yale University in collaboration with Hong Kong University, New Haven, October 3–5, 2008, and Hong Kong, March 14–16, 2008. Later versions were presented at the 5th Beijing Forum, Beijing, November 7–10, 2008 and at the APU Conference on 'Reflections on the Asia Pacific: Past, present and future', Ritsumeikan Asia Pacific University, Beppu, December 12–13, 2009. Parts of this article were published as 'Subaltern Olympics and the changing imagination of the Far East'. In: Beijing Forum Organizing Committee, ed.: *Olympic spirit and world harmony*. Beijing: Beijing Forum Organizing Committee 2008, 221–233; and 'Global movements, sports spectacles and the transformation of representational power'. In: *Asia Pacific World* 1/1 (2010), 37–55, being reproduced with permission by Berghahn Books.
2. Within intellectual history, the notion of the spectacle is most famously associated with the meta-social critique of Guy Debord (1978) and the Situationalists, whereas in sport studies John MacAloon first advocated a reading of the Olympic spectacle as a cultural performance of its own rights, 'engaged in complex dialectical and functional dynamics with the other master genres' of performativity, i.e. games, ritual and festival (MacAloon 2006:15).
3. For example, see Niehaus and Seinsch 2007 on Japan's Olympics in general; Collins 2007 on the Tokyo Olympics 1940; Tagsold 2002 on the Tokyo Olympics 1964; Ahn 1990 and Manheim 1990 on the Seoul Olympics 1988; Horne and Manzenreiter 2002a on the Football World Cup in Japan/Korea; Brownell 2008 and Price and Dayan 2008 on the Beijing Games 2008.

4. It even took some time until the political elites in East Asia came to appreciate the symbolic meaning of getting access to the inner circles of the international sport movement, which is in marked contrast to the hurry in which postcolonial states or the successors of falling states nowadays hasten to set up National Olympic Committees in order to be eligible for membership at the IOC or to gain admittance to other international sport associations, thereby gaining the worldwide reputation of being a recognized member of the community of modern states (cf. Taki 1995; Bairner 2001).
5. Dreams of hosting the Olympic Games in China date back to the early years of the 20th century, when Chinese writers used the lines to provoke their readership (Brownell 2007).
6. For the IOC, the decision to ban Wushu from the Olympics was first of all based on concerns with competition from karate, another martial art of probably much wider global spread, seeking its way into the Olympic programme. The IOC request that any Olympic sport must be able to guarantee a certain ratio of TV coverage, should generate substantive revenues and be able to secure sponsorship from multinational companies unintentionally revealed the premises on which respect and appreciation for the core elements of the Olympic contests are based.
7. Part of the moral campaigns ahead of the Tokyo Games 1964 was the instruction of the public in restraining from urinating at waysides or against trees. This was just a small section of an ongoing process of disciplining and managing the human body as clean and proper in line with Japan's modernization politics (Otomo 2007:117). The issue of sanitization standards was also high on the agenda in South Korea prior to the Football World Cup in 2002. The National Council Better Korea Movement forged a comprehensive strategy on public health and sanitation to revitalize a South Korean society still suffering from the aftermath of the Asian financial crisis in the late 1990s (Choi 2004). In 2008, a newspaper report heralded Beijing's world city status in terms of the number of public restrooms, having bypassed contenders like New York or Tokyo. Similarly, in the context of changing body politics, spurred by the rising fear of global pandemics, spitting in public has increasingly become an object of critical surveillance throughout East Asia.
8. A 'place of remembrance' is never a fixed reality but constituted within rearranging social, political, cultural or imaginary spaces. Generated by the mnemonic technologies of memorizing, recording and projection, the Beijing Olympic Games are more than likely to condense a generation's future collective memories of their people's past.
9. Riefenstahl produced the well-known documentary of the 1936 Olympics in Berlin, along with other Nazi propaganda films.

NOTES TO CHAPTER 11

1. Sections of this chapter were presented to students of International Development Studies and Global History at the University of Vienna and the University of Graz in April 2010. I also read a paper on this subject to the graduate students at Ritsumeikan University, Kyoto and Chung-Ahn University, Seoul, in July 2010. A previous version was published in 2010 in German as 'A(sian) Race to the Bottom? Asiatische Produktionsnetzwerke im globalen Sportartikelmarkt'. In: Karin Fischer, Christoph Reiner and Cornelia Staritz, eds.: *Globale Güterketten. Weltweite Arbeitsteilung und ungleiche Entwicklung.* Vienna: Promedia, 157–178.

References

Abe Ikuo (1988) 'A study of the chronology of the modern usage of "sportsmanship" in English, American and Japanese dictionaries'. In: *International Journal of the History of Sport* 5/1, 3–28

Abe Ikuo, Kiyohara Yasuharu und Nakajima Ken (1992) 'Fascism, sport and society in Japan'. In: *International Journal of the History of Sport* 9/1, 1–28

Abe Ikuo and J. A. Mangan (2003) '"Sportsmanship"—English inspiration and Japanese response: F. W. Strange and Chiyosaburo Takeda'. In: Fan Hong and J. A. Mangan, eds.: *Sport in Asian society. Past and present.* London: Frank Cass, 99–128

Adams, Francis Ottiwell (1914) 'The schools of Japan'. In: Eva March Tappan, ed.: *China, Japan, and the islands of the Pacific. The world's story: A history of the world in story, song and art.* Vol. I. Boston: Houghton Mifflin, 443–446

Adidas (2012a) *Geschäftsbericht 2011.* Online at http://www.adidas-group.com/de/investorrelations/assets/pdf/annual_reports/2011/GB_2011_De.pdf (accessed December 14, 2012)

Adidas (2012b) *Performance counts. 2011 sustainability progress report.* Online at http://www.adidas-group.com/en/ser2011/ (accessed December 12, 2012)

Adorno, Theodor W. (1991) 'The schema of mass culture'. In: J. M. Bernstein, ed.: *The culture industry: Selected essays on mass culture.* London: Routledge, 85–92

Ahn Min-Seok (1990) *The 1988 Seoul Summer Olympic Games: A critical commentary.* PhD diss., University of Illinois

Aigaki Yukihira (1994) 'Sākitto to chiiki okoshi' [The race track and regional vitalization]. In: *Toshi Mondai* 85/12, 59–69

Akamatsu Kaname (1935) 'Wagakuni yōmō kōgyōhin no bōeki sūsei' [Trends of textile trade in Japan]. In: *Shōgyō Keizai Ronsō* 13, 129–212

Akamatsu Kaname (1962) 'A historical pattern of economic growth in developing countries'. In: *The Developing Economies* 1, 3–25

Alkemeyer, Thomas (1996) *Körper, Kult und Politik. Von der 'Muskelreligion' Pierre de Coubertins zur Inszenierung von Macht in den Olympischen Spielen von 1936.* Frankfurt/New York: Campus

Alkemeyer, Thomas (1997) 'Sport als Mimesis von Gesellschaft: Zur Aufführung des Sozialen im symbolischen Rahmen des Sports' [Sport as mimesis of society: Social performance in the symbolic framework of sport]. In: *Zeitschrift für Semiotik* 19/4, 365–396

Amagai Kenichi (2002) 'W-hai kaisai kikanchū no keizai kōka' [Economic impact during the World Cup finals]. In: *NEC Monthly Report* 14, 1–2

Amaha Keisuke (2003) 'Supōtsu de rōka o fusegō' [Fending off aging by sport]. In: *Supōtsu Shisutemu Kōza* 4, 15–40

Amariglio, Jack L. (1988) 'The body, economic discourse, and power: An economist's introduction to Foucault'. In: *History of Political Economy* 20/4, 583–613

Amsden, Alice H. (1989) *Asia's next giant. South Korea and late industrialization.* Oxford: Oxford University Press

Andranovich, Greg, Matthew Burbank and Charles Heying (2001) 'Olympic cities: Lessons learnt from mega-event politics'. In: *Journal of Urban Affairs* 23/2, 113–131

Andreff, Madeleine and Wladimir Andreff (2009) 'Global trade in sports goods: International specialisation of major trading countries'. In: *European Sport Management Quarterly* 9/3, 259–294

Andreff, Wladimir and Stefan Szymanski (2006) 'Introduction: Sport and economics'. In: Wladimir Andreff and Stefan Szymanski, eds.: *Handbook on the ecomomics of sport.* Cheltenham: Edward Elgar Publishing, 1–8

Andrews, David L. and John W. Loy (1993) 'British cultural studies and sport'. In: *Quest* 45/2, 255–276

Andrews, David L. and George Ritzer (2007) 'The grobal in the sporting glocal'. In: *Global Networks* 7/2, 113–153

Appadurai, Arjun (1990) 'Disjuncture and difference in the global cultural economy'. In: *Theory, Culture and Society* 7/2–3, 295–310

Appadurai, Arjun (1993) 'Patriotism and its futures'. In: *Public Culture* 5, 411–429

Appadurai, Arjun (1996) *Modernity at large. Cultural dimensions in globalization.* Minneapolis: University of Minnesota Press

Appelbaum, Richard (2009) 'Big suppliers in Great China: A growing counterweight to the power of giant retailers'. In: Hung Ho-Fung, ed.: *China and the transformation of global capitalism.* Baltimore, MD: Johns Hopkins University Press, 65–85

Arai Setsuo, Naitō Junko and Morita Shigeru (1988) *Kenkō bunka taiikugaku* [Sports science health culture]. Kōbe: Rokkō Shuppan

Armstrong, David (1995) 'The rise of surveillance medicine'. In: *Sociology of Health and Illness* 17/3, 393–404

Arimoto Takeshi (2004) 'Narrating football'. In: *Inter-Asia Cultural Studies* 5/1, 63–76

Arnaud, Pierre (1988) 'Sport—A means of national representation'. In: Pierre Arnaud and James Riordan, eds.: *Sport and international politics. Impact of fascism and communism on sport.* London: SPON Press, 3–13

Arrighi, Giovanni (1994) *The long twentieth century: Money, power and the origins of our times.* London: Verso

Asada Takao and Kataoka Akio (1975) 'Sport consciousness and behavior of Japanese people'. In: *Research Journal of Physical Education* 19/6, 317–328

Asai Motofumi (2004) 'Primary responsibility for the worsening in Japan-China relations lies with Japan: Reflections on recent conflicts'. In: *Japan Focus*, February 25, 2004. Online at http://japanfocus.org/products/details/2307 (accessed May 20, 2006)

Asics (2009) *Annual report 2009.* Online at http://www.asics.com/global/img/investors/ ar2009.pdf (accessed March 4, 2010)

Asics (2012a) *Annual report 2012.* Online at http://www.asics.com/ global/img/investors/ar2012.pdf (accessed December 14, 2012)

Asics (2012b) *Sound mind sound body sound world. ASICS CSR report 2012.* Online at http://www.asics.com/global/img/responsibility/G12/csr2012_global.pdf (accessed December 14, 2012)

Baade, Robert A. (1996) 'Professional sports as catalysts for metropolitan economic development', *Journal of Urban Affairs* 18/1, 1–17

Bair, Jennifer (2005) 'Global capitalism and commodity chains: Looking back, going forward'. In: *Competition and Change* 9/2, 153–180

Bairner, Alan (2001) *Sport, nationalism and globalisation. European and North American perspectives.* Albany: State University of New York Press

Bakhtin, Michail (1987) *Rabelais und seine Welt. Volkskultur als Gegenkultur* [Rabelais and his world]. Frankfurt: Suhrkamp

Bale, John (1993a) 'The spatial development of the modern stadium'. In: *International Review of the Sociology of Sport* 28/2–3, 121–133

Bale, John (1993b) *Sport, space and the city.* London/New York: Routledge

Bale, John and Mike Cronin, eds. (2003) *Sport and postcolonialism.* Oxford: Berg

Bale, John and Joe Sang (1996) *Kenyan running. Movement culture, geography and global change.* London: Frank Cass

Bassino, Jean-Claude (2006) 'Inequality in Japan (1892–1941): Physical stature, income, and health'. In: *Economics and Human Biology* 4/1, 62–88

Beck, Ulrich (1986) *Risikogesellschaft. Auf dem Weg in eine andere Moderne* [Risk society: Towards a new modernity]. Frankfurt: Suhrkamp

Ben-Ari, Eyal (1997) *Body projects in Japanese childcare: Culture, organization and emotions in a preschool.* Richmond: Curzon Press

Berkowitz, Pere et al. (2007) 'Brand China: Using the 2008 Olympic Games to enhance China's image'. In: *Place Branding and Public Diplomacy* 3/2, 164–178

Bernard, Mitchell and John Ravenhill (1995) 'Beyond product cycles and flying geese: Regionalization, hierarchy, and the industrialization of East Asia'. In: *World Politics* 47/2, 171–209

Bernstein, Alina (2002) 'Women in sports media: Time for a victory lap?' Paper delivered at the 3rd Play-the-Game Conference, Denmark, November 10–12. Online at http://www.play-the-game-org (accessed October 20, 2003)

Bette, Karl Heinz and Uwe Schimank (2000) 'Sportevents. Eine Verschränkung von "erster" und "zweiter" Moderne' [Sportevents. Entanglement of 'first' and 'second' modernity]. In: Winfried Gebhardt, Ronald Hitzler and Michaela Pfadenhauer, eds.: *Events. Soziologie des Außergewöhnlichen.* Opladen: Leske und Budrich, 307–323

Binkley, Sam (2007) 'Governmentality and lifestyle studies'. In: *Sociology Compass* 1/1, 111–126

Binkley, Sam (2009) 'Governmentality, temporality and practice. From the individualization of risk to the "contradictory movements of the soul"'. In: *Time & Society* 18/1, 86–105

Bhabha, Homi K. (1996) 'Unsatisfied: Notes on vernacular cosmopolitanism'. In: Laura Garcia-Moreno and Peter Pfeiffer, eds.: *Text and nation: Cross-disciplinary essays on cultural and national identities.* Columbia, SC: Camden House, 191–207

Blackwood, Thomas (2003) 'The reproduction and naturalisation of sex-based separate spheres in Japanese high schools: The role of female "managers" of high school baseball teams'. In: *Social Science Japan* 25, 22–26

Bourdieu, Pierre (1977) *Outline of a theory of practice.* London: Cambridge University Press

Bourdieu, Pierre (1986) 'Historische und soziale Voraussetzungen modernen Sports' [Historical and social conditions of modern sport]. In: Gert Hortleder and Gunter Gebauer, eds.: *Sport—Eros—Tod.* Frankfurt: Suhrkamp, 91–112

Bourdieu, Pierre (1987) *Die feinen Unterschiede. Kritik der gesellschaftlichen Urteilskraft* [Distinctions. A social critique of the judgement of taste]. Frankfurt: Suhrkamp

Bourdieu, Pierre (1990) *The logic of practice.* Stanford: Stanford University Press

Bourdieu, Pierre (1992) 'Programm für eine Soziologie des Sports' [Outline of a sociology of sports]. In: Pierre Bourdieu: *Rede und Antwort.* Frankfurt: Suhrkamp, 193–207

Bourdieu, Pierre (1995) *Sociology in question.* London: Sage Publications

Bourdieu, Pierre (2003) 'Culture is in Danger'. In: Pierre Bourdieu, ed.: *Firing back: against the tyranny of the market; 2.* London: Verso, 66–81

Boyle, Raymond and Richard Haynes (2000) *Power play. Sport, the media and popular culture.* Harlow: Longman

Brenke, Karl und Gert Wagner (2007) *Zum volkswirtschaftlichen Wert der Fußball-Weltmeisterschaft 2006 in Deutschland* [The macroeconomic value of the 2006 Football World Cup in Germany]. Berlin: DIW (= Berlin Research Notes; 19)

Brohm, Jean-Marie (1978) *Sport: A prison of measured time.* London: Ink Links

Bromberger, Christian (1995) 'Football as world-view and as ritual'. In: *French Cultural Studies* 6, 293–311

Brownell, Susan (1995) *Training the body for China. Sports in the moral order of the People's Republic.* Chicago: University of Chicago Press

Brownell, Susan (2007) 'China and the Olympic Games. Body culture, east and west'. Paper presented at the Amsterdam School for Social Science Research, May 29

Brownell, Susan (2008) *Beijing's Games: What the Olympicsm mean to China.* Lanham: Rowman and Littlefield

Brownell, Susan (2009) 'Was there a master plan to use the Olympic Games to promote a positive image of China to the world?' Paper presented at the conference on 'The 2008 Beijing Olympic Games: Public diplomacy triumph or public relations spectacle?' Center on Public Diplomacy, US–China Institute, and Center for International Studies at the University of Southern California, January 29–30

Brumann, Christoph (1999) 'Writing for culture: Why a successful concept should not be discarded'. In: *Current Anthropology* 40, 1–13

Butler, Oliver (2001) *Asian football report 2001.* London: Soccer Investor

Butler, Oliver (2002) 'Getting the games: Japan, South Korea and the co-hosted World Cup'. In: John Horne and Wolfram Manzenreiter, eds.: *Japan, Korea and the 2002 World Cup.* London: Routledge, 43–55

Caffrey, Kevin (2008) 'Olympian politics in Beijing: Games but not just games'. In: *International Journal of the History of Sport* 25/7, 807–825

Caillois, Roger (1958) *Les jeux et les hommes* [Games and people]. Paris: Gallimard

Callewaert, Staf (2006) 'Bourdieu, critic of Foucault: The case of empirical social science against double-game-philosophy'. In: *Theory, Culture and Society* 23/6, 73–98

Cameron, Heather, ed. (2004) *Strategies for seniors and sport. Conference report.* Berlin: Anglo-German Foundation

Carney, Michael (2005) 'Globalization and the renewal of Asian business networks'. In: *Asia Pacific Journal of Management* 22, 337–354

Carrigan, Marylin (1998) 'Segmenting the grey market. The case for fifty-plus "lifegroups"'. In: *Journal of Marketing Practice* 4/2, 43–56

Castells, Manuel (1996) *The rise of the network society. The information age: Economy, society and culture.* Oxford: Blackwell

Cave, Peter (2004) '*Bukatsudō*: The educational role of Japanese school sport clubs'. In: *Journal of Japanese Studies* 30/2, 383–415

Chakrabarty, Dipesh (1985) 'Invitation to a dialogue'. In: Ranajit Guha, ed.: *Subaltern studies IV.* Delhi: Oxford University Press, 364–376

Chang Se-Moon (2002) 'Korean economy after the World Cup games'. In: Korean Information Service, ed.: *Korean experience with the World Cup*. Seoul: Korean Information Service, 80–85

Cheska, Alyce Taylor (1979) 'Sports spectacular: A ritual model of power'. In: *International Review for the Sociology of Sport* 14, 51–71

Choi Yoon Sung (2004) 'Football and the South Korean imagination'. In: Wolfram Manzenreiter and John Horne, eds.: *Football goes east. Business, culture and the people's game in China, Japan and South Korea*. London: Routledge, 133–147

Chūtairen (Nihon Chūgakkō Taiiku Renmei) (2004) *Kameikō, kamei seitō sū chōsa shūkeibyō Heisei 16nen* [Membership table of schools and pupils 2004]. Tokyo: Chūtairen

CKSJ (Chūshō Kigyō Sōgō Jigyōdan) (2001) *Juyō dōkō chōsa. Kōrei shakai sangyō yoka amenity bunya* [Demand trend survey. Field of leisure amenities among industries of the aged society]. Tokyo: Chūshō Kigyō Sōgō Jigyōdan

Cohen, Einat Bar-On (2006) 'Kime and the moving body: Somatic codes in Japanese martial arts'. In: *Body & Society* 12/4, 73–93

Collins, Sandra (2007) 'Tōkyō 1940: Non-celebres'. In: Andreas Niehaus and Max Seinsch, eds.: *Olympic Japan. Ideals and realities of (inter)nationalism*. Würzburg: Ergon, 89–110

Collins, Sandra (2008) 'The fragility of Asian national identity in the Olympic Games'. In: Monroe Price and Daniel Dayan, eds.: *Owning the Olympics. Narratives of the new China*. Ann Arbor: University of Michigan Press, 185–209

Collins, Tony (2000) 'Return to manhood. The cult of masculinity and the British Union of fascists'. In: J. A. Mangan, ed.: *Superman supreme. Fascist body as political icon—Global fascism*. London: Frank Cass, 145–162

Cox, Rupert Andrew (1990) *'Dancing for Buddha'—Conceptions of 'self' in a Japanese martial art*. Unpublished dissertation submitted to the Dept. of Social Anthropology at Oxford Brooks University

CSGF (China Sporting Goods Federation) (2009) *CSGF news*. Online at http://en.csgf.org.cn/ News_Center/ (accessed March 12, 2012)

Csikszentmihalyi, Mihaly (1975) *Beyond boredom and anxiety: Experiencing flow in work and play*. San Francisco: Jossey-Bass

Cumings, Bruce (1984) 'The origins and development of the Northeast Asian political economy: Industrial sectors, product cycles, and political consequences'. In: *International Organization* 38/1, 1–40

Darby, Paul (2002) *Africa, football and FIFA: Politics, colonialism and resistance*. London: Frank Cass

Date Yoshimi (2000) 'Kyokutō senshu kyōgi taikai no sekai. Ajia shugiteki supōtsu kan no risō to genjitsu' [The world of the Far East Games. Ideal and reality of the Asianist sport view]. In: Hirai Hajime, ed.: *Supōtsu de yomu Ajia*. Kyōto: Sekai Shisōsha, 206–224

De Garine, Igor and Nancy Pollock, eds. (1995) *Social aspects of obesity*. London: Routledge

De Kloet, Jerome et al. (2008) 'The Beijing Olympics and the art of nation-state maintenance'. In: *China Aktuell/Journal of Contemporary Chinese Affairs* 2006/2, 6–35

Debord, Guy (1978) *Die Gesellschaft des Spektakels* [The society of the spectacle]. Hamburg: Ed. Nautilus.

Degler, Carl N. (1989) *Culture versus biology in the thought of Franz Boas and Alfred L. Kroeber. With comments by Marshall Hyatt and Barbara Duden*. New York: Berg

DeLisle, Jacques (2009) 'After the gold rush: The Beijing Olympics and China's evolving international roles'. In: *Orbis* 53/2, 179–204

Demura Shinichi et al. (2003) 'Physical-fitness declines in older Japanese adults'. In: *Journal of Aging and Physical Activity* 11/1, 112–122

Diefenbach, Katja (1997) *Nikeworld*. Online at www.b-books.de/texteprojekte/txt/ kd-nike.htm (accessed March 4, 2010)

Doi Takeo (1973) *The anatomy of dependence*. New York: Kodansha International

Donnelly, Peter (1996) 'The local and the global: Globalisation in the sociology of sport'. In: *Journal of Sport and Social Issues* 20/3, 239–257

Durkheim, Émile (1971 [1915]) *The elementary forms of the religious life*. London: George Allen and Unwin

Dyck, Noel (2000) 'Games, bodies, celebrations and boundaries'. In: Noel Dyck, ed.: *Games, sports and cultures*. Oxford: Berg, 13–42

Eckstein, Rick and Kevin J. Delaney (2002) 'New sports stadiums, community self-esteem, and community collective conscience'. In: *Journal of Sport and Social Issues* 26/3, 235–247

Ehashi Shōgo (1979) 'Danshi gakusei no seikatsu to supōtsu' [Way of life of male students and sports]. In: *Taiiku Shakaigaku Kenkyū* 8, 123–138

Eisenbürger, Gert (2006) 'Fußballkrieg? Der Konflikt zwischen El Salvador und Honduras 1969' [Football war? The conflict between El Salvador and Honduras in 1969]. In: Dario Azzellini and Stefan Thimmel, eds.: *Fußball und Lateinamerika. Hoffnungen, Helden, Politik und Kommerz*. Berlin: Assoziation A, 48–53

Ekberg, Merryn (2007) 'The parameters of the risk society. A review and exploration'. In: *Current Sociology* 55/3, 343–366

Elias, Norbert (1982) *The civilizing process: State-formation and civilization*. Oxford: Blackwell

Elias, Norbert (1989) 'Die Genese des Sports als soziologisches Problem' [The genesis of sport as sociological problem]. In: Norbert Elias and Eric Dunning, eds.: *Sport im Zivilisationsprozeß*. Münster: LitVerlag, 9–46

Elias, Norbert and Eric Dunning (1989) *Sport im Zivilisationsprozeß* [Sport in the civilization process]. Münster: LitVerlag

Elliott, Anthony (2002) 'Beck's sociology of risk: A critical assessment'. In: *Sociology* 36/2, 293–315

Emi Kōichi (2005) *'Oiru shokku' wa sando kuru!* [The aging shock comes thrice!]. Tokyo: Kanki Shuppan

Enomoto Miyoko (2003) 'Gendai shakai to kenkō no kagaku' [Contemporary society and health sciences]. In: Nomura Kazuo et al., *Kenkō būmu o yomitoku*. Tokyo: Seikyūsha, 185–229

ESRI (Economic and Social Research Institute) (2003) *Shōhi dōkō chōsa* [Survey on trends in consumption]. Tokyo: Economic and Social Research Institute, Cabinet Office, Government of Japan. Online at http://www.esri.cao.go.jp/jp/stat/menu.html#shohi-z (accessed February 20, 2005)

Fält, Olavi K. (1997) 'The social whirl of "white" Yokohama after Iwakura's return, 1874'. Unpublished paper, presented at the EAJS-Konferenz, Budapest, August 27–30

Fan Hong and Tan Hua (2003) 'Sport in China: Conflict between tradition and modernity, 1840s to 1940s'. In: J. A. Mangan and Fan Hong, eds.: *Sport in Asian society. Past and present*. London: Frank Cass, 189–212

Fan Ying (2006) 'Branding the nation: What is being branded?' In: *Journal of Vacation Marketing* 12/1, 5–14

Fetscher, Irving (1996) 'Die Olympischen Spiele, Showbusiness und der Sinn des Sports' [Olympic games, show business and the meaning of sport]. In: Gunter Gebauer, ed.: *Olympische Spiele—die andere Utopie der Moderne zwischen Kult und Droge*. Frankfurt: Suhrkamp, 131–135

Fine, Michael (2005) 'Individualization, risk and the body. Sociology and care'. In: *Journal of Sociology* 41/3, 247–266

Foer, Franklin (2004) *How soccer explains the world. An [unlikely] theory of globalization.* New York: Harper Perennial

Foucault, Michel (1970) *The order of things. An archaeology of the human sciences.* New York: Pantheon Books

Foucault, Michel (1977) *Discipline and punish: The birth of the prison.* New York: Vintage

Foucault, Michel (2003) *Society must be defended. Lectures at the Collège de France, 1975–76.* New York: Picador

Foucault, Michel (2007) *Security, territory, population. Lectures at the Collège de France, 1977–78.* London: Palgrave Macmillan

Frenkel, Stephen J. (2001) 'Globalization, atheletic footwear commodity chains and employment relations in China'. In: *Organization Studies* 22, 531–562

Friedman, Jonathan (1990) 'Being in the world: Globalization and localization'. In: Mike Featherstone, ed.: *Global culture: Nationalism, globalization and modernity.* London: Sage, 311–328

Frost, Dennis (2010) *Seeing stars: Sports celebrity, identity, and body culture in modern Japan.* Cambridge: Harvard University Press

Frühstück, Sabine and Wolfram Manzenreiter (2001) 'Neverland lost: Judo cultures in Austria, Japan and everywhere'. In: Harumi Befu and Sylvie Guichard-Anguis, eds.: *Globalizing Japan. Ethnography of the Japanese presence in Asia, Europe, and America.* London: Routledge, 69–93

Fujita Motoaki (1988) 'Dainihon Taiiku Kyōkai no seijisei ni tsuite no kenkyū' [Research on the political nature of the Greater Japan Amateur Sports Association]. In: *Taiiku Supōtsu Shakaigaku Kenkyū* 7, 35–53

Fukuda Yoshiharu, Nakamura Keiko and Takano Takehito (2005) 'Municipal health expectancy in Japan: Decreased healthy longevity of older people in socioeconomically disadvantaged areas'. In: *BMC Public Health* 5/65. Online at http://www.biomedcentral.com/1471–2458/5/65 (accessed August 15, 2006)

Funck, Carolin (1999) 'When the bubble burst: Planning and reality in Japan's resort industry'. In: *Current Issues in Tourism* 2/4, 333–353

Galtung, Johan (1991) 'The sport system as a metaphor for the world system'. In: Fernand Landry, Marc Landry and Magdeleine Yerlès, eds.: *Sport: The third millenium.* Sainte-Foye: Presses de l'Université Laval, 147–155

Gard, Michael and Jan Wright (2005) *The obesity epidemic: Science, morality, and ideology.* New York: Routledge

Gebauer, Gunter and Thomas Alkemeyer (2001) 'Das Performative in Sport und neuen Spielen' [The performative in sport and new games]. In: *Paragrana. Internationale Zeitschrift für Historische Anthropologie* 10/1, 117–136

Geertz, Clifford (1973) *The interpretation of cultures.* New York: Basic Books

Geertz, Clifford (1987) *Dichte Beschreibung. Beiträge zum Verstehen kultureller Systeme* [Thick description]. Frankfurt: Suhrkamp

Gereffi, Gary (1996) 'Global commodity chains: New forms of coordination and control among nations and firms in international industries'. In: *Competition and Change* 4, 427–439

Gereffi, Gary (2002) *The international competitiveness of Asian economics in the apparel commodity chain.* Manila: Asian Development Bank

Giddens, Anthony (1990) *The consequences of modernity.* Cambridge: Polity Press

Girginov, Vassil (2008) 'Creative tensions: "Join in London" meets "Dancing Beijing". The cultural power of the Olympics'. In: *International Journal of the History of Sport* 25/7, 893–914

Giulianotti, Richard (2002) 'Fußball in Südamerika. Globalisierung, Neoliberalismus und die Politik der Korruption' [Football in South America. Globalization, neoliberalism and the politics of corruption]. In: Michael Fanizadeh, Gerald Hödl and Wolfram Manzenreiter, eds.: *Global players. Kultur, Ökonomie und Politik des Fußballs*. Frankfurt/Vienna: Brandes and Apsel/Südwind, 159–181

Giulianotti, Richard (2005) *Sport. A critical sociology*. Cambridge: Polity Press

Giulianotti, Richard and Roland Robertson, eds. (2007) *Globalization and sport*. Oxford: Blackwell

Goo Research (2002) 'W-hai kaimaku mokuzen! 25,000 nin ankēto kekka' [Immediately before the curtain of the World Cup rises: Results from a survey among 25,000 persons]. Online at http://research.goo.ne.jp/Result/0205op29/01.html (accessed February 10, 2005)

Gratton, Chris, Simon Shabli and Richard Coleman (2006) 'The economic impact of major sport events'. In: *Sociological Review* 54/2, 41–58

Gruneau, Richard (1983) *Class, sports, and social development*. Amherst: University of Massachusetts Press

Größing, Stefan (1998) 'Vom Schulturnen zur Bewegungserziehung' [From school gymnastics towards body education]. In: Ernst Bruckmüller and Hannes Strohmeyer, eds.: *Turnen und Sport in der Geschichte Österreichs*. Vienna: ÖBV Pädagogischer Verlag, 201–211

Guthrie-Shimizu, Sayuri (2012) *Transpacific field of dreams: How baseball linked the United States and Japan in peace and war*. Chapel Hill: University of North Carolina Press

Guttmann, Allen (1979) *Vom Ritual zum Rekord. Das Wesen des modernen Sports*. [From ritual to record. The nature of modern sports]. Schondorf: Hofmann

Guttmann, Allen (1994) *Games and empires. Modern sport and cultural imperialism*. New York: Columbia University Press

Guttman, Allen and Lee Thompson (2001) *Japanese Sports. A history*. Honolulu: University of Hawai'i Press

Hachleitner, Bernhard and Wolfram Manzenreiter (2010) 'The EURO 2008 bonanza: Mega-events, economic pretensions and the sports-media business alliance'. In: *Soccer and Society* 11/6, 843–854

Harada Munehiko (2001) 'Supōtsu to chiiki kaihatsu' [Sports and regional development]. In: Harada Munehiko, ed.: *Supōtsu sangyōron nyūmon. Understanding the sports industry*. Tokyo: Keirin Shoin, 304–314

Harada Munehiko (2002) *Supōtsu ibento no keizaigaku. Mega ibento to hōmuchiimu ga toshi o kaeru* [The economy of sport events. Mega-events and home teams are changing the city]. Tokyo: Heibonsha

Hargreaves, Jennifer (1994) *Sporting females. Critical issues in the history and sociology of women's sports*. London: Routledge

Hargreaves, John (1986) *Sport, power and culture*. Cambridge: Polity Press

Hargreaves, John (1988) 'The state and sport: Programmed and non-programmed interventions in Great Britain'. In: Lincoln Allison, ed.: *The politics of sports*. Manchester: University of Manchester Press, 242–261

Hargreaves, John (2000) *Freedom for Catalonia: Catalan nationalism, Spanish identity and the Barcelona Olympic Games*. Cambridge: Cambridge University Press

Harvey, David (1989) *The conditions of postmodernity*. Oxford: Blackwell

Harvey, Jean, Geneviève Rail and Lucie Thibault (1996) 'Globalization and sport: Sketching a theoretical model for empirical analysis'. In: *Journal of Sport and Social Issues* 20/3, 258–277

Harvey, Jean and Maurice Saint-Germain (2001) 'Sporting goods trade, international division of labor, and the unequal hierarchy of nations'. In: *Sociology of Sport Journal* 18, 231–246

Hashizume Shinya (1987) 'Kurabu no tanjō. Meiji-ki no toshi gōraku sangyō ni kansuru kōsatsu' [The birth of the club. Considerations related to the entertainment industry in urban Meiji Japan]. In: *Ningen to Gijutsu* 4/1, 27–46

Hassler, Markus (2003) 'The global clothing production system: Commodity chains and business networks'. In: *Global Networks* 3/4, 513–531

Hayashi Takatoshi (1982) 'Dainippon Butokukai no seikaku to tokuchō ni tsuite' [On the character and particularities of the Greater Japan Society of Martial Virtues]. In: *Taiiku Supōtsu Shakaigaku Kenkyū* 1, 59–76

Hayashi Takatoshi (1984) 'Dainippon Butokukai butoku gakkō no seiritsu. Sono mezashita ningenzō ni tsuite' [The establishment of the school for martial virtues at the Dainippon Butokukai and its image of the human being]. In: *Supōtsu Shakaigaku Kenkyū* 3, 49–61

Held, David (2000) *A globalizing world? Culture, economics, politics.* London: Routledge in association with the Open University

Held, David et al. (1999) *Global transformations: Politics, economics and culture.* Palo Alto, CA: Stanford University Press

Helmenstein, Christian and Anna Kleissner (2008) *Volkswirtschaftliche Effekte der UEFA EURO 2008 in Österreich. Rahmenstudie im Auftrag des Bundeskanzleramts/Sektion Sport und der Wirtschaftskammer Österreich unter Einbeziehung von Teilstudien des Bundesministeriums für Wirtschaft und Arbeit und der Wirtschaftskammer Wien* [Macroeconomic effects of EURO 2008 in Austria]. Vienna: SportsEconAustria Institut für Sportökonomie

Helmenstein, Christian, Anna Kleissner and Bernhard Moder (2007) *Makroökonomische und sektorale Effekte der UEFA EURO 2008 in Österreich. Studie im Auftrag der Wirtschaftskammer Österreich* [Macroeconomic and sectoral effects of EURO 2008 in Austria]. Vienna: SportsEconAustria Institut für Sportökonomie

Henderson, Jeffrey et al. (2002) 'Global production networks and the analysis of economic development'. In: *Review of International Political Economy* 9/3, 436–464

Herrigel, Eugen (1953) *Zen in the art of archery.* London: Routledge & Kegan Paul

Hess, Martin (2009) 'Investigating the archipelago economy: Chains, networks and the study of uneven development'. In: *Journal für Entwicklungspolitik* 25/2, 20–37

Heywood, Ian (1994) 'Urgent dreams: climbing, rationalization and ambivalence'. In: *Leisure Studies* 13, 179–194

HIFA (Hokkaido Institute for the Future Advancement) (2002) *2002nen Wārudokappu kaisai ni yoru dōnai keizai e no hakyū kōka ni tsuite* [On the diffusion effects of the 2002 World Cup on the economy of Hokkaidō]. Sapporo: Hokkaido Institute for the Future Advancement. Online at http://www.hifa.or.jp/wc2002.pdf (accessed February 20, 2005)

Hirakawa Sumiko (2002) 'Supōtsu, jendā, media imēji. Supōtsu CF ni egakareru jendā' [Sport, gender, media image. Gender depictions in sport TV commercials]. In: Hashimoto Junichi, ed.: *Gendai media supōtsu ron.* Kyōto: Sekai Shisō Sha, 91–115

Hirata Munefumi (1999) 'Wa ga kuni no undōkai no rekishi' [The history of the sport festival in our country]. In: Yoshimi Shunya et al., eds.: *Undōkai to Nihon kindai.* Tokyo: Seikyūsha, 85–128

Hiratsuka Daisuke (2005) *The 'catching up' process of manufacturing in East Asia.* Institute of Developing Economies Discussion Paper No. 22

Hirose Ichirō (2003) 'Wārudokappu kaisai jigo kenshō. Kaisai o keiki ni shita chiiki shinkō' [Ex post evaluation of hosting the World Cup]. Online at http://www.rieti.go.jp/jp/ publications/rr/04r001.pdf (accessed December 20, 2006)

Hirose Ichirō (2004a) *J-riigu no manejimento* [The management of J. League]. Tokyo: Tōyō Keizai Shinpō Sha

Hirose Ichirō (2004b) 'The making of a professional football league: The design of the J. League system'. In: Wolfram Manzenreiter and John Horne, eds.: *Football goes east. Business, culture and the people's game in East Asia*. London: Routledge, 38–53

Hobsbawm, Eric J. (1994) *The age of extremes: The short twentieth century, 1914–1991*. London: Michael Joseph

Holton, Robert (1998) *Globalisation and the nation-state*. Basingstoke: Macmillan

Höpflinger, François (2005) 'Alternde Gesellschaft—verjüngte Senioren. Über die doppelte Dynamik des Alterns' [Aging society—rejuvenated seniors. On the double dynamics of aging]. In: *Neue Zürcher Zeitung*, September 27

Horimatsu Buichi (1975) 'Kokkashugi kyōiku no kakudai to kyōka' [Expansion and strengthening of nationalist education]. In: Umene Satoru, ed.: *Nihon kyōiku shi. Dai 1 kan*. Tokyo: Kōdansha, 7–127

Horne, John (1996) '*Sakka* in Japan'. In: *Media, Culture and Society* 18/4, 527–547

Horne, John (2001) 'Professional football in Japan'. In: Joy Hendry and Massimo Raveri, eds.: *Japan at play. The ludic and the logic of power*. London: Routledge, 199–213

Horne, John (2006) *Sport in consumer culture*. London: Palgrave

Horne, John and Derek Bleakley (2002) 'The development of football in Japan'. In: John Horne and Wolfram Manzenreiter, eds.: *Japan, Korea and the 2002 World Cup*. London: Routledge, 89–105

Horne, John and Wolfram Manzenreiter, eds. (2002a) *Japan, Korea and the football World Cup*. London: Routledge

Horne, John and Wolfram Manzenreiter (2002b) 'The World Cup and television football'. In: John Horne and Wolfram Manzenreiter, eds.: *Japan, Korea and the 2002 World Cup*. London/New York: Routledge, 195–212

Horne, John and Wolfram Manzenreiter (2004) 'Accounting for mega-events: Real and imagined impacts of the 2002 F ootball World Cup finals on the host countries Japan/Korea'. In: *International Review for the Sociology of Sport* 39/2, 187–203

Horne, John, Alan Tomlinson and Garry Whannel (1999) *Understanding sport. An introduction to the sociological and cultural analysis of sport*. New York: E&FN SPON

Horne, John and Garry Whannel (2010) 'The "caged torch procession": Celebrities, protesters and the 2008 Olympic torch relay in London, Paris and San Francisco'. In: *Sport in Society* 13/5, 760–770

Houlihan, Barry (1994) 'Homogenisation, americanisation and creolisation of sports: Varieties of globalisation'. In: *Sociology of Sports Journal* 11/4, 356–375

Houlihan, Barry (2003) 'Sport and globalization. In: Barry Houlihan, ed.: *Sport and society: A student introduction. Oxford: Berg,* 73–90

Huizinga, Johan (1955 [1938]) *Homo ludens. A study of the play element in culture*. Boston: Beacon Press

Hurst, G. Cameron (1998) *Armed martial arts of Japan. Swordsmanship and archery*. New Haven, CT: Yale University Press

Ide Yoshihiro (2002) '2002nen Wārudokappu no keizai kōka 773 oku en' [World Cup has 77.3 billion yen impact on the prefectural economy]. Online at http://www.jsdi.or.jp/ ~y_ide/020222kash_kaizai.htm (accessed February 20, 2005)

IDF (International Diabetes Federation) (2006) *The IDF consensus worldwide definition of the metabolic syndrome*. Brussels: IDF

IHRSA (International Health, Rackets and Sportsclub Association) (2006) *The 2006 IHRSA global report on the state of the health club industry.* Online at http://cms.ihrsa.org/IHRSA/ (accessed July 31, 2006)

Iida Takako (2000) '"Monbushō supōtsu tesuto" ga tsukuru danjosa' [Differences in body strength of men and women created by the Ministry of Education's sport test]. Paper delivered at the Symposium Kyōto supōtsu to josei fōramu, Kokuritsu Fujin Kyōiku Kaikan, Kyōto, October 6–8

Iida Takako (2002) 'Media supōtsu to feminizumu' [Media sports and feminism]. In: Hashimoto Junichi, ed.: *Gendai media supōtsu ron.* Kyōto: Sekai Shisō Sha, 71–90

Iida Takako (2003) 'Shinbun hōdō ni okeru josei kyōgisha no jendā-ka. Sugawara Kyōko kara Narazaki Noriko e' [The gendering of female athletes in newspaper reports. From Ms. Noriko Sugawara to Mrs. Noriko Narazaki]. In: *Journal of Sport and Gender Studies* 1, 4–14

Ikeda Masao (1977) *Sumō no rekishi* [The history of sumo]. Tokyo: Heibonsha

Ikeda Masaru, Yamaguchi Yasuo and Chogahara Makoto (2001) *Sport for all in Japan.* Tokyo: Sasagawa Sports Foundation

Ikei Masaru (1991) *Yakyū to Nihonjin* [Baseball and the Japanese]. Tokyo: Maruzen

IMF (International Monetary Fund) (2007) *Regional economic outlook: Asia and Pacific.* Washington, DC: International Monetary Fund (World Economic and Financial Surveys 07)

Inagaki Masahiro (1987) 'Kindai shakai no supōtsu' [Sport of modern societies]. In: Kishino Yūzō, ed.: *Saishin Supōtsu Jiten.* Tokyo: Taishūkan Shoten, 231–240

Inagaki Masahiro (1995) *Supōtsu no kōkindai. Supōtsu bunka wa soko e iku no ka* [Postmodernity of Sport. Where is the culture of sport heading?]. Tokyo: Sanseidō

Inoue Kazuo, Shono Teiji and Matsumoto Masatoshi (2006) 'Absence of outdoor activity and mortality risk in older adults living at home'. In: *Journal of Aging and Physical Activity* 14/2, 108–119

Inoue Shun (1992) '"Kindai" no hatsumei. Kanō Jigorō to Kōdōkan jūdō o chūshin ni' [The discovery of 'modernity'. Kanō Jigorō and his Kodokan judo]. In: *Soshioroji* 115 (37/2), 111–126

Inoue Shun (1998) 'Budō: invented tradition in the martial arts'. In: Sepp Linhart and Sabine Frühstück, eds.: *The culture of Japan as seen through its leisure.* Albany: State University of New York Press, 83–94

IOC (International Olympic Comitee) (2009) *Olympic marketing fact file. 2009 edition.* Lausanne: IOC Television and Marketing Services SA

Irie Katsumi (1986) *Nihon fashizumu-ka no taiiku shisō* [The idea of physical education under Japanese fascism]. Tokyo: Fumaidō

Irie Katsumi (1988) *Nihon kindai taiiku no shisō kōzō* [The ideational structure of physical education in modern Japan]. Tokyo: Akashi Shoten

Ishizawa Nobuhiro (2004) 'Kōki kōreisha no seikatsu manzoku ni eikyō o oyobosu undō, supōtsu katsudō to nichijō seikatsu dōsa no kēsu sutadii' [A case study of the influence of physical activity and daily life activities on life satisfaction of the old elderly]. In: *Taiikugaku Kenkyū* 49/4, 305–319

Itani Keiko (2003) 'Josei taiiku kyōshi e no mensetsu chōsa kara mita gakkō taiiku no jendā sabukaruchā' [The gender subculture of school physical education as viewed through interviews of women physical educators]. In: *Journal of Sport and Gender Studies* 1, 27–38

Itō Kimio (2001) 'Supōtsu kyōiku to jendā' [Sports education and gender]. In: Sugimoto Atsuo, ed.: *Taiiku kyōiku o manabu hito no tame ni.* Kyōto: Sekai Shisō Sha, 124–141

Iwamoto Yasushi (2004) 'Issues in Japanese health policy and medical expenditure'. In: Tachibanaki Toshiaki, ed.: *The economics of social security in Japan*. Cheltenham: Edward Elger, 219–232

Jacobson, David (1996) *Rights across borders: Immigration and the decline of citizenship*. Baltimore, MD: Johns Hopkins University Press

Japan NGO Report Preparatory Committee (1999) 'B. Women and education'. *Japan NGO report preparatory committee. Women 2000, Japan NGO alternative report*. Online at http://www.jca.apc.org/fem/bpfa/NGOreport/B_en_Education. html (accessed October 10, 2004)

JATA (2002) 'Dai ikkai JATA ryokō shijō dōkō chōsa—kokunai 2002nen 6 gakki' [The first JATA survey on trends of the tourism market, June 2002]. Online at https://www.jata-net.or.jp/tokei/shijo/020805/02.htm (accessed December 10, 2006)

JAWOC (2003) *2002 FIFA World Cup Korea/Japan*. Tokyo: JAWOC

JETRO (Japan External Trade Organization) (2008) *Japan's growing health-food market*. Tokyo: JETRO

Jin Fumio and Kurosu Mitsuru (1986) 'Nihonteki supōtsu no genten ni tsuite—toku ni supōtsu to SPORT no hazama o chūshin to shite' [On the origin of Japanese sport, with particular reference to the gap between sport and supōtsu]. In: *Taiiku Supōtsu Shakaigaku Kenkyū* 5, 109–126

JNTO (2004) 'Hōchi gaikyaku sū, shukkoku Nihonjin sū' [Visitor arrivals and Japanese overseas travellers]. Online at http://www.jnto.go.jp/info/statistics/pdfs/ 030410stat.pdf (accessed December 20, 2006)

Jones, Robin (2004) 'Football in the Republic of China'. In: Wolfram Manzenreiter and John Horne, eds.: *Football goes east. Business, culture and the people's game in East Asia*. London: Routledge, 54–66

JPHA (Japan Public Health Association) (2006) *Public Health of Japan 2005*. Tokyo: Japan Public Health Association

Jung, Koo-Chul (1996) *Erziehung und Sport in Korea* [Education and sport in Korea]. Cologne: Sport und Buch Strauß

Kado Osamu (1998) 'Chūkōnen no supōtsu sanka o meguru tayōka to soshikika ni kansuru kenkyū no matome to teigen' [Summary of research on organization and diversification of sport participation by the middle aged and final declaration]. In: Kado Osamu et al., eds.: *Chūkōnen no supōtsu sanka o meguru tayōka to soshikika ni kansuru shakaigaku kenkyū—dai 3 hō* [A sociological study on organisation and diversification concerning sport participation of the middle-aged]. Tokyo: Nihon Taiiku Kyōkai, Supōtsu I + Kagaku Senmon Iinkai, 96–100

Kaga Hideo (1978) 'Miritarizumu to supōtsu (senzen no mondai)' [Militarism and sport. Prewar problems]. In: Nakamura Toshio, ed.: *Supōtsu nashonarizumu*. Tokyo: Taishūkan Shoten, 145–178

Kaibara Ekiken (2010) *Yōjōkun. Regeln zur Lebenspflege. Aus dem Japanischen übersetzt von Andreas Niehaus und Julian Braun*. Munich: Iudicium

Kalab, Kathleen A. (1992) 'Playing gateball: A game of the Japanese elderly'. In: *Journal of Aging Studies* 6/1, 23–40

Kameda Atsuko (1995) 'Sexism and gender-stereotyping in schools'. In: Kumiko Fujimura-Fanselow and Atsuko Kameda, eds.: *Japanese women. New feminist perspectives on the past, present, and future*. New York: Feminist Press, 107–124

Kameyama Yoshiaki (1991) 'Seisei suru shintai—sakusō shintai, seido shintai to kakuchō shintai, shintō shintai' [The emerging body—intricative body, institutionalised body and expanding body, immediate body]. In: *Soshioroji* 111 (36/1), 17–29

Kamiwada Shigeru (2001) 'Gakkō taiiku shisetsu no bunka shi' [A cultural history of school sport facilities]. In: Sugimoto Atsuo, ed.: *Taiikugaku o manabu hito no tame ni*. Kyōto: Sekai Shisō Sha, 166–182

Kang Shin-pyo (1987) 'Korean culture, the Olympic and world order'. In: Kang Shin-Pyo, John J. MacAloon and Roberto da Matta, eds.: *The Olympics and cultural exchange*. Seoul: Hanyang University, Institute for Ethnological Studies, 85–103

Kang Shin-pyo (1991) 'The Seoul Olympic Games and dae-dae cultural grammar'. In: Fernand Landry et al., eds.: *Sport. The third millennium*. Sainte-Foy, Quebec: Las Presses de L' Universite Laval, 49–66

Katanoda Kōta, Hirota Kōichi and Matsumura Yasuhiro (2005) 'Jichitai kubunbetsu ni mita Kenkō Nihon 21 chihō keikaku ni okeru sūji mokuhyō sakutei jōkyō' [State of the establishment of numerical targets in regional plans of Healthy Japan 21, according to local community type]. In: *Nihon Kōshū Eisei Zasshi* 52/9, 817–823

Kausch, Michael (1988) *Kulturindustrie und Populärkultur. Kritische Theorie der Massenmedien* [Cultural industry and popular culture. A critical theory of the mass media]. Frankfurt: Fischer Tb

Kawaguchi Chiyo, Ikeda Hiroe and Miki Hiromi (1999) 'Women's education and physical education in Japan: Past, present, and perspective'. Unpublished paper presented at the 50th Anniversary Conference, International Association of Physical Education & Sports for Girls and Women, Smith College, Northampton, Massachusetts, July 7–10

Kawaguchi Tomohisa (1962) 'Industrial recreation. Problems of leisure and recreation among the working classes in the florescence of capitalism in Japan'. In: *Hitotsubashi Journal of Arts and Sciences* 3/1, 41–68

Kawaguchi Tomohisa (1966) 'Problems in "sport culture"—An analysis of interior factors'. In: *Hitotsubashi Journal of Arts and Sciences* 7/1, 47–57

Kelly, William W. (1998a) 'Blood and guts in Japanese professional baseball'. In: Sepp Linhart and Sabine Frühstück, eds.: *The culture of Japan as seen through its leisure*. Albany: State University of New York Press, 95–111

Kelly, William W. (1998b) 'Learning to swing: Oh Sadaharu and the pedagogy and practice of Japanese baseball'. In: John Singleton, ed.: *Learning in likely places. Varieties of apprenticeship in Japan*. Cambridge: University of Cambridge Press, 265–285

Kelly, William W. (2000) 'The spirit and spectacle of school baseball. Mass media, statemaking, and 'edu-tainment in Japan, 1905–1935'. In: *Senri Ethnological Studies* 52, 105–115

Kelly, William W. (2004) 'Sense and sensibility at the ball park: What Japanese fans make of professional baseball'. In: William W. Kelly, ed.: *Fanning the flames: Fandoms and consumer culture in contemporary Japan*. Albany: SUNY Press, 79–108

Kelly, William W. (2009) 'Samurai baseball: The vicissitudes of a national sporting style'. In: *International Journal of the History of Sport* 26(3), 1–13

Kelly, William W. (2011) 'The sportscape of contemporary Japan'. In Theodore C. Bestor and Victoria Lyon Bester, eds.: *The Routledge Handbook of Japanese Society and Culture*. New York: Routledge, 251–262

Kelly, William W., with Sugimoto Atsuo, eds. (2007) *This sporting life: Sports and body culture in modern Japan*. New Haven, CT: Yale CEAS

Kiku Kōichi (1984) 'Kindai no puro supōtsu no seiritsu ni kansuru rekishi shakaigakuteki kōsatsu. Wa ga kuni ni okeru senzen no puro yakyū o chūshin ni' [A historical-sociological study on the development of modern professional sports—particularly on the development of professional baseball in Japan before World War II]. In: *Taiiku Supōtsu Shakaigaku Kenkyū* 3, 1–26

Kiku Kōichi (1989) 'Supōtsu no purofesshonarizumu seisei ni kansuru rekishi shakaigakuteki kenkū josetsu—senzen ni okeru puro yakyū shinjō no keisei o chūshin to shite' [Sociological historical considerations on the creation of professionalism in sport. Centring on the formation of professional baseball in prewar Japan]. In: *Taiiku Supōtsu Shakaigaku Kenkyū* 8, 91–117

Kiku Kōichi (1993) *'Kindai puro supōtsu' no rekishi shakaigaku. Nihon puro yakyū no seiritsu o chūshin ni* [Historical sociology of professional sports. The establishment of professional baseball in Japan]. Tokyo: Fumaidō

Kiku Kōichi (1996) 'Kako no supōtsu katsudō no jōkyō' [Situation of former sport activities]. In: Kado Osamu et al., eds.: *Chūkōnen no supōtsu sanka o meguru tayōka to soshikika ni kansuru shakaigaku kenkyū—dai 1 hō* [A sociological study on organisation and diversification concerning sport participation of the middle-aged]. Tokyo: Nihon Taiiku Kyōkai, Supōtsu Kagaku Senmon Iinkai, 31–41

Kiku Kōichi (1997) 'Eriasu-ha supōtsu shakaigaku to shintai/Body' [The Elias school of sport sociology and the body]. In: *Supōtsu Shakaigaku Kenkyū* 5, 15–25

Kiku Kōichi (1998) *Shōgai supōtsu taikei no kōzō to undō ni kansuru Nichiei hikaku kenkyū* [A comparative study on structure and movement of lifelong sport systems in Japan and England]. Research report to a grant-in-aid for scientific research in fiscal 1997

Kiku Kōichi (2007) 'Bushido and the modernization of sports'. In: William W. Kelly, with Sugimoto Atsuo, eds. *This sporting life. Sports and body culture in modern Japan*. New Haven, CT: Yale CEAS, 39–53

Kimura Ki (1978) *Nihon supōtsu bunka shi* [Cultural history of sport in Japan]. Tokyo: Bēsuboru Magajin Sha

Kimura Kichiji (1975) *Nihon kindai taiiku shisō no keisei* [The formation of ideas on modern sport in Japan]. Tokyo: Kyorin Shoin

Kimura Kichiji (1978) 'Kyūsei Ichikō no kōfū ronsō to supōtsu' [Sport and the debate on school tradition at the First Higher School]. In: Nakamura Toshio et al., eds.: *Supōtsu nashonarizumu* [Sport nationalism]. Tokyo: Taishūkan Shoten, 118–144

Kimura Kichiji (1999) 'Meiji seifu no undōkai seisaku' [Sport day policy of the Meiji government. In: Yoshimi Shunya et al., eds.: *Undōkai to Nihon kindai*. Tokyo: Seikyūsha, 127–155

Kimura Yukihiko (2003) 'Oita Trinita, kanshudō no ketsujitsu to kongo' [Oita Trinita—The fruits of bureaucratic leadership and the future]. In: *Sakkā Hihyō* 18, 70–75

Kishino Yūzō et al., eds. (1973) *Kindai taiiku supōtsu nenpyō* [Chronological chart of modern sport and physical education]. Tokyo: Taishūkan Shoten

Klein, Naomi (1999) *No logo. Taking aim at the brand bullies*. New York: Picador

Koiwai Zenichi (1994) 'Sakkā ni yoru machizukuri' [Urban planning by the means of football]. In: *Toshi Mondai* 85/12, 59–69

Komatsu Shūichi (1976) 'Kindai kokumin kyōiku seido no seiritsu' [The establishment of the modern national education system]. In: Umene Satoru, ed.: *Nihon kyōiku shi. Dai 1 kan*. Tokyo: Kōdansha, 187–319

Komiya Shuichi (1997) 'Nihonjin no taisosei' [Body composition of Japanese men and women]. In: *Journal of Health Science* 19 (1997), 1–13

Komlos, John, ed. (1994) *Stature, living standards, and economic development: Essays in anthropometric history*. Chicago: University of Chicago Press

Korhonen, Pekka (1994) 'The theory of the flying geese pattern of development and its interpretations'. In: *Journal of Peace Research* 31/1, 93–108

Korzeniewicz, Miguel (1994) 'Commodity chains and marketing strategies: Nike and the global athletic footwear industry'. In: Gary Gereffi and Miguel Korzeniewicz, eds.: *Commodity chains and global capitalism*. Westport, CT: Praeger Publishers, 247–266

Kōseishō (1999) *Heisei 11 nendo kōsei hakusho. Shakai hoshō to kokumin seikatsu* [White book on welfare 1999. Social security and the life of the people]. Tokyo: Gyōsei

Kōseishō Tairyoku Kyoku (1940) *Tairyoku kōjō shisetsu shirabe* [Survey on facilities for the improvement of physical strength]. Tokyo: Kōseishō

Kōyaren (Nihon Kōtō Gakkō Yakyū Renmei) (2004) *Buin sū tōkei* [Membership statistics]. Online at http/www.jhbf.or.jp/renmei33.doc (accessed October 20, 2004)

Kōzu Masaru (1978) 'Seisaku to shite no supōtsu. Taishō demokurashii to supōtsu no seisakuka' [Sport as politics. Taisho democracy and the political grip on sport]. In: Nakamura Toshio et al., eds.: *Supōtsu seisaku*. Tokyo: Taishūkan Shoten, 35–93

Kōzu Masaru (1980) 'The development of sports in Japanese agricultural districts: From the 1920s to the 1930s'. In: *Hitotsubashi Journal of Arts and Sciences* 21/1, 40–51

Kōzu Masaru (1995) *Nihon kindai supōtsu shi no teiryū* [Undercurrents of Japan's modern sport history]. Tōkyō: Sōbun Kikaku

KRDK (Kōsei Rōdōshō Daijin Kanbō Tōkei Jōhō Bu) (2003) *Heisei 14 nendo kokumin iryōhi no gaikyō* [General conditions of national medical expenses in fiscal 2002]. Tokyo: Kōsei Rōdōshō Daijin Kanbō Tōkei Jōhō Shitsu

Kreitz-Sandberg, Susanne (2000) 'Reformen im japanischen Schulwesen' [Reforms of the Japanese school system]. In: Friederike Bosse and Patrick Köllner, eds.: *Reformen in Japan*. Hamburg: Institut für Asienkunde, 265–285

KTJZ (Kenkō Tairyoku-zukuri Jigyō Zaidan) (2004) *Kōreisha no undō jissensha to hijissensha ni okeru seikatsu ishiki to seikatsu no sōi ni kan suru kenkyū* [Research on life perceptions and differences of lifestyle among aged participants and non-participants in sport activities]. Tokyo: Kenkō Tairyoku-zukuri Jigyō Zaidan

Kubota Akio, Ishikawa-Takata Kazuko and Ohta Toshiki (2005) 'Effect of daily physical activity on mobility maintenance in the elderly'. In: *International Journal of Sport Health Science* 3, 83–90

Kusaka Yūko (1985) 'Meiji-ki ni okeru 'bushi'teki, 'bushidō'teki yakyū shinjō ni kansuru bunkashakaigakuteki kenkyū' [Cultural sociological research into the believes of chivalry baseball and the way of the warriors-style baseball in the Meiji period]. In: *Taiiku Supōtsu Shakaigaku Kenkyū* 4, 23–44

Kusaka Yūko and Maruyama Tomio (1988) 'Ippan seijin no supōtsu kan ni kansuru kenkyū' [Research into adults' sport view]. In: *Taiiku Supōtsu Shakaigaku Kenkyū* 7, 131–158

Kuwamori Hiroshi and Okamori Nobuhiro (2007) *Industrial networks between China and the countries of the Asia-Pacific region*. IDE Discussion paper 110

Lee Jong Young (1997) 'Wārudo kappu kyōsai to Kankoku shakai' [World-Cup co-hosting and Korean society]. in: Nihon Supōtsu Shakai Gakkai, ed.: *Henyō suru gendai shakai to supōtsu*. Kyōto: Sekai Shisō Sha, 138–147

Lee Jong-Young (2002) 'The development of football in Korea'. In: John Horne and Wolfram Manzenreiter, eds.: *Japan, Korea and the 2002 World Cup*. London: Routledge, 73–88

Leitgeb, Manfred (2000) *Sport als Transportmittel nationalsozialistischer Ideologie*. Master thesis submitted to the Faculty of Arts, University of Vienna

Li & Fung (2009) *Annual report 2008*. Online at http://www.irasia.com/listco/hk/lifung/ annual/ar39566–e00494.pdf (accessed March 4, 2010)

Li & Fung (2012) *Annual report 2011*. Online at http:// www.lifung.com/eng/ir/reports/ ar2011/ar2011.pdf (accessed December 14, 2012)

Li Ning (2008) *Annual report 2008*. Online at www.lining.com/EN/download/AR2004.pdf (accessed March 4, 2010)

Li Ning (2012) *Annual report 2011.* Online at http://www.lining.com/eng/ir/reports.php (accessed December 14, 2012)

Liepins, Ruth (2000) 'New energies for an old idea: reworking approaches to 'community' in contemporary rural studies'. In: *Journal of Rural Studies* 16/1, 23–35

Light, Richard (1999) 'Regimes of training, seishin, and the construction of embodied masculinity in Japanese university rugby'. In: *International Sports Studies* 21/1, 39–54

Linz, Juan J. (1976) 'Some notes towards a comparative study of facism'. In: Walter Laquer, ed.: *Fascism: A reader's guide.* Berkeley: University of California Press, 3–121

Lithman, Yngve Georg (2004) 'Anthropologists on home turf: How green is the grass?' In: *Anthropologica* 46, 17–27

Locke, Richard M. (2003) 'The promise and perils of globalization: The case of Nike'. In: Thomas A. Kochan and Richard L. Schmalensee, eds.: *Management—Inventing and delivering its future.* Boston: Massachusetts Institute of Technology, 39–70

Long, Jonathan (2004) 'Sport and the ageing population: Do older people have a place in driving up participation in sport?'. In: Sport England, ed.: *Driving up participation: The challenge for sport.* London: Sport England, 28–38

Lowder, Stella (1999) 'Globalisation of the footwear industry: A simple case of labour?' In: *Tijdschrift voor Economische en Sociale Geografie* 90/1, 47–60

Lupton, Deborah (1999) *Risk.* New York: Routledge

Lupton, Deborah (2006a) 'Risk and governmentality'. In: James F. Cosgrave, ed.: *The sociology of risk and gambling reader.* New York: Routledge, 85–100

Lupton, Deborah (2006b) 'Sociology and risk'. In: Gabe Mythen and Sandra Walklate, eds.: *Beyond the risk society: Critical reflections on risk and human security.* Maidenhead: Open University Press, 11–24

MacAloon, John (1981) *This great symbol. Pierre de Coubertin and the origins of the modern Olympic Games.* Chicago: University of Chicago Press

MacAloon, John (1984) 'Cultural performances, cultural theory'. In: John MacAloon, ed.: *Rite, drama, festivals. Toward a theory of cultural performance.* Philadelphia: Institute for the Study of Human Issues, 1–17

MacAloon, John (2006) 'The theory of spectacle. Olympic ethnography revisited'. In: Alan Tomlinson and Christopher Young, eds.: *National identity and global sports events. Culture, politics and spectacle in the Olympics and the football World Cup.* Albany: State University of New York Press, 15–39

Maeda Hiroko (2001) *W-hai kokunai kaisaichi no kitai to chiketto no dōkō* [Expectations of World Cup host regions and trends in ticketing]. In: *Soccer Social Sciences.* Online at http://www.fslab.jp/social/soci.htm (accessed October 20, 2002)

Maeda Kazushi (1998) 'Kanū kurabu ni yoru ryūiki nettowāku keisei to sono kanōsei' [Regional networking in river areas by means of canoe clubs and related opportunities]. In: *Japan Journal of Sport Sociology* 6, 17–29

Maguire, Joseph (1999) *Global sport: Identities, societies, civilisations.* Cambridge: Polity Press

Makabe, Akio (2002) 'Wārudo Kappu wa, Nihon ni dono yōna keizai kōka o motarasu no deshōka?' [What impact will the World Cup have on Japan?]. *Japan Mail Media*, May 20. Online at http://jmm.cogen.co.jp/jmmarchive/m167001.html (accessed October 31, 2002)

Mallard, John (2002) 'World Cup may give Japan economy a kick, even if no goal'. *Dow Jones Newswires*, June 14

Mangan, J. A. und Komagome Takeshi (2000) 'Militarism, sacrifice and emperor worship: The expendable male body in fascist Japanese martial culture'. In:

J. A. Mangan, ed.: *Superman supreme. Fascist body as political icon—global fascism*. London: Frank Cass, 181–204

Manheim, Jarol B. (1990) 'Rites of passage: The 1988 Seoul Olympics as public diplomacy'. In: *Western Political Quarterly* 43/2, 279–295

Manzenreiter, Wolfram (2000) *Die soziale Konstruktion des japanischen Alpinismus. Kultur, Ideologie und Sport im modernen Bergsteigen* [The social construction of Japanese mountaineering. Culture, ideology and sport in modern alpinism]. Vienna: Centre for Japanese Studies, Dept. of East Asian Studies at Vienna University

Manzenreiter, Wolfram (2001) 'Moderne Körper, moderne Orte. Sport und Nationalstaat in Japan und Österreich 1850–1900'. In: *Minikomi—Informationen des Akademischen Arbeitskreis Japan* 2, 14–21

Manzenreiter, Wolfram (2002) 'Japan und der Fußball im Zeitalter der technischen Reproduzierbarkeit: Die J.League zwischen Lokalpolitik und Globalkultur' [Japan and football in the age of technical reproductability. The J.League between local politics and global culture]. In: Michael Fanizadeh, Gerald Hödl and Wolfram Manzenreiter, eds.: *Global Players. Kultur, Ökonomie und Politik des Fußballs*. Frankfurt/Vienna: Brandes and Apsel/Südwind, 133–158

Manzenreiter, Wolfram (2004a) 'Her place in the "House of Football": Globalisation, sexism and women's football in East Asian societies'. In: Wolfram Manzenreiter and John Horne, eds.: *Football goes east. Business, culture and the people's game in East Asia*. London/New York: Routledge, 197–221

Manzenreiter, Wolfram (2004b) 'Japanese football and world sports: Raising the global game in a local setting'. In: *Japan Forum* 16/2, 289–313

Manzenreiter, Wolfram (2004c) 'Sport zwischen Markt und öffentlicher Dienstleistung. Zur Zukunft des Breitensports in Japan' [Sport between market and public service. On the future of mass sports in Japan]. In: *SWS-Rundschau (Journal für Sozialforschung)* 44/2, 227–251

Manzenreiter, Wolfram (2005) '*Bugei* und *bujutsu*: Kampfkunst im Frieden der Tokugawa-Zeit' [Bugei and bujutsu: martial arts during the peaceful Tokugawa period]. In: *Cultura Martialis: Das Journal der Kampfkünste aus aller Welt* 4, 50–66

Manzenreiter, Wolfram (2007a) 'Die Faschisierung des Körpers: Sport in totalitären Systemen. Wien und Tokyo im Vergleich 1930 bis 1945'. In: Roland Domenig and Sepp Linhart, eds.: *Freizeit und Arbeit in Tokyo und Wien 1930–1945*. Vienna: Abtl. für Japanologie des Instituts für Ostasienwissenschaften, 33–54

Manzenreiter, Wolfram (2007b) 'Die Mangatisierung der Welt: Japans Populärkultur, Kulturdiplomatie und die neue internationale Arbeitsteilung' [The mangatization of the world. Japan's popular culture, cultural diplomacy and the new international division of labour]. In: *Japan Aktuell* 4, 3–23

Manzenreiter, Wolfram (2008) 'Sports, body control and national discipline in prewar and wartime Japan'. In: *Leidschrift* 23/3, 63–83

Manzenreiter, Wolfram (2010) 'The Beijing Games in the Western imagination of China: The weak power of soft power'. In: *Journal of Sport and Social Issues* 34/1, 29–48

Manzenreiter, Wolfram and John Horne (2002) 'Global governance in world sport and the 2002 World Cup Korea/Japan'. In: John Horne and Wolfram Manzenreiter, eds.: *Japan, Korea and the 2002 World Cup*. London: Routledge, 1–25

Manzenreiter, Wolfram and John Horne (2004) 'Football, culture, globalization: Why professional football has been going East'. In: Wolfram Manzenreiter and John Horne, eds.: *Football goes east. Business, culture and the people's game in East Asia*. London: Routledge, 1–17

Manzenreiter, Wolfram and John Horne (2005) 'Public policy, sports investments and regional development initiatives in contemporary Japan'. In: John Nauright and Kimberley S. Schimmel, eds.: *The political economy of sport*. London: Palgrave Macmillan, 152–182

Manzenreiter, Wolfram and John Horne (2007) 'Playing the post-fordist game in/to the Far East: Football cultures and soccer nations in China, Japan and South Korea'. In: *Soccer and Society* 8/4, 561–577

Marschik, Matthias (1998) 'Der Ball birgt ein Mysterium. Vom 'englischen Sport' zur Wiener Fußballschule' [The mystery within the ball. From English sport towards the Vienna football tradition]. In: Ernst Bruckmüller and Hannes Strohmeyer, eds.: *Turnen und Sport in der Geschichte Österreichs*. Vienna: ÖBV Pädagogischer Verlag, 170–186

Martin, Bernd (1999) '"Großostasiatische Wohlstandssphäre", Japan, der Krieg in Asien und im Pazifik'. In: Mathias Münter-Elfner et al., eds.: *Aufbruch der Massen, Schrecken der Kriege*. Leipzig/Mannheim: Brockhaus, 664–677

Maruna, Roland (1998) 'Leichtathletik in Österreich' [Track and field in Austria]. In: Ernst Bruckmüller and Hannes Strohmeyer, eds.: *Turnen und Sport in der Geschichte Österreichs*. Vienna: ÖBV Pädagogischer Verlag, 187–200

Maruyama Masao (1963) *Thought and behaviour in modern Japanese politics*. London: Oxford University Press

Marx, Karl (2003 [1872]) *Das Kapital. Kritik der politischen Ökonomie* [Capital. A critique of political economy]. Cologne: Parkland

Masai Yasuo (1997) 'Meiji jidai ni okeru Tōkyō no dochi riyō henka' [Change of land use in 19th-century Japan]. In: Japanisch-Deutsches Zentrum Berlin, ed.: *Berlin-Tokyo im 19. und 20. Jahrhundert*. Berlin: Springer Verlag, 51–60

Matsunaka Keiko (2001) 'Shirubā bijinesu to supōtsu' [The silver business and sport]. In: Harada Munehiko, ed.: *Supōtsu sangyō nyūmon* [An introduction to the sport industry]. Tokyo: Kyorin Shoin, 332–347

Matsuzawa Yūji (2006) 'Nihonjin no kenkō kadai o metaborikku shindorōmu kara kangaeru' [Reflections about the health problem of the Japanese from the metabolic syndrome]. In: *Kagaku no Dōkō* 2006/5, 8–13

Mauss, Marcel (1989 [1934]) 'Die Techniken des Körpers' [Body techniques]. In: Marcel Mauss, *Soziologie und Anthropologie 2*. Frankfurt: Fischer, 197–220

McCormack, Gavan (2002) 'Breaking the iron triangle'. In: *New Left Review* 13/1, 5–23

McNamara, Dennis L. (1995) *Textiles and industrial transition in Japan*. Ithaca, NY: Cornell University Press

Merk, Jeroen (2005) *The Play Fair at the Olympics campaign: An evaluation of company responses*. Clean Clothes Campaign, ICFTU, Oxfam. Online at http://www.cleanclothes.org/documents/05-07-pfoc_evaluation.pdf (accessed March 4, 2010)

METI (Ministry of Economy, Trade and Industry) (2006) 'This new generation of Japanese seniors is a consumer powerhouse'. Press release delivered by PR Newswire, March 22. Online at http://sev.prnewswire.com/household-consumer-cosmetics/20060322/NYW07322032006-1.html (accessed March 23, 2006)

MEXT (Ministry of Education, Culture, Sports, Science and Technology) (2000) *Supōtsu shinkō kihon keikaku* [Basic plan for the promotion of sports]. Online at http://www.mext.go.jp/b_menu/houdou/12/09/000905.htm (accessed February 8, 2002)

MEXT (Ministry of Education, Culture, Sports, Science and Technology) (2007) *Heisei 19 nendo tairyoku undō nōryoku chōsa no gaiyō* [Outline of the survey of physical fitness and athletic ability 2007]. Tokyo: MEXT

MEXT (Ministry of Education, Culture, Sports, Science and Technology) (2010) *Heisei 21 nendo sōgō-gata chiiki supōtsu kurabu ni kansuru jittai chōsa kekka gaiyō* [Outline of results from the 2009 survey on the state of comprehensive community sports clubs]. Tokyo: Monbukagakushō Supōtsu Seishōnen Kyōku Shōgai Supōtsu Ka

MEXT (Ministry of Education, Culture, Sports, Science and Technology) (2011) *Heisei 22 nendo kōiki supōtsu sentā ni kansuru jittai chōsa kekka gaiyō* [Outline of results from the 2010 survey on the state of wide-area sports centers]. Tokyo: Monbukagakushō Supōtsu Seishōnen Kyōku Shōgai Supōtsu Ka

MHLW (Ministry of Health, Labor and Welfare) (2007) *Heisei 16 nen kokumin kenkō eiyō chōsa kekka no gaiyō* [Summary of results of the National Health and Nutrition Survey, 2004]. Tokyo: MHLW, Kenkōkyoku

MIC, Statistics Bureau (2008) *Nihon tōkei nenkan. Heisei 20 nen. Japan Statistical Yearbook 2008*. Tokyo: Statistics Bureau, MIC

Miller, Phillip (2002) 'The economic impact of sports stadium construction: The case of the construction industry in St. Louis, MO'. In: *Journal of Urban Affairs* 24/2, 159–173

Miller, Toby et al. (2001) *Globalization and sport. Playing the world*. London: Sage Publications

Mills, James (2006) 'Introduction'. In: James Mills, ed.: *Subaltern sports. Politics and sport in South Asia*. London: Anthem Press, 1–15

Ministry of Education, Japan (1996) *Waga kuni no taiiku supōtsu shisetsu* [Sport facilities in Japan]. Tokyo: Monbushō

Miyachi Motohiko (2005) 'Laboratory of physical activity and health evaluation'. In: *Health and Nutrition News* 11, 3

Mizuno (2009) *2009 Factbook Mizuno*. Online at http://www.mizuno.com/aboutus/financial/factbook/2009FACTBOOK.pdf (accessed March 4, 2010)

MOFA (Ministry of Foreign Affairs) (2005) *Japan's official development assistance white paper 2005*. Tokyo: Association for Promotion of International Cooperation

Monbu Daijin Kanbō Eisei Ka (1922) *Taishō nana, hachi, kyū sankanen ni okeru zenkoku kaki taiikuteki shisetsu* [Summer sport programmes in all Japan 1918–1920]. Tokyo: Monbushō

Monbushō (1972) *Gakusei hyakunen shi* [A history of hundred years of the educational system]. Tokyo: Ōkurashō Insatsukyoku

Monbushō (1992) *Heisei 4 nendo waga kuni no bunkyō seisaku. Supōtsu to kenkō—yutaka-na mirai e mukete* [Japanese government policies in education, science and culture. Sport and health—facing a rich future]. Tokyo: Ōkurashō Insatsukyoku

Monbushō (1999a) *Chūgakkō gakushū shidō yōryō* [Outline of teaching instructions at junior high school]. Tokyo: Monbushō. Online at http://www.mext.go.jp/b_menu/ shuppan/sonota/990301/c990301g.htm (accessed November 12, 2004)

Monbushō (1999b) *Kōtō gakkō gakushū shidō yōryō* [Outline of teaching instructions at senior high school]. Tokyo: Monbushō. Online at http://www.mext.go.jp/b_menu/shuppan/sonota/990301/03122603/007.htm (accessed November 12, 2004)

Monbushō (1999c) *Shōgakkō gakushūshido yōryō* [Outline of teaching instructions at elementary school]. Tokyo: Monbushō. Online at http://www.mext.go.jp/b_menu/ shuppan/sonota/990301b/ 990301j.htm (accessed November 12, 2004)

Mori Takemaro (2004) 'Colonies and countryside in wartime Japan: Emigration to Manchuria'. In: *Japan Focus*, July. Online at http://japanfocus.org/ article.asp?id=130 (accessed December 12, 2004)

Mosk, Carl (1996) *Making health work. Human growth in modern Japan*. Berkeley: University of California Press

MSN (Maquila Solidarity Network) (2008) *Die Hürden überwinden. Schritte zur Verbesserung von Löhnen und Arbeitsbedingungen in der globalen*

Sportbekleidungsindustrie [Conquering the barriers. Measures to improve wages and conditions of labour in the global sports apparel industry]. No place: Play Fair

NAASH (National Association for the Advancement of Sports and Health) (2003) *Heisei 15 nendo supōtsu shinkō kuji joseikin no naitei* [Sport promotion lottery grants in 2003]. Online at http://www.naash.go.jp/ sinko/pdf/soukatsu.pdf (accessed February 8, 2004)

NAASH (2010) 'Heisei 22 nendo supōtsu shinkō kuji joseikin' [Sport promotion lottery grants in 2010]. In: *Kōhōshi Supōtsu shinkō kuji* 40. Online at http:// naash.go.jp/sinko/ home/kankou/kouhousi//tabid/369/Default.aspx (accessed February 18, 2011)

Nagazumi Jin (1999) 'Kōkyō supōtsu shisetsu no manejimento' [Management of public sport facilities]. In: Harada Munehiko, ed.: *Supōtsu sangyōron nyūmon.* Tokyo: Keirin Shoin, 157–173

Nagazumi Jin (2000) 'Machizukuri to supōtsu keiei' [Urban planning and sport management]. In: Yamashita Shūji, Hata Osamu and Tomita Yukihiro, eds.: *Supōtsu keiei. Foundation of Sport Management.* Tokyo: Taishūkan, 290–295

Naikaku-fu (2003) 'Heisei 14 nendo Naikaku-fu hōnseifu seisaku hyōka (jigo hyōka)' [Cabinet Office's ex post evaluation of government politics in 2002]. Tokyo: Cabinet Office, Government of Japan. Online at www8.cao.go.jp/ hyouka/h14hyouka/ h14jigo/zenbun.pdf (accessed February 20, 2005)

Naikaku-fu (2004a) *Heisei 16 nen tairyoku supōtsu ni kan suru yoron chōsa* [Opinion survey on sport and physical fitness 2004]. Tokyo: Naikaku-fu

Naikaku-fu (2004b) *Heisei 16 nendo 'ejiresu raifu jissensha' oyobi 'shakai sanka katsudō jirei' senkō kekka* [Results from the selection of 'ageless life practicioners' and examples of 'participation in social activities']. Online at http:// www8.cao.go.jp/kourei/kou-kei/h16ageless/h16agefront.html (accessed August 15, 2006)

Naikaku-fu (2006) *Heisei 18 nenban seishōnen hakusho* [Whitebook on youth 2006]. Tokyo: Kokuritsu Insatsukyoku

Nakamura Toshio (1981) *Supōtsu no fūdo. Nichibei hikaku supōtsu bunka* [Sports climate. A comparison of sport culture in Japan and the US]. Tokyo: Taishūkan Shoten

Nakamura Toshio (1991) *Supōtsu rūru no shakaigaku* [Sociology of sport rules]. Tokyo: Asahi Shinbun Sha

Nakamura Toshio (1994a) *Kendō jiten: gijutsu to bunka no rekishi.* Tokyo: Shimatsu Shobō

Nakamura Toshio (1994b) *Menbā chēnji no shisō* [The idea of player substitution]. Tokyo: Heibonsha

Nakamura Toshio (1995) *Nihonteki supōtsu kankyō hihan* [Critique of the Japanese sport environment]. Tokyo: Taishūkan Shoten

Nakayama Masayoshi (2000) *Chiiki no supōtsu to seisaku* [Regional sport and politics]. Okayama: Okayama Kyōiku Daigaku Shuppan

NDK (Naikaku-fu Daijin Kanbō Seifu Kōkoku Shitsu) (2005) *Heisei 17 nendo kokumin seikatsu ni kan suru yoron chōsa.* Tokyo: Naikaku-fu Daijin Kanbō Seifu Kōkoku Shitsu

Niehaus, Andreas (2003) *Leben und Werk Kanō Jigorōs (1860–1938). Ein Forschungsbeitrag zur Leibeserziehung und zum Sport in Japan* [Life and work of Kanō Jigorō]. Würzburg: Ergon

Niehaus, Andreas, and Max Seinsch, eds. (2007) *Olympic Japan. Ideals and realities of (inter)nationalism.* Würzburg: Ergon

Nihon Taiiku Supōtsu Keiei Gakkai (2004) *Tekisuto. Sōgō-gata chiiki supōtsu kurabu* [Comprehensive community sports club. Texts]. Tokyo: Taishūkan

Nike (2012) *Corporate responsibility report FY 10 11*. Online at http://www.nikeresponsibility.com/report/ (accessed December 12, 2012)

Nitobe Inazō (2001 [1899/1900]) *Bushido—The soul of Japan*. Tokyo: Tuttle

Niwa Takaaki (1985) 'Supōtsu sanka fujin no taidō kara mita supōtsu no bunkateki tokuchō' [Cultural particularities of sport seen from the attitudes of female sport participants]. In: *Taiiku Supōtsu Shakaigaku Kenkyū* 4, 95–121

Niwa Takaaki and Kaneko Hiroko (1983) 'Daigaku undōbuin no taidō kara mita supōtsu no bunkateki tokuchō' [Cultural particularities of sport seen from the attitudes of sport club members among university students]. In: *Taiiku Supōtsu Shakaigaku Kenkyū* 2, 1–23

Nogawa Haruo and Mamiya Toshio (2001) 'Sociology of sports stadiums'. In: Koh Eunha et al., eds.: *Sociology of sport and new global order: Bridging perspectives and crossing boundaries. Proceedings of the 1st World Congress of Sociology of Sport, Seoul July 20–24*. Seoul: Organizing Committee for the 1st World Congress of Sociology of Sport, 201–208

Nogawa Haruo and Mamiya Toshio (2002) 'Building mega-events: Critical reflections on the 2002 World Cup infrastructure'. In: John Horne and Wolfram Manzenreiter, eds.: *Japan, Korea and the 2002 World Cup*. London: Routledge, 177–194

Nogawa Haruo (2004) 'An international comparison of the motivations and experiences of volunteers at the 2002 World Cup.' In: Wolfram Manzenreiter and John Horne, eds.: *Football goes east. Business, culture and the people's game in China, Japan and South Korea*. London: Routledge, 222–242

Noi Shingo and Masaki Takeo (2002) 'The educational experiments of school health promotion for the youth in Japan: Analysis of the "sport test" over the past 34 years'. In: *Health Promotion International* 17/2, 147–160

Noll, Roger and Andrew Zimbalist, eds. (1997) *Sports, jobs, and taxes: The economic impact of sports teams and stadiums*. Washington, DC: Brookings Institute

Nomura, Hataru (2002) 'Sutajiamu kensetsu, zankoku monogatari!' [Stadium construction is a lurid tale!]. In: Asano Tomoaki and Hara Hiroshi, eds.: *Shūshi kessan Wārudokappu. Kaisai shite hajimete wakatta kane, seiji, fukumaden*. Tokyo: Takarajima Sha, 188–199

Nomura, Masaaki (1990) 'Remodeling the Japanese body'. In: *Senri Ethnological Studies* 27, 259–274

Nora, Pierre (1989) 'Between memory and history: les lieux de mémoire'. In: *Representations* 26, 7–25

Norden, Gilbert (1998) 'Breitensport und Spitzensport vom 19. Jahrhundert bis zur Gegenwart' [Mass sport and elite sport from the 19th century towards the present]. In: Ernst Bruckmüller and Hannes Strohmeyer, eds.: *Turnen und Sport in der Geschichte Österreichs*. Vienna: ÖBV Pädagogischer Verlag, 56–72

Nozaki Naohiko (2007) 'Iryō seido kaikaku o fumaeta iryō hokensha no tokutei kenkō shinsa, tokutei kenkō shidō e no junbi jōkyō to sono eikyō yōin ni kansuru kenkyū' [Research into the state of preparation on behalf of health insurers for the Special Health Check-Up and special health guidance based on the medical health care reform and its impact factors]. In: *Hoken Iryō Kagaku* 56/3, 278–279

NPD (2008) *Global sports equipment, apparel and footwear market*. Online at http://www.marketingcharts.com/direct/global-sports-equipment-apparel-and-footwear-market-nearly-280b-5548/ (accessed March 4, 2010)

NTK [Nihon Taiiku Kyōkai Nihon Supōtsu Shōnendan] (2003) *Gaidobukku Supōtsu shōnendan to wa. Supōtsu shōnendan soshiki to katsudō no arikata no kaisetsusho* [Guidebook Kids Sports Network]. Tokyo: Nihon Taiiku Kyōkai

Nunn, Samuel and Mark S. Rosentraub (1995) *Sports wars: Suburbs and center cities in a zero sum game*. Bloomington: Indiana University, Center for Urban Policy and the Environment

OECD (2004) *OECD in figures. 2004 edition. Statistics on the member countries*. Paris: OECD

Ōgushi Yōichi (2007) *Metabo no wana. 'Byōnin' ni sareru kenkō-na hitobito* [The metabo trap—healthy people that are made into patients]. Tokyo: Kadokawa SS Komyunikēshonzu

Ohno Yoshiyuki et al. (2000) 'Successful aging and social activity in older Japanese adults'. In: *Journal of Aging and Physical Activity* 8/2, 129–139

Ohnuki-Tierney, Emiko (1984) *Illness and culture in contemporary Japan: An anthropological view*. Cambridge: Cambridge University Press

Ohnuki-Tierney, Emiko (1989) 'Health care in contemporary Japanese religions'. In: Lawrence E. Sullivan, ed.: *Healing and restoring: Health and medicine in the world's religious traditions*. New York: Macmillan, 59–87

Oikawa Hiroshi (2008) *Empirical global value chain analysis in electronics and automobile industries: An application of Asian international input-output tables*. Institute of Developing Economies Discussion Paper No. 172

Okada Kei (1999) 'Nihon ni okeru supōtsu seisaku no genjō to kadai—ASC (Australia Sports Commission) to no hikakuteki kenchi kara' [Current state and task of Japan's sport politics in comparison with Australia]. In: *Dōshisa Seisaku Kagaku Kenkyū* 1, 111–128

Okada Kei (2004) 'Kankiteki-na kisu. Sakkā ni okeru otokorashisa to homososhiaritii' [Evocative kisses: Masculinitiy and homosocial desire on football]. In: *Supōtsu Shakaigaku Kenkyū* 12, 38–48

Okao Keiichi (1987) 'Ekiden' [Relay race]. In: Kishino Yūzō et al., eds.: *(Saishin) Supōtsu daijiten*. Tokyo: Taishūkan Shoten, 109–110

O'Neill, P. G. (1984) 'Organisation and authority in the traditional arts'. In: *Modern Asian Studies* 18/4, 631–645

Onimaru Masaaki (2001) 'Kōkyōken to shinmitsuken. Supōtsu shakaigaku oyobi shakaigaku ni okeru kōkyōken ron no dōkō' [Public space and private space. Trends of discussing the public sphere in sociology and the sociology of sport]. In: *Hitotsubashi Daigaku Supōtsu Kagaku Kenkyūshitsu Kenkyū Nenpō* 2001, 9–14

Onishi, Norimitsu (2008) 'Japan, seeking trim waists, measures millions'. In: *New York Times*, June 13. Online at http://www.nytimes.com/2008/06/13/world/asia/13fat.html?pagewanted=all&_r=0. (accessed March 3, 2009)

Otomo Rio (2007) 'Narratives, the body and the 1964 Tokyo Olympics'. In: *Asian Studies Review* 31, 117–132

Park, Young-Il and Kym Anderson (1991) 'The rise and demise of textiles and clothing in economic development: The case of Japan'. In: *Economic Development and Cultural Change* 39/3, 531–548

Podoler, Guy (2006) 'Japanese colonialism, national memory and Korean football'. In: *Japan Focus*, February 9. Online at www.japanfocus.org (accessed January 20, 2009)

Price, Monroe and Daniel Dayan, eds. (2008) *Owning the Olympics. Narratives of the new China*. Ann Arbor: University of Michigan Press

Radhakrishnan, R. (2001) 'Globalization, desire and the politics of representation'. In: *Comparative Literature* 53/4, 315–332

Rahmann, Bernd et al. (1998) *Sozio-ökonomische Analyse der Fußball-WM 2006 in Deutschland* [Socioeconomic analysis of the Football World Cup 2006 in Germany]. Cologne: Sport und Buch Strauß

Reischauer, Edwin (1970) *Japan. The story of a nation*. New York: Knopf

Rejeski, W. Jack and Shannon L. Mihalko (2001) 'Physical activity and quality of life in older adults'. In: *Journals of Gerontology Series A: Biological Sciences and Medical Sciences* 56, 23–35

Rivenburgh, Nancy K. (2004) 'The Olympic Games, media and the challenges of global image making'. Paper presented at the Centre d'Estudis Olimpics, Barcelona (n.d.)

Robertson, Roland (1990) 'Mapping the global condition: Globalisation as the central concept'. In: *Theory, Culture and Society* 7/2–3, 15–30

Robertson, Roland (1994) 'Globalisation or glocalisation?' In: *Journal of International Communication* 1/1, 33–52

Roden, Donald T. (1980) *Schooldays in Imperial Japan: A study of the culture of a student elite*. Berkeley: University of California Press

Rohlen, Thomas (1983) *Japan's high schools*. Berkeley: University of California Press

Rosentraub, Mark (1997) *Major League losers: The real costs of sports and who's paying for it*. New York: Basic Books

Ross, John (2008) *The share of developing countries in world trade*. Online at http://ablog.typepad.com/citifc/2008/12/the-share-of-developing-countries-in-world-trade.html (accessed March 4, 2010)

Sage, George (2000) 'Political economy and sport'. In: Jay Coakley and Eric Dunning, eds.: *Handbook of sports studies*. London: Sage Publications, 260–276

Saitō Torao (1994) 'Sukii ni yoru chiiki shinkō' [Regional promotion by means of skiing]. In: *Toshi Mondai* 85/12, 79–85

Saitō Toshiki (2000) *Fubyōdō Nihon shakai. Sayonara sōchūryū* [Unequal society Japan. Goodbye to the all-encompassing middle class]. Tokyo: Chūō Kōron Sha

Sakashita Akakazu (2003) '"Shōnendan" to "Shōnendan Nihon Renmei". Soshiki to katsudō no kenkyū' [Boys groups and the Association of Boy Scouts Japan. A study on organization and activities]. In: *Nihon Daigaku Daigakuin Shakai Jōhōgakka Kiyō* 4, 1–13

Sakaue Yasuhiro (1998) *Kenryoku sōchi to shite no supōtsu. Teikoku Nippon no kokka senryaku* [Sport as power device. The nation-state strategy of Imperial Japan]. Tokyo: Kōdansha

Sakurai Hideya (2003) 'Healthy Japan 21'. In: *Japan Medical Association Journal* 46/2, 47–49

Sanbonmatsu Masatoshi (1979) 'Supōtsu no kachi ni kansuru shakaigakuteki kenkyū josetsu' [Introductory remarks to a sociological study of values in sport]. In: *Taiiku Shakaigaku Kenkyū* 8, 25–40

Sanbonmatsu Masatoshi (1994) 'Waga kuni supōtsu bunka no seishinsei keisei ni kansuru shakaigakuteki kenkyū' [Sociological inquiry into the formation of the spiritual aspect of sport culture in Japan]. In: *Fukuoka Kyōiku Daigaku Kiyō* 43/5, 71–82

Sanderson, Ben, Michelle Webb and Roger Hobkinson (2002) *Home advantage? The impact of the World Cup on real estate markets (= Global Insights 3)*. Online at http://www.am.joneslanglasalle.com/News/2002/05may (accessed August 5, 2002)

Sassen, Saskia (1998) *Cities in a world economy*. Thousand Oaks, CA: Pine Forge/Sage Publications

Satō Makoto (1990) *Rizōto rettō* [Resort archipelago]. Tokyo: Iwanami Shoten

Schimmel, Kimberly (2001) 'Sport matters: Urban regime theory and urban regeneration in the late-capitalist era'. In: Chris Gratton and Ian Henry, eds.: *Sport in the city*. London: Routledge, 259–277

Schmid, Stefan and Thomas Kotulla (2007) *Grenzüberschreitende Akquisitionen und zentrale Konsequenzen für die internationale Marktbearbeitung: Der Fall Adidas/Reebok* [Border-crossing acquisitions and central consequences for the international handling of the market]. ESCP-EAP Working Paper. Online at http://www.escp-eap.eu/uploads/media/ SS_WP_07.pdf (accessed March 4, 2010)

Schröppel, Christian and Nakajima Mariko (2002) 'The changing interpretation of the Flying Geese Model of economic development'. In: *Japanstudien* 14, 203–236

SCK (Sōmuchō Chōkan Kanbō Kōrei Shakai Taisaku Shitsu) (1999) *Heisei 10 nendo koreisha no nichijō seikatsu ni kan suru ishiki chōsa* [Survey on attitudes of the elderly towards everyday life in 1998]. Tokyo: Sōmuchō Chōkan Kanbō Kōrei Shakai Taisaku Shitsu

SCK (2005a) *Heisei 16 nendo koreisha no nichijō seikatsu ni kan suru ishiki chōsa* [Survey on attitudes of the elderly towards everyday life in 2004]. Tokyo: Sōmuchō Chōkan Kanbō Kōrei Shakai Taisaku Shitsu

SCK (2005b) *Heisei 17 nendo kokumin seikatsu ni kan suru yoron chōsa* [Opinion survey on the life of the nation in 2005]. Tokyo: Sōmuchō Chōkan Kanbō Kōrei Shakai Taisaku Shitsu

SCSK (Shinkin Chūō Sangyō Kenkyūjo) (2002) *Kitai sareru shirubā bijinesu* [The expected silver business]. Tokyo: SCB Sōgō Kenkyūjo (= *Sangyō Chōsa Jōhō; 66*)

Seki Harunami (1997) *Sengo Nihon no supōtsu seisaku. Sono kōzō to tenkai* [Sport politics in postwar Japan. Changes and outlook]. Tokyo: Taishūkan Shoten

Shay, Ted (1994) 'The level of living in Japan, 1885–1938: New evidence'. In: John Komlos, ed.: *Stature, living standards, and economic development: Essays in anthropometric history*. Chicago: University of Chicago Press, 173–201

Shibuya Shigeki (2005) 'Opinion: Nihon wa supōtsu senshinkoku?' [Is Japan an advanced sport nation?]. In: *SFEN Online Magazine* Sept. 2005. Online at http://www.sfen.jp/opinion/shibuya/shibuya1_3.html (accessed August 1, 2006)

Shimizu Satoshi (1999) 'Supōtsu ibento to terebi media' [Sport events and TV media]. In: *Japan Marketing Journal* 73 (19/1), 15–23

Shimizu Satoshi (2001) 'Keiryū sareru shintai. Shintai kakō no sōchi to shite no gakkō to shōhi shakai ni okeru no shintai' [The school as device of body processing and the body in the consumer society]. In: Sugimoto Atsuo, ed.: *Taiiku kyōiku o manabu hito no tame ni*. Kyōto: Sekai Shisō Sha, 81–101

Shimizu Satoshi (2002) *Kōshien yakyū no arukeorojii. Supōtsu no 'monogatari', media, shintai bunka* [The archeology of Koshien baseball. The narrative of sport, media, body culture]. Tokyo: Shinhyōron

Shimizu Takahiko and Shirasawa Takuji (2006) 'How to stay young while getting old'. In: *Japan Close-Up* July, 12–18

Shirahata Yōsaburō (1985) 'Ryokō no sangyōka. Kihinkai kara Japan Tsūrisuto Byūrō e' [The commercialization of travelling. From the Japan Welcome Society to the Japan Tourist Bureau]. In: *Gijutsu to Bunmei* 2/1, 79–98

Shirahata Yōsaburō (1994) 'Fukuzawa Yukichi no undōkai (zoku)' [The field sport day of Fukuzawa Yukichi]. In: *Nihon Kenkyū* 2, 57–74

Shirahata Yōsaburō (1999) 'Fukuzawa Yukichi no undōkai. Kindai no supōtsu to Nihonjin no shintaikan kō' [The field sport day of Fukuzawa Yukichi. Thoughts about modern sport and the body perception of the Japanese]. In: Yoshimi Shunya et al., eds.: *Undōkai to Nihon kindai*. Tokyo: Seikyūsha, 55–83

Shirai Shōzō (2000) 'Fittonesu sangyō to wa nani ka' [What is the fitness industry?]. In: Uenishi Yasufumi, ed.: *Supōtsu bijinesu senryaku*. Toyko: Taishūkan, 113–139

Shoji, Kaori (2009) 'Putting the lie to the health of Japanese bodies'. In: *Japan Times*, August 12. Online at http://www.japantimes.co.jp/life/2009/08/12/language/putting-the-lie-to-the-health-of-japanese-bodies/ (accessed March 2, 2010)

Siegfried, John and Andrew Zymbalist (2002) 'A note on the local economic impact of sports expenditures'. In: *Journal of Sports Economics* 3/4, 361–366

Singleton, John (1997) *The world textile industry*. London: Routledge

SKS (Sangyō Kōzō Shingikai) (2000) *21 seiki keizai sangyō seisaku no kadai to tenbō. Kyōsōryoku tasanka shakai no keisei o megutte* [Prospects and tasks of industrial politics for the 21st century. On the formation of a society enhancing its competitive power]. Tokyo: METI

SKSH (Shakai Keizai Seisansei Honbu) (2003) *Rejā hakusho 2003. Arata-na yoka shijō no kanōsei* [White book on leisure 2003. Potentials of new leisure markets]. Tokyo: Shakai Keizai Seisansei Honbu

Spielvogel, Laura (2003) *Working out in Japan. Shaping the female body in Tokyo fitness clubs*. Durham, NC: Duke University Press

Spivak, Gayatri Chakravorty (1985) 'Can the subaltern speak? Speculations on widow sacrifice'. In: *Wedge* 7/8, 120–130

SSF (Sasagawa Sports Foundation), ed. (1997) *Supōtsu hakusho. 2001 nen no supōtsu foa ōru ni mukete* [Whitebook on sports. Towards 'Sports for all' 2001]. Tokyo: Sasagawa Sports Foundation

SSF (Sasagawa Sports Foundation) (2001) *Supōtsu hakusho 2010. Supōtsu foa ōru kara supōtsu fō eburiwan e* [White book on sport 2010. From Sport for All to Sport for Everyone]. Tokyo: Sasagawa Sports Foundation

SSF (Sasagawa Sports Foundation) (2002) *Supōtsu raifu dēta 2002* [Data on sports life 2002]. Tokyo: Sasagawa Sports Foundation

SSF (Sasagawa Sports Foundation) (2004) *Supōtsu raifu dēta 2004* [Data on sports life 2004]. Tokyo: Sasagawa Sports Foundation

SSF (Sasagawa Sports Foundation) (2008) *Supōtsu hakusho. Supōtsu no aratana kachi no hakken* [White book on sports. Discovery of the new value of sport]. Tokyo: Sasagawa Sports Foundation

SSF (Sasagawa Sports Foundation) (2009) *Supōtsu raifu dēta 2008* [Sport life data 2008]. Tokyo: Sasagawa Sports Foundation

Stathi, Aphrodite, Kenneth R. Fox and James McKenna (2002) 'Physical activity and dimensions of subjective well-being in older adults'. In: *Journal of Aging and Physical Activity* 10, 76–92

Steckel, Richard H. (1997) 'Stature and standard of living'. In: *Journal of Economic Literature* 33, 1903–1940

STK (Sōmushō Tōkei Kyoku) (2000) *Kakei chōsa nenpō Heisei 12 nen* [Annual report on household income and expenditure survey 2000]. Tokyo: Sōmushō Tōkei Kyoku

STK (Sōmushō Tōkei Kyoku) (2001) *Heisei 13 nen shakai seikatsu kihon chōsa* [Basic survey on time use and leisure 2001]. Tokyo: Sōmushō Tōkei Kyoku

STK (Sōmushō Tōkei Kyoku) (2005) *Kakei chōsa nenpō Heisei 17 nen* [Annual report on household income and expenditure survey 2005]. Tokyo: Sōmushō Tōkei Kyoku

Strohmeyer, Hannes (1998a) 'Sport und Politik. Das Beispiel der Turnbewegungen in Österreich 1918–1938' [Sport and politics. The turner movement in Austria, 1918–1938]. In: Ernst Bruckmüller and Hannes Strohmeyer, eds.: *Turnen und Sport in der Geschichte Österreichs*. Vienna: ÖBV Pädagogischer Verlag, 212–244

Strohmeyer, Hannes (1998b) 'Vom adeligen zum bürgerlichen Sport in Österrich (16–19. Jh.)' [From feudal towards bourgeois sport in Austria (16th–19th century)]. In: Ernst Bruckmüller and Hannes Strohmeyer, eds.: *Turnen und Sport in der Geschichte Österreichs*. Viena: ÖBV Pädagogischer Verlag, 28–55

Sugden, John and Alan Tomlinson (1998) *FIFA and the contest for world football*. Cambridge: Polity

Sugimoto Atsuo (1995) *Supōtsu bunka no henyō. Tayōka to kakuichika no bunka chitsujo* [Changes of sport culture. The cultural order of diversification and standardisation]. Kyōto: Sekai Shisō Sha

Sugita, Yone (2004) 'Historical lessons from Asian Cup'. In: *Japantoday.com* August 9. Online at http://www.japantoday.com/e/?content=comment&id=620 (accessed August 14, 2004)

Sugiyama Yoshio et al. (1986) 'Kōreisha no supōtsu katsudō to 'ikigai' ishiki no kanren' [The relationship between sport activities of elderly and their sense of purpose in life]. In: *Rōnen Shakaikagaku* 8, 161–176

Suzuki Akihito and Suzuki Mika (2009) 'Cholera, consumer, and citizenship: modernizations of medicine in Japan'. In: Hormoz Ebrahimnejad, ed.: *The development of modern medicine in non-Western countries: Historical perspectives.* London: Routledge, 184–203

Szymanski, Stefan (2002) 'The economic impact of the World Cup'. In: *World Economics* 3/1, 169–177

Tagsold, Christian (2002) *Die Inszenierung der kulturellen Identität in Japan. Das Beispiel der Olympischen Spiele Tokio 1964.* Munich: Iudicium Verlag

Takahashi Hirokazu (2003) *Taiiku supōtsu shisetsu no seibi unei hōhō ga toshi no jizokusei ni ataeru eikyō ni kansuru kenkyū* [Influences of provision and management of PE and sport facilities on urban sustainability]. MA thesis approved by the Division of Environmental Engineering and Architecture, Nagoya University

Takahashi Junichi (1995) '"Supōtsu to hegemonii" ron no chihei' [The horizon of the discourse on sport and hegemony]. In: David Jary et al., eds.: *Supōtsu rejā shakaigaku. Ōrutānatibu no genzai.* Tokyo: Dōwa Shoin, 66–83

Takeda Hiroko (2009) 'The governing of family meals in the UK and Japan'. In: Peter Jackson, ed.: *Changing families, changing food.* Basingstoke: Palgrave Macmillan, 165–184

Takemura Tamio (1998) 'The embryonic formation of a mass consumption society, and innovation in Japan during the 1920s'. In: *Japan Review* 10, 173–197

Takenoshita Kyūzō and Kishino Yūzō (1959) *Nihon kindai gakkō taiiku shi* [History of modern school sport in Japan]. Tokyo: Tōyōkan

Taki Kōji (1995) *Supōtsu o kangaeru. Shintai, taiiku, nashonarizumu* [Thinking about sport. The body, physical education, nationalism]. Tokyo: Chikuma Shinsho

Takizawa Toshiyuki (2011) 'Asian ideas on health promotion and education from historical perspectives of the theory of yojo as an interface of health, self and society'. In: Takashi Muto, Nam Eun Woo and Nakahara Toshitaka, eds.: *Asian perspectives and evidence on health promotion and education.* New York: Springer, 3–12

Tanada Shinsuke (1988) 'Diffusion into the orient: The introduction of Western sports in Kobe, Japan'. In: *International Journal of the History of Sport* 5/3, 372–376

Tanaka Kiyoji et al. (2002) 'Asian perspectives on America's national blueprint: Increasing physical activity among adults age 50 and older'. In: *Bulletin of the Institute of Health and Sport Sciences, University of Tsukuba* 25, 13–22

Tanaka Shigeho, Itō Yukako and Hattori Komei (2002) 'Relationship of body composition to body-fatness estimation in Japanese university students'. In: *Obesity Research* 10/7, 590–596

Taniguchi Masako (2003) 'Supōtsu ni okeru jendā no seisan to saiseisan' [The production and reproduction of gender in sports]. In: *Supōtsu Shakaigaku Kenkyū* 11, 76–86

Takahashi Hirokazu (2003) *Taiiku supōtsu shisetsu no seibi unei hōhō ga toshi no jizokusei ni ataeru eikyō ni kansuru kenkyū* [Influences of provision and management of PE and sport facilities on urban sustainability]. MA thesis approved by the Division of Environmental Engineering and Architecture, Nagoya University

Tazaki Kentarō (2006) 'Nihon no kōteki supōtsu shinkō no genkyō' [Current state of public sport promotion in Japan]. In: *Shidōsha no tame no Supōtsu Jānaru* 267, 41–45

Thun, Eric (2001) *Growing up and moving out: Globalization of 'traditional' industries in Taiwan.* MIT IPC Globalization Working Paper 00–004

TKI (Tosu-shi Kyōiku Iinkai), ed. (2002) *Tosu-shi no kyōiku* [Education in Tosu]. Tosu: Tosu-shi

TKK (Tōkei-kyoku) (2003) *Kakei chōsa* [Survey on household economy]. Tokyo: Statistical Bureau, Ministry of Internal Affairs and Communication, Government of Japan. Online at http://www.stat.go.jp/data/soutan/1.htm (accessed February 20, 2005)

Tokunaga Toshifumi and Ōhashi Yoshikatsu (1982) 'Nihonjin no supōtsu kan ni tsuite—tayōsei to sono henka' [On the sport view of the Japanese. Diversity and change]. In: *Taiiku Supōtsu Shakaigaku Kenkyū* 1, 19–38

Tomlinson, John (1991) *Cultural imperialism.* London: Pinter

Tomlinson, John (1999) *Globalization and culture.* Cambridge: Polity Press

TSKJ (Tosu-shi Sōmu-bu Kikaku Jōhō-ka) (2002) *Tosu-shi tōkeisho Heisei 13 nenban* [Statistical Report Tosu 2001]. Tosu: Tosu-shi

Turner, Victor (1982) *From ritual to theatre. The human seriousness of play.* New York: PAJ Publications

Ubukata Yukio (1994) *J.Riigu no keizaigaku* [The economics of the J.League]. Tokyo: Asahi Shinbun Sha

Uchiumi Kazuo (2002) 'Shijōka to kōkyōka no taikō. 90nendai no supōtu seisaku' [Marketisation and public sphere trends. Sport politics of the 1990s]. In: *Hitotsubashi Daigaku Supōtsu Kagaku Kenkyūshitsu Kenkyu Nenpō* 2002, 13–20

Uchiumi Kazuo (2005) *Nihon no supōtsu fō ōru—mijun-na fukushi kokka no supōtsu seisaku* [Japan's sport for all. Sport politics of an immature welfare state]. Tokyo: Fumaidō Shuppan

Udagawa Kōko, Miyoshi Miki and Yoshiike Nobuo (2008) 'Mid-term evaluation of 'Health Japan 21': Focus area for the nutrition and diet'. In: *Asia Pacific Journal of Clinical Nutrition* 17/S2, 445–452

Uesugi Masayuki (1982) 'Nihonjin no supōtsu kan ishiki to dō, shūgyō no shisō' [The sport view and consciousness of the Japanese and the idea of the way, spiritual work]. In: *Taiiku Supōtsu Shakaigaku Kenkyū* 1, 39–58

van Bottenburg, Martin (2001) Global games. Urbana: University of Illinois Press

van Gennep, Arnold (1960 [1909]) *The rites of passage.* Chicago: University of Chicago Press

Vinnai, Gerhard, ed. (1972) *Sport in der Klassengesellschaft.* Frankfurt: Fischer Tb

Wallerstein, Immanuel (1974) *The modern world system: Capitalist agriculture and the origins of the European world economy in the sixteenth century.* New York: Academic Press

Wang Hong-Zen (2005) 'Asian transnational corporations and labor rights: Vietnamese trade unions in Taiwan-invested companies'. In: *Journal of Business Ethics* 56, 43–53

Watts, Jonathan (1998) 'Soccer *shinhatsubai.* What are the Japanese consumers making of the J.League?' In: D. P. Martinez, ed.: *The worlds of Japanese popular culture: Gender, shifting boundaries and global cultures.* Cambridge: Cambridge University Press, 181–201

Weber, Max (2010 [1921–1922]) *Wirtschaft und Gesellschaft: Grundriß der verstehenden Soziologie* [Economy and society]. Frankfurt: Zweitausendeins

Weiss, Otmar et al. (1999) *Sport und Gesundheit. Die Auswirkungen des Sports auf die Gesundheit—eine sozioökonomische Analyse.* Vienna: Bundesministerium für Gesundheit
Whannel, Garry (2002) *Media sport stars. Masculinities and moralities.* London: Routledge
Wheatley, Elizabeth E. (2005) 'Disciplining bodies at risk. Cardiac rehabilitation and the medicalization of fitness'. In: *Journal of Sport and Social Issues* 29/2, 198–220
Whiting, Robert (1989) *You gotta have wa.* New York: Vintage Departures
Whitson, David and John Horne (2006) 'Underestimated costs and overestimated benefits? Comparing the outcomes of sports mega-events in Canada and Japan'. In: *Sociological Review* 54/2: 73–89
WHO (World Health Organization) (2002) *The world health report 2002: Reducing risks, promoting healthy life.* Geneva: WHO
WHO Centre for Health Development (2005) *Public health policy and approaches for noncommunicable disease prevention and control in Japan: a case study.* Kōbe: WHO Centre for Health Development
Willensky, Marcus (2005) 'Japanese fascism revisited'. In: *Stanford Journal of East Asian Affairs* 5/1, 58–77
Wright, George (1999) 'The impact of globalisation'. In: *New Political Economy* 4/2, 268–272
Yaguchi Kōichi (1988) 'Kōreisha no undō, supōtsu katsudō to mentaru herusu' [Sport activities of the elderly and mental health]. In: *Rōnen Shakaikagaku* 10/2, 161–176
Yamamoto Hidenori (2008) 'Iryō seido kaikaku ni okeru tokutei kenshin, hoken shidō no ichizuke' [Health check-ups and healthcare advice with a particular focus on the metabolic syndrome in the health care system reform]. In: *Hoken Iryō Kagaku* 57/1, 3–8
Yamamoto Takuji (1999) 'Kokuminka to gakkō shintai kensa ni tsuite' [Nationalisation and physical examinations at school]. In: *Ōhara Skakai Mondai Kenkyūjo Zasshi* 488, 30–43
Yamamoto Yasuteru (2002) *Wārudo Kappu no keizai kōka ni tsuite* [On economic impacts of the World Cup]. Tokyo: Sumitomo Seimei Sōgō Kenkyūjo
Yamashita Takayuki (1995) 'Posuto forudizumu no moto de no supōtsu, rejā' [Sport and leisure on the basis of postfordism]. In: David Jary et al., eds.: *Supōtsu rejā shakaigaku. Ōrutānatibu no genzai.* Tokyo: Dōwa Shoin, 84–128
Yamashita Takayuki (1997) 'Buritishu karuchuraru sutadiizu to supōtsu kenkyū' [British Cultural Studies and sport research]. In: *Supōtsu Shakaigaku Kenkyū* 5, 3–15
Yamashita Takayuki and Saka Natsuko (2002) 'Another kick off: The 2002 World Cup and soccer voluntary groups as a new social movement'. In: John Horne and Wolfram Manzenreiter, eds.: *Japan, Korea and the 2002 World Cup.* London: Routledge, 147–161
Yano Masakazu et al. (1995) *Seikatsu jikan no shakaigaku. Shakai no jikan, kojin no jikan* [Sociology of time. Social time and individual time]. Tokyo: University of Tokyo Press
Yasunaga Akitomo (2006) 'Yearlong physical activity and health-related quality of life in older Japanese adults: the Nakanojo study'. In: *Journal of Aging and Physical Activity* 14/3, 38–51
Yasunaga Akitomo, Yaguchi Kōichi and Tokunaga Mikio (2002) 'Kōreisha no shukanteki kōfukukan ni oyobosu undō kanshū no eikyō' [Effects of exercise habits on subjective well-being among the elderly]. In: *Taiikugaku Kenkyū* 47/2, 173–183
Yokomatsu Muneharu (1996) 'Nihon ni okeru kyōgijō kensetsu no rekishi to genjō' [History and current state of sport facility construction in Japan]. In: Zenkoku

Jichitai Shokuin Sakkā Renmei Kikaku, ed.: *Nihon no sakkā sutajiamu. Kyō soshite asu.* Tokyo: Nihon Sakkā Kyōkai, 276–278

Yōrō, Takeshi (1996) '"Nihon-teki shintai" ron' [Discourse on 'the Japanese body']. In: Inoue Shun et al., eds: *Shintai to kanshintai no shakaigaku.* Tokyo: Iwanami Shoten, 197–207

Yoshimi Shunya (1993) 'Undōkai to iu kindai. Shukusai no seijigaku' [The modernity called sports days. The politics of festival]. In: *Gendai Shisō* 21/7, 55–73

Yoshimi Shunya (1999) 'Nēshon no girei to shite no undōkai' [The sport day as ceremony of the nation]. In: Yoshimi Shunya et al., eds.: *Undōkai to Nihon kindai.* Tokyo: Seikyūsha, 7–53

Yoshimi Shunya (2001) 'Undōkai to gakkō kūkan' [Sports days and school space]. In: Sugimoto Atsuo, ed.: *Taiiku kyōiku o manabu hito no tame ni.* Kyōto: Sekai Shisō Sha, 42–60

Yoshiuchi Kazuhiro et al. (2006) 'Yearlong physical activity and depressive symptoms in older Japanese adults: Cross-sectional data from the Nakanojo study'. In: *American Journal of Geriatric Psychiatry* 14, 621–624

Yu Xiaomin (2008) 'Impacts of corporate code of conduct on labor standards: A case study of Reebok's athletic footwear supplier factory in China'. In: *Journal of Business Ethics* 81, 513–529

Yue Yuen (2009) *A team player in the global supply chain. Annual report 2009.* Online at http://www.yueyuen.com/annual/2009/2009eng_100120_ar.pdf (accessed March 4, 2010)

Yue Yuen (2012) *Annual report 2011.* Online at http://www.yueyuen.com/annual/2011/EW00551AR(1801).pdf (accessed December 14, 2012)

Zen-Kōtairen (Zenkoku Kōtō Gakkō Taiiku Renmei) (2004) 'Heisei 16 nendo kamei tōroku jōkyō' [The state of registered membership in 2004]. Online at http://www.zen-koutairen.com/f_regist.html (accessed October 12, 2004)

Index

Q

R